The Practical Guide to

EVIDENCE
IN
CRIMINAL CASES
Sixth Edition

The Practical Guide to

EVIDENCE
IN
CRIMINAL CASES

Sixth Edition

The Honourable
Roger E. Salhany

CARSWELL

A THOMSON COMPANY

Canadian Cataloguing in Publication Data

Salhany, Roger E.
    The practical guide to evidence in criminal cases

6th ed.
First-3rd eds. published under title: A basic guide to evidence in criminal cases.
Includes bibliographical references and index.
ISBN 0-459-26868-6

1. Evidence, Criminal – Canada.   I. Title.   II. Title: A basic guide to evidence in criminal cases.

KEA9312.S24   2001   345.71'06   C2001-903651-5

♾ The acid-free paper used in this publication meets the minimum requirements of American National Standard for Information Sciences - Permanence of Paper for Printed Library Materials, ANSI Z39.48-1984.

CARSWELL

A THOMSON COMPANY

One Corporate Plaza, 2075 Kennedy Road, Scarborough, Ontario M1T 3V4
Customer Service:
Toronto 1-416-609-3800
Elsewhere in Canada/U.S. 1-800-387-5164
Fax 1-416-298-5094

Foreword

Roger Salhany has always been a student of the law. He was one of the very few of our Osgoode Hall Law School class of 1961 to pursue graduate studies (Cambridge University, where he studied Criminal Procedure under Glanville Williams). His interest in and curiosity about the legal process and the what's and why's of criminal law are evident in this book. As the name of the text suggests, this is a practical guide to evidence in criminal cases. It is both clear and comprehensive.

The anatomy of a criminal trial is set out in a logical and easily understandable fashion. The case references are both timely and relevant in an area of the law that is constantly changing.

This text will be helpful to everyone from the student to the expert in criminal law when trying to either understand the overall scheme of the criminal trial, or when seeking an answer to a specific evidentiary or procedural question. While there are many useful books on criminal evidence, this text's blending of a careful review of the jurisprudence with useful and practical examples of criminal evidentiary issues make it an important addition to the library of anyone who has an interest in criminal law or the trial process.

P.J. LeSage
Chief Justice, Superior Court of Justice
Osgoode Hall, Toronto
February 26, 2002

Preface to the Sixth Edition

This edition brings up to date all of the important decisions rendered by the Supreme Court of Canada, provincial appellate courts and the superior and provincial courts of each province since 1998. Chapter 1, dealing with Admissibility, has a new heading, "Habit or Disposition" and a discussion of the recent authorities. Chapter 7, dealing with Confessions, has a new heading "Exclusion of Evidence Obtained by an Involuntary Confession" and a discussion of the recent cases on this subject. Many of the other chapters have been expanded to deal with a number of issues that have arisen since the last edition: the constitutionality of ss. 278.1-278.91 of the *Criminal Code* dealing with third party records (*Mills*-SCC); recent developments in the modern Hearsay Rule, such as the test for reliability (*Smith*-SCC) (*Merz*-Ont.C.A.); the mentally challenged witness (*Parrott*-SCC) and the requirement that the trial judge assess the threshold reliability of all hearsay statements, even the traditional ones (*Starr*-SCC); the importance of solicitor-client privilege, the limits to the exceptions (*McClure*-SCC), and the constitutional validity of s. 488.1 of the Code; the gatekeeper role of the judge in admitting opinion evidence (*J. (J-L.)*-SCC); the meaning of voluntariness for the admissibility of confessions (*Oickle*-SCC); the limits of the cross-examination of an accused (*Charlebois*-SCC); the explanation of the onus of proof (*Starr*-SCC); and the extent of the trial judge's duty to warn the jury about the character of Crown witnesses (*Brooks*-SCC).

I want to express my thanks to Chief Justice Patrick LeSage for taking the time from his busy schedule to read this edition and to write a foreword. Again, I must express my gratitude to my editor at Carswell, Debbie Bowen, for her patience in correcting my grammatical errors and skill in guiding this edition to its completion.

R.E.S.
February 7, 2002
Kitchener, Ontario

Table of Contents

Table of Cases

PART A

Admissibility

1

General Principles

1. INTRODUCTION

In every criminal trial, there are three things that the Crown must establish in order to prove its case. The first is that a crime was committed or what is called the *"actus reus"*. The second is that it was the accused who committed the crime; the identity of the perpetrator. The third and final thing that must be established is that the accused intended to commit the crime, in the sense that it was his deliberate act, or in some cases, a result of his recklessness or gross negligence. This is what is called the *"mens rea"*. However, intention is not to be confused with motive. Why a person commits a crime is not really something that concerns the court, although it may be relevant in some instances, as a matter of circumstantial evidence, to prove one of the three issues. There are also certain crimes where intention is not a relevant issue; sometimes the accused may not even be aware that he was committing the crime. These are called strict liability offences and are not necessary to this discussion.

Proof of a fact in issue may be made either by way of direct evidence or circumstantial evidence. Direct evidence is simply evidence that directly proves a fact in issue. For example, if the issue is whether A walked across the street, evidence given by B that he saw A walk cross the street is direct evidence. Circumstantial evidence, on the other hand, is evidence of surrounding circumstances from which an inference may be drawn by the judge or jury that a fact in issue occurred. For example, B may not have seen A walk across the street but may have observed him on one side of the street one minute and then on the other side a minute later. In such instance, testimony by B of that observation is circumstantial evidence from which an inference may be drawn by the judge or jury that A must have walked across the street. Circumstantial evidence allows the trier of fact to draw the inference that a fact occurred, provided that the inference is a reasonable one and not inconsistent with any other rational conclusion.

Therefore, the first question that the prosecutor or the defence counsel must ask is this: what does a particular piece of evidence go to prove? That is the very question that police officers must ask themselves when called upon to investigate a crime after arrival at the scene. As the officer looks over the crime scene, he or she will make a number of observations. Items will be seen that arouse suspicion, such as weapons, broken windows, footprints, or injured persons. Someone may come forward and give a statement about their observation. The officer will be advised of certain information and will conduct an investigation that may turn up objects or statements that may or may not be relevant to the case. The officer must continually keep in mind the question: what does this go to prove?

2. TEST OF RELEVANCY

In a criminal trial, neither the Crown nor defence is entitled to introduce, as of right, every piece of evidence in their possession that may or may not be relevant to the case. Evidence is only admissible if it is relevant to prove one of the three issues in the case: the act, the identity or the intent. If the trial judge concludes that the evidence is relevant and should not be excluded because it runs afoul of a specific exclusionary rule, or if a balancing of its probative value against its prejudicial effect does not warrant its exclusion, then the judge will admit it. It then becomes the responsibility of the trier of fact (whether the judge or the jury) to decide what importance or weight should be attached to the evidence.

In other words, the relevance of any piece of evidence must be determined only in relation to the issues that the prosecution must establish.[1] If the evidence is logically probative of one of the three issues, then it is said to be relevant and admissible so long as it is not contrary to one of the exclusionary rules of evidence that will be discussed in the next two sections. No minimum probative value is required for evidence

---

[1] *Cloutier*, [1979] 2 S.C.R. 709, 12 C.R. (3d) 10, 28 N.R. 1, 48 C.C.C. (2d) 1, 99 D.L.R. (3d) 577, 1979 CarswellQue 15.

to be deemed relevant.[2] What is relevant will generally be decided by logic and human experience. In *Corbett,* Mr. Justice La Forest described the rule this way:

> All relevant evidence is admissible, subject to a discretion to exclude matters that may unduly prejudice, mislead or confuse the trier of fact, take up too much time, or that should otherwise be excluded on clear grounds of law or policy. Questions of relevancy and exclusion are, of course, matters for the trial judge, but over the years many specific exclusionary rules have been developed for the guidance of the trial judge, so much so that the law of evidence may superficially appear to consist simply of a series of exceptions to the rules of admissibility, with exceptions to the exceptions, and their subexceptions.[3]

Although evidence, to be relevant and admissible, must be logically probative of one of the three issues, there is no requirement that it must go directly to the proof of one of the three issues. As Doherty J. pointed out in *P.(R.)*:

> Evidence may, however, be relevant even though it does not go directly to the proof of a material fact, or even alone provide the basis for an inference that the material fact exists. Evidence may be relevant by its combination with other evidence adduced in the case. Such is the essence of circumstantial evidence.[4]

This means that where evidence offered by one side is circumstantial in nature, the trial judge, in deciding whether the evidence is relevant and admissible, is required to examine that evidence in the light of all of the factual issues that are raised and the respective position taken by the Crown and the defence in the case.[5] Although, generally, relevance will depend on the ultimate issue in the case (whether it be the act, identity or intent, or a combination of any or all of the three), the evidence, although not directly relevant to one of those issues, may be relevant to another factor that is relevant to one of those issues.

Thus, relevance of any piece of evidence requires a determination by the trial judge whether, as a matter of human experience and logic, the existence of fact A makes the existence of fact B more or less

---

[2]   *Corbett,* [1988] 1 S.C.R. 670, [1988] 4 W.W.R. 481, 85 N.R. 81, 28 B.C.L.R. (2d) 145, 41 C.C.C. (3d) 385, 64 C.R. (3d) 1, 34 C.R.R. 54, 1988 CarswellBC 252, 1988 CarswellBC 756.

[3]   *Ibid.*, at (C.R.) pp. 33-34.

[4]   (1990), 58 C.C.C. (3d) 334 (Ont. H.C.), at pp. 339-40.

[5]   *Sims*, 28 C.R. (4th) 231, 87 C.C.C. (3d) 402, 1994 CarswellBC 574 (C.A.) at (C.C.C.) p. 420-27.

probable than it would be without the existence of fact A. If it does, then fact A is relevant to fact B. As long as fact B is itself a material fact in issue or is relevant to a material fact in issue in the case, then fact A is relevant and *prima facie* admissible.[6]

Unfortunately, even the courts often have difficulty in deciding what is relevant to a fact in issue when it comes to circumstantial evidence. Whether evidence is considered relevant will usually depend upon the facts and the individual view of the judge hearing the case. For example in *Cloutier*,[7] the accused was charged with importing marijuana. Marijuana had been found concealed in a piece of furniture (a dresser) imported into Canada and stored at the home of the accused's mother on the accused's instructions. At trial, the judge had refused to admit certain items found by the police during a search of the accused's home. These included a glass jar containing a green substance analyzed as marijuana, certificates of analysis of a cigarette butt made of marijuana and traces of marijuana found on scales and pipes in the premises. The Supreme Court of Canada, in a majority decision, held that the trial judge was correct in his ruling. The majority said that the fact the accused used marijuana did not create a logical inference that he knew or ought to have known that the dresser contained a narcotic at the time it was imported. All it showed was that a user of a narcotic was more likely to import the substance illegally than a non-user. Nor could the evidence be used to prove motive since it did not "disclose a sufficiently close logical connection between the facts that are to be proven as a motive and the crime committed".[8]

The minority came to the exact opposite conclusion. They concluded that since guilty intent cannot be established by direct evidence in such cases, it is "necessary to admit in evidence every bit of circumstantial evidence".[9] As far as they were concerned, there was a clear connection between the fact that the accused was a user of a prohibited narcotic and the presence of that narcotic concealed in the dresser. So long as there was some connection, even though not conclusive, the evidence had to be admitted for what it was worth. It was up to the trier to decide what weight should be attached to the evidence. If the accused was a marijuana user, then his motive in importing it was obvious.

---

[6] *Morris*, [1983] 2 S.C.R. 190, 1 D.L.R. (4th) 385, 48 N.R. 341, [1984] 2 W.W.R. 1, 7 C.C.C. (3d) 97, 36 C.R. (3d) 1, 1983 CarswellBC 695, 1983 CarswellBC 730; *Watson*, 108 C.C.C. (3d) 310, 50 C.R. (4th) 245, 92 O.A.C. 131, 30 O.R. (3d) 161, 1996 CarswellOnt 2884 (C.A.).

[7] *Supra,* note 1.

[8] *Ibid., per* Pratte J. at (C.R.) p. 81.

[9] *Ibid., per* Pigeon J. at p. 33.

A little over four years later, the Supreme Court, in a majority decision, came to the opposite conclusion on similar facts. In *Morris*,[10] the accused and several others were charged with conspiracy to import and traffic in heroin from Hong Kong. The Crown's case was based on surveillance and wiretap evidence. When the accused was arrested, a newspaper article headed "The Heroin Trade Moves to Pakistan", which had been written two years prior to the offence, was found in the accused's apartment. This time the majority held that an inference could be drawn from the presence of the newspaper article in the accused's apartment that he had informed himself of the sources of supply of heroin, a subject of vital interest to an importer of heroin. It raised the inference that the accused had taken preparatory steps to import heroin or had contemplated it, even though the article referred to the heroin trade in Pakistan and not Hong Kong. The minority, relying on *Cloutier*, held that the sole relevancy of the evidence was to show that it was more likely that persons who are traffickers keep such information than people who are not. Since the newspaper article only went to the disposition of the accused to commit the offence, it should not have been admitted by the trial judge.

A subsequent decision of the Supreme Court in *Lepage*[11] plainly demonstrates that relevancy will usually depend upon the facts and the individual view of the judge hearing the case. Lepage was charged with possession of LSD for the purposes of trafficking. A plastic bag containing the drug was seized from the common area of the home that he shared with two others. One of the co-residents was allowed to testify that the drugs were not his and that Lepage was a drug trafficker, although he could not identify a relationship between Lepage and the specific drugs in issue. Sopinka J., for the majority of the Court, held that the evidence was admissible because it was relevant to show possession "which is a key issue". He wrote:

> In the circumstances of this case, there were three people living in the house and it was clear that the drugs belonged to one of the three. Surely, it is relevant to the issue of possession to have one of the three testify that the drugs were not his and, furthermore, indicate that the respondent is in the business and, therefore, it was more likely that he was the owner of the drugs.[12]

---

[10] [1983] 2 S.C.R. 190, 1 D.L.R. (4th) 385, 48 N.R. 341, [1984] 2 W.W.R. 1, 7 C.C.C. (3d) 97, 36 C.R. (3d) 1, 1983 CarswellBC 695, 1983 CarswellBC 730.

[11] 95 C.C.C. (3d) 385, 36 C.R. (4th) 145, 178 N.R. 81, [1995] 1 S.C.R. 654, 79 O.A.C. 191, 1995 CarswellOnt 3, 1995 CarswellOnt 517.

[12] *Ibid.,* at (C.C.C.) p. 399.

Major J., however, dissented, holding that the evidence was only evidence of propensity and nothing more. It did not provide any evidence that actually connected the accused to the drugs.

Let us assume that an accused is seen crouching down in an empty field, 30 to 40 feet off the highway. The accused then gets up and gets into his automobile parked on the side of the road and drives away. The area where the accused was observed is searched and a bag containing nine pounds of marijuana is found. The accused is later arrested by the police, who search his car and find a small amount of cocaine and a large amount of cash. The accused is charged with possession for the purposes of trafficking of the nine pounds of marijuana found in the field. Is the evidence of the finding of cocaine in the accused's car admissible on the charge of possession of marijuana for the purposes of trafficking? The accused's defence is that it was mere coincidence that the marijuana was in the place where he had been observed.

That very issue faced the Manitoba Court of Appeal in *Caslake*.[13] Here again the Court was divided. Lyons J.A. held that such evidence was admissible. As far as he was concerned, the evidence went beyond mere propensity because it largely discredited the defence's position that the accused's presence at the location of the cache of marijuana was only a coincidence and that he was a mere victim of circumstances. The other two members of the Court, however, disagreed. Helper J.A, who delivered the majority judgment, felt that the evidence was not admissible. The evidence of the possession of cocaine was not probative of any element on the charge of possession of the marijuana for the purposes of trafficking. As far as she was concerned, it had no relevance beyond mere propensity.

3. HABIT OR DISPOSITION

The common law prohibits the prosecution from leading evidence in chief that the accused is a person of bad character and one who is in the habit of committing criminal acts to prove that he committed the particular offence charged.[14] The prohibition is not based on irrelevance.

---

[13]   101 C.C.C. (3d) 240, 45 C.R. (4th) 98, 107 Man. R. (2d) 24, 109 W.A.C. 24, [1995] M.J. No. 383, 1995 CarswellMan 470 (C.A.), affirmed, 121 C.C.C. (3d) 97, 155 D.L.R. (4th) 19, 221 N.R. 281, 13 C.R. (5th) 1, 48 C.R.R. (2d) 189, [1998] 1 S.C.R. 51, 123 Man. R. (2d) 208, 159 W.A.C. 208, [1999] 4 W.W.R. 303, 1998 CarswellMan 1, 1998 CarswellMan 2.

[14]   *Makin v. Attorney General for New South Wales* (1893), [1894] A.C. 57, [1891-94] All E.R. Rep. 24, 17 Cox C.C. 704, 10 T.L.R. 155, 69 L.T. 778, 63 L.J.P.C. 41, 58 J.P. 148,

The disposition of the accused to engage in certain kinds of conduct may be very relevant to the facts in issue. Evidence of an accused's disposition is excluded because of its potential prejudicial effect. The common law has consistently reaffirmed its belief that the overall fairness of the criminal trial process requires an accused to stand trial for what is specifically alleged in the indictment, not for what he may have done in the past. Propensity reasoning alone has been excluded because of the concern that it may impair the proper functioning of the criminal justice system.

Martin J.A. expressed the rule this way in *Scopelliti*:

> The law prohibits the prosecution from introducing evidence for the purpose of showing that the accused is a person who by reason of his criminal character (disposition) is likely to have committed the crime charged, on policy grounds, not because of lack of relevance.[15]

Although evidence of an accused's disposition is generally excluded, not because of lack of relevance, but because of its prejudicial effect, evidence of habit or disposition of a third party may sometimes be relevant and therefore admissible because it is a reliable predictor of conduct. For example, in *Watson*,[16] the accused (who was charged with murder) and two associates, H and C, visited the deceased at his place of business, which consisted of a small office and a large warehouse area behind. The deceased was shot dead by H in a confrontation at the back of the warehouse, while Watson remained in the front office. C was also shot in the chest. At least two of the bullets that hit the deceased came from a different gun than the one used to shoot C. In support of its theory that the deceased was killed during a spontaneous gun battle between H and the deceased, and that the deceased's death was not planned by H, C and Watson, the defence sought to call a witness who had given a statement to the police that the deceased was in the habit of carrying a gun. The purpose was to show that since the deceased always carried a gun, it was less likely that Watson was a party to a plan to kill or harm him. The trial judge, however, refused to allow the defence to call that evidence because there was no evidence that the deceased had a gun on the day in question, or that he fired a gun if he had one.

---

6 R. 373 (New South Wales P.C.) at (A.C.) p. 65; *Koufis*, [1941] S.C.R. 481, 76 C.C.C. 161, [1941] 3 D.L.R. 657, 1941 CarswellNS 24 at (C.C.C.) p. 170.

[15] 34 O.R. (2d) 524, 63 C.C.C. (2d) 481, 1981 CarswellOnt 814 (C.A.) at (C.C.C.) p. 493.

[16] 108 C.C.C. (3d) 310, 50 C.R. (4th) 245, 92 O.A.C. 131, 30 O.R. (3d) 161, 1996 CarswellOnt 2884 (C.A.).

The Ontario Court of Appeal disagreed and held that the trial judge had erred. Doherty J.A., delivering the judgment of the Court, reasoned as follows:

> The fact that a person is in the habit of doing a certain thing in a given situation suggests that on a specific occasion in which those circumstances arose the person acted in accordance with established practice. It makes the conclusion that the person acted in a particular way more likely than it would be without the evidence of habit. Evidence of habit is therefore properly viewed as circumstantial evidence that a person acted in a certain way on the occasion in question.
>
> Evidence of habit is closely akin to, but not identical to, evidence of disposition. Evidence of habit involves an inference of conduct on a given occasion based on an established pattern of past conduct. It is an inference of conduct from conduct. Evidence of disposition involves an inference of the existence of a state of mind (disposition) from a person's conduct on one or more previous occasions and a further inference of conduct on the specific occasion based on the existence of that state of mind. Evidence of habit proceeds on the basis that repeated conduct in a given situation is a reliable predictor of conduct in that situation. Evidence of disposition is premised on the belief that a person's disposition is a reliable predictor of conduct in a given situation.[17]

Doherty J.A. felt that the evidence that the deceased always carried a gun was therefore relevant to the question whether he had a gun when he was shot. The availability of the inference from the deceased's possession of the gun, to the use of it, required a consideration of the rest of the evidence, which revealed that there were only two possibilities. Either C was shot by the deceased or H fired two different guns, hitting the deceased with one and C with the other. The jury, having concluded that the deceased was armed, could have inferred that C was shot, not by his friend H, but by the deceased, who was the target of H's assault. Had the jury inferred that the deceased was armed and fired a weapon, those inferences could logically have influenced their conclusion as to the origins of the shooting. If the deceased was unarmed, the circumstances strongly suggested a preconceived plan to shoot the deceased. If the deceased was armed and used his weapon, then the possibility that the shooting was as a result of a spontaneous competition between H and the deceased, both of whom were armed, became a viable one. Evidence supporting the inferences that the deceased was armed and used a weapon during the confrontation, made the defence position as to Watson's non-involvement in any plan to kill or do harm to the

---

[17] *Ibid.*, at (C.C.C.) p. 325.

deceased more viable than it would have been if those inferences were not available.

Evidence of disposition may also be relevant where the defence advanced blames a third party or a co-accused for the offence. For example, in *McMillan*,[18] the accused, who was charged with the murder of his infant son, denied hurting the child. The trial judge had permitted the defence to call psychiatric evidence to the effect that the accused's wife had a psychopathic personality disturbance with brain damage, that she was immature, impulsive, had poor appreciation of the difference between right and wrong, in order to show that it was more likely that she had committed the offence. It was held that evidence of the disposition of the accused's wife in these circumstances was relevant because it went to the probability of the accused doing or not doing the act charged. At the same time, the door was now opened to permit the Crown to call evidence *in reply* of the accused's disposition for violence.

Disposition has also been permitted where the defence raised is self-defence. For example, in *Scopelliti*,[19] the defence raised was that the accused killed the two deceased in self-defence when they attempted to rob him. The trial judge permitted the defence to lead evidence of previous acts of violence by the deceased, even though at the time of the killing the accused was not aware of those acts. Martin J.A. held that, although evidence of a person's disposition is not generally admissible, it was relevant and admissible in the circumstances to support the accused's version of the events. Again, evidence by the defence of the victim's disposition for violence opened up the door for the Crown to call, *in reply*, evidence of the accused's disposition for violence.

In all of these cases, evidence of the disposition of a third party was permitted where it was relevant to the defence raised. The Crown was not entitled to lead evidence of the accused's disposition as part of its case in chief, even though such evidence may have been relevant to the facts in issue. Policy considerations prevented the Crown from leading evidence of the accused's disposition for violence until the issue of disposition was raised as part of the accused's defence.

Are there occasions where propensity reasoning will be admitted because it is critical to the proper functioning of the criminal trial process? Doherty J.A. has argued that there are. In *Batte*,[20] he wrote:

[18] 7 O.R. (2d) 750, 23 C.C.C. (2d) 160, 29 C.R.N.S. 191, 1975 CarswellOnt 7 (C.A.), affirmed, [1977] 2 S.C.R. 824, 33 C.C.C. (2d) 360, 15 N.R. 20, 73 D.L.R. (3d) 759, 1977 CarswellOnt 474.

[19] 34 O.R. (2d) 524, 63 C.C.C. (2d) 481, 1981 CarswellOnt 814 (C.A.).

[20] 145 C.C.C. (3d) 449, 34 C.R. (5th) 197, 49 O.R. (3d) 321, 134 O.A.C. 1, 2000 CarswellOnt 2113, [2000] O.J. No. 2184 (C.A.).

The criminal law's resistance to propensity reasoning is not, however, absolute. There will be situations in which the probative force of propensity
reasoning is so strong that it overcomes the potential prejudice and cannot be
ignored if the truth of the allegation is to be determined. The probative force
of propensity reasoning reaches that level where the evidence, if accepted,
suggests a very strong disposition to do the very act alleged in the indictment.
For example, if an accused is charged with assaulting his wife, evidence that
the accused beat his wife on a regular basis throughout their long marriage
would be admissible. Evidence of prior beatings does much more than suggest
that the accused is a bad person or that the accused has a general disposition
to act violently and commit assaults. The evidence suggests a strong disposition to do the very act in issue — assault his wife. In such cases, the jury is
permitted to reason, assuming it accepts the evidence of prior assaults, that
the accused was disposed to act violently towards his wife and that he had
that disposition on the occasion in issue. The existence of the disposition is a
piece of circumstantial evidence that may be considered in deciding whether
the accused committed the alleged assault.[21]

4. JUDICIAL DISCRETION TO EXCLUDE EVIDENCE

The general rule at common law was that, apart from the question
of confessions, the court was not concerned with how evidence was
obtained. So long as the evidence was relevant to a fact in issue, the
court allowed the evidence to be admitted. Over the last fifty years,
however, Canadian courts became concerned about whether trial judges
had and should have the discretion to exclude evidence that is otherwise
admissible, where it would operate unfairly to the accused. Finally, in
Wray,[22] the Supreme Court of Canada grudgingly indicated that it was
prepared to recognize a limited judicial discretion to exclude evidence,
but only where that evidence had little probative value and was so
gravely prejudicial to the accused that it would prevent a fair trial.

Following the *Wray* case, Canadian courts struggled over the extent
of a judge's discretion to exclude evidence. Even the Supreme Court
was divided on the issue. That division was summed up by Mr. Justice
La Forest in *Potvin*,[23] in these words:

> As my colleague notes, some have interpreted Martland J.'s dictum (in *Wray*)
> as limiting the discretion solely to situations where the evidence is highly
> prejudicial to the accused and is of only modest value. I do not accept

---

[21] *Ibid.,* at (C.C.C.) p. 481.
[22] (1970), [1971] S.C.R. 272, 11 C.R.N.S. 235, [1970] 4 C.C.C. 1, 11 D.L.R. (3d) 673, 1970
CarswellOnt 22.
[23] 93 N.R. 42, [1989] 1 S.C.R. 525, 21 Q.A.C. 258, 47 C.C.C. (3d) 289, 68 C.R. (3d) 193,
42 C.R.R. 44, 1989 CarswellQue 104.

this restrictive approach to the discretion . . . under English law a judge in a criminal trial always has a discretion to exclude evidence if, in the judge's opinion, its prejudicial effect substantially outweighs its probative value . . . The discretion is grounded in the judge's duty to ensure a fair trial.[24]

Today, the Supreme Court regards the *Wray* formula as superseded by the more expansive formula expressed by La Forest in *Potvin*. In *Seaboyer*,[25] the Court said that "admissibility will depend upon the probative effect of the evidence balanced against the prejudice caused to the accused by its admission".[26] Moreover, when it comes to evidence offered by the defence, the courts have said that the discretion of a trial judge to exclude relevant evidence should only be exercised where the prejudice *substantially* outweighs its probative value.[27]

There are some instances where the right to exclude evidence which is highly prejudicial has been specifically recognized by the Supreme Court. One is where the Crown is seeking to introduce evidence under section 715(1) of the *Criminal Code*.[28] Section 715 allows the Crown to read in at trial evidence given by a witness at the previous trial of the accused on the same charge, or in the investigation of the charge against the accused or on the preliminary inquiry into the charge, where the witness refuses to be sworn or to give evidence, or is dead, insane, too ill to travel or testify, or is absent from Canada. At one time, the rule was that the judge had no discretion to refuse the admission of the evidence where the conditions set out in section 715(1) had been met, even though the section provided that the evidence *may* be admitted. However, in *Potvin*,[29] the Supreme Court decided that the word *may* does confer on the trial judge the discretion not to allow the previous testimony to be admitted in circumstances that would operate unfairly to the accused. An example of the exercise of that discretion would occur where the accused satisfies the judge that he did not have full opportunity to cross-examine the witness. In *Potvin*, Wilson J. described how that discretion should be exercised by the trial judge:

---

[24] *Ibid.*, at (C.R.) p. 243.
[25] 7 C.R. (4th) 117, 48 O.A.C. 81, 128 N.R. 81, 6 C.R.R. (2d) 35, [1991] 2 S.C.R. 577, 66 C.C.C. (3d) 321, 83 D.L.R. (4th) 193, 1991 CarswellOnt 1022, 1991 CarswellOnt 109.
[26] *Ibid.*, at (C.R.) p. 139, quoting *Sweitzer*, [1982] 1 S.C.R. 949, 42 N.R. 550, [1982] 5 W.W.R. 555, 37 A.R. 294, 29 C.R. (3d) 97, 21 Alta. L.R. (2d) 97, 137 D.L.R. (3d) 702, 68 C.C.C. (2d) 193, 1982 CarswellAlta 552.
[27] *Watson*, 108 C.C.C. (3d) 310, 50 C.R. (4th) 245, 92 O.A.C. 131, 30 O.R. (3d) 161, 1996 CarswellOnt 2884 (C.A.).
[28] R.S.C. 1985, c. C-6.
[29] *Supra*, note 23.

> In my view there are two main types of mischief at which the discretion (to refuse to admit evidence under section 715) might be aimed. First, the discretion could be aimed at situations in which there has been unfairness in the manner in which the evidence was obtained . . . An example of unfairness in obtaining the testimony might be a case in which, although the witness was temporarily absent from Canada, the Crown could have obtained the witness's attendance at trial with a minimal degree of effort. Another example might be a case in which the Crown was aware at the time when the evidence was initially taken that the witness would not be available to testify at the trial but did not inform the accused of the fact so that he could make best use of the opportunity to cross-examine the witness at the earlier proceeding . . . A different concern at which the discretion might have been aimed is the effect of the admission of the previously-taken evidence on the fairness of the trial itself. This concern flows from the principle of the law of evidence that evidence may be excluded if it is highly prejudicial to the accused and of only modest probative value . . .[30]

Another instance where the Supreme Court has held that there is a discretion to exclude evidence which may be probative, but also gravely prejudicial, is where the Crown seeks to cross-examine the accused under section 12 of the *Canada Evidence Act*[31] on his criminal record. Section 12 of the Act permits the accused or a witness to be asked whether he has been convicted of any offence and, if he denies or refuses to answer the question, allows the criminal record of the accused or witness to be proved. In *Corbett*,[32] the Supreme Court held that the trial judge has a limited discretion to prevent cross-examination of an accused on his previous criminal record where it might unduly prejudice, mislead or confuse the trier of fact.

5. CONSTITUTIONAL REQUIREMENT TO EXCLUDE EVIDENCE

The *Charter of Rights and Freedoms*,[33] enacted in 1982, has substantially broadened the court's powers to exclude evidence where a right or freedom guaranteed by the *Charter* has been denied or infringed. Section 24 provides:

> 24(1) Anyone whose rights or freedoms, as guaranteed by this Charter, have been infringed or denied may apply to a court of competent jurisdiction

---

[30] *Ibid.,* at (C.R.) pp. 237-38.
[31] R.S.C. 1985, c. C-5.
[32] [1988] 1 S.C.R. 670, [1988] 4 W.W.R. 481, 85 N.R. 81, 28 B.C.L.R. (2d) 145, 41 C.C.C. (3d) 385, 64 C.R. (3d) 1, 34 C.R.R. 54, 1988 CarswellBC 252, 1988 CarswellBC 756.
[33] *Canadian Charter of Rights and Freedoms,* Part 1 of the Constitution Act, 1982, being Schedule B to the Canada Act 1982 (U.K.), 1982, c. 11.

to obtain such remedy as the court considers appropriate and just in the circumstances.

(2) Where, in proceedings under subsection (1), a court concludes that evidence was obtained in a manner that infringed or denied any rights or freedoms guaranteed by this Charter, the evidence *shall* be excluded if it is established that, *having regard to all the circumstances*, the admission of it in the proceedings would bring the administration of justice into disrepute. [Emphasis added].

It is important to note at the outset that section 24(2) is concerned not only with the fairness of an accused's trial, but also with the method by which the evidence was obtained by the prosecution. For example, in *Manninen*,[34] the accused told a police officer that he did not want to say anything until he had seen his lawyer. However, the officer continued to question the accused and obtained an incriminating answer that the trial judge relied upon in convicting him. It was held that the officer's conduct was a deliberate and flagrant disregard of the accused's right to counsel as guaranteed by section 10(b) of the *Charter of Rights and Freedoms*.

Section 24(2), however, does not say that every breach of the *Charter* will result in the exclusion of evidence obtained by that breach. It is only where it is established by the accused that, "having regard to all the circumstances, the admission of it in the proceedings would ["could", *i.e.*, "susceptible" under the French version] bring the administration of justice into disrepute". In *Collins*,[35] the Supreme Court decided that a trial judge should consider three factors in determining whether the administration of justice would [could] be brought into disrepute. The first is whether the admission of the evidence will affect the fairness of the trial. Here the Court drew a distinction between evidence that was already pre-existing, such as a murder weapon, and evidence that was obtained purely as a result of a *Charter* violation, such as a confession. It said that a *Charter* violation relating to pre-existing evidence was not as serious as one where the evidence was obtained after a violation of the *Charter*. The Court reasoned that the use of evidence obtained after a violation of the *Charter*, such as a person's confession, strikes at one of the fundamental tenets of a fair trial: the right against self-incrimination. It stressed that where the evidence existed prior to the *Charter* violation, then the more serious the offence,

[34]   76 N.R. 198, 38 C.R.R. 37, 58 C.R. (3d) 97, 21 O.A.C. 192, 34 C.C.C. (3d) 385, [1987] 1 S.C.R. 1233, 41 D.L.R. (4th) 301, 61 O.R. (2d) 736 (note), 1987 CarswellOnt 967.
[35]   [1987] 3 W.W.R. 699, [1987] 1 S.C.R. 265, 38 D.L.R. (4th) 508, 74 N.R. 276, 13 B.C.L.R. (2d) 1, 33 C.C.C. (3d) 1, 56 C.R. (3d) 193, 28 C.R.R. 122, 1987 CarswellBC 94, 1987 CarswellBC 699.

the less likely the evidence would be excluded, as that, in itself, would bring the administration of justice into disrepute. On the other hand, where the evidence was obtained as a result of a *Charter* violation, the more serious the offence, the more damaging to the system's repute would be an unfair trial, in which case the evidence should be excluded.

Lamer J. wrote:

> The trial is a key part of the administration of justice, and the fairness of Canadian trials is a major source of the repute of the system ... If the admission of the evidence in some way affects the fairness of the trial, then the admission of the evidence would tend to bring the administration of justice into disrepute and, subject to a consideration of other factors, the evidence generally should be excluded.[36]

The second factor that a trial judge must consider is the seriousness of the violation. Relevant to this issue is whether the violation was committed in good faith, whether it was inadvertent or of a merely technical nature, whether it was motivated by urgency or to prevent the loss of evidence, and whether the evidence could have been obtained without a *Charter* violation.

The last factor that the judge must consider is the effect excluding the evidence would have on the administration of justice. Here the focus again is on the fairness of the trial. Evidence should not automatically be admissible even where the breach was trivial, the charge serious and the evidence essential to substantiate the charge, if it would result in an unfair trial.

Lamer J. explained:

> Real evidence that was obtained in a manner that violated the Charter will rarely operate unfairly for that reason alone. The real evidence existed irrespective of the violation of the Charter and its use does not render the trial unfair. However, the situation is very different with respect to cases where, after a violation of the Charter, the accused is conscripted against himself through a confession or other evidence emanating from him. *The use of such evidence would render the trial unfair, for it did not exist prior to the violation and strikes at one of the fundamental tenets of a fair trial, the right against self-incrimination.* [Emphasis added].[37]

Although the *Collins* case required judges to consider all three factors, the Supreme Court in 1992 began to focus its attention on the

---

[36] *Ibid.*, at (C.R.) p. 211.
[37] *Ibid.*

first factor, trial fairness. In *Elshaw*,[38] and *Broyles*,[39] the Court said that where the tainted evidence affects the fairness of the trial, the second set of factors, that is, good faith on the part of the police, cannot reduce the seriousness of the violation. Mr. Justice Iacobucci, delivering the judgment of the Court in *Elshaw*, re-affirmed that the test for the admissibility of self-incriminating evidence under section 24(2) was more stringent than the test for real evidence. This was because the breach of the right against self-incrimination was directly related to a *Charter* violation and its admission would dramatically affect the presumption of innocence of an accused, as well as his or her right not to testify. He wrote:

> A proper approach would have been premised on the principle that, as a general rule, such evidence (self-incriminating remarks as a result of the breach of right to counsel) is not admissible because it would adversely affect the fairness of the trial and bring the administration of justice into disrepute.[40]

In 1995, the Supreme Court again dealt with the issue of the admissibility of self-incriminating evidence obtained through a violation of the accused's section 10(b) right to counsel. In *Burlingham*,[41] the accused, who was charged with first-degree murder, had been repeatedly questioned by the police intensively and in a manipulative way, even though he indicated that he wished to consult with his lawyer. The police had also denigrated the integrity of his counsel. Burlingham ultimately accepted a deal to plead guilty to second-degree murder in exchange for a full confession and assisting the police in locating the murder site and the murder weapon. The accused complied with his end of the agreement. However, the deal fell through because Burlingham misunderstood that he had to plead guilty to second-degree murder. The Crown then tried him for first-degree murder and he was convicted.

At trial, the judge had refused to admit the evidence of Burlingham's confession, the disclosure of the location of the weapon and his directions and gestures to the police. He did, however, admit the fact

---

[38] 7 C.R. (4th) 333, 128 N.R. 241, 67 C.C.C. (3d) 97, 59 B.C.L.R. (2d) 143, 6 C.R.R. (2d) 1, 3 B.C.A.C. 81, 7 W.A.C. 81, [1991] 3 S.C.R. 24, 1991 CarswellBC 215, 1991 CarswellBC 922.

[39] 9 C.R. (4th) 1, 8 C.R.R. (2d) 274, [1991] 3 S.C.R. 595, 120 A.R. 189, 8 W.A.C. 189, [1992] 1 W.W.R. 289, 84 Alta. L.R. (2d) 1, 68 C.C.C. (3d) 308, 131 N.R. 118, 1991 CarswellAlta 212, 1991 CarswellAlta 560.

[40] *Supra*, note 38, at (C.R.) p. 351.

[41] 38 C.R. (4th) 265, 97 C.C.C. (3d) 385, 181 N.R. 1, 124 D.L.R. (4th) 7, 58 B.C.A.C. 161, 96 W.A.C. 161, 28 C.R.R. (2d) 244, [1995] 2 S.C.R. 206, 1995 CarswellBC 71, 1995 CarswellBC 639.

of the finding of the gun and the testimony of the accused's girlfriend regarding statements that he had made to her. Burlingham appealed his conviction to the Supreme Court, arguing that the judge had erred in admitting the evidence of the finding of the gun. The Court set aside his conviction.

Adopting the "but for" approach to derivative evidence, the Court held that such evidence should not have been admitted by the trial judge because it brought the administration of justice into disrepute. The Court observed that "but for" the unconstitutional behaviour of the police, the derivative evidence, that is, the gun would not have been found.

In vigorous dissent, Madam Justice L'Heureux-Dubé expressed concern that the Supreme Court's broad interpretation of the term "trial fairness" in the first branch of the *Collins* test resulted in virtually automatic exclusion of evidence whenever there is a finding of "trial unfairness". She felt that this approach was inconsistent with a court's obligation under s. 24(2) to determine whether the evidence should be excluded "having regard to all of the circumstances". To do so would allow "trial fairness ... to wag the section 24(2) dog". As far as she was concerned, the only evidence that could result in an unfair trial would be evidence that was not reliable by reason of some connection with state action amounting to a *Charter* breach.

Mr. Justice Sopinka felt it necessary to address her concerns. He wrote:

> A fair trial is the sine qua non of our justice system and it is hard to conceive of a situation in which it could be said that an unfair trial resulting in a conviction did not depreciate the repute of our system of justice.[42]

In 1997, the Supreme Court in *Stillman*,[43] finally clarified the direction it had been taking since its seminal interpretation of section 24(2) in *Collins*. In *Stillman*, the Court said that the distinction between real or testimonial evidence is no longer relevant in a section 24(2) remedy analysis. Evidence must now be classified as "conscriptive" or "non-conscriptive" depending upon how the evidence was obtained. Evidence is "conscriptive" when an accused, in violation of his *Charter* rights, is compelled to incriminate himself at the behest of the state by means of a statement, the use of the body, or the production of bodily samples. "Non-conscriptive" evidence is that which the accused was not

---

[42] *Ibid.,* at (C.C.C.) p. 455.
[43] 113 C.C.C. (3d) 321, 144 D.L.R. (4th) 193, 5 C.R. (5th) 1, [1997] 1 S.C.R. 607, 209 N.R. 81, 185 N.B.R. (2d) 1, 472 A.P.R. 1, 42 C.R.R. (2d) 189, [1997] S.C.J. No. 34, 1997 CarswellNB 107, 1997 CarswellNB 108.

compelled to participate in the creation or discovery of, because it existed independently of the *Charter* breach in a form useable by the state. If the evidence is non-conscriptive, its admission will not render the trial unfair and courts will proceed to consider the two other tests in *Collins*, namely, the seriousness of the breach and the effect that exclusion would have on the repute of the justice system. If the evidence is conscriptive, then the Crown must establish on a balance of probabilities that the evidence would have been discovered by alternative non-conscriptive means. If the Crown fails to do so, then its admission will render the trial unfair. In such instance, it will not be necessary to consider the remaining tests, since an unfair trial would automatically bring the administration of justice into disrepute (the third test). However, if the Crown demonstrates on balance that the conscriptive evidence would have been discovered by alternative means, then its admission will generally not render the trial unfair. In such instance, the trial judge will have to go to consider the second and third tests, namely the seriousness of the breach and the effect that exclusion would have on the repute of the justice system.

In *Stillman*, the issue was whether hair samples, buccal swabs and dental impressions taken from the accused, using threats and contrary to his express wishes and the explicit written directions of his lawyers, should be excluded. A majority panel of the Court (6-3) held that they should because they were taken in violation of Stillman's right to security of the person as protected by section 7 of the *Charter* and could not have been obtained otherwise. However, a tissue discarded by the accused that contained nasal mucous suitable for DNA analysis was admissible. Although the tissue was conscriptive, it could have been obtained by a warrant to seize the tissue. Moreover, the violation was not serious and there was no interference with the accused's bodily integrity.

6. ADMISSIBILITY VERSUS WEIGHT

It is important to draw a distinction between the admissibility of evidence and its weight. When one side seeks to introduce evidence and the other side objects, the trial judge must rule as to its admissibility. That decision involves a question of law that only the trial judge can decide. If the judge rules that the evidence is admissible, then the question of what importance or weight should be attached to the evidence is a matter solely for the trier of fact, either a jury or the judge sitting without a jury.

This distinction is of particular importance when we come to Chapter 3 dealing with hearsay evidence and recent developments in the law of hearsay authorizing a trial judge to admit hearsay evidence that meets the twin test of necessity and reliability. Whenever such evidence is admitted, the trial judge must remind the jury (or himself, where he sits alone) of the potential unreliability of such evidence and instruct them that the question of the weight to be attached to such evidence is for them alone.

2

Kinds Of Evidence

1. INTRODUCTION

The law recognizes two methods of proof: direct evidence and circumstantial evidence. There is no particular magic in these terms. Direct evidence is simply evidence that directly proves a fact in issue. For example, if the fact in issue is whether Smith stabbed Jones, a witness who testifies that he saw Smith stab Jones is giving what is known as direct evidence.

Circumstantial evidence, on the other hand, is evidence of surrounding circumstances from which an inference may be drawn that a certain event occurred. If, in our previous example, the witness did not see Smith stab Jones, but saw Smith walking down the street all covered in blood with a knife in his hand and Jones, a short distance away, lying in a pool of blood, it would be reasonable to infer from all of the surrounding circumstances that Smith did in fact stab Jones. This is circumstantial evidence of a fact in issue, as opposed to direct evidence of the fact.

Although both kinds of evidence are admissible, the court scrutinizes circumstantial evidence more carefully. The burden of proof will be discussed in a subsequent chapter. It is only necessary to say at this stage that the burden is always upon the Crown to prove the guilt of an accused, and such proof must be established beyond a reasonable doubt. Where proof is based upon circumstantial evidence, either in whole or in part, a judge will usually caution a jury (or himself when trying the case without a jury) that before they can rely on circumstantial evidence, they must be satisfied that the guilt of the accused is the only logical inference to be drawn from such evidence.

There are three kinds of evidence that are generally recognized as admissible to establish a fact in issue. They are: oral testimony or *viva voce* evidence; real evidence, which includes documents or things such as weapons, etc; and demonstrative evidence, which includes photographs, maps, etc.

2. ORAL TESTIMONY

(a) Generally

The most common way that evidence is given is by a witness entering the witness box and testifying in open court. In Canada, as well as throughout other common law jurisdictions, the order of questioning a witness is strictly controlled. The witness is first examined by the side that calls him; the witness may then be cross-examined by the other side; and finally the witness may be re-examined by the side that called him. Unlike the continental system, which allows a witness to repeat his evidence with little interruption, the evidence of a witness is tightly controlled by the questions asked. This does not mean that the witness must answer either yes or no. However, the witness is expected to be responsive to the questions put to him. He is not entitled to make a speech unconnected with that question.

There is a distinction, however, between the type of questions that may be asked in chief (that is, by the side who calls the witness) and the questions that may be asked in cross-examination (that is, by the opposing side). When a witness is examined in chief, the examiner must not lead the witness or suggest the answer, except on matters that are not disputed or in issue. For example, a witness may be led on all preliminary background matters such as age, marital status, number of children, occupation, *etc.*, unless those issue are disputed or in issue. Often a judge will permit the examiner to lead a witness of tender years or one who is intellectually challenged and is having difficulty expressing him or herself. Such evidence, however, may not be given the same weight as evidence that is not led by the examiner.

On the other hand, there are few restrictions on the cross-examiner. The cross-examiner may lead the witness or suggest answers. One purpose of cross-examination is to test the accuracy of what the witness has said in chief. Another is to bring out new evidence that the witness did not give in chief that is favourable to the cross-examiner's case. Once cross-examination is completed, the side that called the witness is entitled to re-examine him. Here, however, re-examination is restricted solely to matters that were raised in cross-examination and is only allowed in order to clarify those answers that were given.

(b) Competence of the Witness

(i) Generally

Not everyone is allowed to enter the witness box and give oral evidence. A person called as a witness must be competent to give testimony. Competence refers to the legal qualification of a person to give evidence. Competence must also be distinguished from compellability. Compellability refers to the right of either side of a dispute to call a witness to give evidence and the legal obligation of that witness to testify.

Until the end of the last century, there were a great many individuals who were considered not competent to give evidence. For example, a person who had an interest in the case was not allowed to testify because his evidence was not considered reliable. In fact, it was not until 1640 that a person charged with a felony (*i.e.*, a serious crime), was allowed to call witnesses for the defence. And, until the end of that century, witnesses for the defence were not allowed to give their evidence under oath. The theory was that such witnesses, if they contradicted the witnesses for the Crown, were probably lying.

Today, generally all witnesses (subject to the exceptions below) are presumed competent to testify if they understand the nature and obligation of an oath. Until recently, that meant that the proposed witness had to understand the spiritual consequences of an oath. In other words, he or she had to believe in God or a Supreme Being. That requirement is no longer necessary. When a witness takes an oath to tell the truth, it means that he understands the moral obligation to tell the truth.[1] It also means that the witness understands the legal consequences of lying, namely, the possible prosecution for perjury or giving contradictory evidence. As McLachlin J. wrote in *Khan*:

> Before a person can give evidence under oath, it must be established that the oath in some way gets a hold on his conscience, that there is an appreciation of the significance of testifying in court under oath.[2]

For a long time, those who would not or could not take an oath because of their religion, or lack of it, were not allowed to testify at all. In Canada today, a person may give sworn testimony without the necessity of taking an oath. Section 14 of the *Canada Evidence Act*[3] allows a person to solemnly affirm if the traditional oath is objected to on the grounds of conscientious scruples or because the person would not be bound by it. In such instance, the person is required to solemnly affirm that the evidence to be given by him or her "shall be the truth, the whole truth and nothing but the truth". This means that if the witness tells a lie, he or she is liable to prosecution for perjury or giving contradictory evidence, just as if the traditional oath had been taken.

Although all witnesses are now presumed competent to testify, a witness may be declared incompetent if the witness suffers from a mental

---

[1] *Fletcher* (1982), 1 C.C.C. (3d) 370 (Ont. C.A.), leave to appeal refused (1983), 48 N.R. 319n (S.C.C.).
[2] 113 N.R. 53, 79 C.R. (3d) 1, 41 O.A.C. 353, [1990] 2 S.C.R. 531, 59 C.C.C. (3d) 92, 1990 CarswellOnt 108, 1990 CarswellOnt 1001, [1990] S.C.J. No. 81, at (C.R.) p. 7.
[3] R.S.C. 1985, c. C-5.

or psychiatric condition that renders it unsafe for the trier of fact to rely on his or her testimony. However, the mere finding that the witness suffers from a particular mental or psychiatric condition does not necessarily disqualify the witness from giving evidence. In order to disqualify a witness, the court must be satisfied that the particular condition is such as to substantially negative the trustworthiness of his or her evidence on the specific subject.

The general rule, as we shall see later, is that an expert is not permitted to give opinion evidence as to the credibility of a witness. However, where the opposing side seeks to challenge the competency of a witness because of a particular mental or psychiatric condition, experts are permitted to go further and say that the witness suffers from some "hidden defect" which affects the reliability of the testimony. Moreover, the expert's evidence is not confined to a general opinion about the unreliability of the witness. The expert will be permitted to testify about all of the matters necessary to show not only the foundation of and the reasons for the diagnosis, but also the extent to which the credibility of the witness is affected.[4]

(ii) The Accused

Historically, the most serious restriction on the right to testify was on the accused. An accused was not allowed to testify because it was believed that since he or she had an interest in the result, he or she would probably lie. It was not until 1898 that an accused in England was allowed to give evidence under oath on his or her own behalf. In Canada, that right was granted a few years earlier. Today, section 3 of the *Canada Evidence Act* specifically provides that "a person is not incompetent to give evidence by reason of interest or crime".

Section 4(1) of the Act goes on to provide:

> Every person charged with an offence . . . *is a competent witness for the defence* whether the person so charged is charged solely or jointly with any other person. [Emphasis added].

This means that although an accused is competent to testify in his own defence, he is still not competent (and therefore not compellable) at the instance of the prosecution to testify against himself. It also means that

---

[4]   *Hawke*, 7 O.R. (2d) 145, 22 C.C.C. (2d) 19, 29 C.R.N.S. 1, 1975 CarswellOnt 4 (C.A.); *Toohey v. Metropolitan Police Commissioner*, [1965] A.C. 595, [1965] 1 All E.R. 506, 49 Cr. App. R. 148 (H.L.).

an accused who is being jointly tried with others is not competent at the instance of the prosecution to testify against a co-accused; moreover, he is not compellable to testify at the instance of a co-accused.

The fact that an accused is competent to testify in his own defence means that he becomes an ordinary witness like any other witness once he takes the stand. He is required to answer any question asked by the prosecution or counsel for a co-accused regarding his involvement in the offence or the involvement of a co-accused.

(iii) The Spouse of the Accused

Historically, another person who was not allowed to give evidence was the spouse of an accused, unless the offence charged affected the spouse's person, health or liberty. This was initially based on the theory that husband and wife were one. Thus, if the accused was incompetent to testify, so was his spouse. Eventually, this reason was abandoned and justification for the rule was based on the natural repugnance of using the law to compel a wife to betray her husband or *vice versa*, if marital harmony was to be preserved. The rule was even applied if the parties were not husband and wife at the time of the offence, so long as they were married at the time of the trial.[5] Ironically, the same rule was not applied to prevent a child from betraying a parent, or a sister or brother from betraying a sibling.

The rule rendering a spouse incompetent to testify was eventually abolished in Canada at the end of the last century by section 4 of the *Canada Evidence Act*. Section 4(1) of the Act now makes a spouse "a competent witness for the defence", but not for the prosecution, subject to certain exceptions outlined in subsections (2) and (4). Those exceptions relate generally to certain sexual offences or assaults against children under the age of 14. Here a spouse is a competent witness for the prosecution, without the consent of the accused. Another exception is contained in section 4(5). It gives statutory recognition to the common law rule that allowed the prosecution to call a spouse to give evidence where the offence charged affected the spouse's person, health or liberty.

Over the last decade, the courts have indicated that they intend to restrict the spousal non-competency rule to the policy considerations

---

[5] *Hoskyn v. Commissioner of Police for the Metropolis* (1978), [1979] A.C. 474, [1978] 2 All E.R. 136, 67 Cr. App. R. 88 (H.L.).

underlying it. For example, in *Salituro*,[6] the Supreme Court said that if the parties, although legally married, are separated with no reasonable prospect for reconciliation, then the public policy of promoting marital harmony would have no rational foundation and spousal incompetence will no longer apply. It has also been held that the time for determining whether spouses have irreconcilably separated is at the time of the trial.[7] Moreover, the so-called "common law marriage" or "common law relationship" has not been recognized by the courts so as to render one of the parties to that relationship incompetent to testify for the Crown against the other.[8]

Although the Supreme Court has indicated a willingness to adapt and develop common law rules to reflect changing circumstances in society at large, it has also stressed that such changes should only be made incrementally to the common law. A good example of where the Court refused to make any changes was *Hawkins*.[9] There the Crown had suggested that a spouse should be rendered competent if the marriage was solemnized after the issuance of an information or indictment and where an accused married a witness for the purpose of insulating that witness from being called by the prosecution. The Court rejected this suggestion for a number of reasons. First of all, it would strike at the heart of the traditional rule of spousal incompetency. Secondly, such a marriage may be perfectly valid and genuine, a marital bond worthy of protection. Thirdly, even if the marriage was motivated by a desire to take advantage of the incompetency rule, it may nonetheless be a true marriage deserving of the law's protection. Finally, the Supreme Court said that it would be unworkable because it would require the courts to examine the motivation for the marriage and there would be no justification for such an inquiry, unless there was concrete evidence that the marriage was legally invalid. The Court, however, did not absolutely rule out such an inquiry where the evidence clearly established that the only purpose of the marriage was to avoid criminal responsibility by rendering a key witness uncompellable and the partners had no intention of fulfilling their mutual obligations of care and support.

6   38 O.A.C. 241, 78 C.R. (3d) 68, 56 C.C.C. (3d) 350, 1990 CarswellOnt 101 (C.A.), affirmed, 9 C.R. (4th) 324, 8 C.R.R. (2d) 173, 50 O.A.C. 125, [1991] 3 S.C.R. 654, 131 N.R. 161, 68 C.C.C. (3d) 289, 1991 CarswellOnt 124, 1991 CarswellOnt 1031.
7   *Jeffrey*, 12 Alta. L.R. (3d) 153, 84 C.C.C. (3d) 31, 106 D.L.R. (4th) 442, 141 A.R. 299, 46 W.A.C. 299, 25 C.R. (4th) 104, 17 C.R.R. (2d) 95, 1993 CarswellAlta 84 (C.A.).
8   *Duvivier*, 75 O.R. (2d) 203, 60 C.C.C. (3d) 353, 1990 CarswellOnt 958 (Gen. Div.), affirmed, 64 C.C.C. (3d) 20, 6 C.R.R. (2d) 180, 1991 CarswellOnt 1012 (C.A.).
9   111 C.C.C. (3d) 129, 30 O.R. (3d) 641 (headnote only), 2 C.R. (5th) 245, 204 N.R. 241, 96 O.A.C. 81, [1996] 3 S.C.R. 1043, 141 D.L.R. (4th) 193, 1996 CarswellOnt 4063, [1996] S.C.J. No. 117.

In refusing the Crown's suggestion, the Court stressed that complex changes to the law with uncertain ramifications that could result should be left for resolution by Parliament. Although the Crown had relied upon *Salituro*[10] to support the Court's authority to change the law, the Court noted that the change which it made in that case did not strike at the original justifications of marital harmony and repugnance which animated the substance of the common law rule.

As will be discussed later in this chapter (Compellability of the Witness), the *compellability* of a witness must be distinguished from the question of a witness's *competence* to give evidence. Although a spouse of an accused may be competent to testify by common law or statute, he or she is not necessarily compellable to give testimony against the accused at the instance of the Crown.

(iv) Children and Mentally Incompetent Persons

Section 16(1) of the *Canada Evidence Act* contemplates that there are two persons who may not be competent to give evidence: the first is a person under the age of 14 years; the second is a person whose mental capacity is challenged.

Whenever a person under the age of 14 is called to give evidence, the court is required, before permitting the person to testify, to conduct an inquiry to determine,

(a)   whether the person understands the nature of an oath or solemn affirmation; and
(b)   whether the person is able to communicate the evidence.

Similarly, whenever the testimony of a person is challenged on the basis that he or she is mentally incompetent, the same inquiry must be made.

The usual practice is for the trial judge to conduct the inquiry, although there is no rule that says it must necessarily be conducted by the trial judge. The interrogation may be conducted by Crown counsel or defence counsel provided that the inquiry is fairly conducted under the control of the trial judge.[11]

---

[10] *Supra*, note 6.
[11] *Peterson*, 47 C.R. (4th) 161, 89 O.A.C. 60, 27 O.R. (3d) 739, 106 C.C.C. (3d) 64, 1996 CarswellOnt 628 (C.A.), leave to appeal refused, 109 C.C.C. (3d) vi, 96 O.A.C. 79 (note), [1996] 3 S.C.R. xii, 206 N.R. 233 (note); *Ferguson*, 112 C.C.C. (3d) 342, 85 B.C.A.C. 33, 138 W.A.C. 33, 1996 CarswellBC 2888, [1996] B.C.J. No. 2617 (C.A.); *B.(R.J.)*, 77 Alta. L.R. (3d) 1, [2000] 5 W.W.R. 388, 33 C.R. (5th) 166, 255 A.R. 301, 220 W.A.C. 301, 2000 CarswellAlta 286 (C.A.).

Although section 16(1) does not require the inquiry to be conducted in the jury's presence, Canadian practice generally considers it preferable to do so. Support for this practice is usually found in the decision of Lord Goddard C.J. in *Reynolds*, where he noted:

> ...although the duty of deciding whether the child may be sworn or not lies on the judge and is not a matter for the jury, it is most important that the jury should hear the child's answers and see its demeanour when questioned, because those matters will enable the jury to come to a conclusion as to the weight they should attach to its evidence.[12]

That view was echoed by the British Columbia Court of Appeal in *Ferguson*.[13] There the Court noted that the evidence given by a prospective child witness on the inquiry might well assist the jury in weighing the child's evidence on the substance of the complaint, if he or she is subsequently found competent to testify. The Court felt that the subject of the child's competence, which is to be determined by the judge, and the child's credibility, which is to be determined by the jury, are tightly entwined. Evidence relevant to one issue will be relevant to the other. The Court acknowledged that there might be the possibility of prejudice to an accused if the child was found by the trial judge not to be competent to testify. However, it felt that this could be avoided if counsel sat down with the judge before the inquiry began and reviewed ways of avoiding it.

The view that the jury should be present during the inquiry is not universally held by all common law jurisdictions. For example, in Australia, it has been said where "a question of competency is likely to be prejudicial to the accused, it should be received in the absence of the jury".[14] Similarly, the English Court of Appeal in *Hampshire*[15] said that the above passage by Lord Goddard was not necessary for the decision in *Reynolds* and the practice should not be followed. The Court reasoned that since a proposed witness, whose competence is attacked, is not a witness until the judge has investigated and ruled on his or her competency, the jury should not be present during the competency hearing.

On the other hand, where the competency of a witness is questioned and third party experts (such as psychologists or psychiatrists) are called to give evidence on the issue of a witness's competency, the practice is clear that their evidence should be heard on a *voir dire* in the absence of

---

[12] (1950), 34 Cr. App. R. 60 (C.A.), at p. 64.
[13] *Supra*, note 11.
[14] *Demirok*, [1977] 137 Crim. L.R. 21.
[15] [1995] 2 Cr. App. R. 319 (C.A.).

the jury. In this way, the risk that the jury may draw the conclusion that the experts believe that the witness is telling the truth is avoided. Moreover, it would prevent a breach of the rule against oath helping and the likelihood of prejudice to the accused:[16]

The first branch of the test in section 16(1) requires the judge to question the witness to determine if he or she "understands the nature of an oath or solemn affirmation". Here, the judge's (or counsel's) questions must be directed towards determining whether the witness understands the legal consequences of lying under oath and the special obligation to tell the truth in court. As noted earlier, the test is whether "the oath in some way gets a hold on his (the witness) conscience, that there is an appreciation of the significance of testifying in court under oath".[17] Unfortunately the cases offer little assistance to the trial judge on how far he or she must go to satisfy the test. This may be because the nature and extent of the inquiry will generally depend upon the age of the child. In other words, an intensive inquiry may not be necessary when the child is close to 14,[18] while it may be for a younger child of eight.[19]

The second branch of the test obligates the trial judge to determine whether the person under the age of 14 or whose mental competency is challenged "is able to communicate the evidence". Here the inquiry by the judge is into the capacity of the proposed witness to observe, recollect and communicate generally, not into whether the witness actually observes, recollects and can communicate about the events in question.[20] In other words, any deficiencies in the particular witness's perception, recollection or narration of the events in question will go to the weight of the witness's evidence; it will not go to the witness's competence to testify. Moreover, as the Supreme Court stressed in *Marquard*,[21] the test in the case of children should not be based on any presumption of the incompetency of children to be witnesses; nor is it intended to make it difficult for children to testify. The test merely outlines the basic abilities that all individuals need to possess if they are to testify.

---

[16] *Deakin*, [1995] 1 Cr. App. R. 471 (C.A.).

[17] *Khan*, 113 N.R. 53, 79 C.R. (3d) 1, 41 O.A.C. 353, [1990] 2 S.C.R. 531, 59 C.C.C. (3d) 92, 1990 CarswellOnt 108, 1990 CarswellOnt 1001, [1990] S.C.J. No. 81, at (C.R.) p. 7.

[18] *Fletcher* (1982), 1 C.C.C. (3d) 370 (Ont. C.A.), leave to appeal refused (1983), 48 N.R. 319n (S.C.C.).

[19] *L. (J.)*, 54 C.C.C. (3d) 225, 37 O.A.C. 269, 1990 CarswellOnt 895 (C.A.).

[20] *Marquard*, 25 C.R. (4th) 1, 85 C.C.C. (3d) 193, [1993] 4 S.C.R. 223, 108 D.L.R. (4th) 47, 159 N.R. 81, 66 O.A.C. 161, 1993 CarswellOnt 127, 1993 CarswellOnt 995, [1993] S.C.J. No. 119.

[21] *Ibid.*

Nevertheless, the Supreme Court has said that the ability to "communicate the evidence" means more than mere verbal ability.[22] The reference to "the evidence" indicates the ability to testify about the matters before the court. This means that the trial judge is required to explore in a general way whether the witness is capable of perceiving events, remembering events and communicating events to the court. However, the judge is not required to determine, in advance, whether the child perceived and recollects the very events at issue in the trial as a condition of ruling that his or her evidence be received. Since that is not required of adult witnesses, it should not be a requirement for children.[23]

As already noted, section 16(1) of the *Canada Evidence Act* requires the court to be satisfied that the person under the age of 14 or the person whose mental capacity is challenged has the ability to communicate the evidence. Although what is meant by the expression "is able to communicate the evidence" is not defined in section 16, the Ontario Court of Appeal has said that it means that the judge who conducts the inquiry must ensure that the proposed witness has the capacity to give his or her evidence with some independence, and not simply in response to suggestive questions.[24] The Court also said that this requires that the proposed witness demonstrate some ability, not only to distinguish between fact and fiction, but also a capacity and a willingness, limited as it may be in the case of a young child, to relate to the court the essence of what happened to him or her.[25]

For example, in *Caron*, the trial judge conducted an inquiry into the competence of the complainant, a five-and-a-half-year-old girl at the time of the trial. The accused was charged with sexual assault and exposure for a sexual purpose. The child appeared very reluctant to answer any questions. In the judge's first effort to conduct the inquiry, the child gave very few verbal answers. After a recess, the judge requested the Crown to ask the child questions to help her feel more at ease. The trial judge then asked her a few questions, during which she still volunteered very little, but agreed with the suggestion that it was not nice to lie. The judge concluded that the complainant could testify based on her promise to tell the truth. The Ontario Court of Appeal said that she should not have been declared competent to testify, since her

---

[22] *Ibid.*
[23] *Ibid.*
[24] *Caron*, 19 O.R. (3d) 323, 72 O.A.C. 287, 94 C.C.C. (3d) 466, 1994 CarswellOnt 866, [1994] O.J. No. 1591 (C.A.).
[25] *Ibid.*

capacity to communicate her evidence had not been established. It was evident that the complainant would communicate very little of her evidence verbally, and when she did so, would do little more than confirm or deny what was put to her.

If the court is satisfied that the witness "understands the nature of an oath or a solemn affirmation and is able to communicate the evidence", the witness will be entitled to testify under oath or solemn affirmation.[26] However, the fact that a child under the age of 14 or a mentally incompetent person does not understand the nature of an oath or of a solemn affirmation will not necessarily exclude the child's testimony. Section 16(3) of the *Canada Evidence Act* provides that if a witness is "able to communicate the evidence" and promises "to tell the truth", the witness will be allowed to give unsworn or unaffirmed testimony.[27]

What is meant by the phrase "is able to communicate the evidence" has already been discussed. In *McGovern*,[28] it was held that the promise "to tell the truth" requires an understanding on the witness's part of what a promise is and the importance of keeping it "(O)therwise, the promise would be an empty gesture". It has also been held to require an assessment by the trial judge as to whether the witness "understands the duty to speak the truth in terms of every day social conduct".[29] As Robins J.A. pointed out in *Khan*:[30]

> This can be demonstrated through a simple line of questioning directed towards whether the child understands the difference between the truth and a lie, knows that it is wrong to tell a lie, understand the necessity to tell the truth, and promises to do so.

---

[26]   *Canada Evidence Act*, s. 16(2).

[27]   *D.(R.R.)*, 47 C.C.C. (3d) 97, 20 R.F.L. (3d) 1, 72 Sask. R. 142, 69 C.R. (3d) 267, 1989 CarswellSask 66 (C.A.).

[28]   22 C.R. (4th) 359, 88 Man. R. (2d) 18, 82 C.C.C. (3d) 301, 51 W.A.C. 18, 1993 CarswellMan 22 (C.A.), leave to appeal refused (1993), 25 C.R. (4th) 123 (note), 84 C.C.C. (3d) vi (S.C.C.).

[29]   *Farley*, 40 C.R. (4th) 190, 23 O.R. (3d) 445, 80 O.A.C. 337, 99 C.C.C. (3d) 76, 1995 CarswellOnt 119, [1995] O.J. No. 1278 (C.A.); *Ferguson*, 112 C.C.C. (3d) 342, 85 B.C.A.C. 33, 138 W.A.C. 33, 1996 CarswellBC 2888, [1996] B.C.J. No. 2617 (C.A.).

[30]   27 O.A.C. 142, 64 C.R. (3d) 281, 42 C.C.C. (3d) 197, 64 C.R. 281, 1988 CarswellOnt 69 (C.A.) at (C.R.) p. 289, affirmed, 113 N.R. 53, 79 C.R. (3d) 1, 41 O.A.C. 353, [1990] 2 S.C.R. 531, 59 C.C.C. (3d) 92, 1990 CarswellOnt 108, 1990 CarswellOnt 1001, [1990] S.C.J. No. 81, (at p. 206 [42 C.C.C. (3d)]), approved in *Farley, ibid.*, and *A. (K.)*, 123 O.A.C. 161, 137 C.C.C. (3d) 554, 1999 CarswellOnt 2118, [1999] O.J. No. 2640 (C.A.).

In other words, it entails an appreciation by the witness that he or she must answer all questions truthfully in accordance with the witness's recollection of what actually happened.[31]

Ironically, section 16 does not attach any evidentiary distinction in terms of weight to the evidence of someone who is only required to promise "to tell the truth" as opposed to someone who gives evidence under oath or affirmation. Both are entitled to the same weight. Logically, if no lesser weight is to be attached to evidence given after a simple "promise to tell the truth", then it is arguable that the requirement of an oath or a solemn affirmation is redundant and of no significance. Although, the language of section 16 viewed in its totality would appear to indicate that evidence given upon a promise "to tell the truth" is at the bottom of the scale in descending order of weight, the courts have said that the weight to be given to a young person's evidence "is not affected by the form of the witness's commitment to tell the truth".[32] In *D. (R.R.)*, Bayda C.J.S. wrote:

> The purpose of an oath, a solemn affirmation and a promise are the same: to put an additional impact on the person's conscience and to give further motivation for the person to tell the truth . . . There is no reason in logic to treat one class of witness as belonging to a higher level than another class. Nor is there any reason in logic to treat differently, from the standpoint of need and importance, the three prerequisites: an oath, a solemn affirmation and a promise.[33]

(c) Compellability

(i) *The Accused and Co-Accused*

When it is said that a witness is "compellable", it means that the law authorizes either side to call the witness to give evidence. However, the fact that a person may be competent to testify does not necessarily mean that he is automatically compellable to testify. Although the general rule is that all competent witnesses are also compellable, there are a number of exceptions.

The most notable is the accused. Although an accused is competent to testify for the defence, he is not compellable. However, if he elects to testify, he cannot refuse to answer any question that may incriminate him. He must submit to cross-examination on any issue relating to the

---

[31] *Farley, supra,* note 29.
[32] *McGovern, supra,* note 28 *per* Twaddle J.A. at (C.R.) p. 365.
[33] *Supra,* note 27, at (C.R.) pp. 274-75.

case, subject to a limited discretion in the trial judge to prevent cross-examination on a previous criminal record where it might unduly prejudice, mislead or confuse the trier of fact.[34]

A person who is jointly charged and tried with another accused is not compellable to give evidence either by the prosecution or by a co-accused at his own trial. But if his trial is severed from the trial of his co-accused by a judge's order for a separate trial, or if he is charged in a separate information or indictment by the Crown with the same offence as a co-accused, he becomes an ordinary witness at the trial of the co-accused. Although he may not be compelled to testify at his own trial, he is compellable to testify either for the prosecution or for the defence at the separate trial of his co-accused.

(ii) Spouse of the Accused

When section 4(1) of the *Canada Evidence Act* made an accused's spouse a *competent* witness for the defence, that spouse also became a *compellable* witness for the defence. However, since a spouse is not competent to testify for the prosecution, he or she is also not compellable to testify for the prosecution subject to two exceptions.

The first is the common law exception, preserved by section 4(5) of the *Canada Evidence Act*, which allows the prosecution to call the accused's spouse as a witness without the accused's consent where the common law permitted it. The common law made an exception where the evidence disclosed that the spouse's person, liberty or health had been threatened by the accused spouse. The second exception is set out in subsections 4(2) and (4) of the Act. Those subsections make husbands and wives compellable against one another with respect to certain specified offences (generally sexual offences and assaults against children under the age of 14). The purpose is to ensure that spouses will testify against one another where an offence has been committed against children, particularly their own. Before the enactment of these sections, children who had been physically or sexually assaulted by one parent could not count upon the other parent to testify against the accused parent.

It is important at this stage to draw a distinction between a "communication" made by husbands and wives to one another and an "ob-

---

[34] *Corbett*, [1988] 1 S.C.R. 670, [1988] 4 W.W.R. 481, 85 N.R. 81, 28 B.C.L.R. (2d) 145, 41 C.C.C. (3d) 385, 64 C.R. (3d) 1, 34 C.R.R. 54, 1988 CarswellBC 252, 1988 CarswellBC 756.

servation" by one spouse of the conduct of the other. The two exceptions already discussed, which allow the prosecution to compel a husband or wife to testify against the other who may be accused of a crime, are clearly applicable to "observations" made by that spouse. However, section 4(3) of the *Canada Evidence Act* appears to have preserved the common law rule that prohibits a husband or wife from being compelled by the prosecution to disclose a marital "communication". Section 4(3) provides that:

> 4(3) No husband is compellable to disclose any communication made to him by his wife during their marriage, and no wife is compellable to disclose any communication made to her by her husband during their marriage.

Not all authorities have been convinced that section 4(3) was intended to preserve the common law exception relating to marital communications. For example, in *St. Jean*,[35] Kaufman J.A. observed:

> It seems to me that it would not make sense to make a spouse competent and compellable, only to put severe restrictions on the scope of his or her testimony.

However, the appellate courts of Alberta and Ontario have not agreed with that observation.[36]

They have held that the language of section 4(3) is unambiguous and must be given its plain meaning. Although a spouse may be otherwise competent and compellable to give evidence, a spouse is not compellable to disclose any communication (but not observation) made by his or her spouse "during their marriage". Thus a wife who is giving evidence is entitled to invoke the protection of section 4(3) at any time during her testimony and to refuse to disclose a martial communication made to her by her husband.[37] It must be remembered, however, that the privilege extends only to a marital communication received by her from her husband. Section 4(3) does not protect her from revealing any marital communication which she has made to her husband.[38]

[35] 34 C.R.N.S. 378, 32 C.C.C. (2d) 438, 1976 CarswellQue 12 (C.A.) at (C.C.C.) p. 441.
[36] *Jean*, 15 A.R. 147, 7 C.R. 338, 46 C.C.C. (2d) 176, 7 C.R. (3d) 338, 1979 CarswellAlta 169 (C.A.), affirmed, [1980] 1 S.C.R. 400, 20 A.R. 360, 16 C.R. (3d) 193, 51 C.C.C. (2d) 192, 31 N.R. 410, 1980 CarswellAlta 157, 1980 CarswellAlta 312; *Mailloux*, 30 C.R. (3d) 121, 55 C.C.C. (2d) 193 at 196, 1980 CarswellOnt 77 (C.A.); *Zylstra*, 41 C.R. (4th) 130, 99 C.C.C. (3d) 477, 82 O.A.C. 394, 1995 CarswellOnt 124 (C.A.).
[37] *Zylstra, ibid.*
[38] *Lloyd*, 16 C.R. (3d) 221, 53 C.C.C. (2d) 121, 1980 CarswellBC 441 (C.A.), reversed, [1981] 2 S.C.R. 645, 31 C.R. (3d) 157, 35 B.C.L.R. 145, 64 C.C.C. (2d) 169, 131 D.L.R. (3d) 112, 39 N.R. 474, 1981 CarswellBC 633.

It must also be remembered that the protection given by section 4(3) may only be invoked for a verbal communication. If a wife receives a written communication from her husband, the privilege ceases to apply and the written communication is admissible in evidence.[39] Similarly, if a third person overhears a verbal marital communication, the privilege ceases to apply.[40]

(d) Refreshing the Witness's Memory

At the foundation of the common law adversarial system are two notions. The first assumes that a witness will have a memory of the events that he or she is relating to the court. The second assumes that the other side will be allowed to test the accuracy of that memory and the truth of that testimony by cross-examination.

Frequently, a witness who is called upon to testify weeks, months or even years after an event, may find that once he steps into the witness box, his memory has failed on some critical issue. Historically, the rule was that a witness was entitled to refresh his memory while in the witness box from any record of the event which he had with him, provided (a) that he made the note of the event himself or, if it was made by another person, he verified the accuracy of the other person's note, and (b) the note was written by him, or the record of another person was verified by him, *shortly after the event* when the facts were fresh in his memory.[41]

However, the strictness of this rule appears to have relaxed in recent years. The courts no longer require that the note be made by the witness or, if made by another, verified by the witness *shortly after the event*. What now appears to be required is that the note be made either by the witness or by another and verified by the witness, *when the event was fresh in the witness's mind*.[42] Common sense tells us that, unless the note was made at least when the event was fresh in the witness's mind, there is a serious risk that the note will contain errors that the witness will probably rely upon when giving testimony.

---

[39] *Kotapski* (1981), 66 C.C.C. (2d) 78 (Que. S.C.), affirmed (1984), 13 C.C.C. (3d) 185 (Que. C.A.), leave to appeal refused (1984), 13 C.C.C. (3d) 185 (Que. C.A.).

[40] *Jean, supra,* note 36; *Kotapski, ibid.*

[41] *Gwozdowski* (1972), [1973] 2 O.R. 50, 10 C.C.C. (2d) 434, 1972 CarswellOnt 944 (C.A.).

[42] *Coffin,* [1956] S.C.R. 191, 23 C.R. 1, 114 C.C.C. 1, 1956 CarswellQue 1; *Shergill,* 13 C.R. (5th) 160, 23 O.T.C. 218, 1997 CarswellOnt 5225 (Gen. Div.); *B. (K.G.),* 125 C.C.C. (3d) 61, 109 O.A.C. 138, 1998 CarswellOnt 1914, [1998] O.J. No. 1859 (C.A.).

English courts have also relaxed the strictness of the rule.[43] There the question is one for the discretion of the trial judge applying the requirements of fairness and justice. Such a rule is obviously more sensible. It seems rather arbitrary to say that a witness is only entitled to refresh his or her memory if the note is made shortly after the event. A police officer doing undercover work or on surveillance duty may be unable to make notes until hours after the event in question. Nevertheless, the risk of possible error from the delay cannot be ignored and should be the subject of a caution by the judge to the jury when assessing the weight of the witness's testimony.[44]

It is a common and accepted practice for the Crown to give witnesses the transcript of the preliminary inquiry and to ask them to read their testimony at the inquiry in order to refresh their memory of the events in issue before they testify at trial.[45] Although evidence given at the preliminary inquiry is obviously closer to those events in issue, today's preliminary inquiries are often held months or sometimes a year after the event. Presumably, justification for allowing witnesses to refresh their memory from the transcript of the inquiry is based on the fact that before they testified at the inquiry, they refreshed their memory from notes made or a statement given to the police shortly after the event, or at least when the events were fresh in their minds.

At one time, the rule was that a witness was only required to produce the notes to the cross-examiner if the witness relied upon the notes while testifying in court; if the witness used the notes to refresh his or her memory before entering the witness box, the witness did not have to produce them to the cross-examiner.[46]

The logic of this distinction was difficult to understand. All it did was encourage witnesses to memorize their notes before they came to court. Today, it is generally accepted that any witness who refreshes his or her memory from notes or any statement he or she or anyone else prepared prior to trial, or uses those notes to assist during his or her testimony, must produce them to the cross-examiner.[47] This rule makes more sense. If a witness refreshes his or her memory before trial or relies

---

[43] *South Ribble Magistrates, ex p. Cochrane*, [1996] 2 Cr. App. R. 544; *Da Silva* (1990), 90 Cr. App. R. 233 (C.A.).

[44] *B. (K.G.), supra,* note 42.

[45] *Coffin, supra,* note 42.

[46] *Kerenko* (1964), 45 C.R. 291, 51 W.W.R. 53, [1965] 3 C.C.C. 52, 49 D.L.R. (2d) 760, 1964 CarswellMan 65 (C.A.).

[47] *Catling*, 73 A.R. 61, 29 C.C.C. (3d) 168, 1984 CarswellAlta 391 (Q.B.); *Morgan*, 80 C.C.C. (3d) 16, 1993 CarswellOnt 795 (C.A.), leave to appeal refused (1994), 87 C.C.C. (3d) vi (note), 72 O.A.C. 82 (note), 172 N.R. 246 (note) (S.C.C.).

upon notes or any document at trial, then what the witness says when he or she gives testimony may be essentially the information contained in those notes. The cross-examiner should be allowed to examine the notes to consider whether they are consistent with the witness's oral testimony. The cross-examiner may also wish to attack the accuracy of the notes by questioning the timeliness of the record or raising the possibility of invention.

The discussion so far has proceeded on the assumption that the witness has some recollection of the events in issue, but wishes to use the notes to jog or refresh his or her memory. This is what is known as "present memory revived". What happens, however, if the notes do not refresh the witness's memory and that memory is lost forever? Is testimony of that witness lost forever, even though the witness may have made notes of the event? Can the written word ever replace the lost memory?

Professor Wigmore recognized that total memory loss did not necessarily result in lost testimony where certain conditions were met.[48] He called it "past recollection recorded". Those conditions were,

1. The past recollection must have been recorded in some reliable way.
2. At the time, it must have been sufficiently fresh and vivid to be probably accurate.
3. The witness must be able now to assert that the record accurately represented his knowledge and recollection at the time, The usual phrase requires the witness to affirm that "he knew it to be true at the time."
4. The original record itself must be used, if procurable.

In other words, the notes or record made at the time replace the memory of the witness and become "past memory recorded".

Canadian courts have been slow to recognize past recollection recorded as an exception to the hearsay rule.[49] The reason may be because of the difficulty in effectively cross-examining a witness who has made a record of the event, but has no memory of. All that the witness can say is that he or she made a note at the time and, when the note was made, believed it to be true. The witness cannot be cross-examined as to the

---

[48] *Wigmore on Evidence* (Chadbourn rev. 1970), Vol. 3, c. 28, para. 744 *et seq.*
[49] See *Rouse* (1978), [1979] 1 S.C.R. 588, 5 C.R. (3d) 125, [1978] 6 W.W.R. 585, 42 C.C.C. (2d) 481, 23 N.R. 589, 89 D.L.R. (3d) 609, 1978 CarswellBC 508; *Green*, 32 C.R. (4th) 248, 1994 CarswellOnt 96 (Gen. Div.).

accuracy of the contents of the note because the witness cannot recall the contents. Although the necessity for admitting the note is the lack of recollection by the witness, the only basis for the note's reliability is the assurance of the witness that he or she believed the note to be true at the time it was made.

Few Canadian authorities have also paid much attention to the distinction between "present memory revived" and "past recollection recorded".[50] This may be due to the fact that a witness who is asked to refresh his or her memory from a statement or note before testifying will usually be reluctant to admit that he or she has absolutely no memory of an event. The problem is that once the witness has reviewed the statement or the note, it is almost impossible for the cross-examiner to determine whether the witness is relying on the note, or his or her memory of the event, or both.

(e) The Adverse or Hostile Witness

(i) The General Rule

The rule, already noted, is that the side who calls a witness is not allowed to ask that witness leading questions, that is, questions that directly or indirectly suggest the answer to the witness. Nevertheless, there may be occasions when a witness will have a lapse of memory and not be responsive to the questions asked by the examiner. In the case of a written statement, this situation may be remedied by simply showing the witness his previous statement and asking him to read it over.[51] It may jog the witness's memory. When this happens, the witness is, in effect, being allowed to refresh his memory. If the previous statement was an oral one, then counsel is entitled to draw the witness's attention to the circumstances surrounding the making of the statement and ask him if he made it.

---

[50] See *Meddoui* (1990), 77 Alta. L.R. (2d) 97, 111 A.R. 295, 2 C.R. (4th) 316, 61 C.C.C. (3d) 345, [1991] 2 W.W.R. 289, 5 C.R.R. (2d) 294, 1990 CarswellAlta 187 (C.A.), quashed, [1991] 3 S.C.R. ix, [1992] 1 W.W.R. lxv (note), 6 C.R.R. (2d) 192 (note), 82 Alta. L.R. (2d) lxv (note), 69 C.C.C. (3d) vi (note), 137 N.R. 389 (note); *B. (A.J.)*, 90 C.C.C. (3d) 210, 120 Nfld. & P.E.I.R. 147, 373 A.P.R. 147, 1994 CarswellNfld 206 (C.A.), reversed, 98 C.C.C. (3d) 95, 133 Nfld. & P.E.I.R. 231, 413 A.P.R. 231, 182 N.R. 384, [1995] 2 S.C.R. 413, 1995 CarswellNfld 43F, leave to appeal allowed (October 6, 1994), Doc. 24182 (S.C.C.) and *F. (C.)*, 220 N.R. 362, 154 D.L.R. (4th) 13, 120 C.C.C. (3d) 225, 11 C.R. (5th) 209, [1997] 3 S.C.R. 1183, 104 O.A.C. 321, 1997 CarswellOnt 4448, 1997 CarswellOnt 4449, [1997] S.C.J. No. 89.

[51] *Coffin, supra,* note 42.

If the witness cannot remember making the previous inconsistent statement, or denies making it, or admits making it but says that it is false, the examiner is entitled to call other witnesses to contradict the witness's testimony. This remedy is rarely satisfactory since the witness's testimony, although contradicted by the testimony of other witnesses, may still be considered by the trier with all of the testimony. The examiner is now faced with a problem. Unless the examiner is able to impeach his witness's testimony with the prior inconsistent statement, the trier will be entitled to consider the witness's in-court testimony for what it is worth.

Section 9(1) of the *Canada Evidence Act* offers the examiner a solution. It provides:

> 9(1) A party producing a witness shall not be allowed to impeach his credit by general evidence of bad character, but if the witness, in the opinion of the court, proves adverse, the party may contradict him by other evidence, or, by leave of the court, may prove that the witness made at other times a statement inconsistent with his present testimony, but before the last mentioned proof can be given the circumstances of the supposed statement, sufficient to designate the particular occasion, shall be mentioned to the witness, and he shall be asked whether or not he did make the statement.

It should be noted at the outset that section 9(1) starts off by stating the general rule that a person calling a witness may not "impeach his credit by general evidence of bad character". The section then goes on to say illogically, "but if the witness, in the opinion of the court, proves adverse," he may be contradicted by other evidence or a prior inconsistent statement. Unfortunately, the draftsman of this legislation misstated the common law and put the cart before the horse. At common law, an examiner was not required to prove that the witness was *adverse* before the witness could be contradicted by other inconsistent evidence. An examiner was entitled to use the prior inconsistent evidence to prove the witness adverse (or hostile). Fortunately, the courts have ignored this apparent condition precedent and have allowed the calling of other evidence to contradict a witness.

Section 9(1) declares the common law and allows the examiner to use the cross-examination on the previous inconsistent evidence to have the witness declared "adverse" by the trial judge. At common law, the term used was "hostile". Once a witness is declared adverse or hostile, the witness may be cross-examined, not only with respect to his previous inconsistent evidence or statement, but on the whole of his evidence, or what is commonly called "at large".

The traditional view has been that "a hostile witness is a witness who, from the manner in which he gives his evidence, shows that he is not desirous of telling the truth to the court".[52] In other words, the witness must show some manifest hostility or animosity towards the side that has called him to give evidence. The court must determine this hostility by observing the witness's general attitude or demeanour in the witness stand and the substance of his or her evidence.

Section 24 of the Ontario *Evidence Act*[53] also codifies the common law with respect to civil proceedings. Although cast in similar language, it does not require the court to first make a finding of adversity before the witness can be impeached by other evidence. Moreover, in *Hanes v. Wawanesa Mutual Insurance Co.*,[54] the Ontario Court of Appeal said that the word "adverse" should be given its ordinary meaning of "opposed in interest" and not the restricted meaning of "hostile". This means that in determining whether the witness is "adverse", the judge is not limited to a consideration only of the witness's demeanour or attitude in the witness box. The trial judge is also entitled to consider the witness's prior inconsistent statement in determining whether he was adverse.

However, not all courts accepted this interpretation of section 9(1) of the *Canada Evidence Act*. The result was that in 1969, section 9(2) was added. It provides:

> 9(2) Where the party producing a witness alleges that the witness made at other times a statement in writing, reduced to writing, or recorded on audio tape or video tape or otherwise, inconsistent with his present testimony, the court may, without proof that the witness is adverse, grant leave to that party to cross-examine the witness as to the statement and the court may consider the cross-examination in determining whether in the opinion of the court the witness is adverse.

This section is now legislative recognition that the trial judge is not first required to make a finding of adversity before cross-examination may be permitted on a prior inconsistent statement. However, it should be noted that section 9(2) only applies to "a statement in writing, reduced to writing, or recorded on audio tape or video tape or otherwise". It does not apply to an oral statement made by the witness.

[52] *Coles v. Coles* (1866), L.R. 1, p. 70.
[53] R.S.O. 1990, c. E.23.
[54] [1961] O.R. 495, [1963] 1 C.C.C. 176, 28 D.L.R. (2d) 386 (C.A.), reversed, [1963] S.C.R. 154, [1963] 1 C.C.C. 321, 36 D.L.R. (2d) 718, 1963 CarswellOnt 61.

In *Milgaard*,[55] the Saskatchewan Court of Appeal suggested the following procedure be used where this situation arises:

1. Counsel should advise the court that he desires to make an application under section9(2) of the *Canada Evidence Act*.
2. When the court is so advised, the court should direct the jury to retire.
3. Upon retirement of the jury, counsel should advise the trial judge of the particulars of the application and produce for him the alleged statement in writing or the writing to which the statement has been reduced.
4. The trial judge should read the statement, or writing, and determine whether, in fact, there is an inconsistency between the statement or writing and the evidence the witness has given in court. If he decides that there is no inconsistency, then that is the end of the matter. If he finds that there is an inconsistency, he should then call upon counsel to prove the statement or writing.
5. Counsel should then prove the statement or writing. This may be done by producing the statement or writing to the witness. If the witness admits the statement, or the statement reduced to writing, such proof is sufficient. If the witness does not admit it, counsel should then provide the necessary proof by other evidence.
6. If the witness admits making the statement, counsel for the opposing party should have the right to cross-examine as to the circumstances under which the statement was made. A similar right to cross-examine should be granted if the statement is proved by other witnesses. It may be that he will be able to establish that there were circumstances which would render it improper for the trial judge to permit the cross-examination, notwithstanding the apparent inconsistencies. The opposing counsel, too, should have the right to call evidence as to factors relevant to obtaining the statement, for the purpose of attempting to show that cross-examination should not be permitted.
7. The trial judge should then decide whether or not he will permit the cross-examination. If so, the jury should be recalled.

One matter that should be stressed when counsel is proceeding under section 9(2) is that until the witness is declared adverse, cross-examination is limited to the statement that the court finds is a previous

55 [1971] 2 W.W.R. 266, 2 C.C.C. (2d) 206, 14 C.R.N.S. 34, 1971 CarswellSask 26 (C.A.), leave to appeal refused (1971), 4 C.C.C. (2d) 566n (S.C.C.).

inconsistent statement. However, once the court rules that the witness is adverse, the witness may then be cross-examined at large, that is, on his entire evidence.

What steps may counsel take if the previous statement is an oral one? Until the decision of the Ontario Court of Appeal in 1982 in *Cassibo*,[56] the general view was that a judge could not consider a previous inconsistent oral statement in determining whether a witness was adverse because section 9(2) was restricted to previous written statements or ones reduced to writing. However, the *Cassibo* case rejected the notion that section 9(2) was such a compromise and held that a previous oral statement could still be considered under section 9(1) of the *Canada Evidence Act* in deciding whether the witness is adverse.

Finally, as already noted, in deciding whether a witness is adverse, the court is not restricted to relying only on the inconsistency in his testimony with a previous statement or the answers that he gives in his testimony. The court may also determine that a witness is adverse by observing his general attitude or demeanour in the witness stand, the substance of his evidence and any other contradictory evidence.

(ii) Use That Can be Made of a Prior Inconsistent Statement

(A) The Orthodox Rule

What use can be made of a prior inconsistent statement? Until recently, the common law rule was that if the witness denies making the statement or says that it is false, then no use can be made of it on the issue of its truth. The jury is not entitled to accept the prior inconsistent statement for its truth, even if they do not believe the witness's testimony. The jury is only entitled to accept the prior inconsistent statement for its truth if the witness adopts the statement as the truth while giving testimony in the witness stand.[57] Unless adopted as the truth, the prior inconsistent statement can only be used to cancel out or neutralize the witness's damaging testimony given in court. In other words, it can only

[56]   39 O.R. (2d) 288, 70 C.C.C. (2d) 498, 1982 CarswellOnt 850 (C.A.).
[57]   *Deacon*, [1947] S.C.R. 531, 89 C.C.C. 1, 3 C.R. 265, [1947] 3 D.L.R. 772, 1947 CarswellMan 1; *Mannion*, [1986] 6 W.W.R. 525, [1986] 2 S.C.R. 272, 31 D.L.R. (4th) 712, 69 N.R. 189, 47 Alta. L.R. (2d) 177, 75 A.R. 16, 28 C.C.C. (3d) 544, 53 C.R. (3d) 193, 25 C.R.R. 182, 1986 CarswellAlta 190, 1986 CarswellAlta 715; *Kuldip*, 1 C.R. (4th) 285, 1 C.R.R. (2d) 110, 43 O.A.C. 340, 61 C.C.C. (3d) 385, 114 N.R. 284, [1990] 3 S.C.R. 618, 1990 CarswellOnt 62, 1990 CarswellOnt 1010.

be used in assessing the credibility of the harmful testimony given by the witness.

In applying the rule, the courts have been careful to ensure that the prosecution does not try to use a prior inconsistent statement to unfairly cancel out or cast doubt on the credibility of the defence witnesses. For example, in *Soobrian*,[58] two accused, who were friends, were charged with sexual assault. A third friend, who was present during the alleged assault, told the police that he did not observe any sexual activity. Later, however, at the preliminary inquiry, he told the police that he had observed consensual sexual activity between the accused and the complainant. At trial, the Crown called the witness in expectation that he would testify in a manner consistent with his preliminary inquiry testimony. The Crown's purpose in calling the witness was to demonstrate the inconsistency between the witness's first statement to the police and his later testimony at the preliminary inquiry in an effort to obtain leave to cross-examine him under section 9(2) of the *Canada Evidence Act* and possibly have him declared adverse under section 9(1) of the Act. In other words, it was to prove that since the witness was lying, so were his friends, the accused. The Court held that since a finding that the witness was adverse would serve no purpose other than to neutralize his evidence and would have no bearing on whether the accused were credible, the Crown should not have been permitted to proceed in this fashion. It was unfair because it was an attempt by the Crown to prove that the entire defence was a fabrication without any evidence of either accused's involvement in fabricating it.

One reason why a prior inconsistent statement is not admissible for its truth is because what the witness said on a prior occasion is hearsay (which will be discussed in Part B). The courts have been concerned that what the witness said on a prior occasion was not said under oath or solemn affirmation and the judge or jury had no opportunity to observe the witness's demeanour when the statement was made in order to assess the credibility of the witness. Probably the strongest reason why a prior inconsistent statement has not been admissible for its truth is that the other side did not have the opportunity to cross-examine the witness when he made the statement.

---

[58]   76 O.A.C. 7, 96 C.C.C. (3d) 208, 21 O.R. (3d) 603, 1994 CarswellOnt 202 (C.A.).

(B) The Modern Rule

Not everyone has agreed with the logic of the orthodox rule that has restricted the use of a prior consistent statement to an assessment of the credibility of its maker. Mr. Justice Estey, in a dissenting judgment in *Rouse*[59] could not understand why a witness's prior inconsistent statement should not be considered for its truth as well as for the credibility of the witness. Even though the prior inconsistent statement was hearsay, he could not see why the rule should be enforced where the witness was in the witness box and available for cross-examination. Others have argued that the lack of opportunity by the judge and jury to observe the demeanour of the witness at the time that the statement was made, and thus to assess credibility based on that demeanour, is overstated. They point out that the opportunity to observe the witness at trial denying or professing not to remember making the statement can give the judge and jury insight into the truthfulness of the prior statement. They argue that the power of an oath as a means of ensuring reliability of evidence must be discounted. Moreover, they note that the witness is under oath when he testifies at trial.

All of these various attacks on the orthodox rule were finally considered by the Supreme Court of Canada in *B. (K.G.).*[60] There the Court decided that the time had come for the orthodox rule to be replaced by a new one that recognized the changed means and methods of proof in modern society. It was felt that changing the rule was not a matter better left to Parliament, since it was a judge-made rule. The rule lent itself to judicial reform and was a natural and incremental progression in the development of the law of hearsay in Canada.

Chief Justice Lamer, delivering the majority judgment of the Court, stressed that the focal issue for consideration by the trial judge is the comparative reliability of the prior statement and the testimony offered at trial. That criterion of reliability is satisfied when the circumstances in which the prior statement was made provide sufficient guarantees of its trustworthiness with respect to the dangers of the absence of oath and the inability of the trier of fact to assess the declarant's demeanour.

It was his view that there would be sufficient guarantees of reliability to allow the jury to make substantive use of a prior statement if:

1.   It was made under oath, solemn affirmation or solemn declaration

---

[59] *Supra,* note 49.
[60] 19 C.R. (4th) 1, [1993] 1 S.C.R. 740, 61 O.A.C. 1, 148 N.R. 241, 79 C.C.C. (3d) 257, 1993 CarswellOnt 76, 1993 CarswellOnt 975, [1993] S.C.J. No. 22.

following an explicit warning to the witness as to the existence of severe criminal sanctions for the making of a false statement;

2.   It was videotaped in its entirety; and

3.   The opposing party, whether the Crown or the defence, had a full opportunity to cross-examine the witness at trial respecting the statement.

In his reasons, the Chief Justice indicated that he was not restricting the admissibility of a prior inconsistent statement for its truth to the fulfilment of the three conditions. He left it open to the trial judge to consider other guarantees of reliability, provided that the judge was satisfied that the circumstances provided adequate assurances of reliability in place of those which the hearsay rule traditionally required. He summed up the role of the trial judge this way:

> ...in the part of the *voir dire* addressing the new rule, the trial judge must first satisfy him or herself that the indicia of reliability necessary to admit hearsay evidence of prior statements — a warning, oath, solemn affirmation, or solemn declaration, and videotape record, or sufficient substitutes — are present and genuine. If they are, he or she must then examine the circumstances under which the statement was obtained, to satisfy him or herself that the statement supported by the indicia of reliability was made voluntarily if to a person in authority, and that there are no other factors which would tend to bring the administration of justice into disrepute if the statement was admitted as substantive evidence. In most cases, as in this case, the party seeking to admit the prior inconsistent statements as substantive evidence will have to establish that these requirements have been satisfied on the balance of probabilities. The trial judge is not to decide whether the prior inconsistent statement is true, or more reliable than the present testimony, as that is a matter for the trier of fact. Once this process is complete, and all of its constituent elements satisfied, the trial judge need not issue the standard limiting instruction to the jury, but may instead tell the jury that they may take the statement as substantive evidence of its contents, or, if he or she is sitting alone, make substantive use of the statement, giving the evidence the appropriate weight after taking into account all of the circumstances. In either case, the judge must direct the trier of fact to consider carefully these circumstances in assessing the credibility of the prior inconsistent statement relative to the witness' testimony at trial. For example, where appropriate the trial judge might make specific reference to the significance of the demeanour of the witness at all relevant times (which could include when making the statement, when recanting at trial, and/or when presenting conflicting testimony at trial), the reasons offered by the witness for his or her recantation, any motivation and/or opportunity the witness had to fabricate his or her evidence when making the previous statement or when testifying at trial, the events leading up to the making of the first statement and the nature of the

interview at which the statement was made (including the use of leading question, and the existence of pre-statement interview or coaching), corroboration of the facts in the statement by other evidence, and the extent to which the nature of the witness' recantation limits the effectiveness of cross-examination on the previous statement. There may be other factors the trier of fact should consider, and the trial judge should impress upon the trier of fact the importance of carefully assessing all such matters in determining the weight to be afforded prior inconsistent statements as substantive evidence.

Where the prior statement does not have the necessary circumstantial guarantees of reliability, and so cannot pass the threshold test on the *voir dire*, but the party tendering the prior statement otherwise satisfied the requirements of ss. 9(1) or (2) of the *Canada Evidence Act*, the statement may still be tendered into evidence, but the trial judge must instruct the jury in the terms of the orthodox rule.[61]

In *U. (F.J.)*,[62] the Supreme Court re-affirmed the modern rule that when the reliability and necessity criteria are met, prior inconsistent statements of witnesses, other than the accused, are substantially admissible for their truth, provided that they would have been admissible as the witness's sole testimony. The Court noted that the gravest danger associated with hearsay evidence, namely, the absence of contemporaneous cross-examination, simply does not exist in the case of prior inconsistent statements because the witness is available for cross-examination. It also noted that the other two dangers, namely, the absence of an oath and absence of demeanour evidence, can be met through appropriate police procedures and occasionally appropriate substitutes can be found. The Court stressed that a prior statement is necessary evidence when a witness recants.

In *U.(F.J.)* both the accused and the complainant had made separate statements containing similarities to the police. However, both had recanted at trial. The Court held that a threshold of reliability can be established in cases where the witness is available for cross-examination by a striking similarity between two statements. In order to eliminate, or at least substantially reduce, the likelihood of a similarity between two statements arising through coincidence, the similar factual assertion must be so striking that it is unlikely two people would have independently fabricated it. In some cases, the necessary degree of similarity will result from the unique nature of particular factual assertions in both statements. In other situations, it may be that the cumulative combination of similar points renders the overall similarity between the two state-

---

[61] *Ibid.*, at (C.R.) pp. 45-46.
[62] 42 C.R. (4th) 133, 101 C.C.C. (3d) 97, 128 D.L.R. (4th) 121, 186 N.R. 365, 85 O.A.C. 321, [1995] 3 S.C.R. 764, 1995 CarswellOnt 555, 1995 CarswellOnt 1175.

ments sufficiently distinctive to reject coincidence as a likely explanation.

The Court set out the procedure that should be followed where the party invokes section 9 of the *Canada Evidence Act* and fulfils its requirements on the *voir dire* under that section:

1.   The party must state its objectives in tendering the statement. If the statement is only to be used to impeach the witness, the inquiry ends at this point. If, however, the party calling the witness wishes to make substantive use of the statement, the *voir dire* must continue so that the trial judge can assess whether a threshold of reliability has been met. However, the criteria of necessity need not be assessed as it is met whenever a witness recants.

2.   If the reliability criterion is to be met, in rare cases, by the striking similarity between the statement being assessed and another statement which is already clearly substantively admissible, the trial judge must be satisfied on a balance of probabilities that there are striking similarities between the two statements, and there was neither reason nor opportunity for the declarants to collude, nor improper influence by interrogators or other third parties. The trial judge must also ascertain that the prior statement relates to evidence which would be admissible as the witness's sole testimony.

3.   If the trial judge determines that the statement meets the threshold reliability criterion and is thus substantively admissible, he or she must direct the jury to follow a two-step process in evaluating the evidence.

       (a)   The jury must first be certain that the statement which is being used as a reliability referent was made, without taking into account the prior inconsistent statement under consideration.

       (b)   Once the jury are satisfied that the other statement was made, they may compare the similarities between the two statements. If they are sufficiently striking that it is unlikely that the two people independently fabricated them, then they may draw conclusions from that comparison about the truth of the statements.

One of the difficulties with Step 3, which requires that the jury "*must first be certain* that the statement which is being used as a reliability referent, was made", is how the trial judge is to instruct the jury as to the way that the statement may be used by them. The requirement that jury "*must first be certain*" presumably means proof beyond a reasonable doubt. However, the same Court in *MacKenzie*,[63] approved the judgment of the Ontario Court of Appeal in *Minhas*,[64] where Martin J.A. held that "the instruction that the jury must be satisfied beyond a reasonable doubt that the statements alleged to have been made by the appellant were, in fact, made by her ... was ... more favourable to the appellant than the instructions to which she was by law entitled". Moreover, in *Dipietro*,[65] the Supreme Court held that the judge must tell the jury that they must determine whether the Crown has established on a balance of probabilities that the statements were those of the accused, and if that threshold is met, then the jury may consider the statements with all of the other evidence in the case to determine whether or not guilt has been proven beyond a reasonable doubt.[66] In other words, the decision of the Supreme Court in *U.(F.J.)* will undoubtedly create difficulty for the trial judge and confusion for the jury where they must be instructed that *they must be certain* the accused's statement was made when the statement is used as a reliability referent on a *B. (K.G.)* (now *U.(F.J.)*) application, but they must only be satisfied on balance where the statement is tendered by the Crown to prove that the statement, in fact, was made by the accused.

Since the goal of the Crown in attempting to introduce a prior inconsistent statement is to contradict the truth of the declarant's sworn testimony, it would seem to follow that the test for reliability should be more stringent than for other forms of hearsay.[67] On the other hand, authorities have suggested that the trial judge should not apply the same strict standards for reliability of the prior out-of-court statements to the defence as it does to the Crown.[68] As Martin J.A. noted in *Williams*:[69]

---

[63] 18 C.R. (4th) 133, [1993] 1 S.C.R. 212, 146 N.R. 321, 118 N.S.R. (2d) 290, 327 A.P.R. 290, 78 C.C.C. (3d) 193, 1993 CarswellNS 12, 1993 CarswellNS 270.

[64] 16 O.A.C. 42, 53 C.R. (3d) 128, 29 C.C.C. (3d) 193, 1986 CarswellOnt 125 (C.A.), leave to appeal refused (1987), 86 N.R. 320 (note) (S.C.C.).

[65] 13 Alta. L.R. (3d) 1, 145 A.R. 81, 55 W.A.C. 81, 85 C.C.C. (3d) 97, [1993] 3 S.C.R. 653, 158 N.R. 278, 25 C.R. (4th) 46, 108 D.L.R. (4th) 32, 1993 CarswellAlta 111, 1993 CarswellAlta 567.

[66] See also *Dickson* (1993), 13 O.R. (3d) 489, 63 O.A.C. 254 (C.A.).

[67] *Diu*, 144 C.C.C. (3d) 481, 33 C.R. (5th) 203, 49 O.R. (3d) 40, 133 O.A.C. 201, 2000 CarswellOnt 1727, [2000] O.J. No. 1770 (C.A.).

[68] *Eisenhauer*, 165 N.S.R. (2d) 81, 495 A.P.R. 81, 123 C.C.C. (3d) 37, 14 C.R. (5th) 35, 1998 CarswellNS 65 (C.A.), leave to appeal refused (1998), 230 N.R. 400 (note), 171 N.S.R. (2d) 200 (note), 519 A.P.R. 200 (note), 126 C.C.C. (3d) vi (note) (S.C.C.) at (C.C.C.) p. 64; *F. (G.)*, 132 C.C.C. (3d) 14, 116 O.A.C. 345, 43 O.R. (3d) 290, 1999 CarswellOnt 129 (C.A.).

[69] 50 O.R. (2d) 321, 7 O.A.C. 201, 18 C.C.C. (3d) 356, 44 C.R. (3d) 351, 14 C.R.R. 251, 1985 CarswellOnt 86 (C.A.), leave to appeal refused, 50 O.R. (2d) 321n, 44 C.R. (3d) 351n, 18 C.C.C. (3d) 356n, 10 O.A.C. 319 (note), 59 N.R. 160, [1985] 1 S.C.R. xiv.

It seems to me that a court has a residual discretion to relax in favour of the accused a strict rule of evidence which is necessary to prevent a miscarriage of justice and where the danger against which an exclusionary rule aims to safeguard does not exist.[70]

Although the trial judge may be satisfied as to the reliability of the prior inconsistent statement of a witness, it is an error for the judge to tell the jury that he has found it sufficiently reliable to warrant its reception as original evidence.[71] It is up to the jury to assess the reliability of the statement and the weight to be given to it relative to the witness's evidence at trial and the judge is required to instruct them to this effect.

(f) Protection or Privilege from Answering Questions

(i) Generally

When a witness enters the witness box, he is required to answer all questions that are relevant to the facts in issue. The common law, however, has recognized that, for reasons of public policy, certain persons should be protected from answering questions touching on certain matters. This does not mean that the questions asked by examining counsel or the answers counsel seeks are irrelevant to the issues in the case. They may be very relevant. It simply means that the courts have concluded that society, as a whole, would be better served if some witnesses were protected from revealing certain information, even though that information was important and crucial to the determination of the issues in the case.

What kind of information is protected?

(ii) The Privilege Against Self-Incrimination

In the early common law, anyone accused of heresy or some other crime could be brought before a judge or some other public official and ordered to take an oath to answer truthfully all the questions that might be put to him. He was not told of the specific crime that he was suspected to have committed nor the names of the witnesses against him. If he refused to take the oath or answer the questions put to him, he was thrown into prison and kept there until he agreed to answer the questions.

---

[70]   *Ibid.*, at (C.C.C.) p. 378.

[71]   *Gilling*, 101 O.A.C. 297, 117 C.C.C. (3d) 444, 34 O.R. (3d) 392, 1997 CarswellOnt 2353 (C.A.).

By the beginning of the seventeenth century, many persons summoned for questioning refused to take the oath and claimed that "no man should be required to incriminate himself". The prosecution of *John Lilburne*[72] brought the matter to the attention of the courts and Parliament and, by the end of the seventeenth century, the claim of privilege became firmly established in all courts. It was enshrined in the American *Bill of Rights* as the Fifth Amendment on September 25th, 1789. In Canada, it was given constitutional recognition by section 11(c) of the *Charter of Rights and Freedoms* in 1982. Section 11(c) provides that,

> Any person charged with an offence has the right
>
> . . .
>
> (c) not to be compelled to be a witness in proceedings against that person in respect of the offence.

Section 11(c) thus protects an accused from being forced to enter the witness box to give evidence in any proceedings against him or her. However, if the accused chooses voluntarily to testify, then he or she loses the privilege of silence and is treated like any other witness. Once an accused chooses to testify, section 5(1) of the *Canada Evidence Act* requires him or her to answer all questions that are put by counsel or the judge. Any testimony that the accused gives may be considered by the trier in determining his or her guilt or innocence of the charge.

However, section 5(2) of the *Canada Evidence Act* guarantees the accused (or any witness who testifies) that in exchange for being compelled to answer a question, his or her testimony at trial is protected from being used against him or her in any other criminal proceeding, except a later prosecution for perjury in the giving of that evidence or for giving contradictory evidence. Similar protection is guaranteed an accused under provincial evidence statutes. The same protection is also given constitutional recognition by section 13 of the *Charter*.

Section 13 provides:

> A witness who testifies in any proceedings has the right not to have any incriminating evidence so given used to incriminate the witness in any other proceedings, except in a prosecution for perjury or for the giving of contradictory evidence.

---

[72]   (1649), 4 St. Tr. 1270.

It is important to note that although section 5(2) of the *Canada Evidence Act* and section 13 of the *Charter* appear to overlap in their protection of an accused's right to silence, there is a distinct difference between the two sections. Section 5(2) requires the witness at the first proceeding to object to answering the question in order to trigger the protection given by that section. Section 13 of the Charter automatically gives the witness protection.

Although the testimony of an accused or any witness may not be used to incriminate him or her at a later proceeding, there does not appear to be any restriction on the Crown using evidence given by an accused in a prior proceeding to test or impeach his or her credibility at trial. However, the Supreme Court has drawn a distinction between cross-examination on the prior evidence for the purpose of impeaching credibility and cross-examination to incriminate the accused, that is, to establish guilt. Thus, it would appear to be open for the Crown to ask the accused questions about the apparent inconsistencies between testimony given at the previous proceedings and the testimony that he or she is now giving. What the Court seems to frown upon are questions that are designed to incriminate the accused.[73] This imposes upon the trial judge the responsibility of warning the jury that the purpose of the cross-examination is to test the credibility. It must not be used to establish the truth of the prior evidence.

(iii) Spousal Privilege

As noted earlier, an accused's spouse is not competent nor compellable as a witness for the prosecution unless the offence charged is one of those listed in subsections (2) and (4) of section 4 of the *Canada Evidence Act* or is subject to the common law exception preserved by section 4(5) of the Act. The common law exception arises in those cases where the charge affects the person, health or liberty of the spouse of the accused. For a long time, Canadian law was uncertain whether the charge itself had to specifically allege a threat to the spouse, or if it was enough that the evidence itself disclosed such a threat. In England, the Court of Criminal Appeal had decided that the nature of the charge had to affect a spouse's health or liberty.[74] Canadian authorities, however, eventually began to adopt a liberal approach allowing a spouse to testify

---

[73]   *Kuldip*, 1 C.R. (4th) 285, 1 C.R.R. (2d) 110, 43 O.A.C. 340, 61 C.C.C. (3d) 385, 114 N.R. 284, [1990] 3 S.C.R. 618, 1990 CarswellOnt 62, 1990 CarswellOnt 1010; *Dhaliwal*, 60 C.C.C. (3d) 302, 1990 CarswellBC 658 (C.A.).

[74]   *Director of Public Prosecutions v. Blady*, [1912] 2 K.B. 89 (K.B.).

where the evidence revealed that his or her health or liberty was affected.[75]

Although the common law exception extends to cases involving the health or liberty of a spouse, it does not, ironically, apply where the health or liberty of a child of the accused is involved. In other words, at common law, a wife was able to testify against her husband where he assaulted her, but not where he assaulted their child. An attempt to rectify this situation was made in 1903 by an amendment to the *Canada Evidence Act*. That amendment listed a number of offences, primarily sexual offences, where a spouse was both competent and compellable for the prosecution, but it omitted simple assaults. In 1983, that omission was corrected by a further amendment to section 4(4).

Spousal privilege against compellability by the prosecution will extend only as long as the parties are married at the time of trial and are living together. If the parties are married at the time of the offence, but are divorced at the time of trial, then the privilege does not apply.[76] Since the modern justification for the rule is that it promotes marital harmony, it is against common sense that spousal privilege should continue after divorce.

That view has given support to the argument that spousal privilege should not continue if the parties are separated and there is no reasonable possibility of reconciliation;[77] nor should spousal incompetence or non-compellability be extended to so-called "common law marriages" or similar relationships since they are not recognized by law.[78]

In *Salituro*, Mr. Justice Iacobucci wrote:

> Absent parliamentary intervention, I would conclude that changing the common law rule to make spouses who are irreconcilably separated competent witnesses for the prosecution would be appropriate. Although the principles upon which this change is based would appear to favour abolishing the rule entirely and making all spouses competent witnesses under all circumstances, policy considerations and uncertainty as to the consequences of such change suggest that a more cautious approach is appropriate. The parties before us

---

[75] *Sillars* (1978), [1979] 1 W.W.R. 743, 45 C.C.C. (2d) 283, 12 C.R. (3d) 202, 1978 CarswellBC 541 (C.A.); *Czipps*, 25 O.R. (2d) 527, 12 C.R. (3d) 193, 101 D.L.R. (3d) 323, 48 C.C.C. (2d) 166, 1979 CarswellOnt 56 (C.A.).

[76] *Marchand*, 39 N.S.R. (2d) 700, 71 A.P.R. 700, 55 C.C.C. (2d) 77, 115 D.L.R. (3d) 403, 1980 CarswellNS 95 (C.A.); *Bailey*, 32 C.R. (3d) 337, 4 C.C.C. (3d) 21, 1983 CarswellOnt 62 (C.A.).

[77] *Salituro*, 38 O.A.C. 241, 78 C.R. (3d) 68, 56 C.C.C. (3d) 350, 1990 CarswellOnt 101 (C.A.), affirmed, 9 C.R. (4th) 324, 8 C.R.R. (2d) 173, 50 O.A.C. 125, [1991] 3 S.C.R. 654, 131 N.R. 161, 68 C.C.C. (3d) 289, 1991 CarswellOnt 124, 1991 CarswellOnt 1031.

[78] *Duvivier*, 75 O.R. (2d) 203, 60 C.C.C. (3d) 353, 1990 CarswellOnt 958 (Gen. Div.), affirmed, 64 C.C.C. (3d) 20, 6 C.R.R. (2d) 180, 1991 CarswellOnt 1012 (C.A.).

did not argue for such a change, and in my opinion a far reaching change of this kind is best left to the legislature. However, expanding the exceptions to the common law rule to include irreconcilably separated spouses is precisely the kind of incremental change which the courts can and should make. The courts are custodians of the common law, and it is their duty to see that the common law reflects the emerging need and value of our society.[79]

As noted previously, a distinction must be drawn between a "communication" made by husbands and wives to one another and an "observation" by one spouse of the conduct of the other. Section 4(3) of the *Canada Evidence Act* provides that no spouse is compellable "to disclose any communication made [to him or her by the other spouse] during their marriage". The prevailing view seems to be that all marital communications continue to be protected by section 4(3) of the Act;[80] What is clear, however, is that any protected marital communication must be testimonial in nature. Spousal privilege will not prevent the admission into evidence of a document written by the accused and sent to his wife which is found during a search of the accused's house.[81] Moreover, the privilege is limited to the spouses themselves. Third persons who overhear, either intentionally or accidentally, a marital communication are compellable by the prosecution to testify about what they overheard.[82]

It should be noted that section 4(3) speaks of "any communication made...during their marriage". This would seem to exclude communications made before marriage. However, since the purpose of the section is to promote marital harmony, then it would seem to follow that it should include all communications made prior to or during marriage provided that the marriage is *bona fide* and subsisting at the time of the trial of the accused spouse.[83]

[79] *Supra,* note 77, at (C.R. (4th)) p. 344.
[80] *Jean,* 15 A.R. 147, 7 C.R. 338, 46 C.C.C. (2d) 176, 7 C.R. (3d) 338, 1979 CarswellAlta 169 (C.A.), affirmed, [1980] 1 S.C.R. 400, 20 A.R. 360, 16 C.R. (3d) 193, 51 C.C.C. (2d) 192, 31 N.R. 410, 1980 CarswellAlta 157, 1980 CarswellAlta 312; *Mailloux,* 30 C.R. (3d) 121, 55 C.C.C. (2d) 193 at 196, 1980 CarswellOnt 77 (C.A.); *Zylstra,* 41 C.R. (4th) 130, 99 C.C.C. (3d) 477, 82 O.A.C. 394, 1995 CarswellOnt 124 (C.A.).
[81] *Kotapski* (1981), 66 C.C.C. (2d) 78 (Que. S.C.), affirmed (1984), 13 C.C.C. (3d) 185 (Que. C.A.), leave to appeal refused (1984), 13 C.C.C. (3d) 185 (Que. C.A.).
[82] *Rumping v. Director of Public Prosecutions* (1962), [1964] A.C. 814, [1962] 2 All E.R. 233 (Eng. C.A.), (1962), [1964] A.C. 814 at 822, [1962] 3 All E.R. 256, 46 Cr. App. R. 389 (H.L.).
[83] *Hawkins, supra,* note 9.

(iv) Solicitor/client Privilege

What a person says to his or her lawyer in the latter's professional capacity and intended to be confidential is privileged. Neither the lawyer nor the client can be compelled to disclose the contents of that information.[84] Such communications are protected not because they are irrelevant, but because there are overriding policy reasons for upholding the confidentiality. The rule is based on the fact that the relationship and the communications between solicitor and client are essential to the effective operation of the legal system.[85] It is in the best interests of society as a whole that a person be allowed to consult with his or her legal adviser openly and freely, knowing that what the person tells their legal adviser cannot be revealed.

Despite its importance, solicitor-client privilege is not absolute. It is subject to certain clearly defined exceptions, where other societal values are compelling.[86] Danger to the public could, in appropriate circumstances, provide the requisite justification for setting aside the privilege. Here three factors must be considered: the first is whether there is a clear risk to an identifiable person or group of persons; the second is whether there is a risk of serious bodily harm or death; the last is whether there is imminent danger.

Nevertheless, the Supreme Court has said that solicitor-client privilege must be as close to absolute as possible to ensure public confidence and retain relevance.[87] It does not involve a balancing of interests on a case-by-case basis. In order for the communication to be privileged, it must arise from a communication between a lawyer and his client where the client seeks *lawful* advice.[88] For example, privilege does not attach to a communication by a client to his lawyer seeking advice on how to commit a crime.[89] Such a communication is outside the scope of the rule and is not protected from being revealed by the lawyer.

---

[84] *Bencardino*, 2 O.R. (2d) 351, 15 C.C.C. (2d) 342, 24 C.R.N.S. 173, 1973 CarswellOnt 51 (C.A.).

[85] *Fosty*, [1991] 6 W.W.R. 673, 67 C.C.C. (3d) 289, 130 N.R. 161, 8 C.R. (4th) 368, 75 Man. R. (2d) 112, 6 W.A.C. 112, [1991] 3 S.C.R. 263, 7 C.R.R. (2d) 108, 1991 CarswellMan 206, 1991 CarswellMan 285, [1991] S.C.J. No. 80.

[86] *Smith v. Jones*, 169 D.L.R. (4th) 385, 60 C.R.R. (2d) 46, 132 C.C.C. (3d) 225, 22 C.R. (5th) 203, 236 N.R. 201, 120 B.C.A.C. 161, 196 W.A.C. 161, [1999] 1 S.C.R. 455, 62 B.C.L.R. (3d) 209, [1999] 8 W.W.R. 364, 1999 CarswellBC 590, 1999 CarswellBC 591, [1999] S.C.J. No. 15.

[87] *McClure*, 2001 SCC 14, 151 C.C.C. (3d) 321, 195 D.L.R. (4th) 513, 40 C.R. (5th) 1, 266 N.R. 275, [2001] 1 S.C.R. 445, 142 O.A.C. 201, 2001 CarswellOnt 496, 2001 CarswellOnt 497, [2001] S.C.J. No. 13.

[88] *McClure, ibid.*

[89] *Cox* (1884), 14 Q.B.D. 153, 33 W.R. 396, 15 Cox C.C. 611 (C.C.R.).

The Supreme Court has said that the appropriate test to determine whether to set aside solicitor-client privilege is whether the accused's innocence is at stake.[90] It is so stringent a test that the privilege should only be infringed where core issues going to the guilt of the accused are involved and there is a genuine risk of a wrongful conviction. Unless the solicitor-client communication goes directly to one of the elements of the offence, it will not be sufficient to meet the stringent requirements.

The communication does not have to be given directly to the lawyer. It may be given to the lawyer's assistant or anyone acting under the lawyer's supervision. For example, privilege has been held to extend to statements made by a client to a law clerk to obtain legal aid.[91] Moreover, even if a person changes lawyers, the information that the person gave to his previous lawyer is still protected from disclosure.[92] The protection also extends to information given by two or more persons to their lawyer in connection with the same matter.

It is important to stress that the privilege extends only to a communication made by the client to his or her solicitor. It does not extend to any real evidence that a client may have given to his or her solicitor for safekeeping. For example, a client cannot claim privilege with respect to any item he or she has given to his or her solicitor that is evidence of a crime, such as a weapon or bloody shirt. Indeed, the solicitor may be compelled to testify for the prosecution that he or she received these items from the client, although he or she need not reveal what the client revealed about the items.

The client, but not the lawyer, may waive a solicitor-client privilege either intentionally or even inadvertently. For example, waiver may occur where the accused asks his solicitor to send the communication to a third person, such as his wife, even though he does not intend to waive the privilege.[93] Moreover, the accused is not entitled to pick and chose which part of the communication he will waive. Once the accused waives part of the communication, he cannot claim protection for the balance of the communication. If he waives any part of the privilege, he loses protection for the entire communication.[94]

---

[90]   *McClure, supra,* note 87.
[91]   *Littlechild* (1979), [1980] 1 W.W.R. 742, 11 C.R. (3d) 390, 19 A.R. 395, 51 C.C.C. (2d) 406, 108 D.L.R. (3d) 340, 1979 CarswellAlta 265 (C.A.).
[92]   *Bell v. Smith,* [1968] S.C.R. 664, 68 D.L.R. (2d) 751, 1968 CarswellOnt 79.
[93]   *Kotapski, supra,* note 81.
[94]   *Ibid.*

(v) Identity of Informers

Law enforcement officers often depend upon professional inform-
ers to furnish them with information about criminal activities. The law
therefore recognizes that it is in the best interests of society as a whole
that people with important information about the commission of a crime
be encouraged to come forward and give that information to the police
without fear of disclosure. The law thus protects a witness for the Crown
from answering questions that would have the effect of disclosing the
identity of the informer.[95]

This protection, however, is not absolute. If the court is persuaded
that the identity of the informant would be material to demonstrate the
innocence of the accused, then the court may order the witness to disclose
the informant's identity.[96] Section 7 of the *Charter of Rights and Freedoms* ensures that everyone has the right "to life, liberty and security of
the person and the right not to be deprived thereof except in accordance
with the principles of fundamental justice". The principles of fundamental justice entitle everyone accused of a crime to make "full answer
and defence".

The informer privilege is thus subject only to the "innocence at
stake" exception. In order to raise this exception, there must be a basis
on the evidence for concluding that the disclosure of the informer's
identity is necessary to demonstrate the innocence of the accused. For
example, in *Leipert*,[97] the police had investigated the accused following
a "Crime Stoppers" tip that drugs were being grown in his house. The
tip was mentioned in the information to obtain a warrant to search the
accused's house. The Crown had refused to produce the tip sheet on the
ground of informer privilege. The trial judge viewed the document and
attempted to edit out all references to the identity of the informer and
then ordered disclosure. When the Crown ceased to call evidence, the
trial judge acquitted the accused. The British Columbia Court of Appeal
ordered a new trial and that order was upheld by the Supreme Court of
Canada. The Supreme Court said that the rule of informer privilege is
of such importance to the workings of a criminal justice system that it

---

[95] *Hunter*, 57 C.R. (3d) 1, 59 O.R. (2d) 364, 19 O.A.C. 131, 34 C.C.C. (3d) 14, 1987
      CarswellOnt 89 (C.A.); *Escoffery*, 47 C.R. (4th) 40, 89 O.A.C. 394, 28 O.R. (3d) 417,
      1996 CarswellOnt 935 (C.A.); *Leipert*, 143 D.L.R. (4th) 38, 207 N.R. 145, 4 C.R. (5th)
      259, [1997] 3 W.W.R. 457, 112 C.C.C. (3d) 385, 41 C.R.R. (2d) 266, 85 B.C.A.C. 162,
      138 W.A.C. 162, [1997] 1 S.C.R. 281, 1997 CarswellBC 101, 1997 CarswellBC 102.
[96] *Bisaillon c. Keable*, [1983] 2 S.C.R. 60, 2 D.L.R. (4th) 193, 51 N.R. 81, 4 Admin. L.R.
      205, 7 C.C.C. (3d) 385, 37 C.R. (3d) 289, 1983 CarswellQue 28, 1983 CarswellQue 96.
[97] *Supra,* note 95.

cannot be balanced against other interests relating to the administration of justice. There was concern that it would undermine the efficacy of programs such as Crime Stoppers, which depends on guarantees of anonymity to those who volunteer information on crimes. The Court said that where it is impossible, in the case of the anonymous informer, to determine which details of the information provided by the informer will or will not result in that person's identity being revealed, none of those details should be disclosed, unless there is a basis to conclude that the innocence at stake exception applies.

A police informer must be distinguished from a police agent.[98] Unlike an informer who merely furnishes information to the police, an agent will usually act on the direction of the police and go "into the field" to gather information about a criminal activity, or may even participate in an illegal transaction which will be the subject of the charge against an accused. Although the police informer is protected by a *strong privilege that is not disclosable subject to the innocence at stake exception*, the identity of the agent is disclosable to the defence.

Another claim of privilege that has become the subject of judicial discussion in recent years is "surveillance location privilege". Persons who assist the police by providing them with a safe location from which to conduct the surveillance of suspected criminal activity have been held to be entitled to the same protection as persons assisting the police by providing information.[99] Such people are vulnerable to retribution from criminals who may resent the fact that they have cooperated with the police and may attempt to make an example of them in order to discourage others from doing the same. Unless their identities are kept confidential, they may be reluctant to help the police. Moreover, disclosure could destroy the value of the location and possibly threaten the safety of officers using that location.

Against these considerations must be balanced the right of an accused to full answer and defence. Whether the officer was able to make the observations claimed in his evidence may depend on the location of the observation post. Unless the defence is provided with the location of the post, it would be virtually impossible for the defence to test the credibility of the officer when he gives evidence of his observation. Thus, it would appear that the admissibility of the location and

[98] *B. (G.)*, 146 C.C.C. (3d) 465, 2000 CarswellOnt 2750 (C.A.), leave to appeal refused, 2001 CarswellOnt 874, 2001 CarswellOnt 875 (S.C.C.).
[99] *Thomas*, 124 C.C.C. (3d) 178, 1998 CarswellOnt 1331, [1998] O.J. No. 1400 (Gen. Div.); *Lam*, 2000 BCCA 545, 148 C.C.C. (3d) 379, 38 C.R. (5th) 189, 143 B.C.A.C. 193, 235 W.A.C. 193, 2000 CarswellBC 1928 (C.A.).

the reliability of the officer's observations has to be decided on a case-by-case basis.[100] Once the privilege has been established, neither the police nor the court possess the discretion to abridge it. The privilege belongs to the Crown and cannot be waived without the informer's consent.[101] The privilege prevents not only disclosure of the informer's name, but also any information that might implicitly reveal his or her identity.[102]

An example of where disclosure of the name of the informant was ordered is *Hunter*.[103] There the defence were seeking to attack a search warrant that had been used to search the accused's residence where narcotics were discovered. It was held that, in the circumstances of that case, disclosure of the identity of the informer was crucial to the defence. The Crown was given the option of either disclosing the informant's identity, proceeding on a warrantless search or withdrawing the prosecution.

Another exception that allows the court to order disclosure is where the informer has acted as an *agent provocateur*. Disclosure may also be ordered where the accused seeks to establish that a search and seizure of his premises was not undertaken on reasonable grounds and therefore contravened section 8 of the *Charter*.[104]

(vi) Public Interest Privilege

The law recognizes that it is not in the public interest to disclose certain information regarding governmental activities. At the same time, it also recognizes that litigants should have access to all evidence that may be of assistance to the fair disposition of issues arising in litigation, in order for the administration of justice to operate properly and fairly. What the court must try to do is balance these two competing interests. It will depend, as one judge has said, on "changing social conditions and the role of government in society at various times".[105]

Section 37(3)(b) of the *Canada Evidence Act* gives to the superior court of the province the right, upon application, to determine a public

---

[100] *Lam, ibid.*
[101] *Gordon*, 136 C.C.C. (3d) 64, 1999 CarswellOnt 1146 (Gen. Div.).
[102] *Leipert, supra,* note 95.
[103] *Supra,* note 95.
[104] *Scott*, 116 N.R. 361, 1 C.R.R. (2d) 82, 43 O.A.C. 277, 2 C.R. (4th) 153, 61 C.C.C. (3d) 300, [1990] 3 S.C.R. 979, 1990 CarswellOnt 65, 1990 CarswellOnt 1012.
[105] *Carey v. Ontario*, 22 Admin. L.R. 236, [1986] 2 S.C.R. 637, 35 D.L.R. (4th) 161, 72 N.R. 81, 20 O.A.C. 81, 30 C.C.C. (3d) 498, 14 C.P.C. (2d) 10, 58 O.R. (2d) 352n, 1986 CarswellOnt 1011, *per* La Forest J. at (C.C.C.) p. 506.

interest privilege where there is an objection to the information being disclosed. However, section 37(3)(b) does not give the superior court exclusive jurisdiction.[106] Where the issue is raised at the preliminary inquiry, the judge is required to rule on the issue. Usually, the ruling will be in favour of the Crown, since the innocence at stake exception rarely arises at this stage of the proceedings.

(vii) Other Privileges

The common law recognizes two other instances where persons may be protected from disclosing information. The first involves deliberations carried out by jurors in the jury room. No juror may be required to divulge what another juror said during deliberations except for the purposes of an investigation of a juror for obstructing justice. Not only is a juror protected from being compelled to disclose that information, the juror is guilty of contempt of court if he or she does. Moreover, section 649 of the *Criminal Code* now makes it an offence for a juror to disclose such information.

There are several reasons for the rule. One reason is that verdicts are intended to be final and jurors should not be required to explain why they reached a particular verdict. If a juror was required to disclose what took place during deliberations, it would encourage dissatisfied litigants from using every means to find out what went on in the jury room in an effort to show that the result was not according to law and this would be contrary to public policy.[107] Another reason is to encourage jurors while deliberating their verdict to engage in frank discussion without fear that what they say may be publicly disclosed by another juror. Finally, the recent attention by the media to high-profile cases gives added importance to the rule. It ensures that jurors are protected from harassment by investigative reporters and prevents jurors from financially exploiting their duties by selling accounts of their deliberations to the media.

Diplomats are also protected from disclosure of information. The basis of this common law rule is that the courts should respect representatives of the government of another country, even though they have jurisdiction over foreign subjects who are present in Canada. Such im-

---

[106] *Richards*, 115 C.C.C. (3d) 377, 100 O.A.C. 215, 34 O.R. (3d) 244, 1997 CarswellOnt 1841 (C.A.).

[107] *Perras (No. 2)*, [1974] 5 W.W.R. 187, 18 C.C.C. (2d) 47, 48 D.L.R. (3d) 145, 1974 CarswellSask 69 (C.A.); *Pan* (2001), 155 C.C.C. (3d) 97 (S.C.C.).

munity, however, is not absolute where the safety of the country is imperilled.[108]

(viii) No Privilege

There is a misconception by the public generally that persons such as doctors, psychiatrists, priests and journalists are entitled to claim privilege and to refuse to divulge information given to them by patients, penitents and informants. No such common law privilege exists. The reason is that the courts have considered that the public interest in the search for truth far outweighs the protection of confidentiality in such cases.[109]

Similarly, the privilege contained in section 10(5) of the *Divorce Act* which precludes the admissibility of "anything said or of any admission or communication made in the course of assisting spouses to achieve a reconciliation" only applies where the statements for which the claim is made are "in a divorce proceeding" and to a "person nominated by a court under this section to assist spouses to achieve a reconciliation".[110] Although the common law recognizes a privilege in matrimonial disputes for the purpose of promoting spouses to reconcile, there is no such common law privilege recognized by the criminal law outside of the plea bargaining structure.

Nevertheless, some judges, particularly in civil cases, have been loath to compel witnesses to disclose information given in confidence to them;[111] other judges have ordered the information to be disclosed but have refused to impose any penalty, or have imposed a nominal one, for the refusal to do so. By doing so, the judges have not recognized a legal privilege. They have simply refused to impose sanctions on the witness for refusing to divulge the confidential information.

In recent years, however, the Supreme Court of Canada has recognized that there may be case-by-case instances where a judge may allow a person to withhold disclosure of a confidential communication. In *Fosty*,[112] the Court recognized that there are two types of privilege: the first is "blanket privilege" (or what is also known as *prima facie*,

---

[108] *Rose*, 3 C.R. 277, 88 C.C.C. 114, [1947] 3 D.L.R. 618, 1946 CarswellQue 16 (K.B.).

[109] *S. (R.J.)*, 45 C.R. (3d) 161, 8 O.A.C. 241, 19 C.C.C. (3d) 115, 1985 CarswellOnt 93 (C.A.), leave to appeal refused (1985), 61 N.R. 266n, 11 O.A.C. 317n (S.C.C.).

[110] *Pabani*, 17 O.R. (3d) 659, 29 C.R. (4th) 364, 89 C.C.C. (3d) 437, 70 O.A.C. 118, 1994 CarswellOnt 69 (C.A.), leave to appeal refused (1994), 33 C.R. (4th) 405n, 91 C.C.C. (3d) vi (note), 19 O.R. (3d) xvi (note), 77 O.A.C. 400 (note), 179 N.R. 79 (note) (S.C.C.).

[111] *Dembie v. Dembie*, 21 R.F.L. 46, 1963 CarswellOnt 50 (S.C.).

[112] *Supra*, note 85.

common-law or class privilege); the other is "case-by-case privilege". Blanket privilege has been discussed previously. On the other hand, an accused may be able to show that the relationship between himself and his confessor satisfies certain pre-conditions. In such instance, the courts will generally rule that the communication was privileged.

In *Fosty*, the Supreme Court recognized that the courts may declare a confidential communication protected from disclosure where the witness satisfies the following pre-conditions set out by the late Professor Wigmore in his text, *Evidence in Trials at Common Law*:

1. The communication must originate in a confidence that it will not be disclosed;
2. The element of confidentiality must be essential to the full and satisfactory maintenance of the relationship between the parties;
3. The relationship must be one which in the opinion of the community ought to be sedulously fostered;
4. The injury that would inure to the relationship by the disclosure of the communication would be greater than the benefit gained for the correct disposal of the litigation.

3. DOCUMENTARY EVIDENCE

(a) Generally

Direct or circumstantial evidence of a fact in issue may also be proved by a document. In order to prove the authenticity of a document, it is usually necessary to call the person who made the document as a witness so that he can identify it. However, proof as to authorship can also be established by circumstantial evidence, such as the finding of the document in the possession of the accused, an admission by the accused of ownership or authorship, or proof by a handwriting expert.[113] In such instance, it is still necessary for a witness to be asked to identify the document and to give evidence that will tend to connect it with a fact in issue.

Let us assume, for example, that the accused is charged with forging a cheque. If someone is able to testify that he saw the accused writing out the cheque and can identify the particular document, that is direct evidence from which a judge or jury can conclude that the accused committed the crime. However, if no one saw the accused write the

---

[113] *Bloomfield*, 6 N.B.R. (2d) 5, 21 C.R.N.S. 97, 10 C.C.C. (2d) 398, 1973 CarswellNB 1 (C.A.); *Emes* (2001), 157 C.C.C. (3d) 124 (Ont. C.A.).

cheque, but a witness is familiar with the accused's handwriting and that witness is able to identify the writing and signature on the cheque as belonging to the accused, that is circumstantial evidence from which a judge or jury can draw the inference that the accused wrote the cheque.

Quite often, however, a document may be found in the possession of the accused that is incriminating in nature, but no one is able to say that they saw the accused prepare it and no one can identify his signature. Assume, for example, that the accused, a butcher, is charged with selling horsemeat that he fraudulently represented as beef. A search warrant is executed by the police at his home and they find invoices from a horse rancher in Texas indicating that certain horses were sold to the accused on a certain date. It is obvious that these invoices are relevant to the issue of whether the accused has been buying horses and selling them as beef. On the other hand, there is also the possibility that the documents are not relevant to the prosecution at all and simply indicate that the accused purchased some horses that he may still own or that he may have sold intact to someone else. It is also possible that the documents were fabricated by someone who wished to harm the accused.

Nevertheless, the courts have held that all documents found in the possession of an accused, which are relevant to an issue before the court, are admissible as evidence of the accused's knowledge of their contents, connection with, or complicity in, the transactions to which they relate, or his or her state of mind, and may be considered by the judge and jury on the issue of his or her guilt. The prosecution is not required to prove, as a condition of admissibility, that the accused has knowledge of the contents of the document.[114] However, the weight to be attached to those documents by the trier of fact will depend upon all of the circumstances of the case.

(b) Best Evidence Rule

The best evidence rule is a rule of evidence that requires the side that relies upon a document to produce the original of it, unless the original was destroyed or cannot be found, or it is impossible or impractical to produce. For example, it may be impossible or impractical to produce the original if it is in the possession of someone in another country, since a Canadian court has no jurisdiction to order its production.

---

[114] *Turlon*, 32 O.A.C. 396, 49 C.C.C. (3d) 186, 70 C.R. (3d) 376, 1989 CarswellOnt 96 (C.A.).

The rule dates back to the very early common law when witnesses did not testify before juries. It was connected to the doctrine of "profert" in pleading, which required a party relying upon a document as a ground of action or defence to produce it bodily to the court. As the law developed and witnesses were allowed to testify, the rule was justified on the basis that it prevented fraud. In other words, it was presumed that if the original document existed, then it was likely being withheld for some sinister motive. As well, there was a concern that a copy of a document, made by hand in those days, might be inaccurate.

Today, with modern technology, it is possible to produce a document that cannot be distinguished from the original and the best evidence rule is often relaxed. On the other hand, the same technology allows production of an authentic-looking "copy" that may actually be a forgery made up of several documents pasted together. Nevertheless, counsel will frequently admit that a particular document is a photocopy of the original and that it will not be necessary to comply with the best evidence rule. However, if the opposing side is not prepared to agree to the production of a photostat or a copy, then the witness through whom the document is introduced must give some explanation as to why the original cannot be produced. He or she must, at least, be able to say that the copy is an exact reproduction of the original. In such instance, the court will generally admit it and the issue as to whether it is an exact copy of the original will go to the question of the weight of the evidence.

4. ARTICLES AND THINGS

Another form of evidence, in addition to oral and documentary evidence, may be an article or thing that is connected with the crime, such as a gun or a knife, or in the case of a stolen article, the thing itself. This is known as real evidence because it can be seen, heard or touched by the judge and jury. Where such evidence is being tendered, it is generally necessary for a witness to identify it and explain its relevancy to a fact in issue. It will then be made an exhibit (just as a document will be made an exhibit) so that if the verdict is appealed, it will be available for examination by the Court of Appeal.

There may be circumstances where it is impossible or inconvenient to produce the original article. For example, it would hardly add to the decorum of a trial to produce a stolen cow for inspection by the judge and jury, nor would it be practical to produce a stolen automobile. The usual practice is for the police to take a photograph of the particular article and to introduce the photograph in its place. Unless the other side agrees that the photograph is an accurate depiction of the article, here again a witness must be called to testify that he or she took the photograph of the article or is familiar with it, and the photograph is accurate.

5. DEMONSTRATIVE EVIDENCE

Visual aids such as photographs, maps, diagrams or flow charts will often be admitted by the judge to assist the judge and jury in reaching their verdict. Whether the photograph, diagram, map, flow chart or any other item will assist the judge or jury will often depend on the facts of the particular case. A judge may also permit an experiment or demonstration in the courtroom. For example, in *Brooks*,[115] where the defence attacked the testimony of a police officer who said that he took a statement from the accused in eight minutes, the trial judge permitted defence counsel to conduct an experiment and have the officer duplicate as far as possible the taking of the statement.

Sometimes opposing counsel will object to the introduction of a diagram or a map because it is not drawn to scale or a photograph because it is misleading. In each case, the question of admissibility will depend upon whether the judge determines that the document will assist him and the jury in better understanding the evidence. If it is so distorted that it gives a wrong or a misleading impression, then the judge should refuse to admit it.[116]

The most difficult question arises in the case of photographs. The first thing that must be established by the side that wishes to introduce a photograph is that the photograph is an accurate depiction of the scene or the subject and is being offered to assist the triers in determining the fact in issue before them. Often the main objection will be that the photograph, particularly of a victim, may inflame the jury and divert them from their main task or cause them to be prejudiced against the accused. For a long time, the main concern of the court was one of admissibility, not prejudice. Mr. Justice Masten pointed out over sixty years ago in *O'Donnell*:

> The only question to be considered is were they admissible under the rules of evidence. If they are the effect which they may have on the jury cannot interfere with their admission.[117]

---

[115] 81 C.C.C. (3d) 428, 1993 CarswellOnt 797 (Gen. Div.).

[116] *Valley*, 13 O.A.C. 89, 26 C.C.C. (3d) 207, 1986 CarswellOnt 822 (C.A.), leave to appeal refused, 67 N.R. 158 (note), 15 O.A.C. 240 (note), 26 C.C.C. (3d) 207 (note), [1986] 1 S.C.R. xiii.

[117] 65 C.C.C. 299, [1936] 2 D.L.R. 517 (Ont. C.A.) at (C.C.C.) p. 383.

However, with the development of judicial discretion, has arisen the view that the trial judge has the right to exclude photographs if they are of minor assistance and their prejudicial effect far outweighs that assistance. On the other hand, the corollary of this is that, if the photograph will assist the judge and jury in understanding the evidence, it will generally be admitted, even it is inflammatory.[118] In each case, the judge must use his or her discretion to ensure that the accused receives a fair trial.[119]

With the rapid development of photographic equipment, the question arises whether the Crown or the defence should be permitted to use such equipment to re-enact its version of the events that are the subject of disputed issues. For example, a videotaped re-enactment of a crime may be of greater assistance to a jury in understanding the facts in issue than an oral recitation by the witnesses to the crime. On the other hand, the video re-enactment will undoubtedly have an immediate visual impact, such that the jurors may be induced to give it more weight than it deserves.[120] It may also cause the jury to discount less compelling or less vivid evidence that may be more probative of the facts in issue. Here, the Courts have been reluctant to lay down any rigid rules governing the admissibility of such evidence.[121] What has been said is that the overriding principle is whether the prejudicial effect of the video re-enactment outweighs its probative value having regard to its relevance, accuracy, and whether what it portrays can be verified under oath and the necessity of the evidence.

---

[118] *D. (No. 2)*, 35 C.C.C. (2d) 464, [1977] 4 W.W.R. 47, 3 A.R. 409, 1977 CarswellAlta 210 (C.A.), leave to appeal refused, [1977] 1 S.C.R. vii.

[119] *Kendall*, 20 O.A.C. 134, 35 C.C.C. (3d) 105, 57 C.R. (3d) 249, 1987 CarswellOnt 93, [1987] O.J. No. 388 (C.A.); *Wade*, 29 C.R. (4th) 327, 18 O.R. (3d) 33, 89 C.C.C. (3d) 39, 69 O.A.C. 321, 1994 CarswellOnt 68 (C.A.), reversed in part, 23 O.R. (3d) 415, [1995] 2 S.C.R. 737, 41 C.R. (4th) 100, 98 C.C.C. (3d) 97, 182 N.R. 387, 82 O.A.C. 182, 1995 CarswellOnt 123, 1995 CarswellOnt 527; *C.(R.)*, 31 C.R. (5th) 306, 2000 CarswellOnt 363 (S.C.C.).

[120] *MacDonald*, 35 C.R. (5th) 130, 49 O.R. (3d) 417, 146 C.C.C. (3d) 525, 134 O.A.C. 167, 2000 CarswellOnt 2416 (C.A.).

[121] *MacDonald, ibid.*

PART B

Excluded Evidence

3

Hearsay

1. THE ORTHODOX RULE

Probably no rule of evidence is more misunderstood than the rule against hearsay. It is misunderstood because it is commonly believed that the rule means that a witness is not allowed to repeat in court what he or she was told by someone else. Because this is only a partial explanation of the rule, it is important to start at the beginning.

The first question that must be asked whenever a possible hearsay problem arises is "what is the side calling the witness seeking to prove"? If the purpose in calling the witness is to prove the truth of what the witness was told by a third party, then a hearsay problem arises. However, if the purpose of calling the witness is to prove only that a statement was made by the third party, not that the statement was true, then a hearsay problem does not arise. There is no potential hearsay problem because the fact in issue is not the truth of the statement, but whether the statement was made. If the witness is allowed to repeat in court what a third party said only to prove that he or she made a statement, then it is not hearsay. It is original evidence of the fact that the statement was made.

For example, let us assume the accused is charged with robbing a bank at five minutes after 12:00 noon and X saw the accused enter the bank at noon. Such evidence is offered, not as direct evidence that the accused robbed the bank, but rather as circumstantial evidence from which a jury can infer that the accused was in the bank at the time of the robbery. Together with other evidence, it may establish that the accused was the robber. The rule is that only X may be called to testify that he saw the accused enter the bank at noon.

Let us assume, however, that X is unavailable to testify, but told Y that he saw the accused enter the bank at 12:00 noon. If the Crown seeks to introduce what X saw through the testimony of Y, that is hearsay. Y will not be permitted to testify that X told him he saw the accused enter the bank at noon to prove that very fact.

Why do we prohibit hearsay evidence? Clearly, the fact that X saw the accused enter the bank at noon is logically probative of one of the three issues that the Crown must prove. Yet the rules of evidence do not permit Y to tell the court what X told him. The reason is that Y cannot be effectively cross-examined about what X told him. All Y can do is to repeat what X told him. There is no way that Y can assure the court that X's observation was reliable and his statement honest, when he told him that he saw the accused going into the bank at noon. Unless X is compelled to come to court, where his oath can be taken and his demeanour observed while his evidence is being tested by cross-examination, there is no way of ensuring the reliability and honesty of his evidence. Moreover, everyone knows that whenever information is passed from one person to the next, there is a risk that it may be misunderstood. Our system of justice recognizes that someone's life or liberty should not depend upon second-hand information.

Let us assume, however, that X also told Z that he saw the accused enter the bank at 2:00 p.m. and the defence wishes to call Z to say exactly what X told him. Is it hearsay? That will depend upon what the evidence is attempting to prove. Assume that the defence wishes to call the evidence to show that X should not be believed, or is confused about having seen the accused enter the bank at noon because he also told Z that he saw him enter the bank at 2:00 p.m. Here it is not being offered to prove that the accused entered the bank at 2:00 p.m., but to show that X was mistaken or lying when he testified that the accused entered the bank at noon. In such instance, it is admissible. It does not offend the hearsay rule. It is original or first-hand evidence because it is being offered to prove only that X *told* Z that the accused entered the bank at 2.00 p.m., not the fact that the accused entered the bank at 2.00 p.m.

What the law of evidence seeks to ensure is that only original or first-hand evidence is admitted to prove a fact in issue. Second-hand evidence will not suffice. On the other hand, where the fact in issue is whether a statement was made by a third party, the statement will be admitted because it bears directly on the issue to be proved. It is still original or first-hand evidence — not second-hand evidence.

Although the hearsay rule is relatively straightforward, its application often seems to create difficulties for the Court. A classic example of that difficulty was *Ly*.[1] At issue in *Ly* was the admissibility of a telephone conversation between an unidentified person and a police officer, in which the unidentified person made arrangements to deliver drugs to the police officer at a certain time and place. The trial judge had rejected the evidence as hearsay and acquitted the accused of possession for the purposes of trafficking because there was no evidence that the person who met the officer was the same person who spoke to the officer over the phone. On appeal by the Crown to the Alberta Court of Appeal, the acquittal was set aside and a new trial ordered. McClung J.A. for the Court held that the conversation was properly admissible as part of the narrative or the *res gestae* since it would have been impossible to understand the development of the later events without the evidence of the telephone conversation preceding them. Moreover, even if it was hearsay, the particulars of the telephone conversation were still admissible because it had the circumstantial guarantees of reliability, necessity and truthfulness.

Although the Supreme Court of Canada dismissed a further appeal by the accused, McLachlin J., giving the judgment of the Court, felt that the statement was not hearsay at all. Rather, it was a statement of intention or a statement tendered to establish the alleged drug transaction, and hence not tendered for the truth of its contents. It was merely one of the circumstances which, combined with others, was capable of establishing that when the accused appeared at the time and place with drugs in his possession, he did so for the purpose of trafficking.

The first step in an analysis of whether the evidence was hearsay is whether the evidence was relevant to a fact in issue. If the drug dealer

---

[1] 219 N.R. 237, 119 C.C.C. (3d) 479, 206 A.R. 309, 156 W.A.C. 309, [1997] 3 S.C.R. 698, 1997 CarswellAlta 942, 1997 CarswellAlta 943.

had spoken to the officer face to face and made arrangements to meet and deliver drugs, then what the drug dealer said would not only be relevant to a fact in issue, it would be admissible for its truth as an incriminating statement going towards the issue of intent. The difficulty here was that the identity of the drug dealer was unknown. Until his identity was known, the statement was not admissible against the accused for its truth.

What the Alberta Court of Appeal and Supreme Court did not seem to consider was that the statement by the person who spoke to the officer had two aspects to it. The first was that he would meet the officer at a certain time and place. The second was that he would deliver drugs to the officer. The first aspect went to the issue of the identity of the person who offered to traffick in drugs. The second aspect went to his intention. Thus, the statement that he would meet the officer at a certain time and place, along with the fact that the accused met the police officer at the place and time stated, was circumstantial evidence from which it could be inferred, along with other evidence, if any, that the person who spoke to the officer over the telephone was the accused. Thus, the first aspect of the statement was admissible, not necessarily for the truth of its contents, but for the fact that it was made. It showed an intention by someone purporting to traffick in drugs to meet the officer. Once it was admitted for that purpose and the trier was satisfied that it was made by the accused, then the issue of identity was satisfied.

However, there was a second aspect of the statement, namely, the intention to deliver drugs to the officer. Once the identity of the person was established, then surely the evidence was admissible for its truth as evidence of the accused's intention to traffick in drugs. Although hearsay, it constituted an incriminating admission by the accused and was receivable as one of the exceptions to the hearsay rule.

2. WHEN IS HEARSAY ALLOWED?

Most legal historians believe that the hearsay rule, like all exclusionary rules, owes its origin to the jury system. The jury was allowed to hear only evidence that was given under oath and subjected to cross-examination. Some scholars argue that these two reasons have little substance today. For example, a witness who feels that his or her moral conscience cannot be bound by the oath is permitted to testify by affirmation. Moreover, juries today are sophisticated enough to know that the mere fact that a person takes an oath does not ensure the truth of the testimony. If anything does promote truth, it is the fear of a prosecution for perjury.

The real reason, today, why hearsay is still excluded is because it cannot be tested by cross-examination. The law requires the person who has first-hand knowledge of the facts to come forward and to testify so that the reliability and honesty of his or her evidence can be subjected to the scrutiny of cross-examination. As indicated earlier, a witness who has second-hand information cannot be cross-examined to test the truth of the information given to him or her by a third party. All that the witness can say is that he or she was given information by a third party.

However, what if that person is dead or unavailable to testify or, if available, unable to communicate his or her evidence because of some mental or physical incapacity? Should the law, confronted with a choice of either accepting second-hand evidence or no evidence at all, choose the latter? No sooner was the exclusionary rule of hearsay invented in the late seventeenth century than judges began to realize that, unless certain types of hearsay were admitted, serious crimes might go unpunished or litigants denied justice. The result was that the courts began to create a number of exceptions to the strict application of the hearsay rule where the declarant was dead. Professor Wigmore explained the rationale underlying the exceptions this way:

> The purpose and reason of the Hearsay rule is the key to the exceptions to it. The theory of the Hearsay rule is that many possible sources of inaccuracy and untrustworthiness which may lie underneath the bare untested assertion of a witness can best be brought to light and exposed, if they exist, by the test of cross-examination. But this test or security may in a given instance be superfluous; it may be sufficiently clear, in that instance, that the statement offered is free enough from the risk of inaccuracy and untrustworthiness, so that the test of cross-examination would be a work of supererogation. Moreover, the test may be impossible of employment - for example, by reason of the death of the declarant - so that, if his testimony is to be used at all, there is a necessity for taking it in the untested shape.[2]

For almost three centuries, these exceptions to the hearsay rule were applied strictly by the courts. So long as a hearsay statement fell within one of the recognized exceptions, the trial judge was obliged to admit it. However, in 1970 the Supreme Court of Canada delivered its landmark decision in *Ares v. Venner*,[3] a civil case. There the court

---

[2] *Wigmore on Evidence* (3rd ed.), Vol. 5, (Boston: Little, Brown and Co., 1974) para. 1420, p. 202.

[3] [1970] S.C.R. 608, 12 C.R.N.S. 349, 73 W.W.R. 347, 14 D.L.R. (3d) 4, 1970 CarswellAlta 80, 1970 CarswellAlta 142.

permitted a plaintiff to introduce hospital records of his treatment for a broken leg as declarations made in the ordinary course of duty and as "*prima facie* proof of the facts stated therein" even though the nurses who had made the records were alive and were, in fact, waiting outside the courtroom to testify.

Unfortunately, *Ares v. Venner* lay dormant for another twenty years until another landmark decision of the Supreme Court of Canada, *Khan*.[4] This time the court decided to strike out in a new direction. Instead of extending the old exceptions created centuries earlier, the court adopted a new test — "necessity and reliability". The role of the trial judge was no longer restricted to determining whether the hearsay statement that counsel was seeking to introduce fell within one of the recognized exceptions. If it could be established that a declarant was unavailable or unable to give evidence and the statement had the indicia of reliability, the trial judge had the discretion to admit what the declarant had said through a third party.

In *Smith*,[5] Chief Justice Lamer characterized the *Khan* decision as signalling "an end to the categorical approach to the admission of hearsay evidence".[6] However, a year later, speaking for the majority of the Court in *B.(K.G.)*,[7] he was quick to affirm that the "new approach shares the same principled approach basis as the existing exceptions"[8] and some textbook writers[9] took this statement as affirming the continued existence of the traditional exceptions.

Although not formally abolished, the recent decision of the Supreme Court in *Starr*,[10] has effectively delivered the quietus to the traditional exceptions. In *Starr*, at issue was the admissibility of a traditional exception to the hearsay rule — the present intention exception. Delivering the majority judgment of the Court, Iacobucci J. held that, although historically, there has been no requirement for the trial judge to assess

---

[4]   113 N.R. 53, 79 C.R. (3d) 1, 41 O.A.C. 353, [1990] 2 S.C.R. 531, 59 C.C.C. (3d) 92, 1990 CarswellOnt 108, 1990 CarswellOnt 1001, [1990] S.C.J. No. 81.

[5]   15 C.R. (4th) 133, 75 C.C.C. (3d) 257, [1992] 2 S.C.R. 915, 55 O.A.C. 321, 139 N.R. 323, 94 D.L.R. (4th) 590, 1992 CarswellOnt 103, [1992] S.C.J. No. 74.

[6]   *Ibid.,* at (S.C.R.) p. 993.

[7]   19 C.R. (4th) 1, [1993] 1 S.C.R. 740, 61 O.A.C. 1, 148 N.R. 241, 79 C.C.C. (3d) 257, 1993 CarswellOnt 76, 1993 CarswellOnt 975, [1993] S.C.J. No. 22.

[8]   *Ibid.,* at (S.C.R.) p. 798.

[9]   See Sopinka, Lederman and Bryant, *The Law of Evidence in Canada*, 2nd ed., (Toronto: Butterworths, 1992) at p. 19 and Schiff, *Evidence in the Litigation Process*, 4th ed., (Toronto: Carswell, 1993).

[10]   2000 SCC 40, 36 C.R. (5th) 1, 147 C.C.C. (3d) 449, 190 D.L.R. (4th) 591, [2000] 11 W.W.R. 1, 148 Man. R. (2d) 161, 224 W.A.C. 161, 258 N.R. 250, [2000] 2 S.C.R. 144, 2000 CarswellMan 449, 2000 CarswellMan 450, [2000] S.C.J. No. 40.

the reliability of a traditional exception to hearsay before admitting it, it was now necessary to do so. It was his opinion that the concern for reliability and necessity should be no less present when the hearsay is introduced under an established exception. It would compromise trial fairness and raise the spectre of wrongful convictions if the Crown was allowed to introduce unreliable hearsay against the accused, regardless of whether it happens to fall within an existing traditional exception.

Before turning to the modern rule, it is important to further discuss the traditional exceptions.

3. TRADITIONAL EXCEPTIONS TO THE HEARSAY RULE

(b) Dying Declarations

Should a victim of a homicide be allowed to identify his killer before he dies? A strict application of the hearsay rule would say "no" because his identification evidence would have to be given second-hand by the person who overheard him. However, if such evidence was not admitted, a murderer might be able to escape punishment for his crime. On the other hand, there is always the danger that a person who is dying might try to settle a score with an enemy by falsely accusing him of murder.

Faced with these two policy considerations, the courts in the 19th century decided to opt in favour of admitting the evidence for what it was worth. It was argued that anyone going to his maker was unlikely to perjure his soul by dying with a lie on his lips. At the same time, the courts were anxious to ensure that there would be no danger of mistake or an attempt to settle old scores.[11] They did this by creating two conditions that must be satisfied before such evidence would be admitted.

The first was that a dying declaration could only be admitted in a trial for the murder or manslaughter of the victim who made the declaration. This rule was so strictly applied that, in one case, the court refused to accept the dying declaration of a woman on the trial of the person charged with procuring her abortion, even though it resulted in her death. The other condition was that the victim must have had a settled hopeless expectation of impending death at the time that he or she made the declaration. It was believed that a victim's apprehension of death when the declaration was made would ensure its trustworthiness. In other

---

[11] *Schwartzenhauer*, [1935] S.C.R. 367, 64 C.C.C. 1, [1935] 3 D.L.R. 711, 1935 CarswellBC 84.

words, a person is unlikely to tell a deliberate lie when he knows that he is dying and has no hope of recovery.

Unfortunately, this latter condition has restricted the admissibility of a dying declaration because it cannot always be assumed that a person who is dying knows that he is dying. Moreover, it is unlikely that even the most seriously injured person can appreciate that his life is in danger or that he will be told this by anyone who comes to his aid. Indeed, it is more likely that he will be encouraged to "hang on" until help comes.

Nevertheless, these conditions were, and continue to be, strictly applied by the courts under this exception. A famous example where a dying declaration was not admitted is *Bedingfield*.[12] Bedingfield was charged with murdering a woman by cutting her throat. At his trial, a prosecution witness testified that she saw the victim running out of the house where she had just been with Bedingfield. Her throat was almost completely severed. Just before the victim died, she said, "Look what Bedingfield has done to me". However, Chief Justice Cockburn refused to permit the witness to repeat what she heard the victim say. The fact that the wound itself was very serious was not enough for the court to draw the inference that the victim knew that she was dying. Fortunately, Bedingfield was convicted on other evidence.

Kharsekin[13] is another strict application of this rule. Here the victim of a knife attack told a physician who was attending him that he had been wounded by the accused. An hour later, in response to an inquiry, the victim again identified the accused as his attacker. Two hours later, the victim died. It was held by the Newfoundland Court of Appeal that, since the victim did not have a settled hopeless expectation of death at the time that he made his statement, the trial judge was correct in not admitting the statement under this exception. However, the Court went on to hold that the trial judge should have admitted the statement under the new *Khan* rule. Here, necessity arose because of the death of the victim. Reliability existed because the victim had a peculiar means of knowledge, there was little time to falsify and the medical evidence supported the position that the victim knew what he was saying.

Not only are restrictive conditions imposed on the admissibility of dying declarations, the courts have also imposed restrictions on what may be said if the declaration is admitted. The general rule is that the dying declaration must be confined to the circumstances that led to the

---

[12] (1879), 14 Cox C.C. 341.
[13] 74 C.C.C. (3d) 163, 99 Nfld. & P.E.I.R. 70, 315 A.P.R. 70, 1992 CarswellNfld 147 (T.D.), reversed, 88 C.C.C. (3d) 193, 117 Nfld. & P.E.I.R. 89, 365 A.P.R. 89, 30 C.R. (4th) 252, 1994 CarswellNfld 17 (C.A.).

victim's death. On the other hand, a dying declaration is not only admissible against an accused, it is also admissible in his favour. Under this exception, everything that occurred immediately before and after the incident is generally allowed into evidence. However, the courts have imposed some restrictions. For example, in *Buck*,[14] the accused was charged with manslaughter arising out of an illegal operation on a young girl. Although the court was prepared to allow the young girl's dying declaration as to what occurred at the time of the operation, it did not permit that part of her declaration that said that the accused attempted to procure an abortion on her some weeks before.

(b) Declarations Made in the Course of Duty

This exception to the hearsay rule allows the use of an oral or written record or statement made by a deceased person in the usual and ordinary course of his or her business. One rationale for this exception was that if an agent or servant routinely does something, it is likely to be accurate. Another was that an agent or servant has an interest in making an accurate record because an employer will probably keep a check upon its accuracy and fire him or her if it is not accurate.

One might seriously question whether these reasons are sound enough to support this exception to the hearsay rule. We all know that people do make errors when they are making reports, and there is no way of checking the accuracy of the record once it is admitted. There is also the possibility that an employee may be trying to cheat or defraud an employer. In such instance, an innocent accused might discover that he or she has no way of attacking the record's accuracy. However, error or deliberate fraud were considered to be such rare occurrences in comparison to usual or customary conduct, that it was felt to be in the public interest generally that the evidence be admitted.

Let us assume that Detective Jones sends out Officer Smith to make certain observations as to what is happening at the home of a suspect and to report to him. In due course, Officer Smith returns and reports his observations to Detective Jones. If Officer Smith dies before the case comes to trial, then Detective Jones would be entitled to repeat in court what he was told by Officer Smith, because it was a report made in the usual and ordinary course of business.

Are the notes prepared by a police officer admissible under this exception? It is well known that police officers, when conducting an

---

[14] [1940] O.R. 444, 74 C.C.C. 314, [1941] 1 D.L.R. 302, 1940 CarswellOnt 32 (C.A.).

investigation, make notes of everything that they observe in order to enable them to refresh their memories of the events when called upon to testify days, weeks, months or even years after the event. We assume that an officer would try to be as accurate and as comprehensive as possible in the preparation of those notes. Are such notes admissible in evidence if the officer dies before the trial of the accused? It is arguable that the notes are made in the usual and ordinary course of business. However, the notes are for the officer's personal use. Unless he or she is required to file those notes with a superior officer who can check their accuracy, it cannot be said that it is unlikely that the notes will be false or inaccurate.

This common law exception must be distinguished from the provisions of sections 29 and 30 of the *Canada Evidence Act*. Those sections permit any financial record (s. 29) or business record (s. 30) made in the usual or ordinary course of business to be admitted whether the person who made them is dead or alive. A typical example involves a person's bank records. Let us assume that Smith purchased a television set with a cheque that was returned N.S.F. and was charged with either false pretences or fraud. To establish that Smith had insufficient funds in his account, and that in the course of his dealings with the bank, Smith never did put in sufficient monies to honour the cheque, the prosecution would have to produce his bank records. However, the bank records by themselves are hearsay. They are merely notations or records made by bank employees who dealt with Smith. Normally, the prosecution would be required to call every employee of the bank who ever dealt with Smith to show what he deposited in his account or withdrew from it.

Section 29 of the *Canada Evidence Act* allows the prosecution to introduce a copy of any entry in any book or record kept in any financial institution if it is established that, at the time of making the entry, the record was one of the ordinary records of the bank, that the entry was made in the usual and ordinary course of business, that the record was in the custody or control of the bank, and that the copy is a true copy of the entry. Proof of the entry may be given by the manager or accountant of the bank, either orally or by affidavit.

Section 30 further permits the introduction of a business record made in the usual and ordinary course of business, provided that seven days' notice is given before its production.[15]

---

[15] *Bicknell*, 41 C.C.C. (3d) 545, 1988 CarswellBC 781 (C.A.).

(c) Declarations against Interest

Another recognized exception to the hearsay rule is a declaration against penal, pecuniary or proprietary interest. What someone says that might affect his or her liberty, pocketbook, or right or interest to certain property will be admitted in evidence if that person dies before he or she can be called upon to give evidence at trial.

This was not always the rule. For a long time, only declarations affecting a person's pecuniary or proprietary interest, but not his penal interest, were admissible in court.[16] However, in 1977, the Supreme Court of Canada decided in *O'Brien*[17] that it was only logical and proper that it should extend to a penal interest. There Mr. Justice Dickson wrote:

> The effect of the rule in *The Sussex Peerage Case*, as it has been generally understood, is to render admissible the statement by a deceased that he received payment of a debt from another or that he held a parcel of land as a tenant and not an owner, but to render inadmissible a confession by a deceased that he and not someone else was the real perpetrator of the crime. The distinction is arbitrary and tenuous. There is little or no reason why declarations against penal interest and those against pecuniary or proprietary interests should not stand on the same footing. A person is as likely to speak the truth in a matter affecting his liberty as in a matter affecting his pocket book. For these reasons and the ever-present possibility that a rule of absolute prohibition could lead to grave injustice I would hold that, in a proper case, a declaration against penal interest is admissible according to the law of Canada; the rule as to absolute exclusion of declarations against penal interest, established in *The Sussex Peerage case*, should not be followed.[18]

In the same year, the Supreme Court also endorsed the following test for determining what was a declaration against penal interest.[19]

1. The declaration must be made to a person in such circumstances that the declarant could be said to apprehend being vulnerable to penal consequences. For example, if someone says something to a member of his family, such as a parent or a spouse, or even a child, one does not expect that person to report him to the police and expose him to the risk of prosecution.

---

[16] *Sussex Peerage Case* (1844), 8 E.R. 1034, [1843-60] All E.R. Rep. 55, 11 Cl. & Fin. 85 (H.L.).

[17] (1977), [1978] 1 S.C.R. 591, [1977] 5 W.W.R. 400, 38 C.R.N.S. 325, 35 C.C.C. (2d) 209, 16 N.R. 271, 76 D.L.R. (3d) 513, 1977 CarswellBC 403.

[18] *Ibid.,* at (C.C.C.) p. 214.

[19] *Demeter* (1977), [1978] 1 S.C.R. 538, 38 C.R.N.S. 317, 16 N.R. 46, 34 C.C.C. (2d) 137, 75 D.L.R. (3d) 251, 1977 CarswellOnt 15.

2.   The declarant's vulnerability to penal consequences must not be too remote. In other words, one must be able to say that the person who hears the declaration will probably inform the police and expose the declarant to prosecution.

3.   Not every declaration that appears to be against penal interest will be admitted. The court must look at the totality of the words spoken and conclude that the whole tenor of its weight is against the declarant's penal interest.

4.   In a doubtful case, the court must look at all of the circumstances and consider whether or not there is any other evidence connecting the declarant with the crime, and whether there is evidence connecting the declarant and the accused.

It is of significance to note that the Court also said that the exception was not restricted only to declarants since deceased. The declaration was admissible if the declarant was alive but unavailable to testify by reason of insanity, grave illness that prevented the giving of testimony even from a bed, or absence in a jurisdiction where he could not be compelled by an order of the court to attend the accused's trial.

One can easily understand why the courts have carefully scrutinized declarations against penal interest. Just as a person who is about to die may wish to settle an old score with an enemy by accusing him of a crime, a person about to die may wish to save a member of his family or a friend from prosecution by falsely confessing to the crime. The law does not accept the former as evidence unless it is a dying declaration. The latter is accepted because the consequences are less severe. The possibility of convicting an innocent man based on a false accusation of guilt is far worse than the acquittal of a person who might be guilty.

(d) Declarations as to Physical or Mental Condition

As was pointed out initially in this chapter, a statement is hearsay and excluded only when it is offered to prove a fact in issue. If, however, the statement is offered only to prove that the statement is made, it is not hearsay and is clearly admissible. This is what is known as original evidence. The failure to understand the difference between hearsay evidence and original evidence is a problem that frequently arises when one side seeks to call evidence of a statement or declaration made with respect to a physical or mental condition.

Let us assume that X says to Y, "I am afraid because Z has threatened to kill me". X is subsequently found dead and Z is charged with
his murder. Is the statement that X made to Y admissible? The first part
of the statement — "I am afraid" — is a declaration as to a mental
condition, namely, a fear. If the only purpose of admitting the statement
is to show that X has a fear, then it would be clearly admissible. In that
sense, it is original evidence. What is objectionable are the words "because Z has threatened to kill me." If admitted, these words would permit
the jury to infer that X's fear of Z was justified. But without those added
words, the declaration "I am afraid" standing alone would have no
probative value.

The judge has three options. The first is to exclude the statement
altogether. The second is to admit only the statement, "I am afraid." The
third is to admit the entire statement and then to tell the jury that they
are entitled to use it as evidence of X's fear, but not evidence that it was
Z who was the cause of that fear.

Occasionally, the choices are not so straightforward. An example
is the decision of the Privy Council in *Ratten*.[20] Ratten was charged with
the murder of his wife by deliberately shooting her. His defence was
that he shot her accidentally. Shortly before her death, Mrs. Ratten made
a telephone call during which she said, "get me the police, please". Mr.
Ratten denied that his wife ever made a telephone call. The trial judge
allowed the telephone operator who had received that call to testify that
she had received a telephone call, that the voice on the other end was
hysterical and sobbing, and what the person said. It was held by the
Privy Council that the evidence was relevant to prove the state of mind
or emotion of Mrs. Ratten and to rebut the defence of accident.

Another example is a Canadian case, *Wysochan*.[21] There the issue
was whether a woman was killed by her husband or by the accused.
Each blamed the other. About a half an hour after the woman had been
shot, her husband appeared on the scene and the woman stretched out
her arms to him and said, "Stanley, help me out because there is a bullet
in my body", and later, "Stanley, help me. I am too hot." The Crown
applied to have what she said admitted into evidence. The trial judge
admitted her statements to show her state of mind. As he put it, "Would
it not have been a most improbable thing had he been the author of her
death that night?"

One might ask, "What was the relevance of the statements in both
cases?" In the *Ratten* case, the fact that the victim wanted the police was

---

[20]   [1971] 3 All E.R. 801, [1971] 3 W.L.R. 930, [1972] A.C. 378 (Australia P.C.).
[21]   (1930), 54 C.C.C. 172 (Sask. C.A.).

not relevant to the question of whether her death was deliberate or an accident. In *Wysochan*, the fact that the victim wanted her husband to help her or that she was too hot was not relevant as to who shot her. If the victim in each case had named her killer, then her statement would have been clearly hearsay and excluded unless it fell within one of the exceptions, such as a dying declaration or the *res gestae* (which will be discussed later). In both cases, the court held that it fell into neither exception.

In each case, the statement was admitted because it was a declaration as to the victim's physical or mental condition, even though her physical or mental condition was not a fact that the Crown was required to prove to establish its case against the accused. What the Crown had to establish was that a murder had been committed, that the accused had committed it and that he had the requisite mental intent. Because, in each case, the victim's statement was as to her physical or mental condition, the court said that it was original evidence as to that issue, not hearsay. However, by allowing the statement to be admitted as original evidence of the victim's state of mind, the court, in effect, also allowed it to be used for its hearsay content: in *Ratten*, to show that the killing was deliberate, not an accident; and, in *Wysochan*, to show that it was the accused and not the victim's husband who committed the murder.[22]

(e) Declarations as to Present Intention

If A says to B that he intends to go and visit C and is later found dead outside C's residence, the logical inference is that he was able to carry out his intention *to visit C*. This traditional exception to the hearsay rule permits B to tell the court what A told him as proof that A expressed an intention to visit C. However, what the exception has forbidden is the inference that A, in fact, met C where C is charged with causing the death of A, unless C was present when the statement was made.

One of the earliest cases dealing with this rule was an English case, *Wainwright*.[23] There Chief Justice Cockburn refused to admit a statement by the deceased victim that she intended to visit the accused. He ruled it out because "it was only a statement of intention which might or might not have been carried out". Although one might have thought that the Chief Justice should have been more concerned with the question of

---

[22]   See also *Collins*, 118 C.C.C. (3d) 514, 96 B.C.A.C. 49, 155 W.A.C. 49, 1997 CarswellBC 1800 (C.A.).
[23]   (1875), 13 Cox C.C. 171.

weight, rather than relevance, the view that such evidence is not admissible continues to influence Canadian authorities.

Some common law jurisdictions have rejected this restrictive view of such evidence. In *Walton*,[24] the High Court of Australia permitted evidence that the murder victim had stated that she intended to meet her husband (the accused) at the Town Centre, as evidence from which the jury could draw the inference that the two met at the appointed place. As Chief Justice Mason noted, "... her belief that she was to meet the applicant made it more probable that she travelled to the Town Centre".[25]

Over a century ago, the Supreme Court of the United States was prepared to permit inferences to be drawn from a declarant's intention. In *Mutual Life Insurance Co. of New York v. Hillmon*,[26] John Hillmon's wife had sued Mutual Life to recover on an insurance policy issued by them on the life of her husband, whose body had been found in Kansas. The defence was that the body in the grave was not that of Hillmon, but of one Walters, who had also disappeared and who had been killed by Hillmon to allow Mrs. Hillmon to collect on the policy. The Supreme Court held that letters written by Walters to his sister indicating an intention to accompany Hillmon on a trip out west were admissible as evidence of his intention to go with Hillmon, "which made it more probable both that he did go and that he went with Hillmon".

Canadian courts, however, have continued to apply the strict common law rule. In *Smith*,[27] the Supreme Court of Canada considered the Hillmon case but decided to reject it in favour of the English position.[28] In *Smith*, the victim of a murder had driven from Detroit to Canada with the accused where they spent the weekend together in a hotel. According to the theory of the Crown, the accused abandoned the victim at a hotel when she refused to take cocaine back to the United States. He then picked her up and drove her to a service station where he strangled her. To support this theory, the Crown relied upon four telephone calls made by the victim to her mother just before she was murdered discussing her association with the accused. On the first two occasions, the victim told her mother that she had been abandoned at a hotel by the accused and needed transportation home. On the third occasion, she called her mother and said that the accused had just returned and she would not need a

---

[24] (1989), 166 C.L.R. 283, 63 A.L.J.R. 226, 38 A. Crim. R. 276, 84 A.L.R. 59 (Australia H.C.).

[25] *Ibid.*, at (A.L.R.) p. 65.

[26] (1892) 145 U.S. 285, 12 S. Ct. 909, 36 L. Ed. 706 (U.S. Kan.).

[27] 15 C.R. (4th) 133, 75 C.C.C. (3d) 257, [1992] 2 S.C.R. 915, 55 O.A.C. 321, 139 N.R. 323, 94 D.L.R. (4th) 590, 1992 CarswellOnt 103, [1992] S.C.J. No. 74.

[28] *Kearley*, [1992] 2 All E.R. 345 (H.L.).

ride home after all. On the fourth occasion, she called and told her mother that she was on her way home. She was later found dead near the service station where she made her last call.

The Ontario Court of Appeal held that the first two calls were admissible as statements of the victim's existing state of mind and of her intention to go home; they were not evidence that the accused left her at the hotel. Although it was argued that the third call was evidence of the victim's state of mind and her intention to leave with the accused, from which it could be inferred that she did go with the accused, the Court held that it was not admissible to prove that the accused picked her up. The fourth call was also held inadmissible for the same reason. A further appeal to the Supreme Court of Canada was dismissed. The Court agreed that a declaration of intention by the deceased could not be used to prove that someone other than the deceased probably acted in accordance with that intention. That rule was recently reaffirmed by the Supreme Court in *Starr*.[29]

In summary then, Canadian authority does not permit B to tell the court that A told him that he was going to visit C for the purpose of drawing the inference that he probably met C. There is no prohibition, however, against B stating that A told him that he intended to visit C as evidence of his personal intention to visit C. If, for example, the fact in issue is whether C killed A, what is frowned upon is allowing B to tell the court that A told him that he intended to visit C for the purpose of inferring that A probably met C. The reason is that it would permit the trier to infer that A and C must have met and that C caused A's death. The difficulty is that once the evidence is introduced, it would be difficult for the jury not to draw that inference, even if they were instructed not to do so by the judge.

4. THE MODERN RULE

(a) History of the Modern Rule

As already noted, traditional exceptions to the hearsay rule were only allowed where the speaker was dead and therefore unable to testify. However, in the 1970s the Supreme Court decided that the hearsay rule should be relaxed and hearsay statements admitted, even where the declarant was alive but was unable for some reason to come to the court

---

[29] 2000 SCC 40, 36 C.R. (5th) 1, 147 C.C.C. (3d) 449, 190 D.L.R. (4th) 591, [2000] 11 W.W.R. 1, 148 Man. R. (2d) 161, 224 W.A.C. 161, 258 N.R. 250, [2000] 2 S.C.R. 144, 2000 CarswellMan 449, 2000 CarswellMan 450, [2000] S.C.J. No. 40.

to testify. One of the earliest cases where it was allowed was *O'Brien*.[30] There Chief Justice Dickson of the Supreme Court of Canada suggested that declarations against penal interest were admissible where the declarant was unavailable to testify by reason of insanity, grave illness or absence from the jurisdiction of Canadian courts.

The first Canadian decision to actually relax the rigidity of the hearsay rule was an Alberta civil case, *Ares v. Venner*,[31] dealing with declarations made in the course of duty. In that case, the plaintiff, who had fractured his leg while skiing, had sued the doctor, who had reduced the fracture and applied a plaster cast, for not removing the cast in time to prevent muscle necrosis from a lack of blood supply. The plaintiff's leg had to be amputated below the knee. The issue before the court was whether records kept by nurses at the hospital were admissible to show their observations of the pulse, temperature and condition of the plaintiff. Alberta at that time had no provision similar to that of other provinces, such as Ontario, allowing the admission of medical records of a patient. Although the nurses who made the records were alive and were, in fact, waiting outside the courtroom to testify, the plaintiff had not called them, but had been permitted by the trial judge to introduce the nurses' notes. The Supreme Court of Canada held that such records were admissible as declarations made in the ordinary course of duty and were "*prima facie* proof of the facts stated therein" even though the nurses were available to give oral testimony.

In reaching that conclusion, the Court rejected the reasoning of the House of Lords in *Myers v. Director of Public Prosecutions*,[32] where it was held that judges should not change the law to meet modern conditions, but should leave that responsibility to Parliament. Ironically, it was not really necessary for the Supreme Court to have extended the rule at all. The issue in *Ares v. Venner* was whether the doctor was negligent in failing to remove the cast from the plaintiff's leg after he had read the nurses' notes describing the plaintiff's condition (*i.e.*, toes were swollen, numb, blue, *etc.*), not whether the contents of the notes were correct. In other words, had the nurses' notes been admitted, not as proof of the contents, but to show that the doctor should have been alerted by what he read in those notes to look at the plaintiff's leg, no hearsay problem would have arisen.

---

[30] (1977), [1978] 1 S.C.R. 591, [1977] 5 W.W.R. 400, 38 C.R.N.S. 325, 35 C.C.C. (2d) 209, 16 N.R. 271, 76 D.L.R. (3d) 513, 1977 CarswellBC 403.

[31] [1970] S.C.R. 608, 12 C.R.N.S. 349, 73 W.W.R. 347, 14 D.L.R. (3d) 4, 1970 CarswellAlta 80, 1970 CarswellAlta 142.

[32] (1964), [1965] A.C. 1001, [1964] 3 W.L.R. 145, [1964] 2 All E.R. 881, 48 Cr. App. R. 348 (H.L.).

Twenty years later, the Supreme Court of Canada relied on *Ares v. Venner* to approve the reception of statements made by children to others about sexual abuse, provided that the twin requirements of "necessity" and "reliability" were met. In *Khan*,[33] Madam Justice McLachlin, delivering the judgment of the Court, noted that Canadian law was moving towards a more flexible attitude to the reception of the hearsay evidence of children, particularly where the statement concerned sexual abuse. She wrote:

> The hearsay rule has traditionally been regarded as an absolute rule, subject to various categories of exceptions, such as admissions, dying declarations, declarations against interest and spontaneous declarations. While this approach has provided a degree of certainty to the law on hearsay, it has frequently proved unduly inflexible in dealing with new situations and new needs in the law. This has resulted in courts in recent years on occasion adopting a more flexible approach, rooted in the principle and policy underlying the hearsay rule rather than the strictures of traditional exceptions.[34]

In *Khan*, a three-year-old girl had been examined privately in the office of Dr. Khan, a medical doctor. After the examination, the child's mother had noticed a wet spot on the sleeve of her daughter's clothing. About ten to fifteen minutes after the mother and daughter left Khan's office, they had a conversation about the visit and the child described an incident that could have amounted to a sexual assault. The trial judge had refused to permit the mother to testify as to what her daughter had told her because it was hearsay. McLachlin J. held that the judge should have admitted that evidence even though it was hearsay because it met the twin tests of necessity and reliability. The requirement of "necessity" had been met by the fact that, unless admitted, the child's evidence would be inadmissible, and to require the child to testify would be traumatic to her. She found the requirement of "reliability" in the fact that the child had no motive to falsify her story, which emerged naturally and without prompting, and the fact that she could not have knowledge of such sexual acts. McLachlin J. also noted that the child's statement was corroborated by real evidence. Although some provincial appellate courts after *Khan* continued to strictly apply the traditional exceptions to the hearsay rule,[35] the Supreme Court suggested that courts should

---

[33]   113 N.R. 53, 79 C.R. (3d) 1, 41 O.A.C. 353, [1990] 2 S.C.R. 531, 59 C.C.C. (3d) 92, 1990 CarswellOnt 108, 1990 CarswellOnt 1001, [1990] S.C.J. No. 81.

[34]   *Ibid.,* at (S.C.R.) p. 540.

[35]   *Crossley*, 117 C.C.C. (3d) 533, 95 B.C.A.C. 61, 154 W.A.C. 61, 1997 CarswellBC 1677 (C.A.) and *Collins*, 118 C.C.C. (3d) 514, 96 B.C.A.C. 49, 155 W.A.C. 49, 1997 CarswellBC 1800 (C.A.).

strike out into new territory and apply the twin tests of necessity and reliability whenever a hearsay problem arose. In *Smith*,[36] the Court said that hearsay evidence of statements made by persons who are not available to give evidence at trial ought generally to be admissible where the circumstances under which the statements are made satisfy the criteria of necessity and reliability set out in *Khan*, subject to the residual discretion of the trial judge to exclude the evidence where its probative value is slight and undue prejudice may result to the accused.

In *Kharsekin*,[37] the Newfoundland Court of Appeal followed the suggestion. There the victim of a knife attack told a physician who was attending him that he had been wounded by the accused. An hour later, in response to an inquiry, the victim again identified the accused as his attacker. Two hours later, the victim died. The trial judge refused to admit the statements to the physician as a dying declaration or as part of the *res gestae*. The Newfoundland Court of Appeal held that the trial judge was correct in not admitting the statements made to the physician under the old established exceptions. They said, however, that he was wrong in not admitting the statements under the *Khan* exception. Necessity arose because of the death of the victim. Reliability existed because the victim had a peculiar means of knowledge of the identity of his attacker, there was little time to falsify the statements and the medical evidence supported the position that the victim knew what he was saying.

Similarly, in *Chahley*,[38] the accused, who was charged with murder by slitting the deceased's throat, had sought unsuccessfully at trial to adduce evidence of statements made by the deceased to his common law wife several days before his death to the effect that a black man had pulled a knife on him and he could not go downtown for a while. In fact, the deceased had remained in his apartment for several days until he received a telephone call and had left telling his common law wife that, "everything's okay now". It was held that such evidence was not admissible as a dying declaration. However, since the statements met the twin tests of necessity and reliability, they should have been admitted as evidence for their truth to support the accused's defence that the murder had been committed, not by him, but by someone else. The test of necessity was satisfied because the declarant was dead. Reliability was met because the statements made by the declarant were not in favour

[36] *Supra*, note 27.
[37] 74 C.C.C. (3d) 163, 99 Nfld. & P.E.I.R. 70, 315 A.P.R. 70, 1992 CarswellNfld 147 (T.D.), reversed, 88 C.C.C. (3d) 193, 117 Nfld. & P.E.I.R. 89, 365 A.P.R. 89, 30 C.R. (4th) 252, 1994 CarswellNfld 17 (C.A.).
[38] 72 C.C.C. (3d) 193, 13 B.C.A.C. 213, 24 W.A.C. 213, 1992 CarswellBC 1094 (C.A.).

of his interest, were made before dispute or litigation and the declarant had the peculiar means of knowledge not possessed in ordinary cases.

As already observed, recently the Supreme Court, in *Starr*,[39] has effectively abolished the traditional exceptions. In *Starr*, it was held that although, historically, there has been no requirement for the trial judge to assess the reliability of a traditional exception to hearsay before admitting it, it was now necessary to do so. The Court said that concern for reliability and necessity should be no less present when the hearsay is introduced under an established exception.

(b) The Requirement of Necessity

Following the *Khan* decision, it was naturally assumed by the trial courts that if the witness was competent and available to testify, then the element of necessity no longer existed and the hearsay declaration was not admissible through a third party. In fact, when Dr. Khan was re-tried, the victim was nine years old and found competent by the trial judge to testify. Since she was competent to testify, the trial judge held that her statement to her mother was now inadmissible because there was no longer any necessity for it.

In one of the earliest cases, *S.(K.O.)*,[40] Wetmore J. interpreted the word "necessity" in the context of the *Khan* case to have a two-fold meaning. The hearsay evidence, he said, had to be necessary in the sense of being crucial to the case. It also had to be "reasonably necessary" in the sense that direct evidence was not available.

The second part of his test, however, was rejected by the Ontario Court of Appeal in *Khan v. College of Physicians & Surgeons (Ontario)*,[41] a case involving Dr. Khan's discipline proceedings before the Ontario College of Physicians. There the Court decided that it was "reasonably necessary" to admit an out-of-court statement, in addition to the direct evidence of the child, in order to obtain an accurate and frank rendition of the child's version of the events. The Court said that a child, though competent to testify, may be unable to express himself or herself with frankness, accuracy, fullness or candidness. Unless the child's out-of-court statement is admitted, despite legal competency, the child's version of the events may not be adequately placed before the

---

[39] *Supra*, note 29.
[40] 4 C.R. (4th) 37, 63 C.C.C. (3d) 91, 1991 CarswellBC 416 (S.C.).
[41] 9 O.R. (3d) 641, 94 D.L.R. (4th) 193, 76 C.C.C. (3d) 10, 11 Admin. L.R. (2d) 147, 57 O.A.C. 115, 1992 CarswellOnt 914, [1992] O.J. No. 1725 (C.A.).

trier of fact. Mr. Justice Doherty delivering the judgment of the Court wrote:

> In my view, if that tribunal is satisfied that despite the viva voce evidence of the child, it is still 'reasonably necessary' to admit the out-of-court statement in order to obtain an accurate and frank rendition of the child's version of the relevant events, then the necessity criterion set down in *Khan* is satisfied.[42]

A mentally disabled person may also be unable to express himself fully and accurately. This was recognized in a British Columbia case, *Pearson*.[43] There the issue was the identity of the perpetrator of a sexual assault upon an 18-year-old mentally disabled person. The trial judge had admitted statements made by the complainant to his mother shortly after the assault and several weeks later concerning the identity of his attacker. The British Columbia Court of Appeal said that the trial judge was correct in admitting the evidence. Necessity arose from the fact that the complainant was unable, because of his mental disability, to give a full and coherent account of the assault and his credibility could not be assessed by applying the traditional tests of demeanour, consistency, perception and accuracy of recollection of other events. There was reliability in the circumstances in which it could be expected that a person in his position would tell the truth.

Similarly, in *Parkinson*,[44] Mossop J. permitted a police officer to give evidence of what a 96-year-old victim of an assault in his own home told him about his assailant. Necessity was found in the fact that the victim's health was so fragile that there was a risk that he might have a stroke if called to testify.

Necessity has been held to apply where the declarant is unavailable to testify at trial and where the party seeking to introduce a hearsay statement of a third party is unable to obtain evidence of a similar nature from another source. For example, in *Biscette*,[45] it was held that the trial judge properly admitted a witness's preliminary inquiry evidence for its truth when the witness recanted her testimony at trial, since the necessity arose out of the witness's recantation.

---

[42] *Ibid.,* at (C.C.C.) p. 24.
[43] 36 C.R. (4th) 343, 95 C.C.C. (3d) 365, 82 B.C.A.C. 1, 133 W.A.C. 1, 1994 CarswellBC 597 (C.A.).
[44] (August 11, 1995), (Ont. Gen. Div.).
[45] (1995), 99 C.C.C. (3d) 326, 169 A.R. 81, 97 W.A.C. 81, 31 C.R.R. (2d) 38 (C.A.), affirmed, 110 C.C.C. (3d) 285, 39 C.R.R. (2d) 187, 187 A.R. 392, [1996] 3 S.C.R. 599, 127 W.A.C. 392, 203 N.R. 244, 1996 CarswellAlta 1113, 1996 CarswellAlta 1114, leave to appeal allowed (1995), 101 C.C.C. (3d) vi (S.C.C.).

Similarly, in *Hawkins*,[46] unavailability was found in the fact that the spouse of the accused was incompetent to testify against him. There, a woman who had given evidence for the Crown at Hawkins' preliminary inquiry, subsequently married him before trial. Since the woman was now a spouse and incompetent to give testimony for the Crown against her husband, and her evidence at the preliminary inquiry could not be read in at trial pursuant to section 715 of the *Criminal Code*, the Crown sought to introduce the evidence which she gave at the inquiry as a hearsay statement pursuant to the *Khan* rule. It was held by the Supreme Court that necessity arose because of her incompetency to give evidence as a spouse and was admissible provided that it also met the test of reliability.

One question that seems to have created difficulty for trial judges is the extent of the inquiry that must be conducted before hearsay testimony of a witness will be admitted. Is the trial judge entitled to rely on the fact that the witness of a tender age is probably unable to communicate his or her evidence fully or accurately, or may be traumatized if required to give evidence in a courtroom, or should the trial judge first hold a *voir dire* and see what evidence the child may be able to give? Similarly, in the case of a person who may be mentally challenged and unable to communicate his or her testimony fully or accurately, should the trial judge first hear that witness in the absence of the jury, before deciding whether to permit a hearsay statement of that witness from a third party? Should the Crown be required to call expert testimony on the witness's competence to testify or even be permitted to do so? In *Khan v. College of Physicians & Surgeons (Ontario)*,[47] the Ontario Court of Appeal was satisfied based on the age of the child that the child's hearsay statement should be admitted. Similarly, in *Rockey*,[48] the Supreme Court held that the trial judge had not erred in admitting the out-of-court statements of a two-and-a-half-year-old child on the basis of *Khan*. Although the child was five years old at the time of the trial, the Court was satisfied that the trial judge would have inevitably concluded that the child would have been traumatized by actually being called to

---

[46]   111 C.C.C. (3d) 129, 30 O.R. (3d) 641 (headnote only), 2 C.R. (5th) 245, 204 N.R. 241, 96 O.A.C. 81, [1996] 3 S.C.R. 1043, 141 D.L.R. (4th) 193, 1996 CarswellOnt 4063, [1996] S.C.J. No. 117.

[47]   *Supra*, note 41.

[48]   110 C.C.C. (3d) 481, 30 O.R. (3d) 577 (note), 204 N.R. 214, 95 O.A.C. 134, 140 D.L.R. (4th) 503, 2 C.R. (5th) 301, [1996] 3 S.C.R. 829, 1996 CarswellOnt 4284, 1996 CarswellOnt 4285.

give evidence, even though there was no evidence before the judge to that effect.[49]

Similarly, in *F. (W.J.)*,[50] the Supreme Court said that an insistence on evidence to support necessity in every case cannot be reconciled with the values underlying the hearsay rule and the increasing difficulties children face when called upon to testify. Necessity may be established either on the basis of what has happened at trial or on the basis of evidence. If the circumstances reveal that the child cannot, for whatever reason, give evidence in a meaningful way, then the trial judge may conclude that it is self-evident, or evident from the proceedings, that the out-of-court statements are necessary, if the court is to get the evidence and discover the truth of the matter. Lamer C.J.C., in a strong dissent, was concerned that this would place a heavy burden on trial judges who have no expertise in evaluating the risk of harm to a child witness giving evidence. He felt that it was incumbent on counsel seeking to introduce such evidence to make a reasonable attempt to establish such a foundation.

The rule, however, appears to be a different one where the complainant is an adult, even one who may suffer from a mental disability. In *Parrott*,[51] the accused was charged with offences in relation to a woman who suffered from Down's Syndrome. Although expert evidence before the trial judge had established that the woman had the mental development of a three-or-four-year-old child, the Supreme Court, in a majority decision, held that the trial judge had erred in concluding that the witness was unable to communicate the evidence within the meaning of section 16 of the *Canada Evidence Act* on the basis of expert testimony. The majority said that if a witness is *physically* available to testify and there is no suggestion that he or she would suffer trauma by attempting to give evidence, that evidence should generally not be pre-empted by hearsay, unless the trial judge has first had an opportunity to hear the potential witness and form his or her own opinion as to testimonial competence. There is no automatic necessity for calling

[49] See also *P. (J.)*, 13 C.R. (4th) 79, 74 C.C.C. (3d) 276, 150 N.R. 379, 54 Q.A.C. 82, 1992 CarswellQue 6, 1992 CarswellQue 338 (C.A.), affirmed, [1993] 1 S.C.R. 469, 54 Q.A.C. 81, 150 N.R. 378, 20 C.R. (4th) 397, 1993 CarswellQue 12, 1993 CarswellQue 153, where the Quebec Court of Appeal (2-1) came to a similar conclusion.
[50] [1999] 3 S.C.R. 569, 138 C.C.C. (3d) 1, 178 D.L.R. (4th) 53, 27 C.R. (5th) 169, 247 N.R. 62, [1999] 12 W.W.R. 587, 180 Sask. R. 161, 205 W.A.C. 161, [2000] 2 S.C.R. 275, 1999 CarswellSask 625, 1999 CarswellSask 626, [1999] S.C.J. No. 61.
[51] 2001 SCC 3, 150 C.C.C. (3d) 449, 194 D.L.R. (4th) 427, 39 C.R. (5th) 255, 265 N.R. 304, 198 Nfld. & P.E.I.R. 260, 595 A.P.R. 260, [2001] 1 S.C.R. 178, 2001 CarswellNfld 13, 2001 CarswellNfld 14, [2001] S.C.J. No. 4.

expert testimony on the issue of a mentally challenged person's competence to testify under section 16 of the Act. It was felt that trial judges are eminently qualified to assess such matters as "childlike mental condition" or "poor ability to sustain questioning" without expert evidence.

The dissenting members of the Court, however, felt that in cases involving young children or people with mental disabilities, neither direct evidence of the trauma, nor compulsory attendance of the witness to demonstrate it, should become a requirement. The role of the trial judge should be to assess the whole condition of the witness and balance the potential value of the evidence that may result from *viva voce* testimony against the potential prejudice to the witness. Potential trauma or circumstances in which it would be harmful to the witness or serve no real purpose are instances where it should not be necessary to call the complainant to give direct testimony.

(c) The Requirement of Reliability

A threshold test for establishing the requirement of "reliability" undoubtedly creates more difficulty. Critics of the modern rule argue that without the opportunity of cross-examination, that traditional method of testing the accuracy and truthfulness of a witness's testimony is lost. As Professor Wigmore noted:

> The theory of the Hearsay rule is that many possible sources of inaccuracy and untrustworthiness which may lie underneath the bare untested assertion of a witness can best be brought to light and exposed, if they exist, by the test of cross-examination.

However, in the next sentence, Wigmore also went on to suggest:

> But this test or security may in a given instance be superfluous; it may be sufficiently clear, in that instance, that the statement offered is free enough from the risk of inaccuracy and untrustworthiness, *so that the test of cross-examination would be a work of supererogation.* [Emphasis added.][52]

When would *the test of cross-examination be a work of supererogation*? In *Smith*,[53] Chief Justice Lamer, after referring to this passage, suggested that the trial judge, in determining whether the hearsay evidence is reliable, is required to conduct a search for alternative hypoth-

---

[52] *Supra*, note 2, at p. 202.
[53] 15 C.R. (4th) 133, 75 C.C.C. (3d) 257, [1992] 2 S.C.R. 915, 55 O.A.C. 321, 139 N.R. 323, 94 D.L.R. (4th) 590, 1992 CarswellOnt 103, [1992] S.C.J. No. 74.

eses (to the point of speculation) that might give an explanation for the hearsay statements inconsistent with their reliability. It was only where that search failed to the point that cross-examination, the traditional method of testing the accuracy of a witness's evidence, would be superfluous, that the evidence passed the threshold of reliability. In other words, to use the language of Gravely J. in *Cassidy*,[54] "the circumstances then will provide equivalence to the reliability normally insured by cross-examination".

In *Smith*,[55] the victim of a murder had driven from Detroit to Canada with the accused where they spent the weekend together in a hotel. According to the theory of the Crown, the accused abandoned the victim at a hotel when she refused to take cocaine back to the United States and then picked her up and drove her to a service station where he strangled her. To support this theory, the Crown relied upon four telephone calls made by the victim to her mother during which the victim discussed her association with the accused. On the first two occasions, the victim told her mother that she had been abandoned at a hotel by the accused and needed transportation home. On the third, she called her mother and said that the accused had just returned and she would not need a ride home after all. On the fourth occasion, she called and told her mother that she was on her way home. She was later found dead near the service station where she made her last call.

Lamer C.J.C. found that the first two calls had the necessary indicia of reliability because there was no known reason for the victim to lie. However, he rejected the third telephone call because *the circumstances under which it was made* were such that the victim might have been mistaken or might have intended to deceive her mother. His search for alternative hypotheses (to the point of speculation) that might give an explanation for the hearsay statements inconsistent with their reliability was in these words:

> I wish to emphasize that I do not advance these alternative hypotheses as accurate reconstructions of what occurred on the night of Ms. King's murder. I engage in such speculation only for the purpose of showing that the circumstances under which Ms. King made the third telephone call to her mother were not such as to provide that circumstantial guarantee of trustworthiness that would justify the admission of its contents by way of hearsay evidence, without the possibility of cross-examination. Indeed, at the highest, it can only be said that hearsay evidence of the third telephone call is equally

---

[54]   26 C.R. (4th) 252, 1993 CarswellOnt 139, [1993] O.J. No. 3231 (Gen. Div.) at (C.R.) p. 254.
[55]   *Supra*, note 53.

consistent with the accuracy of Ms. King's statements, and also with a number of other hypotheses. *I cannot say that this evidence could not reasonably have been expected to have changed significantly had Ms. King been available to give evidence in person and subjected to cross-examination.* I conclude, therefore, that the hearsay evidence of the contents of the third telephone conversation did not satisfy the criterion of reliability set out in *Khan*, and therefore were not admissible on that basis.[56]

In assessing the reliability of an out-of-court statement made by an accused, some trial courts have looked at other evidence that may reinforce that reliability. For example, in *Stark*,[57] Glithero J. admitted the utterance of the deceased to her female friend that she intended to meet the accused for lunch. In considering the reliability of the statement, he noted that the accused denied any meeting to the police, but admitted to his wife and mother that he met the deceased for lunch. In *Parkinson*, discussed earlier, Mossop J. considered other evidence connecting the accused to the victim's residence at the time of the assault as demonstrating sufficient reliability to admit the 96-year-old victim's statement to the police officer.

However, the Ontario Court of Appeal has said that this approach is the wrong one. The trial judge is only entitled to look at the circumstances surrounding the making of the statement and not any confirmatory evidence that may arise after. In *Merz*,[58] where the accused was charged with the murder of his former common-law spouse, at issue was whether the trial judge had erred in admitting three hearsay statements of the deceased for their truth. The first statement was the testimony of the deceased, at an earlier trial of the accused on a charge of threatening her son, to the effect that the accused had threatened her on January 31, 1993 and again on February 5, 1993. The second was her statement to a friend about the threat on January 31st. The third was her statement to her lawyer about the threat on February 5th. The Ontario Court of Appeal said that the trial judge should not have relied upon the second and third statements as confirmatory of the reliability of the deceased's evidence at the accused's trial for threatening her son. The Court noted that in *Smith*,[59] Lamer C.J.C. had said that in determining the reliability of a hearsay statement, the trial judge must look at the circumstances under which the statement was made to determine whether the circumstances "substantially negate the possibility that the statement was untruthful or

---

[56] *Ibid.*, at (C.R.) p. 151.

[57] (August, 1994), Glithero J. (Ont. Gen. Div.).

[58] 30 C.R. (5th) 313, 46 O.R. (3d) 161, 140 C.C.C. (3d) 259, 127 O.A.C. 1, 1999 CarswellOnt 3620, [1999] O.J. No. 4039 (C.A.), leave to appeal refused, 263 N.R. 391 (note), 141 O.A.C. 398 (note), 2000 CarswellOnt 3925, 2000 CarswellOnt 3926 (S.C.C.).

[59] *Supra*, note 53.

mistaken".[60] This means that the trial judge is not to rely on any other confirmatory evidence.

The British Columbia Court of Appeal, however, has not considered it necessary to impose that same stringent test on the issue of reliability. In *Misir*[61] the accused was charged with stabbing his wife to death. The trial judge had admitted evidence from various members of the victim's family and co-workers that the accused and the victim had a troubled marriage. This included evidence that the accused had physically and verbally abused the victim. The physical abuse included an incident of choking and forced intercourse. A good deal of the evidence came from conversations the victim had with family members and co-workers. Without referring to either *Smith* or *Merz*, it was held that although the evidence of the victim's family members must be treated with caution as it might be "coloured", the evidence of co-workers that supported the evidence of the victim's family, which carried less suggestion that it was coloured, provided support for the trustworthiness of all the victim's statements. The British Columbia Court of Appeal did not consider it necessary to examine the circumstances under which the statements were made to determine whether the circumstances "substantially negate the possibility that the statement was untruthful or mistaken". Relying upon *F. (W.J.)*[62] the Court seemed to be saying that so long as there is a sufficient indication of trustworthiness from all of the other evidence, the hearsay statements will meet the requisite threshold of reliability. In other words, the overwhelming evidence of complaints of abuse by the victim to family and friends was a sufficient indication of the reliability of her statements to them.

Where the out-of-court statement is tendered by the defence, the court will usually take a more relaxed view of the prerequisites to admissibility. Although the rules of evidence generally apply equally to the Crown and the defence, a trial judge is entitled to relax those rules in favour of the defence where it is necessary to prevent a miscarriage of justice.[63] However, as was stressed by Doherty J.A. in *Kimberley*[64]

---

[60]   *Ibid.*, at (C.C.C.) p. 270.

[61]   2001 BCCA 202, 86 B.C.L.R. (3d) 332, 153 C.C.C. (3d) 70, 150 B.C.A.C. 52, 245 W.A.C. 52, 2001 CarswellBC 511 (C.A.). But see *Larson* (2001), 42 C.R. (5th) 49 (B.C. S.C.) and *Nguyen* (2001), 42 C.R. (5th) 35, 153 C.C.C. (3d) 495 (Alta. C.A.) where it was held that the surrounding circumstances must be examined to see if they provide sufficient guarantees of trustworthiness. See also *Stark* (2001), 147 C.C.C. (3d) 499 (S.C.C.) at para. 217.

[62]   *Supra,* note 50.

[63]   *Williams* (1985), 18 C.C.C. (3d) 356 (Ont. C.A.).

[64]   (2001), 157 C.C.C. (3d) 129 (Ont. C.A.).

they do invite an abandonment of the threshold reliability inquiry altogether.

Where a party seeks to introduce hearsay under the *Khan* rule, the judge's role is limited to determining whether the particular hearsay statement exhibits sufficient indicia of reliability so as to afford the trier of fact a satisfactory basis for evaluating the truth of the statement. The judge must identify the specific dangers raised by the statement and then determine whether the facts surrounding the utterance of the statement offer sufficient circumstantial guarantees of trustworthiness to compensate for those dangers. However, the judge must remember that it is not his or her function to decide whether the hearsay statement is, in fact, reliable. That issue is one that must be decided by the jury. Once the trial judge is satisfied that the out-of-court statement is sufficiently reliable to be admitted, then the jury will be entitled to consider evidence from other witnesses in determining the ultimate reliability of the hearsay statements.

5. ASSERTIONS OF LIVING PERSONS

(a) Co-conspirators

Where an accused is charged with the crime of conspiracy to commit an illegal act, proof that he or she agreed to commit the illegal act is sufficient to obtain a conviction. It is not necessary for the prosecution to prove that the accused also committed the illegal act which the conspirators planned to commit. But proving a conspiracy is generally very difficult, because such agreements are usually made in secret and the only witnesses present are the conspirators themselves. Thus, an exception to the hearsay rule has developed which allows the prosecution to prove the conspiracy by introducing evidence of the acts and declarations of fellow members of the conspiracy, performed and made in pursuance of the objects of the conspiracy.

This exception is very confusing because it first requires proof of membership in the conspiracy by direct evidence other than hearsay before the acts and declarations of co-conspirators may be introduced. However, this initial proof of membership need only be made on a balance of probabilities. Once proof has been established, then the hearsay exception kicks in and the prosecution is allowed to introduce evidence of acts and declarations of co-conspirators to prove the conspiracy beyond a reasonable doubt.

In practice what happens is that all of the evidence (including the hearsay) is admitted and, at the conclusion of the case, the trial judge is required to instruct the jury (or himself where trial is by judge alone) that they must conduct their deliberations in two stages. They must first look at only the direct evidence of membership and determine whether the accused is probably a member of the conspiracy. If they are satisfied that he is, then and only then are they allowed to consider the hearsay evidence in determining whether proof has been established beyond a reasonable doubt.[65]

(b) Identification Parades

Where a fact in issue is the identity of the perpetrator of the crime, it may be necessary for the prosecutor to ask a witness, who is able to identify the person, to point him out to the jury. A typical question is "Do you see the person who ... in this courtroom"? In such instances, it will usually not be very difficult for the witness to identify the accused because the accused will be sitting by himself (or with a co-accused) in the prisoner's dock.

However, those involved in the administration of justice know from experience that the identification of an accused for the first time in the prisoner's dock is notoriously suspect and can lead to a miscarriage of justice.[66] The ordinary juror on the other hand may not be aware of this. For this reason, a rule has developed which permits police officers, or anyone else who is present when a prior identification is made by a witness, to give evidence not only that the witness identified the accused but also of the surrounding circumstances of that identification. For example, the officer who was present during an identification parade (a lineup) or when a witness was shown a photo-lineup, or when a composite drawing was prepared, is entitled to give evidence that the witness identified a particular person in the lineup or the composite drawing, whether or not the witness hesitated before making the identification, what words the witness used in making the identification, etc. Such evidence will give the trier of fact a complete picture of all of the surrounding circumstances which led to the accused's ultimate identi-

---

[65] *Carter*, [1982] 1 S.C.R. 938, 31 C.R. (3d) 97, 137 D.L.R. (3d) 387, 46 N.B.R. (2d) 142, 121 A.P.R. 142, 47 N.R. 288, 67 C.C.C. (2d) 568, 1982 CarswellNB 13, 1982 CarswellNB 55.

[66] *Browne*, 11 C.R. 297, 1 W.W.R. (N.S.) 449, 99 C.C.C. 141, 1951 CarswellBC 25 (C.A.).

fication in the prisoner's dock and will enable the trier to properly assess the value of that identification.[67]

Some text writers[68] and authorities[69] have suggested that evidence by a police officer of a prior identification by a witness is hearsay and the rule which allows such evidence is an exception to the hearsay rule. The better view, it is submitted, is that it is really an exception to the rule which prohibits a witness from giving evidence of a prior consistent statement.[70] It is not hearsay because the evidence is not tendered to prove the truth of what the identifying witness has said: simply the fact that it was said. The officers are not saying that the accused committed the crime, only that the witness said that the accused is the person who committed the crime. In other words, the evidence is offered only to prove that the witness has identified the accused as the person who committed the crime, not that the identification is necessarily a correct one. Such evidence is thus original or first-hand evidence of identification by the witness; it is not second hand or hearsay evidence that the accused committed the crime. Nevertheless, because of the concern that the trier may infer from the officer's testimony that the witness must have picked out the right person, the trial judge is required to instruct the jury as to the limited use of such evidence.

The more difficult question arises where the witness is unable to remember making the identification. Should the police officers be permitted to give evidence that the witness made a positive identification, even if the witness is unable to remember doing so? In *Starr*,[71] the two murder victims had given witness B a ride home in their car shortly before they were murdered in a gang-related execution. Soon after the murders, B was shown three photos by two police officers and pointed to one of them and said the person (who was the accused) looked familiar. At trial, B was not asked by the prosecutor to identify the accused at trial, why the person in the photo looked familiar, where she had seen the person or whether she had seen the accused on the night of the murder. However, police officers were permitted to give evidence that

[67] *Langille* (1990), 75 O.R. (2d) 65, 40 O.A.C. 355, 59 C.C.C. (3d) 544 (C.A.); *McCay* (1990), 91 Cr. App. R. 84 (C.A.).
[68] Sopinka, Lederman and Byrant, *The Law of Evidence* (Toronto: Butterworths, 1992) at pp. 313-14.
[69] *T. (W.P.)*, 14 O.R. (3d) 225, 16 C.R.R. (2d) 49, 83 C.C.C. (3d) 5, 63 O.A.C. 321, 1993 CarswellOnt 1056 (C.A.).
[70] *Langille, ibid.; Tat*, 117 C.C.C. (3d) 481, 103 O.A.C. 15, 35 O.R. (3d) 641, 14 C.R. (5th) 116, 1997 CarswellOnt 5434 (C.A.).
[71] 2000 SCC 40, 36 C.R. (5th) 1, 147 C.C.C. (3d) 449, 190 D.L.R. (4th) 591, [2000] 11 W.W.R. 1, 148 Man. R. (2d) 161, 224 W.A.C. 161, 258 N.R. 250, [2000] 2 S.C.R. 144, 2000 CarswellMan 449, 2000 CarswellMan 450, [2000] S.C.J. No. 40.

when B identified a photo (of the accused) shortly after the murders, she stated that it looked like the man she had seen at the gas station talking to one of the deceased and who was also probably driving the other car. It was held by the Supreme Court that the trial judge had erred in admitting the officer's evidence of identification by B.

Iacobucci J., delivering the judgment of the majority, held that what B told the officers was hearsay and inadmissible unless reliable and necessary, because the Crown sought to use the statements to show that the accused was present at the gas station, thus creating an inference that he followed them from the station and was driving the car she saw when she was let off at her home. The issue, as he saw it, was whether the prior identification exception to the hearsay rule permitted the reception of an out-of-court identification by a trial witness, where the witness does not testify at trial that she made the identification. After reviewing the authorities, he concluded that it did not. However, he said that the out-of-court identification would have been permitted, even if she was unable to identify the accused at trial, if she could testify that she previously gave an accurate description or made an accurate identification.[72] His rationale for the distinction was this:

> If the witness can at least testify that at some point she made an accurate identification, then a police officer's testimony that he or she observed the identifying witness in the act of identification is *original evidence* that the identifying witness did indeed select a particular person, and that that person is the accused. However, for this rationale to apply, the identifying witness must confirm that the person he or she identified in the police officer's presence was the person who committed an act that is relevant in the immediate proceedings.[73]

As far as the admissibility of the statements under the principled approach, they were neither necessary nor reliable. They were not necessary because B was a witness at trial. Moreover, there were too many inconsistencies in the identification to make the statements reliable.

It is not easy to understand how a witness who is unable to identify the accused at trial is able to say with assurance that he or she made an accurate identification of the accused at the police station. The issue becomes more problematic for the defence who will undoubtedly find it difficult to cross-examine the witness, unless the witness is able to say what factors at the time led him or her to be satisfied the identification was an accurate one. It is unfortunate that the Supreme Court in *Starr*

---

[72] See *Tat, supra,* note 70.
[73] *Ibid.,* at (C.C.C.) p. 537.

failed to address this potential problem and provide more assistance to trial judges.

(c) Past Memory Recorded

In Chapter 2, dealing with "Refreshing The Witness's Memory", it was noted that the present rule is that a witness may refresh his or her memory while in the witness box from any record of the event that he or she has brought, provided, (a) that he or she made the note of the event or, if it was made by another person, he or she verified the accuracy of the other person's note, and (b) the note was personally written, or the record of another person was verified by the witness when the facts were fresh in his or her memory.[74] The question was also asked — what happens if the witness has no recollection of the events at all?

At the foundation of the common law adversarial system is the notion that a witness will have a memory of the events that he or she is relating to the court and that the other side will be allowed to test the accuracy of that memory and the truth of that testimony by cross-examination. Is the testimony of that witness lost forever, even though the witness may have made notes of the event? Can the written word ever replace the lost memory?

Professor Wigmore recognized that total memory loss did not necessarily result in lost testimony where certain conditions were met.[75] He called it "past recollection recorded". Those conditions were:

1.   The past recollection must have been recorded in some reliable way.
2.   At the time, it must have been sufficiently fresh and vivid to be probably accurate.
3.   The witness must be able now to assert that the record accurately represented his knowledge and recollection at the time, The usual phrase requires the witness to affirm that "he knew it to be true at the time".
4.   The original record itself must be used, if procurable.

In other words, the notes or record made at the time replaces the memory of the witness and becomes "past memory recorded".

---

[74]   *B.(K.G.)*, 125 C.C.C. (3d) 61, 109 O.A.C. 138, 1998 CarswellOnt 1914, [1998] O.J. No. 1859 (C.A.); *Coffin*, [1956] S.C.R. 191, 23 C.R. 1, 114 C.C.C. 1, 1956 CarswellQue 1; *Shergill*, 13 C.R. (5th) 160, 23 O.T.C. 218, 1997 CarswellOnt 5225 (Gen. Div.).
[75]   *Wigmore on Evidence* (Chadbourn rev. 1970), Vol. 3, c. 28, para. 744.

The admissibility of "past memory recorded" is, in effect, an exception to the hearsay rule. It is an exception because the original record is admissible as proof of the truth of the contents, even though the recorder of the note cannot be tested as to the accuracy or truth of the note. The note is considered to have a substantial guarantee of trustworthiness or reliability because it was made by the recorder when it was sufficiently fresh in his or her mind to be probably accurate. It is necessary because the recorder of the note has no memory of the event.[76]

6. RES GESTAE

The term "*res gestae*" is a Latin phrase that is too often used and misused by judges and lawyers. Professor Wigmore called it useless "because every rule of Evidence to which it has ever been applied exists as a part of some other well established principle and can be explained in the terms of that principle".[77] He also called it harmful "because by its ambiguity it invites the confusion of one rule with another and thus creates uncertainty as to the limitations of both". He suggested that it should be wholly repudiated. Regrettably, judges and lawyers continue to use it more than ever.

The rule has been expressed this way.[78]

Acts, declarations, and incidents which constitute, or accompany and explain, the fact or transaction in issue, are admissible, for or against either party, as forming part of the *res gestae*.

In *Teper*,[79] Lord Normand attempted to justify the reception of evidence that forms part of the *res gestae* this way:

It appears to rest ultimately on two propositions, that human utterance is both a fact and a means of communication, and that human action may be so interwoven with words that the significance of the action cannot be understood without the correlative words, and the dissociation of the words from the action would impede the discovery of truth.

The above passages suggest that the term *res gestae* refers to words that give significance to or explain conduct or action. In *Bedingfield*,[80]

---

[76] See E.M. Morgan "Hearsay and Preserved Memory", (1926) 40 Harv. L.R. 712.
[77] *Supra*, note 75, Vol. 6, para. 1767.
[78] *Phipson on Evidence*, (11th ed.), para. 171.
[79] [1952] A.C. 480, 68 L.Q.R. 433, [1952] 2 All E.R. 447 (British Guyana P.C.) at (All E.R.) p. 449.
[80] (1879), 14 Cox C.C. 341.

the victim, who was Bedingfield's mistress, came out of a room where Bedingfield was subsequently found, pointed to her throat which was cut and said to one of her assistants "see what Harry has done". She died ten minutes later. Bedingfield's first name was Harry. The trial judge, Chief Justice Cockburn, would not permit the statement to be admitted in evidence because the transaction, that is the cutting of her throat, was over and completed when she made the statement. Later decisions accepted this restriction and argued that a statement or declaration could not be admitted as part of the *res gestae* unless it accompanied the act and explained it.

Professor Wigmore strongly criticized this restriction. He argued that it arose out of a failure to understand the distinction between what may be described as a verbal act and a spontaneous exclamation. A verbal act is simply words that accompany an act and explain it. As Wigmore pointed out:

> Without the words, the act as a whole may be incomplete; and until the words are taken into consideration, the desired significance can not be attributed to the wordless conduct.[81]

Without the accompanying words, the act has no significance. The words explain the act. This means that when a witness who has seen the act and heard the accompanying words testifies as to what he or she has seen and heard, he or she is giving first-hand or original evidence, not second-hand or hearsay evidence. Thus, in a strict sense, *res gestae* is not really an exception to the hearsay rule because it allows the admission of a statement, that would otherwise be hearsay, as first-hand or original evidence to explain conduct or actions that might otherwise be ambiguous.

Professor Wigmore, however, argued that spontaneous exclamations ought to be admitted as an exception to the hearsay rule. His reasons were these:

> Under certain external circumstances of physical shock, a stress of nervous excitement may be produced which stills the reflective faculties and removes their control, so that the utterance which then occurs is a spontaneous and sincere response to the actual sensations and perceptions already produced by the external shock. Since this utterance is made under the immediate and uncontrolled domination of the senses, and during the brief period when considerations of self interest could not have been brought fully to bear by reasoned reflection, the utterance may be taken as particularly trustworthy,

---

[81]   *Supra,* note 75, at Vol. 6, para. 1772.

(or, at least, as lacking the usual grounds of untrustworthiness), and thus as expressing the real tenor of the speaker's belief as to the facts just observed by him; and may therefore be received as testimony to those facts.[82]

Using the *Bedingfield* case as an example, Professor Wigmore would argue that Bedingfield's mistress' exclamation as to "what Harry has done" was "a spontaneous and sincere response to the actual sensations and perceptions already produced by the external shock" of having her throat cut. It was also made "during the brief period when considerations of self interest could not have been brought fully to bear by reasoned reflection". Thus, he would argue that the utterance should be taken as particularly trustworthy and should be admitted as an exception to the hearsay rule.

For almost seventy years, *Bedingfield* was religiously followed by Canadian and English courts. In 1950, there was some attempt to introduce the concept of "spontaneous exclamation" in an Ontario case, but it was quickly rejected. In *Leland*[83] the accused and her husband were jointly charged with manslaughter arising out of the stabbing of one Monteith, in whose house both were residing as roomers. During a quarrel between Monteith and the accused's husband, all of the lights in the house were turned off. When the lights were turned on again, Monteith was heard to say to his wife, "Rose, she stabbed me". He died a few minutes later. Monteith's wife's name was Rose. The trial judge admitted the statement without specifically referring to it as a "spontaneous exclamation". However, the Ontario Court of Appeal said that the judge was wrong to do so because "our rules of evidence do not seem to extend to cover a case of spontaneous exclamation, in the broad terms stated by Wigmore". Nor was the Court prepared to admit it as part of the *res gestae* because, "[t]he fight had ceased. No one was pursuing the deceased or seeking to continue the struggle".

However, in 1972, the House of Lords in *Ratten*[84] concluded that the *Bedingfield* rule was too restrictive. In *Ratten*, the Crown sought to introduce the evidence of a telephone operator who had received a telephone call from the deceased's home ten minutes before she was shot. The call came from a woman who sounded hysterical and who said, "get me the police, please", gave her address but, before a connection was made, hung up. The trial judge admitted the statement. Lord Wilberforce, delivering the judgment of the House, said that the judge

---

[82] *Ibid.*, at para. 1747.
[83] (1950), [1951] O.R. 12, 11 C.R. 152, 98 C.C.C. 337, 1950 CarswellOnt 21 (C.A.).
[84] [1971] 3 All E.R. 801, [1971] 3 W.L.R. 930, [1972] A.C. 378 (Australia P.C.).

was correct in doing so. It was his view that the admissibility of such statements did not depend on there being exact contemporaneity with the act to be explained.

> ...hearsay evidence may be admitted if the statement providing it is made in such conditions (always being those of approximate but not exact contemporaneity) of involvement or pressure as to exclude the possibility of concoction or distortion to the advantage of the maker or the disadvantage of the accused.[85]

The test that the trial judge had to apply was whether there was the possibility of concoction or fabrication, not whether the statement was part of the event or transaction.

> ... if the drama, leading up to the climax, has commenced and assumed such intensity and pressure that the utterance can safely be regarded as a true reflection of what was unrolling or actually happening, it ought to be received.[86]

Ratten was re-affirmed 14 years later by the House of Lords in *Blastland*[87] and again, a year later, by the House of Lords in *Andrews*.[88] In *Andrews*, *Bedingfield* was specifically overruled.

The concept of "spontaneous exclamation" espoused by Wigmore and the relaxation of the narrow "exact contemporaneity" test of *Bedingfield* was finally accepted by the Ontario Court of Appeal in *Clark*,[89] There it was held that the evidence of a witness that she heard the victim yell: "Help! Help! I've been murdered! I've been stabbed!" was admissible as a spontaneous statement made in such circumstances as to exclude the possibility of concoction or distortion. The statements were contemporaneous with the unfolding events even though they did not accompany the actual stabbing.

However, in *Khan*,[90] the Supreme Court of Canada cast doubt upon the correctness of *Clark* by re-affirming that the traditional tests of contemporaneity and pressure or emotional intensity must exist before

---

[85] *Ibid.*, at (A.C.) p. 391.

[86] *Ibid.*, at 390.

[87] (1985), [1986] 1 A.C. 41, [1985] 2 All E.R. 1095, 81 Cr. App. R. 266, Crim. L.R. 727 (H.L.).

[88] [1987] 1 All E.R. 513, [1987] A.C. 281, [1987] 2 W.L.R. 413 (H.L.).

[89] 42 O.R. (2d) 609, 7 C.C.C. (3d) 46, 1 D.L.R. (4th) 46, 35 C.R. (3d) 357, 1983 CarswellOnt 96 (C.A.), leave to appeal refused (1983), 42 O.R. (2d) 609 (note), 7 C.C.C. (3d) 46 (note), 1 D.L.R. (4th) 46 (note), 39 C.R. (3d) xxvii (S.C.C.).

[90] 113 N.R. 53, 79 C.R. (3d) 1, 41 O.A.C. 353, [1990] 2 S.C.R. 531, 59 C.C.C. (3d) 92, 1990 CarswellOnt 108, 1990 CarswellOnt 1001, [1990] S.C.J. No. 81.

a hearsay statement will be admitted under this exception. There, a three-and-one-half year-old girl had been examined privately by Dr. Khan, a medical doctor. About 15 minutes after the child and her mother had left Khan's office, the child described to her mother an incident that took place in his office that could amount to a sexual assault. The mother was not allowed by the trial judge to repeat what her daughter told her because it was not, in his opinion, a spontaneous utterance. The Court of Appeal, however, disagreed.[91]

Mr. Justice Robins wrote:

> The time that may elapse before a statement following an event capable of rendering it spontaneous is rendered inadmissible will depend on a variety of factors. These include, for instance, the nature and circumstances of the act or event, the nature and circumstances of the statement, the place where the event occurred or the statement was made, the possible influence of intervening events, and the condition and age of the declarant. Each case must depend on its own circumstances; no two cases are identical, and the exact length of time is not subject to mathematical measurement. In any given case, the ultimate question is whether the statement relating to the alleged startling event was made near enough in time to the event to exclude any realistic opportunity for fabrication or concoction.[92]

However, McLachlin J., delivering the judgment of the Supreme Court,[93] held that the trial judge was correct in rejecting the statement as a spontaneous utterance because it was neither contemporaneous nor made under pressure or emotional intensity. She was not prepared to relax the strict requirements as to the admissibility of a spontaneous utterance, as had been done in the United States, particularly in cases of sex offences against children. It was her concern that admissibility under this exception to the hearsay rule did not impose the twin conditions of necessity and reliability before such utterances could be received. She preferred to admit such utterances only where they met those requirements that had been earlier imposed by the Supreme Court in *Ares v. Venner*.[94]

---

[91]   27 O.A.C. 142, 64 C.R. (3d) 281, 42 C.C.C. (3d) 197, 64 C.R. 281, 1988 CarswellOnt 69 (C.A.).

[92]   *Ibid.*, at (C.C.C.) p. 210.

[93]   *Supra*, note 90.

[94]   [1970] S.C.R. 608, 12 C.R.N.S. 349, 73 W.W.R. 347, 14 D.L.R. (3d) 4, 1970 CarswellAlta 80, 1970 CarswellAlta 142: see discussion under heading 3 "The Modern Rule".

7. STATUTORY EXCEPTIONS

(a) Generally

As noted earlier, some statutes permit the introduction of hearsay evidence by affidavit or certificate where it would be inconvenient or even impossible to call the witness who is able to give direct evidence of the fact in issue. Although the evidence is hearsay, once admitted, the evidence becomes admissible for the truth of the contents.

For example, if what has to be established is that X made certain deposits and withdrawals from his account at the Bank of Montreal, a strict application of the hearsay rule would require each bank teller who dealt with X to come forward and give evidence of that specific transaction so that he or she could be subjected to the test of cross-examination. But we know that it would be unlikely that any of the tellers would remember the details of those transactions.

Section 29(1) of the *Canada Evidence Act*, however, authorizes either the Crown or the defence to introduce proof of those transactions by production of "a copy of any entry in any book or record kept in any financial institution" notwithstanding that the copy of the entry, or even the actual entry itself is, in a strict sense, hearsay. But before a copy of the entry is admitted, section 29(2) requires that certain conditions be established. Those conditions are considered crucial to the twin tests of necessity and reliability or trustworthiness discussed earlier. They include the requirement that the book or record be one of the ordinary books or records of the financial institution, that the entry was made in the usual and ordinary course of business, that the book or record be in the custody or control of the financial institution and that the copy be a true copy of the book or record. When these conditions are established, proof of the entry may be given by the bank manager or the accountant, either orally or by affidavit. Similar provisions are contained in section 26 of the Act dealing with Government of Canada records and in section 30 with respect to business records.

Another common exception to the hearsay rule is section 50 of the *Controlled Drugs and Substances Act*.[95] Section 50(1) permits the results of the analysis of a controlled substance to be given by a certificate or report purporting to be signed by a qualified analyst, provided that the other side has been given reasonable notice of the intention to rely on certificate evidence together with a copy of the certificate or report.

---

[95] S.C. 1996, c. 19.

Section (2) does, however, give the court the right to order the attendance of the analyst for the purpose of cross-examination.

(b) Videotaped Evidence of a Complainant

Section 715.1 of the *Criminal Code* permits an out-of-court statement to be admitted at the trial of an accused charged with certain enumerated offences if

1. the complainant was under the age of eighteen years at the time the offence is alleged to have been committed;
2. a videotape of the complainant's statement was made within a reasonable time after the alleged offence;
3. the complainant in the videotape describes *the acts complained of*; and
4. the complainant, while testifying, *adopts* the contents of the videotape.

Following the enactment of section 715.1, one issue that the courts were asked to consider was the meaning of the phrase "adopts the contents of the videotape". This required the courts to determine the nature of a videotaped statement. In *Meddoui*,[96] the Alberta Court of Appeal said that section 715.1 was a statutory exception to one of the conditions for the past recollection recorded exception to the hearsay rule; namely, that to be admitted as past recollection recorded at the time the witness testifies, the witness must have had no recollection of the events recorded. The Court reasoned that this meant that it was not necessary for the complainant to be able, based on a present memory of the events referred to in the videotape, to verify the accuracy and contents of the statement, so long as she recalls giving the statement and her attempt then to be truthful. The Court went further and argued that, if the complainant had a present memory of the events, then her videotape evidence was not necessary because it added nothing to her evidence and would infringe the rule against the admission of prior consistent statements.

---

[96] 77 Alta. L.R. (2d) 97, 111 A.R. 295, 2 C.R. (4th) 316, 61 C.C.C. (3d) 345, [1991] 2 W.W.R. 289, 5 C.R.R. (2d) 294, 1990 CarswellAlta 187 (C.A.), set aside, [1991] 3 S.C.R. ix, [1992] 1 W.W.R. lxv (note), 6 C.R.R. (2d) 192 (note), 82 Alta. L.R. (2d) lxv (note), 69 C.C.C. (3d) vi (note), 137 N.R. 389 (note).

In *T. (W.P.)*,[97] Doherty J.A disagreed with that reasoning. He was of the view that section 715.1 is a statutorily created exception to the rule prohibiting the admission of a prior consistent statement. He could not agree that a witness who has no recollection of the events referred to in a prior statement can be said to *adopt* that statement. He was, understandably, concerned that a complainant who has no recollection of the events, and who was only required to *vouch* for the accuracy of the videotaped statement, could not be cross-examined about the actual events because he or she has no memory of those events. He felt that the requirement that the complainant while testifying, "adopt(s) the contents of the videotape", meant that she must not only acknowledge making the statement but also be able, *based on a present memory of the events referred to in the statement*, to verify the accuracy of the contents of the statement. This did not mean that the admission of the videotaped statement adds nothing to the testimony. The videotaped statement may communicate additional information to the trier of fact that could assist in determining the truth of the allegations.

However, Cory J. in *F. (C.)*,[98] disagreed with the reasoning in both cases. He described section 715.1 as "a statutory exception to the rule that hearsay is admissible". He said that, "it permits an out-of-court statement to be admitted for the truth of its contents, provided that certain conditions are met".[99] Nevertheless, he did approve the interpretation of "adopts" in *Meddoui* and said that the complainant need not have a present memory of the events referred to in the statement, so long as she is able to recall giving the statement and her attempt then to be truthful. He felt that since children, particularly younger ones, are prone to forget details of an event with the passage of time, it was precisely in this situation that a videotaped statement is needed. It was his view that a videotaped statement made shortly after the event is more likely to be accurate than a child's *viva voce* testimony, given months later, at trial.

He also rejected the view expressed in *Meddoui* that the videotaped evidence added nothing to the testimony when the complainant has an independent *present* memory of the events. He concluded that *the adopted videotaped statement, together with the viva voce evidence given at trial, will comprise the whole of the evidence in chief of the complainant.*

---

[97]   14 O.R. (3d) 225, 16 C.R.R. (2d) 49, 83 C.C.C. (3d) 5, 63 O.A.C. 321, 1993 CarswellOnt 1056 (C.A.).
[98]   220 N.R. 362, 154 D.L.R. (4th) 13, 120 C.C.C. (3d) 225, 11 C.R. (5th) 209, [1997] 3 S.C.R. 1183, 104 O.A.C. 321, 1997 CarswellOnt 4448, 1997 CarswellOnt 4449, [1997] S.C.J. No. 89.
[99]   *Ibid.*, at (C.C.C.) p. 232.

On closer analysis, it would appear that section 715.1 is probably a statutory exception to both the hearsay rule and the rule that prohibits introduction of a prior consistent statement. In other words, when the complainant has no recollection of the events and the evidence is admitted as past recollection recorded, then it is a statutory exception to the rule rendering hearsay inadmissible. On the other hand, when the complainant has an independent present memory of the events, then the admissibility of the videotape is a statutory exception to the rule prohibiting a prior consistent statement.

4

Previous Consistent Statements

1. THE RULE

The general rule at common law is that a witness may not be asked in chief whether he previously made a statement consistent with his present testimony. For example, the prosecutor is not entitled to ask the victim of an assault whether she made a statement to the police consistent with her present testimony; nor may any other prosecution witness be permitted to repeat the victim's prior consistent statement. When it comes to the defence, there are two aspects of this rule. The first is that the defence is not allowed to call the accused or any other witness to testify that the accused made a statement before trial declaring his innocence. Secondly, the defence is not allowed to ask a prosecution witness during cross-examination about any statement made by the accused declaring his innocence.[1]

The rule, often called the rule against self-serving evidence, explains one of the reasons for it. It is to prevent witnesses, particularly an accused, from manufacturing or inventing evidence that serves their interests. It is only human nature for a jury to believe that because a victim previously declared the accused's guilt or an accused protested his innocence before trial, their previous statements must be true. Another purpose of the rule is to avoid opening the trial process to the time-

---

[1] *Campbell*, 38 C.C.C. (2d) 6, 17 O.R. (2d) 673, 1 C.R. (3d) 309, 1 C.R. (3d) S-49, 1977 CarswellOnt 5 (C.A.), varied, 17 O.R. (2d) 673 at 699, 1 C.R. (3d) S-49, 38 C.C.C. (2d) 6 at 32, 1977 CarswellOnt 6 (C.A.).

consuming and confusing consideration of a collateral issue. It also prevents the jury from being swayed by this side issue.

A good example of the application of this rule against an accused is in *Roberts*.[2] Roberts was charged with the murder of his girlfriend. His defence was that he had shot her accidentally while they were making up after a quarrel. Two days after the shooting, he told his father that his defence was that the shooting had been an accident. His father was not permitted to give evidence of that conversation because it was self-serving.

Evidence from an accused that he offered to take a polygraph test to demonstrate his innocence is another example of a self-serving statement which is not admissible, even where his offer is refused by the police.[3] Although the probative value of such evidence is to enable the defence to argue that the accused was prepared to do something which a guilty person would not do, it is generally rejected because the results are inadmissible and accordingly the accused risks nothing.[4] On the other hand, such an offer might have probative value if the accused honestly believed that a negative test could be used against him.[5]

Instances where a prior consistent statement has been rejected by the courts usually occur where the statement was made after the event. Nevertheless, if the purpose of the rule is to prevent a witness or an accused contriving evidence to serve their interest, then it would follow that any statement made either before or after the event should be rejected. Unfortunately, a strict application of the rule may seem illogical where it is clear on the evidence that there was no possibility of contrivance. For example, in *Ferguson*[6] the issue was the identity of the person with whom the complainant said she had sexual intercourse twenty years before. The accused had not only denied that he had intercourse with the complainant, but also the fact that he even knew her. However, although the trial judge was satisfied that the contents of a letter sent by the complainant to a friend before the event, identifying the accused as one with whom she had a developed a friendship could not, in the

[2] [1942] 1 All E.R. 187, 86 Sol. Jo. 98, 28 Cr. App. R. 102, 58 T.L.R. 138 (C.A.).
[3] *Beland*, 79 N.R. 263, 9 Q.A.C. 293, [1987] 2 S.C.R. 398, 36 C.C.C. (3d) 481, 60 C.R. (3d) 1, 43 D.L.R. (4th) 641, 1987 CarswellQue 14, 1987 CarswellQue 96; *Richards*, 87 B.C.A.C. 21, 6 C.R. (5th) 154, 143 W.A.C. 21, [1997] B.C.J. No. 339, 1997 CarswellBC 272 (C.A.); *B.(S.C.)*, 119 C.C.C. (3d) 530, 10 C.R. (5th) 302, 104 O.A.C. 81, 36 O.R. (3d) 516, 1997 CarswellOnt 3907, [1997] O.J. No. 4183 (C.A.).
[4] *Beland, ibid.*, at (C.C.C.) pp. 494-95.
[5] *B.(S.C.), supra,* note 3 (C.R.) at p. 310.
[6] June 8, 1994, (Ont. Gen. Div.).

circumstances, have been manufactured, he felt that he was bound by authority not to admit it.

Another reason for the rule, particularly where it affects the defence, is to prevent an accused from avoiding the witness box by having someone else advance his or her defence. If the accused wishes to tell what happened, he or she must do so by entering the witness box where he or she will be required to testify under oath and be subject to cross-examination.

However, the rule will not apply where the prosecution chooses to make the accused's explanation part of its case. For example, if the Crown decides, for whatever reason, to introduce the accused's statement at trial, it will be admissible, even if it is self-serving. Once the Crown chooses to introduce the accused's self-serving statement as part of its case, then the Crown must accept the consequences of its decision.

The strict application of the rule is not without its critics, particularly where it is applied to the evidence of children. For example, in *B. (D.C.)*,[7] the Manitoba Court of Appeal felt that the common law rule should be changed where charges of sexual abuse involve children because it fails to recognize the difficulty of obtaining a full account from the child of the events in question. The Court noted that the rule ignores the fact that credibility may more readily be judged in the case of a child by considering the circumstances in which a complaint was first made. For example, evidence of a spontaneous account of abuse by a child may be highly relevant to the trial judge's difficult task of assessing the credibility of that child. The prior consistent statement may tend to confirm the consistency of the testimony of a young victim who is required to recall and recount dramatic events in an intimidating and hostile courtroom environment. It was the Court's view that a new rule of admissibility would ensure that, in appropriate cases, and for a limited purpose, this kind of evidence would not be excluded from the court's truth-seeking process. It was suggested that the evidence should be received subject to such safeguards as the judge may consider necessary and subject always to considerations affecting the weight that should be accorded to the evidence.

---

[7] [1994] 7 W.W.R. 727, 95 Man. R. (2d) 220, 70 W.A.C. 220, 32 C.R. (4th) 91, 91 C.C.C. (3d) 357, 1994 CarswellMan 150, [1994] M.J. No. 403 (C.A.).

2. EXCEPTIONS TO THE RULE

(a) To Rebut the Suggestion of Recent Fabrication

There are undoubtedly instances where a prior consistent statement should be admitted. The first is where the defence suggests that the complainant is testifying to events that one would have expected the complainant to have mentioned at an earlier time, or where the prosecution suggests that the defence was recently invented or contrived. Here, it is only fair that the Crown or defence be allowed to rebut that suggestion by leading evidence that the complainant's evidence or the accused's defence has been consistent throughout.[8] At the same time, the judge must remind the jury (or him or herself) of the limited use of such evidence. It can only be used to rebut the suggestion of recent fabrication or concoction. It must not be used as proof of its contents or to confirm or show the consistency in the testimony of the witness being impeached.[9]

As a practical matter, the suggestion by the Crown that the defence was recently invented or contrived will not arise very often because of an accused's right to remain silent. It would be very unfortunate if police officers were required to warn an accused of his or her right to remain silent and then be allowed to use that silence to complain of recent fabrication when the defence is revealed for the first time at trial. However, an exception will arise where the defence is alibi. Here, it is generally prudent for the defence to give to the prosecution particulars of that alibi at the earliest opportunity.[10] Indeed, the failure to do so at a time that is early enough to allow the Crown to investigate the alibi will permit the trier of facts to drawn an adverse inference against an alibi defence.[11]

The usual time that the defence will suggest that a victim recently fabricated a complaint against the accused is during the course of the cross-examination of that witness. However, the suggestion need not be

---

[8]   *Garofoli*, 27 O.A.C. 1, 41 C.C.C. (3d) 97, 64 C.R. (3d) 193, 43 C.R.R. 252, 1988 CarswellOnt 68 (C.A.), reversed, 80 C.R. (3d) 317, [1990] 2 S.C.R. 1421, 116 N.R. 241, 43 O.A.C. 1, 36 Q.A.C. 161, 60 C.C.C. (3d) 161, 50 C.R.R. 206, 1990 CarswellOnt 119, 1990 CarswellOnt 1006; *Campbell, supra*, note 1.

[9]   *Collins*, 9 C.R.(4th) 377, 1991 CarswellOnt 126 (C.A.); *F. (J.E.)*, 26 C.R. (4th) 220, 85 C.C.C. (3d) 457, 67 O.A.C. 251, 16 O.R. (3d) 1, 1993 CarswellOnt 137, [1993] O.J. No. 2509 (C.A.).

[10]   *Robertson*, 29 C.R.N.S. 141, 21 C.C.C. (2d) 385, 1975 CarswellOnt 6 (C.A.), leave to appeal refused (1975), 21 C.C.C. (2d) 385 (note) (S.C.C.).

[11]   *Cleghorn*, 41 C.R. (4th) 282, 100 C.C.C. (3d) 393, 186 N.R. 49, 85 O.A.C. 129, [1995] 3 S.C.R. 175, 32 C.R.R. (2d) 41, 1995 CarswellOnt 126, 1995 CarswellOnt 802.

raised only at that time. In *Campbell*, the Ontario Court of Appeal noted that:

> ...an express allegation of recent fabrication in cross-examination is not necessary before the exception, with respect to rebutting an allegation of recent fabrication, becomes operative, and that a suggestion that the accused's story has been recently contrived may also arise implicitly from the whole circumstances of the case, the evidence of the witnesses who have been called and the conduct of the trial.[12]

However, it has also been recognized that a prior consistent statement should not be admitted under the guise of rebutting an allegation of recent fabrication unless the door is clearly opened.[13] But it may be opened through cross-examination of the complainant or other Crown witnesses, or by the allegation of recent fabrication becoming implicit from the defence's conduct of the case or by an opening statement of the defence.

Once the suggestion of recent fabrication is raised, the Crown is required to apply to the court to be allowed to lead the evidence. If the trial judge is satisfied, after hearing submissions from both sides, that there has been a clear suggestion of recent fabrication by the defence, then the Crown will be entitled to lead the evidence through its witnesses. The same procedure will apply where the Crown has made a similar suggestion about the defence.

(b) To Show Consistency of Identification

The rule preventing the admissibility of a prior consistent statement is regularly breached in cases where the identification of the accused is in dispute. Evidence by a witness that the person standing in the prisoner's dock "is the man" is generally regarded as valueless, because it is open to "honest mistake and self-deception".[14]

Therefore, if the prosecution is relying on eyewitness identification, the police will usually attempt, in the initial stages of the investigation, to have the witness view a series of photographs or attend a lineup. The purpose is to see if the witness is able to pick the suspect out of the photographs or the lineup, without any suggestion by the police. When the matter goes to trial, the witness will then be able to

---

[12] *Supra*, note 8 at (C.R.) p. 325.
[13] *Owens*, 18 O.A.C. 125, 55 C.R. (3d) 386, 33 C.C.C. (3d) 275, 1986 CarswellOnt 145 (C.A.).
[14] *Browne*, 11 C.R. 297, 1 W.W.R. (N.S.) 449, 99 C.C.C. 141, 1951 CarswellBC 25 (C.A.).

testify that he or she was shown a series of photographs or attended a lineup and picked out the accused without prompting.

Where the witness gives such evidence at trial, he or she is, in effect, giving evidence of his or her own prior consistent statement. Similarly, police officers present at the out-of-court identification are regularly allowed to testify that the witness viewed a series of photographs or attended a lineup and picked out the accused. This is also evidence of a prior consistent statement. It has been suggested by some text writers that the evidence of the police officers is an exception to the hearsay rule because they are telling the court what the witness said.[15] With respect, such evidence is not hearsay at all. The officers are giving original evidence, not hearsay evidence.[16] The evidence is not being tendered to prove that the witness correctly identified the accused as the person who committed the offence, only the fact that the identification was made by the witness. In other words, when the officer repeats in court that the witness said — "that is the man" — the officer is not verifying the accuracy of the identification. That would be hearsay. He is only verifying or confirming as to the fact of an identification by the witness.[17] That is not hearsay; it is original or first-hand evidence.

When a police officer is permitted to give evidence that the witness identified the accused, the evidence is offered, as one writer has said, only to prove that the "witness identified the accused before the sharpness of his recollection was dimmed by time".[18] Its purpose is to strengthen the value of the identification evidence given in court by the witness. It is not to prove that the witness identified the right person, which would be hearsay.[19]

If the purpose of such evidence is to prove only that the witness has made an out-of-court identification, but not necessarily the correct one, then it would follow that such evidence would not be admissible if the witness denies at trial that he made the previous identification and that the accused is not the person who committed the offence.[20] If the officer's evidence is admitted as original evidence only for the purpose

---

[15] McWilliams, *Canadian Criminal Evidence*, 3rd ed., para. 10130.
[16] *Langille* (1990), 75 O.R. (2d) 65, 40 O.A.C. 355, 59 C.C.C. (3d) 544 (C.A.); *Tat*, 117 C.C.C. (3d) 481, 103 O.A.C. 15, 35 O.R. (3d) 641, 14 C.R. (5th) 116, 1997 CarswellOnt 5434 (C.A.).
[17] *T. (W.P.)*, 14 O.R. (3d) 225, 16 C.R.R. (2d) 49, 83 C.C.C. (3d) 5, 63 O.A.C. 321, 1993 CarswellOnt 1056 (C.A.), at (C.C.C.) p. 27.
[18] See Libling, "Evidence of Past Identification", [1977] Crim L.R. 268 at pp. 271-72.
[19] *Alexander* (1981), 145 C.L.R. 395, 55 A.L.J.R. 355, 34 A.L.R. 289 (Australia H.C.), at (C.L.R.) p. 407.
[20] *McGuire*, [1975] 4 W.W.R. 124, 29 C.R.N.S. 282, 23 C.C.C. (2d) 385, 1975 CarswellBC 98 (C.A.); *Tat, supra*, note 16.

of strengthening the witness's earlier out-of-court identification, then the foundation for the officer's evidence would not exist. There would be nothing to strengthen or confirm. An exception might arise where the prior out-of-court identification was held to be admissible under the rule in *B.(K.G.)*.[21] Under that rule, a prior inconsistent statement made by the witness and not adopted at trial as true could, in some circumstances, be received as original (not hearsay) evidence for its truth. Once admitted for its truth, then there would be a foundation for the confirmatory or strengthening evidence of the officer present at the out-of-court identification.

What happens if the witness is able to identify the accused at trial, but cannot recall identifying the accused out-of-court? Alternatively, what happens if the witness can recall making an accurate identification out-of-court, but is unable to identify the accused in court or cannot positively do so? In the first situation, it has been held that the police officer's evidence of a prior identification by the witness is admissible.[22] Such evidence is admissible to allow the jury to make an informed assessment of the witness's identification of the accused at trial. In other words, the fact that the witness identified the accused as the offender on a earlier date, even though the witness does not remember doing so, will strengthen and confirm the witness's identification of the accused at trial. Similarly, evidence by the police officer of the prior identification of the witness is also admissible as original evidence even though the witness is unable to identify the accused at trial.[23]

There is some authority that in the second instance, that is, where the witness identified the accused on a previous occasion but is unable or cannot positively identify the accused at trial, a police officer will be permitted to testify as to the previous identification by the witness.[24] Since there is no in-court testimony of the witness to confirm, it has been held that such evidence is *independent evidence of identity*.[25] The rationale underlying the admissibility of such evidence as independent evidence of identity is that the earlier identification has greater probative value than an identification made in the courtroom "after the suggestions

[21] 19 C.R. (4th) 1, [1993] 1 S.C.R. 740, 61 O.A.C. 1, 148 N.R. 241, 79 C.C.C. (3d) 257, 1993 CarswellOnt 76, 1993 CarswellOnt 975, [1993] S.C.J. No. 22.
[22] *Tat, supra*, note 16; *Starr* (2001), 147 C.C.C. (3d) 449 (S.C.C.).
[23] *Ibid.*
[24] *Swanston*, [1982] 2 W.W.R. 546, 33 B.C.L.R. 391, 25 C.R. (3d) 385, 65 C.C.C. (2d) 453, 1982 CarswellBC 12 (C.A.); overruling *McGuire, supra*, note 20; *Osbourne*, [1973] 1 Q.B. 678, [1973] 1 All E.R. 649, 57 Cr. App. R. 297 (C.A.).
[25] *Swanston, ibid.*, following *People v. Gould* (1960), 7 Cal. Rptr. 273, 354 P.2d 865 (U.S. Cal. Sup. Ct.).

of others and the circumstances of the trial may have intervened to create a fancied recognition in the witness' mind ...".[26] The difficulty with this view is that it virtually precludes effective cross-examination of the witness by the defence. If the witness is unable to identify the accused at trial, then it would difficult to probe what led the witness to make the original identification.

Although the rationale underlying the admission of an officer's testimony would apply equally to the case where the witness is unavailable to testify, the rule appears to be different in such instance. Here it has been held that, since the purpose of such evidence is only to confirm or corroborate the out-of-court identification of the witness, then in the absence of testimony by the witness, there would be nothing to strengthen or confirm.[27] Moreover, there would be the danger that the jury might use the evidence to infer that the witness correctly identified the accused, even though the purpose of the evidence would be to only confirm that the witness on an earlier occasion said — "that is the man". In the absence of admissible evidence by the witness that he or she on a prior occasion identified the accused as the perpetrator, there would be nothing to confirm or strengthen.

Where evidence of prior identification is admitted, the officers are not restricted to merely testifying that the witness identified a particular person or photograph. They are also entitled to give evidence with respect to all of the relevant circumstances surrounding the identification. On the other hand, the defence will usually wish to cross-examine the officers on the circumstances surrounding the identification. By showing that the witness may have hesitated before making the identification or was uncertain about it, the defence will wish to submit to the trier of fact that not much weight should be given to the evidence.

(c) As Part of the Res Gestae

Although *res gestae*, discussed earlier, is commonly linked with the hearsay rule, it has also been regarded as an exception to the rule against previous consistent statements. Thus an exculpatory statement that is part of the *res gestae* may be admitted, even though it is self-serving. The theory is that a self-serving statement which is uttered

---

[26] *People v. Gould, ibid., per* Traynor J. at (P.2d) p. 867.
[27] *Timm,* [1981] 2 S.C.R. 315, 21 C.R. (3d) 209 (Eng.), 28 C.R. (3d) 133 (Fr.), [1981] 5 W.W.R. 577, 37 N.R. 204, 29 A.R. 509, 59 C.C.C. (2d) 396, 124 D.L.R. (3d) 582, 1981 CarswellAlta 309.

contemporaneously with, and is explanatory of, the act is unlikely to be contrived or manufactured.[28]

An explanation given by an accused to the police, when first found in possession of stolen property or narcotics is regularly admitted, at the instance of the defence, as part of the *res gestae*. Such evidence is admitted even if the accused does not choose to go into the witness box and give any evidence at trial.[29]

One rationale for this exception to the rule against the admission of a prior consistent statement is that an explanation given spontaneously at the moment of discovery is unlikely to be given upon reflection and therefore contrived.[30] If the accused chooses to go into the witness box and give the same explanation that he gave immediately upon discovery, that will be strong proof of the consistency of the accused's evidence.

Another rationale for this exception in possession of stolen property cases probably lies in the *inference* that may be drawn from the unexplained possession of recently stolen property. The doctrine of recent possession provides that the unexplained possession of recently stolen goods entitles the trier of fact to draw the inference that the possessor stole the goods.[31] If a contemporaneous explanation of possession by the possessor of the goods was not admissible, then the trier of fact, unaware that an innocent explanation had been given, could well draw the inference that the accused had the requisite knowledge.[32]

(d) To Rebut the Presumption of Consent in Sexual Assaults

At common law, the fact that a complaint was made by the victim of a sexual assault, but not what she actually said, was admissible at the trial of her attacker to show consistency in the victim's testimony. This rule developed from the ancient requirement that the victim of an attack should raise the "hue and cry" if a prosecution of rape was to succeed.

---

[28] *Slugoski*, 43 C.R. (3d) 369, 17 C.C.C. (3d) 212, 1985 CarswellBC 438 (C.A.).

[29] *Graham* (1972), [1974] S.C.R. 206, 7 C.C.C. (2d) 93, 19 C.R.N.S. 117, [1972] 4 W.W.R. 488, 26 D.L.R. (3d) 579, 1972 CarswellBC 123, 1972 CarswellBC 321; *Risby* (1976), 32 C.C.C. (2d) 242 (B.C. C.A.), affirmed, [1978] 2 S.C.R. 139, 39 C.C.C. (2d) 567, 1978 CarswellBC 563.

[30] *Crossley*, 117 C.C.C. (3d) 533, 95 B.C.A.C. 61, 154 W.A.C. 61, 1997 CarswellBC 1677 (C.A.).

[31] *Newton* (1976), [1977] 1 S.C.R. 399, [1976] 3 W.W.R. 199, 34 C.R.N.S. 161, 28 C.C.C. (2d) 286, 8 N.R. 431, 66 D.L.R. (3d) 639, 1976 CarswellBC 148.

[32] *Kowlyk*, 86 N.R. 195, [1988] 2 S.C.R. 59, 65 C.R. (3d) 97, [1988] 6 W.W.R. 607, 43 C.C.C. (3d) 1, 55 Man. R. (2d) 1, 1988 CarswellMan 162, 1988 CarswellMan 259; *Crossley*, *supra*, note 30.

It was based on the belief and the legal presumption that a woman who did not complain of rape at the earliest opportunity must have consented to intercourse. The judge was required to instruct the jury and the jury was entitled to infer that a woman who failed to complain at the earliest opportunity must have consented. The fact of the complaint, so long as it was made at the earliest opportunity, was admitted to show that the victim acted as one would normally expect her to do after a sexual attack and thereby rebut the inference of consent. It allowed the judge and jury to infer that her consistency in repeating the same story at trial that she did after her attack was because she was a credible person.

Initially, the rule only allowed the fact of the complaint to be admitted, but not what the victim actually said. Eventually, in *Lillyman*,[33] what the victim actually said was admitted, although the jury were instructed that it was only relevant to show that her conduct in complaining was consistent with her testimony in the witness box negativing her consent. In other words, although the particulars of the complaint were now admissible, the emphasis was still on the fact of the complaint rather than the details of it. The jury were not entitled to infer that because the details of the complaint and her testimony were the same, the witness must be credible. That would infringe the rule prohibiting the admission of a prior consistent statement. The details could only be used to show consistency in conduct, not in credibility.

Not surprisingly, this archaic rule was finally abrogated by Parliament in 1983. Its abolition does not mean that a complaint by a victim of a sexual assault is no longer ever admissible. It only means that there is no longer a presumption of consent that the Crown must attempt to rebut by leading evidence-in-chief of a recent complaint.

The abolition of the rule has raised a number of difficult issues for trial judges. One is whether the defence should now be allowed to cross-examine a complainant as to the timeliness of her complaint. Where consent is in issue, the defence may wish to suggest to the complainant that she delayed making a complaint, or made no complaint at all, because she really consented to sexual activity with the accused and later changed her mind. Some courts have refused to permit the defence to cross-examine the complainant as to the timeliness of her complaint because it evokes the stereotypical response that a woman who has not promptly complained must have consented.[34]

---

[33]   [1896] 2 Q.B. 167, [1895-99] All E.R. Rep. 586 (C.C.R.).

[34]   *James*, 24 C.R. (4th) 229, 18 C.R.R. (2d) 128, 1993 CarswellOnt 123 (Gen. Div.).

That view, however, has been rejected by the Ontario Court of Appeal.[35] In *H. (J.)*, the Court said that a delayed complaint is different from prior sexual conduct, as it relates to the timing of the disclosure of the very accusations that are before the court. Although there may be a number of reasons why a complainant has not complained promptly or at all, and the assumption that all victims of sexual aggression will promptly report the acts against them is stereotypical and flawed, that does not mean that exploring the issue of the timeliness of a complaint should be foreclosed. On the contrary, the timeliness of the complaint should be an issue that both the Crown and the defence can explore. It will be for the trier of fact to determine what to make of the explanation.

If there is no longer any presumption of consent and thus no necessity for the Crown to lead any evidence-in-chief of a complaint, then it would seem to follow that evidence-in-chief of a prior complaint, in the absence of a suggestion by the defence of recent concoction, would breach the rule against admitting a prior consistent statement. That reasoning was accepted by Finlayson J.A. in *F.(J.E.)*.[36] There he wrote:

> Now what is the effect of the abrogation of this exception to the rule against past consistent statements? Since the exception was only applicable in sexual offences, and only to the case-in-chief for the Crown, surely the consequences of abrogation must be that evidence of recent complaint by the complainant is no longer admissible as part of the Crown's case when the sexual offences enumerated in the present s. 275 of the Code are alleged. This is a result which was probably not anticipated by the proponents of the abrogation of the rule against recent complaint because it has resulted in the Crown being unable to lead this evidence, where it exists, to show consistency on the part of the complainant and rebut the possible adverse inference...that her allegations were true.[37]

However, Mr. Justice Finlayson went on to conclude that evidence of recent complaint could still be admissible in some instances as part of the narrative "in the sense that it advances the story from offence to prosecution". To put it another way, the Crown was entitled to lead evidence that the alleged victim complained to someone that she had

---

[35] *H. (J.)*, 108 C.C.C. (3d) 97, 29 O.R. (3d) 740, 92 O.A.C. 94, 1996 CarswellOnt 2601 (C.A.), additional reasons at, 29 O.R. (3d) 740 at 751, 110 C.C.C. (3d) 533, 94 O.A.C. 68, 1996 CarswellOnt 3663 (C.A.), over ruling *James* and approving *Ross*, 1996 CarswellOnt 1306, [1996] O.J. No. 1366 (Gen. Div.).

[36] 26 C.R. (4th) 220, 85 C.C.C. (3d) 457, 67 O.A.C. 251, 16 O.R. (3d) 1, 1993 CarswellOnt 137, [1993] O.J. No. 2509 (C.A.); see also *Jones*, 66 C.R. (3d) 54, 29 O.A.C. 219, 44 C.C.C. (3d) 248, 1988 CarswellOnt 84 (C.A.).

[37] *F. (J.E.)*, *ibid.*, at (C.C.C.) p. 469.

been sexually assaulted by the accused in order to show the sequence of events leading up to the charge against the accused, even though that evidence might also infringe the rule against self-serving evidence.

That view was also echoed by Mr. Justice Wood in *Ay*.[38]

> If the full purpose underlying Parliament's abrogation of this particular rule relating to evidence of recent complainant is to be achieved, then evidence of when a complaint was first made, why it was not made at the first available opportunity if that was the case, and what it was that precipitated the complaint eventually made, *must be receivable as part of the narrative*, in order to ensure that the jury have all of the evidence of the complainant's conduct necessary to enable them to draw the right inference with respect to her credibility.[39]

Wood J.A. then went on to summarize what he understood to be the law:

> ... the fact that a prior complaint was made, when it was made, and why it was or was not made in a timely fashion, are all matters relevant and admissible to establish the conduct of the complainant in a criminal case, from which conduct the trier of fact is entitled to draw inferences relative to the credibility of that complainant's evidence. However, the content of any prior statement cannot be used to demonstrate its consistency with, and therefore, the probable truthfulness of, the complainant's evidence at trial, and thus, such content is inadmissible unless relevant for some other purpose such as providing necessary context for other probative evidence.[40]

What Wood J.A. seemed to be saying is that evidence of the fact of a complaint, but not the full particulars of what the complainant said, is still admissible. It is admissible as part of the Crown's case-in-chief to show the sequence of events leading up to the charge against the accused. It is admitted, not as recent complaint, but as part of the narrative of those events. As part of the narrative, only evidence of the fact of the complaint is admissible, not the particulars of that complaint. As part of the narrative, it is admissible to show the credibility of the complainant in the sense that her conduct was credible. However, it cannot be used by the Crown to show that her evidence at trial is consistent with her earlier complaint. In fact, the jury must be instructed to that effect by the trial judge.

---

[38] 93 C.C.C. (3d) 456, 59 B.C.A.C. 161, 98 W.A.C. 161, 1994 CarswellBC 1112, [1994] B.C.J. No. 2024 (C.A.).

[39] *Ibid.,* at (C.C.C.) p. 470.

[40] *Ibid.,* at p. 471.

Unfortunately, in sexual offences, the credibility of the complainant is usually the central issue and consistency is regarded as a hallmark of credibility. Thus the distinction between use of a prior complaint as part of the narrative for the purpose of assessing her conduct, but not for consistency in her testimony at trial, may be difficult for a jury to grasp. It is difficult to understand how the jury is able to distinguish between conduct and consistency. An instruction less confusing to a jury might focus on the use of the evidence as part of the narrative and avoid any reference to question of the complainant's credible conduct. In other words, an instruction more consistent with the purpose of the evidence would be to tell the jury that the prior complaint is only admissible to show the sequence of events that brought this matter to court and not to show consistency in the complainant's testimony.

(e) As Part of the Narrative

At common law, victims of an offence were routinely permitted to give evidence that they complained to the police. Similarly, the police were permitted to say that the victim made a complaint to them about a certain matter and they proceeded to investigate the complaint. Such evidence is technically a prior consistent statement, but is admitted as an exception to the rule, not to show a consistency of conduct, but simply as part of the narrative. To put it another way, it is admitted by the court to show the sequence of events leading up to how the police became involved in the investigation.

In the past, the admission of a complaint by a victim under this exception was not necessarily restricted to a complaint to the police. Nevertheless, where the prior complaint was made to someone other than a police officer, such as a member of the family or a social worker, it was only admitted "if it was so inextricably interwoven with their (the complainant's) evidence that the case could not have been properly presented to the court without admitting this evidence".[41] Allowing a complaint to be admitted simply as part of the sequence of events leading up to the arrest of the accused without the condition that it be "inextricably interwoven" with the complainant's evidence was considered a breach of the general rule prohibiting the admission of a prior consistent statement.

---

[41] *Per* Martin J.A. in *Cassibo*, 39 O.R. (2d) 288, 70 C.C.C. (2d) 498, 1982 CarswellOnt 850 (C.A.).

An example of where the evidence was "inextricably interwoven" is *George*.[42] There, a 14-year-old girl complained to her grandmother and her parents that her cousin had sexual intercourse with her without her consent. The cousin was then confronted with the allegation and admitted that it was true and that he was sorry. When the defence suggested to the girl in cross-examination that she had consented but changed her mind overnight, the trial judge permitted the Crown to call her grandmother, the girl's father and a doctor who had examined her, to repeat what she had told them about what had happened.

MacFarlane J.A., who delivered the judgment of the British Columbia Court of Appeal, said that the fact of the complaint, but not the contents, was admissible not to show consistency in conduct, but as part of the narrative. In other words, it was to show the sequence of events beginning with the complaint to the grandmother, who in turn confronted the accused with the allegation. A similar view was expressed by the same Court in *Beliveau*.[43]

However, in *F. (J.E.)*,[44] the complainant, who was 16, testified that her stepfather had sexually assaulted her over a period of three years, commencing when she was nine. The trial judge had permitted the Crown to lead evidence from the complainant and from other witnesses that the complainant had told a number of persons over the years that the accused was hurting her. The complainant was also permitted to testify that after she had left the province and had gone to Saskatchewan, she had told her teacher, a friend at school and a social worker that the accused had sexually assaulted her. The Ontario Court of Appeal said that the statements of abuse made to the school friend and teacher should not have been admitted because they "neither advance nor enlarge upon the narrative." However, the balance of the statements was held to be admissible.

Finlayson J.A. for the Court wrote:

> The story that unfolds in this case is that of a vulnerable child who has been sexually abused, has been physically abused as a disciplinary matter, has seen her mother assaulted by her tormentor, and has been threatened with injury if she complains about the sexual assaults. She had every reason to believe that the appellant would carry out his threats. This explains her early silence. After her mother separated from the appellant and she returned to the west and her father, we have her account of how she had trouble dealing with the knowledge of what she had been subjected to and had difficulty in discussing

---

[42]   23 C.C.C. (3d) 42, 1985 CarswellBC 714 (C.A.).
[43]   30 C.C.C. (3d) 193, 1986 CarswellBC 665 (C.A.).
[44]   *Supra*, note 36.

the matter with her father from whom she had been estranged. With a proper limiting instruction to the jury, I think that this evidence was properly admissible as part of the unfolding of events from the alleged offences to the inception of this prosecution.[45]

Apparently, Mr. Justice Finlayson did not feel that it was necessary that the complaint be "inextricably interwoven" with the events leading up to the arrest of the accused. All that was necessary was that the complaint be "part of the unfolding of events from the alleged offences to the inception of this prosecution".

Similarly, in *F. (H.P.)*,[46] evidence of a written complaint of sexual abuse given by an 11-year-old complainant to her mother two weeks after the alleged offence, was admitted as part of the narrative, even though the formal complaint to the police was not lodged until 18 months later. The accused was the 33-year-old common law husband of the complainant's mother. Both the complainant and her mother were permitted by the trial judge to testify that, two weeks after the alleged offence, the complainant had given her mother a written complaint of the sexual abuse. Gibbs J.A., for the British Columbia Court of Appeal, held that the evidence was properly admitted as part of the narrative.

As in the case of the other exceptions to the rule against prior consistent statements, the trial judge is required to explain to the jury about the limited value of the evidence. Arguably, if the evidence is admitted simply "to show the sequence of events leading up to how the police became involved in the investigation", then the judge's charge to the jury should be limited to that instruction, with an added instruction that it may not be used by the jury as evidence of the consistency of the complainant's testimony. However, in *F. (J.E.)*,[47] Finlayson J.A. noted that the trial judge was obliged to instruct the jury as to the limited value of the evidence and then, surprisingly, went on to add:

The fact that the statement was made is admissible to assist the jury as to the sequence of events from the alleged offence to the prosecution *so that they can understand the conduct of the complainant and assess her truthfulness.*[48]

In a similar vein, Wood J.A. wrote in *Ay*:[49]

[45]   *Ibid.,* at (C.C.C.) p. 475.
[46]   39 C.R. (4th) 80, 59 B.C.A.C. 24, 98 W.A.C. 24, [1995] B.C.J. No. 831, 1995 CarswellBC 90 (C.A.).
[47]   *Supra,* note 36.
[48]   *Ibid.,* at (C.R.) p. 241.
[49]   *Supra,* note 38, at (C.C.C.) p. 470.

If the full purpose underlying Parliament's abrogation of this particular rule relating to evidence of recent complainant is to be achieved, then evidence of when a complaint was first made, why it was not made at the first available opportunity if that was the case, and what it was that precipitated the complaint eventually made, must be receivable as part of the narrative, *in order to ensure that the jury have all of the evidence of the complainant's conduct necessary to enable them to draw the right inference with respect to her credibility.*

(f) Answers of an Accused When Taxed with the Situation

If the reason for excluding a prior consistent statement of an accused is to prevent him or her from manufacturing or inventing a defence, one might ask why a statement by an accused when taxed with the situation either by a policeman or someone else is not admissible, if it is made spontaneously and without time for reflection? In England, such an exception to the rule has been recognized and is not limited to a statement made on the first encounter with the police.[50]

The rationale underlying this exception was discussed in *McCarthy*.[51] There the accused, charged with robbery, was arrested three days after the offence and questioned by the police. He denied the charge and gave details of an alibi orally and in writing. The trial judge refused to admit the statement. In holding that the trial judge had erred, the English Court of Appeal wrote:

> One of the best pieces of evidence that an innocent man can produce is his reaction to an accusation of a crime. If he has been told, as the appellant was told, that he was suspected of having committed a particular crime at a particular time and place and says at once, 'That cannot be right, because I was elsewhere' and gives details of where he was, that is something which the jury can take into account.[52]

Admissibility of a statement under this exception will usually depend upon whether the statement was given spontaneously or after "careful reflection". A good example of the distinction is *Tooke*.[53] There, the accused was charged with unlawful wounding. He had been involved in an altercation in the lavatory of a public house during which he and the victim were injured. The bar manager gave evidence that, immediately after the incident, the two men blamed each other. The accused then went voluntarily to the police station and made a statement setting out

---

[50] *Pearce* (1979), 69 Cr. App. R. 365.

[51] (1980), 71 Cr. App. R. 142 (Eng. C.A.).

[52] *Ibid.,* at p. 145.

[53] (1990), 90 Cr. App. R. 417 (Eng. C.A.).

his version of the events. The bar manager had been permitted to tell the court what the accused had said, but the trial judge had refused to allow defence counsel to elicit from the officer what the accused had said at the police station. The English Court of Appeal said that his ruling was correct. The statement to the bar manager was spontaneous and showed the accused's reaction shortly after the incident. Although the statement at the police station was also spontaneous, it would add nothing to his reaction to the suggestion that he had committed the assault. Lord Chief Justice Lane, delivering the judgment of the Court, laid down a threefold test for admissibility — spontaneity, relevance and whether the statement which is sought to be admitted added any weight to the other testimony which had been given in the case.

Canadian courts have been generally reluctant to recognize such an exception unless it forms part of the *res gestae*. In *Lucas*,[54] Chief Justice Kerwin of the Supreme Court of Canada had no difficulty in accepting that "it was open to the defence to obtain evidence from the appellant to the effect that he had made a statement to the police, following his arrest, which was similar to the evidence which he had given at trial".[55] However, in *Pappin*,[56] Chief Justice Gale held that the trial judge was correct in refusing to permit the accused to testify concerning statements made by him to the police at the police station after his arrest, as to his knowledge of what was in a package taken from him, because the statements were self-serving. Similarly, in *Keeler*,[57] the Alberta Court of Appeal specifically refused to acknowledge such an exception to the rule against admitting a prior consistent statement unless it was part of the *res gestae*.

Although there appears to be a close connection between an exception to the rule based on "answers given by an accused as part of the *res gestae*" and "answers given by an accused when taxed with the situation", the distinction between the two is probably one of degree. Both exceptions restrict admissibility to the situation where the accused has not had time to reflect upon an explanation. However, Canadian courts have only allowed an exception to the rule where the statement has been a spontaneous reaction by the accused, made contemporaneously with discovery by the police of incriminating evidence in the accused's possession. English courts, on the other hand, have not always applied such a strict test, permitting the admission of a statement made

---

[54] (1962), 39 C.R. 101, [1963] 1 C.C.C. 1, 1962 CarswellOnt 26 (S.C.C.).
[55] *Ibid.*, at (C.C.C.) pp. 10-11.
[56] 12 C.R.N.S. 287, 1970 CarswellOnt 34 (C.A.).
[57] [1977] 5 W.W.R. 410, 4 A.R. 449, 36 C.C.C. (2d) 9, 1977 CarswellAlta 230 (C.A.).

by the accused when questioned by a police officer, provided that it is a spontaneous response to the officer's inquiry.[58]

---

[58] *Storey* (1968), (1968), 52 Cr. App. R. 334, 112 Sol. Jo. 417 (Eng. C.A.) *per* Widgery C.J at (Cr. App. R.) pp. 337-38.

5

Character Evidence

1. THE RULE

One of the most important rules of evidence is that the prosecution is generally not allowed to lead evidence of an accused's bad character or previous convictions to show that he or she probably committed the offence charged. One exception to that rule is section 360 of the *Criminal Code*.[1] It contains an unusual provision that allows the Crown, in prosecutions for possession of stolen property or stolen mail, to introduce evidence of an accused's prior convictions for theft or possession of stolen property within the previous five years for the purpose of proving that he or she knew that the property was unlawfully obtained.

The general rule excluding evidence of the accused's bad character is unique to the common law system of criminal justice. In many countries, evidence of an accused's character is not only admissible, it is the first to be adduced at trial. Those countries believe that a person's previous history and conduct is relevant to the issue of whether he or she may be guilty of the charge he or she is now facing.

Arguably, there is a great deal of merit in that view. As a matter of common sense, people usually take into account the history and character of someone with whom they are dealing. The common law, however, has historically rejected the view that the disposition of a person is relevant to his or her guilt. The common law rule does not purport to be based on common sense, but rather on a number of policy considerations. The first consideration is one of fairness. It is obviously fairer to compel the prosecution to try a person on the facts of the particular case than on that person's whole life. The second is that it

---

[1] R.S.C. 1985, c. C-46.

allows the trier to focus on the particular issues to be proved, rather than be sidetracked by what the accused may have done on other occasions. There is always the risk, particularly in trials by jury where jurors have no legal training or experience, that the trier may be unduly influenced by the accused's previous conduct. The trier may conclude that because of the accused's previous criminal habits, he or she is probably guilty of the offence. As one judge has said:

> The evidence is relevant to the issue, but is excluded for reasons of policy and humanity; because although by admitting it you may arrive at justice in one case out of a hundred, you would probably do injustice in the other ninety-nine.[2]

The general rule prohibiting evidence of an accused's bad character was stated by Lord Herschell L.C. in *Makin v. Attorney General for New South Wales*:

> It is undoubtedly not competent for the prosecution to adduce evidence tending to show that the accused has been guilty of criminal acts other than those covered by the indictment, for the purpose of leading to the conclusion that the accused is a person likely from his criminal conduct or character to have committed the offence for which he is being tried. On the other hand, the mere fact that the evidence adduced tends to show the commission of other crimes does not render it inadmissible if it be relevant to an issue before the jury, and it may be so relevant if it bears upon the question whether the acts alleged to constitute the crime charged in the indictment were designed or accidental, or to rebut a defence which would otherwise be open to the accused. The statement of these general principles is easy, but it is obvious that it may often be very difficult to draw the line and to decide whether a particular piece of evidence is on one side or the other.[3]

However, as Lord Herschell also pointed out, the court will not automatically exclude evidence of the accused's bad character, even though it may show the accused's disposition or propensity to commit the offence, if the evidence is also relevant to an issue at trial. For example, in *Lepage*,[4] three persons were living in a house in which drugs were found. At issue was which of them was in possession of the drugs. The Supreme Court of Canada could find nothing wrong with the trial judge allowing one of three persons to testify that the drugs were not his

---

[2] *Rowton* (1865) L.& C. 520, *per* Willes J., at p. 541.
[3] (1893), [1894] A.C. 57, [1891-94] All E.R. Rep. 24, 17 Cox C.C. 704, 10 T.L.R. 155, 69 L.T. 778, 63 L.J.P.C. 41, 58 J.P. 148, 6 R. 373 (New South Wales P.C.) at (A.C.) p. 65.
[4] 95 C.C.C. (3d) 385, 36 C.R. (4th) 145, 178 N.R. 81, [1995] 1 S.C.R. 654, 79 O.A.C. 191, 1995 CarswellOnt 3, 1995 CarswellOnt 517.

and that the accused was in the business of dealing in drugs, so that the inference could be drawn that it was more likely that the accused was the owner of the drugs. Such evidence was admissible against the accused, even though incidentally it was evidence of the accused's propensity to traffic in narcotics.

The policy rule also has no application where a co-accused seeks to lead evidence of an accused's propensity for violence in order to show that it was more likely that it was the accused, not he, who committed the offence.[5] However, even in such instance, the trial judge is required to minimize the prejudice to the accused by explaining to the jury in clear terms the reason why the evidence has been permitted.

There are four well-established exceptions to the rule.

2. EXCEPTIONS TO THE RULE

(a) When the Accused Puts His or Her Character in Issue

Although the rule is that the Crown may not adduce evidence of bad character, that rule applies only to the prosecution. An accused is always entitled to introduce evidence of his or her own good character. Indeed, the fact that the accused may have lived a good and honest life to date may be the only defence that the accused has to the offence charged. Evidence of good character may be considered by the trier in determining the credibility of the accused and whether he or she is the kind of person who would have committed the offence.[6]

On the other hand, the weight that the courts attach to evidence of good character will usually depend upon the nature of the offence and the age of the victim. For example, in a case involving the sexual assault of children, evidence of good character will not, as a matter of common sense, have very much weight. Since sexual misconduct upon young children usually occurs in private, it will not be reflected in the reputation of a person in the community.[7] Yet, even in cases of sexual misconduct involving children, trial judges are required to tell the jury that they must

---

[5] *Valentini*, 132 C.C.C. (3d) 262, 118 O.A.C. 1, 43 O.R. (3d) 178, 1999 CarswellOnt 271, [1999] O.J. No. 251 (C.A.).

[6] *McMillan*, 7 O.R. (2d) 750, 23 C.C.C. (2d) 160, 29 C.R.N.S. 191, 1975 CarswellOnt 7 (C.A.), affirmed, [1977] 2 S.C.R. 824, 33 C.C.C. (2d) 360, 15 N.R. 20, 73 D.L.R. (3d) 759, 1977 CarswellOnt 474; *Molnar*, 76 C.R. (3d) 125, 55 C.C.C. (3d) 446, 38 O.A.C. 62, 1990 CarswellOnt 91, [1990] O.J. No. 339 (C.A.).

[7] *Profit*, 24 C.R. (4th) 279, [1993] 3 S.C.R. 637, 159 N.R. 395, 85 C.C.C. (3d) 232 at 248, 68 O.A.C. 37, 15 O.R. (3d) 803, 1993 CarswellOnt 126, 1993 CarswellOnt 993.

not ignore character evidence altogether; it is simply not entitled to the same weight as it would have with other offences.[8]

An accused may lead evidence of character in one of three ways. The first is by leading evidence of good character through the cross-examination of Crown witnesses. The second is by going into the witness stand and testifying, not only that he or she did not commit the crime, but that he or she is not *the kind of person* who would commit such a crime. For example, in *Farrant*,[9] where the charge was second degree murder, the accused, during examination-in-chief testified, "It's not my character to be violent, you know, use violence or a rifle, you know, to get my own way. That's not my character." It was held by Dickson J. that the accused had put his non-violent character in issue.

On the other hand, the accused's mere denial of guilt and repudiation of the allegations against him or her alone does not amount to placing his character in issue.[10] Nor do introductory routine questions as to education, marital status and religious affiliation have the effect of putting the accused's character is issue.[11] Similarly, an admission by the accused to having a criminal record is not an assertion of good character.[12]

It should also be stressed that the evidence of good character must come from the accused while giving testimony. The Crown is not permitted to lead evidence of out-of-court statements of good character made by the accused to the police and then argue that the accused has put his or her character in issue.[13]

Finally, the accused may put that character in issue by calling witnesses to attest to that good character. The Crown, however, is not entitled by clever cross-examination of the accused or a witness called by the defence to claim that the accused has put his or her character in

---

[8] *Norman*, 26 C.R. (4th) 256, 16 O.R. (3d) 295, 87 C.C.C. (3d) 153, 68 O.A.C. 22, 1993 CarswellOnt 140, [1993] O.J. No. 2802 (C.A.).

[9] [1983] 1 S.C.R. 124, 147 D.L.R. (3d) 511, 46 N.R. 337, [1983] 3 W.W.R. 171, 21 Sask. R. 271, 4 C.C.C. (3d) 354, 32 C.R. (3d) 289, 1983 CarswellSask 132, 1983 CarswellQue 235.

[10] *Shortreed*, 75 C.R. (3d) 306, 54 C.C.C. (3d) 292, 37 O.A.C. 144, 1990 CarswellOnt 83 (C.A.).

[11] *McNamara (No. 1)* (1981), 56 C.C.C. (2d) 193 (Ont. C.A.), affirmed, 45 C.R. (3d) 289, 9 O.A.C. 321, 19 C.C.C. (3d) 1, 19 D.L.R. (4th) 314, 59 N.R. 241, [1985] 1 S.C.R. 662, 1985 CarswellOnt 939.

[12] *Bricker*, 90 C.C.C. (3d) 268, 71 O.A.C. 383, 1994 CarswellOnt 921 (C.A.), leave to appeal refused (1994), 92 C.C.C. (3d) vi (note), 180 N.R. 399 (note), 82 O.A.C. 400 (note) (S.C.C.).

[13] *Wilson*, 136 C.C.C. (3d) 252, 138 Man. R. (2d) 139, 202 W.A.C. 139, [1999] 10 W.W.R. 334, 1999 CarswellMan 243 (C.A.), leave to appeal refused (1999), 252 N.R. 193 (note), 148 Man. R. (2d) 158 (note), 224 W.A.C. 158 (note) (S.C.C.).

issue. For example, in *A. (W.A.)*,[14] the accused's wife was asked by the Crown why she supported the accused and she replied, "because I know my husband". In the circumstances in which that response was elicited, it would have been clearly unfair to allow the Crown to lead evidence of the accused's bad character. It was held by the Manitoba Court of Appeal that the character of accused is not put in issue where a witness for defence gives evidence of character during cross-examination by Crown counsel. The Court said that evidence of defence witnesses can only put the accused's character in issue through examination-in-chief. In this latter respect, the Court probably went a little too far. It would hardly be fair to the Crown if a defence witness gratuitously volunteered evidence of the accused's good character during cross-examination, precluding the Crown from leading evidence of the accused's bad character.

Where witnesses are called by the accused to attest to his or her good character, the witnesses are not allowed to give their personal opinion of the accused's good character. Nor are they permitted to point out specific incidents of good character or citizenship, such as the fact that the accused may have saved the life of a child or returned a wallet found in the street (although this rule is not always strictly enforced). The rule is that a character witness for an accused can only swear to the general reputation of the accused in the community and not give his or her personal opinion. In this respect, the courts have not confined the "community" to the actual community where the accused lives. In *Lavasseur*,[15] the Alberta Court of Appeal said that evidence of the accused's reputation in the business community is admissible because it reflects the modern metropolitan reality, in which frequently not even neighbours' names are known, let alone their general reputation.

Evidence of a person's character is generally handled in the following manner. The witness will be asked whether he or she knows the accused's reputation for honesty (where the crime is one of dishonesty) or peacefulness (where the crime is one of violence), *etc.*, in the community. If the witness answers in the affirmative, he or she will then be asked, "What is that reputation?" and the witness will be allowed to give evidence of the community's view.

Once the accused calls evidence of his or her good character, that character is put in issue. In such instance, it is considered to be only fair

---

[14] 113 Man. R. (2d) 153, 131 W.A.C. 153, 112 C.C.C. (3d) 83, 3 C.R. (5th) 388, [1997] 2 W.W.R. 305, 1996 CarswellMan 535 (C.A.).
[15] 51 Alta. L.R. (2d) 226, 35 C.C.C. (3d) 136, 56 C.R. (3d) 335, 77 A.R. 241, 1987 CarswellAlta 75 (C.A.).

that the prosecution be allowed the right to answer that evidence by calling evidence of the accused's bad character. Evidence of the accused's bad character may be led in the same way, that is, by witnesses who disagree with the witnesses for the accused and who testify as to the accused's bad reputation in the community. The Crown is not permitted to lead evidence of specific acts of bad conduct, unless it is of acts that would also constitute evidence of similar facts. (See (d) "When the Evidence is of Similar Facts", *post*). The Crown is limited to leading evidence of general reputation.[16] Section 666 of the *Criminal Code* also gives the Crown the right to call evidence of the accused's bad character by introducing evidence of the accused's previous convictions for offences. Section 667 of the *Code* sets out the method by which such previous convictions may be proved. If the accused gives evidence in his defence, he or she may also be cross-examined with respect to specific acts of previous misconduct or previous convictions (see (c) "When the Accused Testifies", *post*).

Although the general rule is that the cross-examination of an accused on a prior criminal record is restricted to the nature of the offence, the date and place of the conviction and the penalty imposed, the same restrictions do not apply where the accused puts his character in issue.[17] If the accused puts his character in issue, the Crown is entitled to cross-examine the accused on prior acts of discreditable conduct, including details of prior convictions,[18] subject to the right to exclude such evidence where its prejudicial effect outweighs its probative value.

Finally, it should be noted that where the Crown is permitted to adduce evidence of an accused's bad character to rebut evidence of good character and that evidence does not constitute similar fact evidence, the jury must be instructed that the reply evidence can only be used to neutralize the evidence of good character and to assess the accused's credibility. It must not be used as affirmative evidence of the accused's disposition to commit the offence charged.[19]

[16] *Brown*, 123 O.A.C. 258, 137 C.C.C. (3d) 400, 177 D.L.R. (4th) 170, 27 C.R. (5th) 151, 1999 CarswellOnt 2443, [1999] O.J. No. 2983 (C.A.).
[17] *W. (L.K.)*, 138 C.C.C. (3d) 449, 126 O.A.C. 39, 1999 CarswellOnt 3014 (C.A.), leave to appeal refused, 264 N.R. 393 (note), 2000 CarswellOnt 4252, 2000 CarswellOnt 4253 (S.C.C.).
[18] *McNamara (No. 1)*, *supra*, note 11; *Farrant*, [1983] 1 S.C.R. 124, 147 D.L.R. (3d) 511, 46 N.R. 337, [1983] 3 W.W.R. 171, 21 Sask. R. 271, 4 C.C.C. (3d) 354, 32 C.R. (3d) 289, 1983 CarswellSask 132, 1983 CarswellQue 235.
[19] *Brown*, *supra*, note 16.

(b) Where the Accused Puts the Victim's or a Third Party's Character in Issue

The general rule is that a victim's character is not admissible on the issue of whether the accused committed the offence. Even bad people are entitled to protection from having crimes committed against them. However, there may be instances where the character of the victim is relevant to the defence of the accused. For example, if the accused is charged with a crime of violence, such as murder, manslaughter or assault, and claims self-defence, the victim's disposition for violence may be relevant to the issue of who was the aggressor.[20] Similarly, if the defence says that it was not the accused who committed the offence, but a third party, evidence of the third party's character for violence would have probative value provided that the third party had the propensity to commit the type of act in question and was connected with the circumstances surrounding the charge.[21] Evidence of a third party's character or violent disposition has been held to be admissible even if it refers only to one event.[22]

The admissibility of the deceased's or the victim's disposition for violence is not restricted only to those instances where the accused claims that he or she acted in self-defence. It may, in some instances, be led where the defence advanced is accident. For example, in *Sims*,[23] the defence was that the deceased was killed when he lunged at the accused with a knife during an altercation and was accidently stabbed by the accused during a struggle to prevent the deceased from using the knife. It was held that evidence of the deceased's disposition for violence was admissible because, if accepted by the jury, it tended to support the accused's evidence that it was the deceased who produced the knife and attacked.

Evidence of the victim's disposition for violence may be elicited through the cross-examination of Crown witnesses or by the defence calling evidence of the victim's general reputation in the community for violence. In such instance, it is only fair that the prosecution be allowed, by way of reply, to establish that the accused also has a propensity for violence and that it was he, not the victim, who was the aggressor. The

---

[20] *Scopelliti*, 34 O.R. (2d) 524, 63 C.C.C. (2d) 481, 1981 CarswellOnt 814 (C.A.).

[21] *Arcangioli*, 27 C.R. (4th) 1, 111 D.L.R. (4th) 48, 69 O.A.C. 26, 162 N.R. 280, [1994] 1 S.C.R. 129, 87 C.C.C. (3d) 289, 1994 CarswellOnt 51, 1994 CarswellOnt 1151.

[22] *Yaeck*, 10 C.R. (4th) 1, 6 O.R. (3d) 293, 50 O.A.C. 29, 68 C.C.C. (3d) 545, 1991 CarswellOnt 65 (C.A.) at (C.C.C.) p. 563, leave to appeal refused, 139 N.R. 240n, [1992] 1 S.C.R. xii, 71 C.C.C. (3d) vii.

[23] 28 C.R. (4th) 231, 87 C.C.C. (3d) 402, 1994 CarswellBC 574 (C.A.).

prosecution is also entitled to lead reputation evidence by way of reply as to the peaceable disposition of the victim or the third party. The Crown, however, is not entitled to lead such evidence in chief, in anticipation of the defence. The Crown must wait until the defence first leads evidence of the violent disposition of the victim or the third party.[24]

Courts have been generally reluctant to permit the Crown to lead evidence-in-chief of the victim's peaceable disposition in the absence of an attack by the defence on the victim's general character for violence. This has raised the question of whether the Crown should be entitled to introduce evidence of the victim's peaceful disposition where the defence raised is one of self-defence. Since self-defence by necessary implication involves an allegation that the victim was the aggressor, it would seem to follow, logically, that the Crown should be entitled to lead evidence of the victim's peaceful disposition. Indeed, that was the opinion expressed in the "Report of the Federal/Provincial Task Force on Uniform Rules of Evidence" (1982). The Report noted:

> In homicide cases the victim will not be there to deny it, and reputation evidence as to his peaceable nature is therefore an important factor in determining what weight to be given to the evidence of the accused.[25]

Courts, however, have not been prepared to lay down a clear rule dealing with the evidence of the peaceful disposition of a victim. Rather, the preferred rule has been to deal with the issue on a case-by-case basis, assessing the relevance of the disposition evidence to the issues raised.[26] As Rowles J.A. observed in *Dejong*:

> Having an inflexible rule governing the admissibility of such evidence would eliminate the discretion to excluded evidence where its probative value is outweighed by its prejudicial value.[27]

---

[24] *Dejong*, 125 C.C.C. (3d) 302, 108 B.C.A.C. 126, 176 W.A.C. 126, 16 C.R. (5th) 372, 1998 CarswellBC 1208 (C.A.). But see *K. (H.W.)*, 2000 BCCA 209, 32 C.R. (5th) 359, 2000 CarswellBC 661 (B.C. C.A.), leave to appeal refused, 263 N.R. 396 (note), 2000 CarswellBC 2173, 2000 CarswellBC 2174 (S.C.C.), a murder case, where it was held that the trial judge did not err in permitting the Crown to lead evidence-in-chief regarding the absence of paedophilic propensities of the deceased, where the defence was that the accused said that "he lost it" after he expressed paedophilic intentions towards his son.
[25] At p. 91.
[26] *Soares*, 19 O.A.C. 97, 34 C.C.C. (3d) 403, 1987 CarswellOnt 1058 (C.A.); *Diu*, 144 C.C.C. (3d) 481, 33 C.R. (5th) 203, 49 O.R. (3d) 40, 133 O.A.C. 201, 2000 CarswellOnt 1727, [2000] O.J. No. 1770 (C.A.).
[27] *Supra*, note 24 at (C.C.C.) p. 323.

In England, the accused is protected from questions about his previous criminal convictions or questions tending to show previous bad character unless he puts his own character in issue or attacks the character of the Crown witnesses. The English rule is essentially a "tit-for-tat" rule. So long as the defence does not attack the prosecution, the prosecution is not entitled to attack the defence. This rule is contained in the *Criminal Evidence Act of 1898*.

Canada has no similar provision. The suggestion that a Crown witness may not be telling the truth does not give the prosecution, under Canadian law, the right to attack the accused by leading evidence of bad character. As already noted, the only recognized exception arises where the defence is one of self-defence and possibly accident.[28] Here the Crown is only allowed to call evidence of the accused's disposition for violence by way of reply to the defence's suggestion that it was the victim who was the aggressor.

(c) When the Accused Testifies

At common law, an accused was not allowed to give evidence in his or her own defence. This rule was based on the civil practice that prohibited persons from testifying in a case that affected their interest. In Canada, the right of an accused to testify on his or her own behalf was first recognized in 1886 with respect to some offences, and later in 1893 by the *Canada Evidence Act*[29] with respect to all offences. Sections 3 and 4(1) of the *Canada Evidence Act*[30] provide that:

> 3. A person is not incompetent to give evidence by reason of interest or crime.
>
> 4(1). Every person charged with an offence and, except as otherwise provided in this section, the wife or husband, as the case may be, of the person so charged, is a competent witness for the defence whether the person so charged is charged solely or jointly with any other person.

This means that although an accused has the right to give evidence on his or her own behalf, the accused cannot be forced to go into the witness box if he or she does not wish to do so. Nor can he or she be forced to do so by a co-accused, where they are jointly charged. However, once an accused chooses to testify on his or her own behalf, he or

---

[28] *Sims, supra*, note 23.

[29] S.C. 1893, c. 31.

[30] R.S.C. 1985, c. C-5.

she is in the same position as any other witness. When an accused testifies, he or she puts themselves forward as a credible person and asks the jury to take his or her word. The accused's credibility becomes relevant to the truth and accuracy of the testimony. His or her credibility is thus subject to attack by cross-examination, as any other witness's would be.

Nevertheless, it has been recognized that the right of the Crown to attack the credibility of an accused is not superior to the policy rule that protects an accused against an attack upon his character. This means that although an accused, like any ordinary witness, is generally open to cross-examination at large as to credibility, he may not be cross-examined by the prosecution as to previous misconduct or discreditable associations for the purpose of attacking his credibility, unless such cross-examination is relevant to prove the falsity of his own evidence.[31] That protection, however, does not extend to the case of an accused who gives damning evidence against a co-accused. In such instance, it is open for the co-accused to ask the accused questions about his character to show that the accused is a disreputable person not worthy of belief.[32] The policy of the law is that the right of an accused to full answer and defence does not allow him to hide under that umbrella of protection thereby impairing the right of his co-accused to full answer and defence by asking questions pertinent to his defence.

The criminal record of a witness or the accused stands on a different level. Section 12(1) and (1.1) of the *Canada Evidence Act* provides:

> 12(1) A witness may be questioned as to whether the witness has been convicted of any offence, excluding any offence designated as a contravention under the *Contraventions Act*, but including such an offence where the conviction was entered after a trial on an indictment.
> (1.1) If the witness either denies the fact or refuses to answer, the opposite party may prove the conviction.

In England, section 1(f) of the *Criminal Evidence Act, 1898* forbids cross-examination of an accused on his record unless it is relevant to a fact in issue; the accused leads evidence of his own good character; the defence impugns the character of the prosecutor or a Crown witness; or the accused gives evidence against a co-accused. In Canada, there is no

---

[31] *Davison*, (1974), 6 O.R. (2d) 103, 20 C.C.C. (2d) 424 (C.A.), leave to appeal refused, 6 O.R. (2d) 103n, 20 C.C.C. (2d) 424n, [1974] S.C.R. viii.
[32] *Jackson*, 9 C.R. (4th) 57, 51 O.A.C. 92, 68 C.C.C. (3d) 385, 1991 CarswellOnt 119 (C.A.), affirmed, 26 C.R. (4th) 178, [1993] 4 S.C.R. 573, 162 N.R. 113, 86 C.C.C. (3d) 385, 68 O.A.C. 161, 109 D.L.R. (4th) 318, 1993 CarswellOnt 136, 1993 CarswellOnt 997.

such protection. Section 12(1) of the *Canada Evidence Act* permits the Crown to cross-examine an accused on his criminal record even if the defence does not attack the Crown witnesses or lead evidence of the accused's good character. The rationale for section 12 is that a prior conviction is a relevant factor in assessing the reliability of the witness. In other words, there is no reason why the jury should not be informed of what sort of person is asking them to accept his word, particularly one who has shown contempt of the law by a previous violation of it.

For a long time, it was believed that a trial judge had a general discretion to exclude evidence of an accused's prior convictions where revealing those convictions would prejudice him in the eyes of the jury.[33] However, four years before the enactment of the *Charter of Rights and Freedoms*,[34] the Ontario Court of Appeal decided that a trial judge had no discretion to prevent the Crown from cross-examining the accused as to prior convictions for any offence.[35] That Court also held that the word "any offence" in section 12(1) included convictions for offences committed outside of Canada provided that the process of adjudication of guilt constituted a conviction under Canadian law.[36] In an earlier case, that Court had also decided that a "conviction" included the sentence so that the accused could be cross-examined on the penalty imposed.[37]

However, in 1988, the Supreme Court of Canada decided that section 12(1) was not so absolute in its terms. In *Corbett*,[38] the Supreme Court said that a trial judge did have a discretion to exclude evidence of previous convictions in those cases where a mechanical application of section 12 would undermine the right to a fair trial as guaranteed by the *Charter*. The Court also accepted, "as a useful catalogue of factors", certain criteria which La Forest J. felt should be considered by the trial judge in determining how his discretion was to be exercised.

La Forest J. acknowledged that it was impossible to provide an exhaustive catalogue of the factors that are relevant in assessing the probative value or prejudice of such evidence. Nevertheless, he felt that among the most important factors is the nature of the previous convic-

---

[33] *Powell* (1977), 37 C.C.C. (2d) 117 (Ont. Gen. Div.); *Skehan* (1978), 39 C.C.C. (2d) 196 (Ont. H.C.).

[34] Part 1 of the Constitution Act, 1982, being schedule B to the Canada Act 1982 (U.K.), 1982, c. 11.

[35] *Stratton*, 42 C.C.C. (2d) 449, 21 O.R. (2d) 258, 3 C.R. (3d) 289, 90 D.L.R. (3d) 420, 1978 CarswellOnt 29 (C.A.).

[36] *Stratton, ibid.*

[37] *Boyce*, 7 O.R. (2d) 561, 23 C.C.C. (2d) 16, 28 C.R.N.S. 336, 1974 CarswellOnt 46 (C.A.).

[38] [1988] 1 S.C.R. 670, [1988] 4 W.W.R. 481, 85 N.R. 81, 28 B.C.L.R. (2d) 145, 41 C.C.C. (3d) 385, 64 C.R. (3d) 1, 34 C.R.R. 54, 1988 CarswellBC 252, 1988 CarswellBC 756.

tion, its similarity to the conduct for which the accused is on trial and the remoteness or nearness of the prior conviction to the charge before the court. La Forest J. reasoned that if the purpose of permitting cross-examination on a prior conviction is to test credibility, then a conviction which involves an act of deceit, fraud, cheating or stealing is more probative of a person's credibility than an act of violence which had little or no direct bearing on a person's veracity or integrity. As far as he was concerned, the similarity of the prior conviction to the charge before the court created a potential for prejudice, unless the evidence met the stringent test for admitting similar fact evidence.[39] He also felt that a conviction, even one which involved an act of dishonesty, which occurred long before and was followed by a legally blameless life, should be generally excluded on the ground of remoteness.

As noted previously, section 1(f) of the English *Criminal Evidence Act, 1898* forbids cross-examination of an accused on his record unless it is relevant to a fact in issue, the accused leads evidence of his own good character, the defence impugns the character of the prosecutor or a Crown witness, or the accused gives evidence against a co-accused. In *Corbett*, Mr. Justice La Forest acknowledged that Canada had no similar rule and accepted the potential unfairness to the Crown of prohibiting the cross-examination of the accused on prior convictions where the defence has made a deliberate attack upon the credibility of a Crown witness, particularly where the case boils down to a credibility contest between the accused and that witness. He was prepared to recognize that, in such instance, the jury was entitled to have before it the record of the person attacking the character of the Crown witness in order to determine whether he was any more worthy of belief than the person attacked and avoid a distorted picture being presented to the jury. Nevertheless, he felt that this was not a factor that should override the concern for a fair trial. In other words, in such instance, cross-examination of an accused on his record should only be permitted "where to do so would render the trial more, and not less, fair".[40] The general rule is that cross-examination of an accused on a criminal record is restricted to the nature

---

[39] See also *P. (G.F.)*, 29 C.R. (4th) 315, 18 O.R. (3d) 1, 89 C.C.C. (3d) 176, 70 O.A.C. 350, 1994 CarswellOnt 67 (C.A.); *Trudel*, 60 Q.A.C. 138, [1994] R.J.Q. 678, 90 C.C.C. (3d) 318, 1994 CarswellQue 167, [1994] A.Q. No. 114 (C.A.); *Brooks*, 113 O.A.C. 201, 20 C.R. (5th) 116, 129 C.C.C. (3d) 227, 41 O.R. (3d) 661, 1998 CarswellOnt 3866, [1998] O.J. No. 3913 (C.A.), reversed, 141 C.C.C. (3d) 321, 182 D.L.R. (4th) 513, 30 C.R. (5th) 201, 2000 SCC 11, 46 O.R. (3d) 640 (headnote only), 129 O.A.C. 205, 250 N.R. 103, [2000] 1 S.C.R. 237, 2000 CarswellOnt 292, 2000 CarswellOnt 293, [2000] S.C.J. No. 12.

[40] See the judgment of Weiler J.A. in *Brooks, ibid.*

of the offence, the date and place of the conviction, and the penalty imposed.[41]

Since the purpose of allowing cross-examination on a record is to test the credibility of the accused, the details surrounding the commission of the offences are irrelevant. Where, however, the accused puts his or her character in issue, the same restrictions do not apply. Details of the prior convictions are relevant to the accused's character. Here, it is permissible for the Crown to cross-examine the accused, not only on the details of the prior convictions, but on prior acts of discreditable conduct.[42] Nevertheless, the trial judge does have the right and the duty to exclude such evidence where its prejudicial effect outweighs its probative value.[43]

(d) When the Evidence is of Similar Facts

At the outset of this chapter, it was pointed out that although, as a matter of common sense, the disposition of a person may be relevant to his or her guilt or innocence, such evidence is excluded because the law considers it unfair to allow the prosecution to try a person on his or her whole life, rather than on the facts of the case. Another reason is to ensure that the jury's attention is not diverted from the central issue in the case. On the other hand, there may be instances where evidence of a person's bad character or disposition is so probative of the particular issues in the case that it should be admitted. As Lord Herschell L.C. pointed out in the second part of his classic statement of the rule in *Makin v. Attorney General for New South Wales*:

> On the other hand, the mere fact that the evidence adduced tends to show the commission of other crimes does not render it inadmissible if it be relevant to an issue before the jury, and it *may be so relevant if it bears upon the question whether the acts alleged to constitute the crime charged in the indictment were designed or accidental, or to rebut a defence which would otherwise be open to the accused.* The statement of these general principles is easy, but it is obvious that it may often be very difficult to draw the line

---

[41] *Laurier*, 1 O.A.C. 128, 1983 CarswellOnt 825 (C.A.); *W. (L.K.)*, 138 C.C.C. (3d) 449, 126 O.A.C. 39, 1999 CarswellOnt 3014 (C.A.), leave to appeal refused, 264 N.R. 393 (note), 2000 CarswellOnt 4252, 2000 CarswellOnt 4253 (S.C.C.).

[42] *McNamara (No. 1)* (1981), 56 C.C.C. (2d) 193 (Ont. C.A.), affirmed, 45 C.R. (3d) 289, 9 O.A.C. 321, 19 C.C.C. (3d) 1, 19 D.L.R. (4th) 314, 59 N.R. 241, [1985] 1 S.C.R. 662, 1985 CarswellOnt 939, at (C.C.C.) p. 350.

[43] See *McNamara (No. 1), ibid.*, at (C.C.C.) p. 352; *Farrant*, [1983] 1 S.C.R. 124, 147 D.L.R. (3d) 511, 46 N.R. 337, [1983] 3 W.W.R. 171, 21 Sask. R. 271, 4 C.C.C. (3d) 354, 32 C.R. (3d) 289, 1983 CarswellSask 132, 1983 CarswellQue 235.

and to decide whether a particular piece of evidence is on the one side or the other. [Emphasis added.][44]

In the years that followed Lord Herschell's classic statement of the rule, judges, lawyers and legal scholars attempted "to draw the line" in an effort to make some sense of the rule. Judges approached their task by creating categories of relevance in an effort to place each case in a particular pigeonhole. Evidence was admitted if the prosecution was able to show that the evidence went "to prove intent" or "to prove a system" or "to prove a plan" or "to show malice" or "to rebut the defence of accident or mistake" or "to prove identity" or "to rebut the defence of innocent association". However, in 1975, the House of Lords in *Boardman v. Director of Public Prosecutions*,[45] decided that although the categories were useful illustrations of the similar fact rule, they were no longer an automatic ticket to admissibility.

Boardman, the headmaster of a boarding school for boys, had been accused of buggery and attempted buggery by two of the students. His defence was that the boys had made up the story because he had threatened to discipline them; in other words, that no offences had been committed. The House of Lords said that the proper approach to be followed in the future was for the trial judge to balance the probative value of the evidence against the prejudice that the accused might suffer if the evidence was admitted. In one of the speeches, Lord Wilberforce said:

> The basic principle must be that the admission of similar fact evidence ... is exceptional and requires a strong degree of probative force. This probative force is derived, if at all, from the circumstances that the facts testified to by the several witness bear to each other such a striking similarity that they must, when judged by experience and common sense, either all be true, or have arisen from a common cause to the witnesses or from pure coincidence. The jury may, therefore, properly be asked to judge whether the right conclusion is that all are true, so that each story is supported by the other.[46]

Three years later, the *Boardman* approach was adopted by the Supreme Court of Canada in *Guay*,[47] and reaffirmed again by the Court

---

[44]   17 Cox C.C. 704, [1984] A.C. 57.
[45]   (1974), [1975] A.C. 421, [1974] 3 All E.R. 887, 60 Cr. App. R. 165 (H.L.).
[46]   *Ibid.*, at (Cr. App. R.) p. 175.
[47]   (1978), [1979] 1 S.C.R. 18, 42 C.C.C. (2d) 536, 6 C.R. (3d) 130, 23 N.R. 451, 89 D.L.R. (3d) 532, 1978 CarswellQue 39.

in *Sweitzer*.[48] In *B. (C.R.)*,[49] Madam Justice McLachlin, writing for the majority, added:

> The judge must consider such factors as the degree of distinctiveness or uniqueness between the similar fact evidence and the offences alleged against the accused, as well as the connection, if any, of the evidence *to issues other than propensity*, to the end of determining whether, in the context of the case before him, the probative value of the evidence outweighs its potential prejudice and justifies its reception.[50]

Before the trial judge can begin to weigh the probative value of the evidence versus its potential prejudice, he must first identify the fact in issue that the evidence is adduced to prove. In Chapter 1, it was pointed out that in every criminal trial, there are three factual issues which the Crown must prove to establish a successful prosecution: the act, that is, whether a crime was committed; the identity of the perpetrator; and the intent of the perpetrator. Whenever the Crown seeks to have similar fact evidence admitted, the judge should be told by the prosecution of the issue or issues towards which the evidence is directed. In some instances, the similar fact evidence will be relevant to a single issue; in others, it may be relevant to all three issues.

However, the Crown may be foreclosed in proving a particular issue by similar fact evidence where the defence is prepared to admit that issue, or where it seeks to rebut a defence that on the evidence is not realistically open to the accused. In *Thompson*,[51] Lord Sumner observed:

> The prosecution cannot credit the accused with fancy defences in order to rebut them at the outset with some damning piece of evidence.[52]

Mr. Justice Martin echoed that view in his Law Society of Upper Canada lecture on "Similar Fact Evidence":

> The Crown ought not, however, to be permitted to introduce evidence of similar facts to the prejudice of the accused under the guise of rebutting a defence, which on the evidence is not realistically open to the accused, and upon which he has given no indication that he intends to rely. To permit the

---

[48] [1982] 1 S.C.R. 949, 42 N.R. 550, [1982] 5 W.W.R. 555, 37 A.R. 294, 29 C.R. (3d) 97, 21 Alta. L.R. (2d) 97, 137 D.L.R. (3d) 702, 68 C.C.C. (2d) 193, 1982 CarswellAlta 552.

[49] [1990] 3 W.W.R. 385, 109 A.R. 81, 73 Alta. L.R. (2d) 1, 55 C.C.C. (3d) 1, 76 C.R. (3d) 1, [1990] 1 S.C.R. 717, 107 N.R. 241, 1990 CarswellAlta 35, 1990 CarswellAlta 650.

[50] *Ibid.*, at (C.R.) p. 25.

[51] [1918] A.C. 221, 13 Cr. App. R. 61 (H.L.).

[52] *Ibid.*, at (Cr. App. R.) p. 78.

Crown to introduce similar fact evidence to rebut a possible defence in those circumstances would gravely undermine the accused's right to a fair trial. If a defence is raised by the accused which could not reasonably be anticipated, and which is properly rebutted by similar fact evidence, the evidence is admissible in reply.[53]

The *Makin*[54] case is a good example of where the court permitted the admission of similar fact evidence to prove all three issues. Makin and his wife were charged with the murder of a child whose body had been found in their back garden. The Makins had agreed to look after the child and had received a very small amount of money from the child's mother. The bodies of eleven other infants who had been entrusted to the care of the Makins for a very small amount of money were also found buried in the gardens of houses occupied by them at various times. Although no one had seen the Makins kill any of the children, it was held that such evidence was admissible to show that the children had died, not from natural causes or by accident, but by design. The evidence was tendered to show that the only natural or irresistible inference that the jury could draw was that the child had died by design (the act) and that it was the Makins who had killed him (identity) and that they intended to do so (intent).

On the other hand, in the famous "Brides in the Bath" case, *Smith*,[55] similar fact evidence was admitted to prove that a crime had been committed. Smith had married successively three women all of whom had drowned, supposedly accidentally, in a bath that he had arranged to have installed. In each case, Smith benefited financially from their deaths. He was charged with the murder of his first wife and the prosecution was granted the right to call evidence as to the circumstances surrounding the deaths of his second and third wives. The English Court of Criminal Appeal held that the evidence was admissible to rebut the defence of accident, that is, whether it was a crime at all. Although there was no evidence directly establishing that the deaths of Smith's three wives were not accidental, the court held that it was highly unlikely that all three could have died by accident. The trial judge, Scrutton J., charged the jury this way:

> If you find an accident which benefits a person and you find that the person has been sufficiently fortunate to have that accident happen to him a number of times, benefiting him each time, you draw a very strong, frequently and

---

[53]   (1984) at p. 16.
[54]   *Supra,* note 44.
[55]   (1915), 11 Cr. App. R. 229.

irresistible inference, that the occurrence of so many accidents benefiting him is such a coincidence that it can not have happened unless it was designed.

Although *Makin* and *Smith* are often regarded as straightforward examples of the application of the similar fact evidence exception, it is significant to note that in both cases the similar acts were not evidence of criminal acts on their face. They only became evidence of crimes when the jury inferred, because of the similarity and number of incidents, that the death of the victims was as a result of the deliberate act of the accused.

Once the fact in issue is identified by the Crown, the next question which must be considered is whether there is a link between the accused and the similar fact evidence. This issue becomes particularly important in cases where the issue is the identity of the offender. Canadian authorities have required the Crown to lead, on the threshold question of admissibility, some evidence directly linking or connecting the accused with the similar fact evidence before it will be admitted. For example, in *Sweitzer*,[56] a decision of the Supreme Court, the accused was originally charged in an indictment containing fifteen counts of sexual assault on women. Before the trial began, the trial judge severed the various counts. The prosecution then elected to proceed on the first count and was permitted by the judge to lead evidence of the other fourteen assaults as similar fact evidence. Although there was some direct evidence identifying Sweitzer as the assailant in four of the assaults, the victims in the eleven other assaults were unable to identify their assailant. Mr. Justice McIntyre, giving the judgment of the Court, held that even though there was some similarity between the conduct of the assailant in those four episodes with the conduct of the assailant in the eleven episodes where he could not be identified, the trial judge had erred in admitting evidence of the eleven episodes. Since the eleven episodes were not shown to be connected to Sweitzer, they were not admissible. The admissibility of such evidence had to be confined to cases where there was some evidentiary link, direct or circumstantial, with the accused. He wrote:

> ... there must be some evidence upon which the trier of fact can make a proper finding that the similar facts to be relied upon were in fact the acts of the accused for it is clear that if they were not his own but those of another they have no relevance to the matters at issue under the indictment ...[57]

---

[56] *Supra,* note 48.
[57] *Ibid.,* at (C.C.C.) p. 197.

English cases have not imposed a direct-link requirement as a threshold of admissibility. There the issue of an evidentiary link has been left to the jury to assess in the light of all of the evidence. The classic example is *Straffen*.[58] Straffen was accused of the murder of a little girl who was found strangled. No attempt had been made to assault her sexually or to conceal her body, although it might easily have been done. Straffen, who had just escaped from Broadmoor and was in the neighbourhood at the time of the crime, had previously committed two murders of young girls. These murders had the same peculiar features. The Court of Appeal reasoned that it would have been a most extraordinary coincidence if, while Straffen was temporarily at large, another madman in the same area had killed the little girl by strangulation, and had neither assaulted her nor made any attempt to conceal her. It was held that the trial judge did not err in leaving it up to the jury to decide whether the distinctive features between the similar fact evidence and the offence charged supported the conclusion that it was the accused who had committed the offence.

Since the facts in *Straffen* were highly unusual, it might be said that the decision was correct because of the peculiar features of the case. Let us take a simpler example and assume that strikingly similar sexual assaults are committed against two women and the evidence proves that one man committed both offences, but there is only positive evidence identifying the accused as the perpetrator of one offence. In England, the law is clear that the jury may be instructed that, if they are satisfied beyond a reasonable doubt that the accused committed one offence, they may use the identification on that offence to support the identification on the other.[59]

However, what seems to be in dispute is whether there must be some positive evidence that the accused is guilty of at least one offence. For example, in *McGranaghan*,[60] Glidewell L.J. said:

> ... an identification about which the jury are not sure cannot support another identification of which they are also not sure however similar the facts of the two offences may be. The similar facts go to show that the same man committed both offences, not that the defendant was that man.

However, in *Downey*,[61] Evans L.J. came to the opposite conclusion. He said:

---

[58] [1952] 2 Q.B. 911, 36 Cr. App. R. 132, [1952] 2 All E.R. 657 (Q.B.).
[59] *Barnes*, [1995] 2 Cr. App. R. 491 (C.A.).
[60] [1995] 1 Cr. App. R. 559 at p. 572.
[61] [1995] 1 Cr. App. R. 547.

> If there is evidence which entitles the jury to reach the conclusion that it was the same man, even though the evidence in either case does not enable them to be sure who the man was then it follows that they can take account of evidence relating to both offences in deciding whether the man was the defendant.[62]

The next threshold issue of admissibility for the trial judge is the degree of distinctiveness that the evidence must bear to the charges against the accused to be regarded as a similar fact. In *Boardman*, the House of Lords suggested that similar fact evidence might be introduced where it was strikingly similar, or had common unusual and highly distinctive features. An example given in *Boardman* was the *Straffen* case referred to above.

However, a requirement of striking similarity was subsequently rejected by the House of Lords in *Director of Public Prosecutions v. P.*[63] There, Lord McKay of Clashfern L.C., after reviewing *Boardman*, concluded that all that the judges were saying in that case was that "striking similarity" was only one way of showing that the similar fact sought to be admitted possessed the necessary high degree of probative force. The degree of similarity required before such evidence would be admitted was never constant, but varied with the nature of the similar fact evidence and the issue which it was lead to prove.

Two cases by the Ontario Court of Appeal shortly after *Boardman* decided that the "strikingly similar" test was only applicable where the Crown is attempting to prove the identity of the accused,[64] but not where the evidence is tendered to prove a state of mind, knowledge, intent, authority or system or where the defence raised was that of accident.[65] Although a requirement of striking similarity was suggested by McLachlin J. in *C. (M.H.)*,[66] the matter was eventually settled by the decision of the Supreme Court in *Arp*.[67] There it was held that the striking similarity test was only necessary where identity was in issue. In such in-

---

[62] *Ibid.,* at (Cr. App. R.) p. 552.

[63] (1990), 93 Cr. App. R. 267 (C.A.), reversed, [1991] 2 A.C. 447, [1991] 3 All E.R. 337, [1991] 3 W.L.R. 161, 93 Cr. App. R. 267 at 272 (H.L.).

[64] *McNamara (No. 1)* (1981), 56 C.C.C. (2d) 193 (Ont. C.A.), affirmed, 45 C.R. (3d) 289, 9 O.A.C. 321, 19 C.C.C. (3d) 1, 19 D.L.R. (4th) 314, 59 N.R. 241, [1985] 1 S.C.R. 662, 1985 CarswellOnt 939.

[65] *Carpenter*, 31 C.R. (3d) 261, 142 D.L.R. (3d) 237, 1 C.C.C. (3d) 149, 1982 CarswellOnt 97 (C.A.).

[66] 4 C.R. (4th) 1, [1991] 1 S.C.R. 763, 123 N.R. 63, 63 C.C.C. (3d) 385, 1991 CarswellBC 917, at (C.R.) p. 7.

[67] 232 N.R. 317, 20 C.R. (5th) 1, 166 D.L.R. (4th) 296, 129 C.C.C. (3d) 321, 114 B.C.A.C. 1, 186 W.A.C. 1, [1998] 3 S.C.R. 339, 58 B.C.L.R. (3d) 18, [1999] 5 W.W.R. 545, 1998 CarswellBC 2545, 1998 CarswellBC 2546, [1998] S.C.J. No. 82.

stance, the jury is asked to infer from the distinctiveness or uniqueness that exists between the manner in which the crime under consideration was committed and the similar act that the accused is the very person who committed the crime. This inference is made possible only if the high degree of similarity between the acts renders the likelihood of coincidence objectively improbable. Similarity between the acts may consist of a unique trademark or signature on a series of significant similarities.

In *Arp*, the Supreme Court stressed that in assessing the similarity of the acts, the trial judge should only consider the manner in which the acts were committed and not the evidence as to the accused's involvement in each act. Once the trial judge concludes that the similar acts were *likely* committed by one person and there is evidence linking the accused to those acts, it is not necessary to conclude that the acts were *likely* committed by the accused. This question was a matter to be decided by the trier of fact on the basis of all the evidence relating to the acts.

Another area of difficulty for the trial judge in deciding whether the similar acts have passed the threshold test of admissibility occurs when the accused is a member of an abnormal group with the same propensities as the perpetrator of a crime. At one time, the courts considered that evidence of a man's homosexuality was admissible on a charge of indecent assault to rebut the defence of innocent association[68] or to prove identity.[69] However, that view was rejected by the House of Lords in *Boardman* and by the Supreme Court of Canada in *Morin*.[70] In *Morin*, Mr. Justice Sopinka said that there also had to be some further distinguishing feature.

> Accordingly, if the crime was committed by someone with homosexual tendencies, it is not sufficient to establish that the accused is a practising homosexual, or indeed is engaged in numerous homosexual acts. The tendered evidence must tend to show that there was some striking similarity between the manner in which the perpetrator committed the criminal act and such evidence.[71]

In those instances where the accused is charged with more than one offence involving more than one alleged victim, such as in a case of sexual assault, the defence may suggest that the victims have con-

---

[68] *King* (1966), 51 Cr. App. R. 46.
[69] *Glynn* (1971), [1972] 1 O.R. 403, 15 C.R.N.S. 343, 5 C.C.C. (2d) 364, 1971 CarswellOnt 15 (C.A.).
[70] 66 C.R. (3d) 1, [1988] 2 S.C.R. 345, 88 N.R. 161, 30 O.A.C. 81, 44 C.C.C. (3d) 193, 1988 CarswellOnt 82, 1988 CarswellOnt 967.
[71] *Ibid.*, at (C.R.) p. 23.

spired or collaborated to bring false charges against the accused. This has raised the question whether there should be an onus upon the Crown, before the evidence is admitted, to negative any suggestion of collaboration or conspiracy. In *Boardman*, Lord Wilberforce suggested that before the evidence was admitted, the trial judge should find "absence of proved conspiracy ... if this evidence is to be allowed". In *B. (C.R.)*,[72] Sopinka J., delivering the minority judgment of the Court, adopted that view, although the majority expressed no opinion on the point. However, in *Director of Public Prosecutions v. P.*,[73] the House of Lords changed their opinion and held that the possibility of collusion among complainants was an issue that should be left for the jury to decide. In *Burke*,[74] Sopinka J., now delivering the majority judgment of the Supreme Court, opted for this approach and held that it should be left to the jury to determine the reliability of the evidence having regard to all of the circumstances, including the opportunities for collusion or collaboration to concoct the evidence.

Until the decision of the Supreme Court of Canada in *Arp*,[75] trial judges struggled with the degree of proof that the Crown is required to establish to the satisfaction of the jury, before they may use the similar fact in relation to the charge against the accused. Before *Arp*, the weight of authority suggested that the onus was not proof beyond a reasonable doubt, but something akin to the civil onus. Juries were customarily told that they could use similar fact evidence to assist them in deciding whether the accused committed the offence charged "if they believe it".[76]

That view, however, was difficult to reconcile with authorities which said that if an accused had been acquitted of a previous incident in another trial, evidence of that previous incident could not be used as similar fact evidence against him.[77] Those authorities reasoned that since

---

[72] [1990] 3 W.W.R. 385, 109 A.R. 81, 73 Alta. L.R. (2d) 1, 55 C.C.C. (3d) 1, 76 C.R. (3d) 1, [1990] 1 S.C.R. 717, 107 N.R. 241, 1990 CarswellAlta 35, 1990 CarswellAlta 650.
[73] *Supra*, note 63 at (Cr. App. R.) p. 272.
[74] 194 N.R. 247, 139 Nfld. & P.E.I.R. 147, 433 A.P.R. 147, 46 C.R. (4th) 195, 105 C.C.C. (3d) 205, [1996] 1 S.C.R. 474, 1996 CarswellNfld 85, 1996 CarswellNfld 85F, [1996] S.C.J. No. 27, reconsideration refused (May 23, 1996), Doc. 24071 (S.C.C.).
[75] *Supra*, note 67.
[76] *Simpson* (1977), 16 O.R. (2d) 129, 35 C.C.C. (2d) 337, 77 D.L.R. (3d) 507, 2 L.M.Q. 40 (C.A.); *Lawson*, [1971] 4 W.W.R. 350, 3 C.C.C. (2d) 372, 14 C.R.N.S. 377, 1971 CarswellAlta 51 (C.A.); *Arp, ibid.*
[77] *Cullen*, 52 C.C.C. (3d) 459, 36 O.A.C. 195, 1989 CarswellOnt 853 (C.A.); *M. (R.A.)*, (1994), [1995] 1 W.W.R. 509, 94 C.C.C. (3d) 459, 97 Man. R. (2d) 70, 79 W.A.C. 70,

an acquittal is considered the equivalent of a finding of innocence,[78] such similar fact evidence could not be used by the trier of fact because another court has found that the accused did not commit the offence. Indeed, the Ontario Court of Appeal went so far as to say that if the trial judge admitted evidence of a similar act that was later prosecuted resulting in an acquittal, then any conviction based on evidence of that similar act resulted in a new trial.[79]

For example, in *G. (K.R.)*,[80] the accused was charged with sexually assaulting two children and an adult. The Crown was allowed to introduce, as similar fact evidence, the testimony of a child who said that he was also sexually assaulted by the accused. The accused was convicted. He was then tried on a charge of sexually assaulting that child, based on the evidence that had been introduced as similar fact evidence and acquitted of the charge. On the appeal of his conviction, the accused applied to introduce as fresh evidence the fact of his acquittal on the similar fact evidence charge and the Court granted application. It was held that if the accused had been tried and acquitted of the charge of sexual assault upon the child before the trial which gave rise to the appeal, that child's evidence would not have been admissible as similar fact evidence.[81] The Court also noted the well-established principle that an acquittal is the equivalent of a finding of innocence.[82] Therefore, it had to be assumed that the accused was innocent of the allegations made against him by the child.

In *Arp*, the Supreme Court decided that the proper standard to apply to the primary inference drawn from the similar fact evidence is proof on a balance of probabilities. Cory J., delivering the judgment of the Court, reasoned that since the probative value of similar fact evidence, as circumstantial evidence, lies in the unlikelihood of coincidence, it simply did not make sense to require one of the allegations to

1994 CarswellMan 174 (C.A.); *Verney*, 67 O.A.C. 279, 87 C.C.C. (3d) 363, 1993 CarswellOnt 1157 (C.A.); *Merdsoy*, 91 C.C.C. (3d) 517, 121 Nfld. & P.E.I.R. 181, 377 A.P.R. 181, 1994 CarswellNfld 131 (C.A.) and *N. (R.S.)*, 31 Alta. L.R. (3d) 424, 169 A.R. 378, 97 W.A.C. 378, 1995 CarswellAlta 263 (C.A.).

[78] *Grdic*, [1985] 1 S.C.R. 810, [1985] 4 W.W.R. 437, 19 D.L.R. (4th) 385, 59 N.R. 61, 19 C.C.C. (3d) 289, 46 C.R. (3d) 1, 1985 CarswellBC 737, 1984 CarswellBC 827, [1985] S.C.J. No. 41; *Grant*, 31 M.V.R. (2d) 309, [1991] 3 S.C.R. 139, 93 Nfld. & P.E.I.R. 181, 292 A.P.R. 181, 7 C.R. (4th) 388, 5 C.R.R. (2d) 193, 130 N.R. 250, 67 C.C.C. (3d) 268, 1991 CarswellPEI 98, [1991] S.C.J. No. 78.

[79] *G. (K.R.)*, 5 O.R. (3d) 406, 51 O.A.C. 294, 68 C.C.C. (3d) 268, 1991 CarswellOnt 727 (C.A.).

[80] *Ibid.*

[81] *Cullen, supra*, note 77.

[82] *Grant, supra*, note 78.

be proved beyond a reasonable doubt as a prerequisite to the trier's consideration of it. Although the similar fact evidence, standing alone, may fall short of proof beyond a reasonable doubt, it can be relied upon to assist in proving another allegation beyond a reasonable doubt. In other words, the correct approach to a consideration of similar fact evidence is the pooling or cumulative approach.

6

Opinion Evidence

1. THE RULE

A witness is not allowed to express personal beliefs or give an opinion about a fact in issue unless the matter calls for his or her special skill or knowledge, and he or she is an expert in such matters. This rule is based upon the notion that it is possible to draw a distinction between a fact and the inference to be drawn from that fact. Witnesses are supposed to testify as to matters which they observe through their senses, that is, the eyes, ears, nose, *etc.* It is for the jury or judge (in trials by judge alone) to decide what is the proper inference to be drawn from the facts established by the witness.

The difficulty with the rule is that it is not always easy to draw a line between a fact and an opinion. For example, when a witness says that "the car was going very fast" or that "the accused was angry" or that "the girl was very pretty" or "the person is very old", the witness is really expressing a personal opinion based on his or her own experience and view of matters. Yet, such evidence is routinely given in court without objection. Indeed, in an Ontario case, *German*,[1] a witness was allowed to give evidence that the accused was intoxicated. Chief Justice Robertson justified the reception of that evidence in this way:

> No doubt, the general rule is that it is only persons who are qualified by some special skill, training or experience who can be asked their opinion upon a matter in issue. The rule is not, however, an absolute one. There are a number of matters in respect of which a person of ordinary intelligence may be

---

[1] [1947] O.R. 395, 3 C.R. 516, 89 C.C.C. 90, [1947] 4 D.L.R. 68, 1947 CarswellOnt 15 (C.A.).

permitted to give evidence of his opinion upon a matter of which he has personal knowledge. Such matters as the identity of individuals, the apparent age of a person, the speed of a vehicle, are among the matters upon which witnesses have been allowed to express an opinion, notwithstanding that they have no special qualifications, other than the fact they have personal knowledge of the subject matter, to enable them to form an opinion.

Not all courts have adopted this liberal approach to the general rule. For example in *Browne*,[2] the question was whether a witness could identify a person as the perpetrator of a crime. O'Halloran J.A. argued:

> A positive statement 'that is the man', when rationalized, is found to be an opinion and not a statement of single fact. All a witness can say is, that because of this or that he remembers about a person, he is of opinion that person is 'the man'. A witness recognizes a person because of a certain personality that person has acquired in the eyes of the witness. That personality is reflected by characteristics of the person, which, when associated with something in the mind of the witness, causes the latter to remember that person in a way the witness does not remember any other person.
> Unless the witness is able to testify with confidence what characteristics and what 'something' has stirred and clarified his memory or recognition, then an identification confined to 'that is the man', standing by itself, cannot be more than a vague general description and is untrustworthy in any sphere of life where certitude is essential.

Nevertheless, the courts have continued to allow an ordinary witness to give evidence on a "subject about which most people should be able to express an opinion from their ordinary day-to-day experience of life". These include such matters as disputed handwriting, if the witness has acquired previous knowledge of the handwriting of a person whose handwriting is in dispute,[3] the age of another person, his own mental or physical condition, whether a person is intoxicated or impaired by alcohol, the degree of intoxication, and whether the person's ability to drive is impaired,[4] and estimates of such things as speed, distance, size, *etc.*

2. EXPERT OPINION

An exception to the rule exists in favour of witnesses who are classified as experts. The theory underlying expert testimony is that

---

[2] 11 C.R. 297, 1 W.W.R. (N.S.) 449, 99 C.C.C. 141, 1951 CarswellBC 25 (C.A.).

[3] *Derrick* (1910), 5 Cr. App. R. 162.

[4] *Graat*, [1982] 2 S.C.R. 819, 18 M.V.R. 287, 31 C.R. (3d) 289, 2 C.C.C. (3d) 365, 144 D.L.R. (3d) 267, 45 N.R. 451, 1982 CarswellOnt 101, 1982 CarswellOnt 745.

experts, because of their knowledge, training and experience, are able to form better opinions on a given state of facts than opinions formed by those not so well equipped, such as ordinary jurors. Their opinions are admitted in evidence to aid the jury to understand questions which uninformed and inexperienced persons are not likely to decide correctly without such assistance. However, if the subject is one of common knowledge and the facts can be intelligibly described to the jury, and they can form a reasonable opinion for themselves, the opinion of an expert will be rejected. An expert is therefore someone who is qualified by study or experience to form a definite opinion respecting a division of science, branch of art or department of trade, which persons having no particular training or special study are incapable of accurately forming. It is not a university degree that makes a person an expert; it is special knowledge acquired through study or practical experience. The expert, however, is not required to have had some experience as a clinician or to have written articles with respect to his or her particular area of expertise before he or she may be qualified and allowed to testify as an expert.[5]

On the other hand, the fact that a witness may have knowledge about a subject, or understand it better than the judge or jury, does not necessarily justify receiving his or her evidence. If the judge or jury can become sufficiently informed about the subject during the trial, so that they can reach an accurate conclusion, there is really no basis for the expert opinion.

Over the last decade, some judges have cautioned against opening the doors too quickly to the admission of expert evidence. For example, in *McIntosh*,[6] Finlayson J.A. observed:

> In my respectful opinion, the courts are overly eager to abdicate their fact-finding responsibilities to 'experts' in the field of behavioural sciences. We are too quick to say that a particular witness possesses special knowledge and experience going beyond that of the trier of fact without engaging in an analysis of the subject-matter of the expertise .... simply because one has lectured and written extensively on a subject that is of interest to him or her does not constitute him or her an expert for the purpose of testifying in a court of law on the subject of that specialty. It seems to me that before we even get

---

[5] *R. (W.D.)*, 35 C.R. (4th) 343, 95 C.C.C. (3d) 190, 77 O.A.C. 59, [1994] O.J. No. 2934, 1994 CarswellOnt 121 (C.A.).

[6] 117 C.C.C. (3d) 385, 102 O.A.C. 210, 35 O.R. (3d) 97, 1997 CarswellOnt 2682, [1997] O.J. No. 3172 (C.A.), leave to appeal refused (1998), 227 N.R. 279 (note), 111 O.A.C. 395 (note) (S.C.C.).

to the point of examining the witness's expertise, we must ask ourselves if the subject-matter of his testimony admits of expert testimony.[7]

And later, he wrote:

... I would caution courts to scrutinize the nature of the subject-matter of the expert testimony. Any natural or unnatural phenomenon may become the subject of an investigation conducted according to the scientific method. The scientific method requires the formation of a hypothesis, the testing of the hypothesis using reliable methodology, the examination of the results (usually with statistical analysis) and the formation of a conclusion. However, the fact that the testimony recites the application of the scientific method does not necessarily render the original object of study a matter requiring opinion evidence at trial.[8]

At issue in *McIntosh* was whether the trial judge had erred in refusing a request by the defence to admit evidence of a psychologist on the question of eyewitness identification. The psychologist's evidence on the *voir dire* included evidence of the factors present at the time of the robbery that would impair the witness's ability to make an accurate identification, and the problem of cross-racial identification. It was held that the trial judge did not err in refusing to admit the evidence. Since the opinion evidence was only directed to instructing the jury that all witnesses have problems in perception and recall with respect to what occurred during any given circumstance that is brief and stressful, such evidence was not outside the normal experience of the trier of fact.

The admissibility of expert evidence will depend upon four criteria: relevance; necessity in assisting the trier of fact; absence of any exclusionary rule; and a properly qualified expert.[9]

This imposes on the trial judge the duty to act as gatekeeper and carefully scrutinize the admissibility of the proposed expert testimony.[10] In *J. (J.-L.)*,[11] the Supreme Court suggested that trial judges should apply the *reliable foundation* test adopted by the U.S. Supreme Court in *Daubert v. Merrell Dow Pharmaceuticals Inc.*[12] and listed a number of factors

[7]   *Ibid.*, at (C.C.C.) p. 392.
[8]   *Ibid.*, at pp. 393-94.
[9]   *Mohan*, 29 C.R. (4th) 243, 71 O.A.C. 241, 166 N.R. 245, 89 C.C.C. (3d) 402, 114 D.L.R. (4th) 419, [1994] 2 S.C.R. 9, 18 O.R. (3d) 160 (note), 1994 CarswellOnt 66, 1994 CarswellOnt 1155.
[10] *Mohan, ibid.*; *J. (J.-L.)*, 2000 SCC 51, 37 C.R. (5th) 203, 148 C.C.C. (3d) 487, 192 D.L.R. (4th) 416, 261 N.R. 111, [2000] 2 S.C.R. 600, 2000 CarswellQue 2310, 2000 CarswellQue 2311.
[11] *Ibid.*
[12] (1993), 113 S. Ct. 2786, 509 U.S. 579, 125 L. Ed. 2d 469, 61 U.S.L.W. 4805, 27 U.S.P.Q.2d 1200 (U.S. Cal.).

that could be helpful to the trial judge in evaluating the soundness of novel science:

1.   whether the theory or technique can be tested;
2.   whether it has been subjected to peer review and publication;
3.   the known or potential rate of error or existence of standards; and
4.   whether the theory or technique used has been generally accepted.

In *J. (J.-L.)*,[13] the accused was charged with sexual offences involving two young boys who were between three and five years old. The Crown alleged anal penetration. The defence sought unsuccessfully to call expert evidence from a psychiatrist to establish that in all probability a serious deviant had inflicted anal intercourse on two children of that age, and that no such deviant personality traits were disclosed in the psychiatrist's testing of the accused. It was held that the trial judge had not erred in excluding the psychiatrist's evidence.

Although the Court was prepared to accept that psychiatric evidence of disposition is admissible where the particular disposition in issue is characteristic of a distinctive group, the characteristics of which fall within the expertise of the psychiatrist, this alone does not establish admissibility. The changing nature of scientific knowledge requires that novel science be evaluated on a case-by-case basis. Novel science is subject to special scrutiny, especially where the psychiatrist's opinion is close to the ultimate issue of guilt or innocence. Where the crime could only, or in all probability would only, be committed by a person having identifiable peculiarities that the accused does not possess, the personality profile of the perpetrator group must be sufficiently complete to identify distinctive psychological elements that were in all probability present and operating in the perpetrator at the time of the offence. In other words, what exactly differentiates or distinguishes the perpetrator class from the rest of the population must be clearly identified, *i.e.*, a standard profile. The range and distinctiveness of personality traits attributable to perpetrators of different offences will vary greatly. The issue for the trial judge will be whether the profile is sufficient for the expert to identify and describe with workable precision what exactly distinguishes the distinctive or deviant perpetrator from other people.

The trial judge must then weigh the relevance, reliability and necessity of the expert evidence against the consumption of time, prejudice and confusion it may cause. In determining relevance, the trial judge must consider whether the probative value of the evidence is overborne

[13]   *Supra*, note 10.

by its prejudicial effect and whether it can influence the trier of fact out of proportion to its reliability.[14] If there is the danger that the expert evidence would be misused, distort the fact-finding process or confuse the jury, then the trial judge should not admit it. Moreover, the trial judge has the duty to subject a novel scientific theory or technique to special scrutiny to ensure that it meets the four criteria.

Before a witness is permitted to give expert evidence, he or she must first be properly qualified as an expert by the side that calls him or her. He or she must also be accepted by the court as an expert in the particular area about which he or she is to testify. Although the other side will often admit the witness's qualifications, there is still an obligation upon the trial judge to be satisfied that the expert's testimony meets the four criteria.

Once qualified and accepted by the court to give expert testimony, the witness may be permitted to express his or her opinion with respect to the conclusion that should be drawn from certain facts. The expert may have personal knowledge of the facts; but more often than not, he or she will have to rely on information received from others. In this later instance, the expert will be asked to give an opinion on what is called a hypothesis or a hypothetical question. He or she will be asked to assume certain facts that will be outlined and will then be asked for an opinion on the conclusion that should be drawn from those facts. However, the opinion expressed must only relate to the facts. The expert is not entitled to give an answer that amounts to a conclusion of law.

If the opinion of an expert is premised upon the truth of facts that he or she has assumed hypothetically, those assumed facts must be established by evidence in the usual way, otherwise the basis of the expert's opinion collapses. Indeed, the judge must warn the jury (or instruct him or herself in trials by judge alone) that before the opinion can be considered, they must be satisfied as to the truth of the facts upon which the expert is relying. Thus an attack on the facts assumed by the expert is usually one of the ways a cross-examiner will attempt to discredit the expert's opinion.

For example, it is the usual practice for a psychiatrist who is called upon to give an opinion as to the mental state of an accused to rely upon interviews with the accused and with others, all of which form part of the accused's psychiatric history. The fact that the expert's opinion is dependant upon the truth of statements made by the accused and others will not affect the admissibility of the opinion, although it is a factor in

---

[14]   *Melaragni* (1992), 73 C.C.C. (3d) 348 (Ont. Gen. Div.).

assessing the weight of it.[15] Nevertheless, the trial judge must be careful to warn the jury that in considering the weight of the opinion, they must be satisfied of the truth of the statements relied upon by the psychiatrist.

On the other hand, if the psychiatrist (or any other expert) is present during the course of the trial and is asked at the conclusion to give an opinion based on the evidence he or she has heard, such evidence is not admissible. The reason is that what the expert is being asked to do is to pass on the truthfulness of the witnesses who have testified and that is within the exclusive jurisdiction of the trier of fact.[16]

A common complaint about expert evidence is that the expert may give an opinion on the very issue which the jury must decide and thus usurp their function. Whether the evidence is simply opinion to assist the jury in deciding the ultimate issue or evidence of the very issue itself, is not often easy to determine. For example, if the issue is whether the accused was criminally responsible for an act committed while suffering from a mental disorder, a psychiatrist called as an expert will be asked to give his or her opinion about whether the accused was capable of "appreciating the nature and quality of his acts" or "of knowing that his acts were wrong" in accordance with section 16 of the *Criminal Code.* Such evidence is regularly received even though it would appear to be on the very issue which the judge or jury must decide.

The courts have always had difficulty with the application of the ultimate issue rule. For example, in *Lupien,*[17] the accused was charged with gross indecency. His defence was that he thought that the male person with whom he was found was, in fact, a female, and attempted to introduce psychiatric evidence to show that he had a strong aversion to homosexual practices and therefore would not knowingly engage in homosexual acts. The Supreme Court of Canada was divided on the issue.

The dissenting judges felt that the psychiatric opinion ought not to be admitted because it came too close to the very question that the jury had to decide on the whole of the evidence. The majority, however, decided that the expert testimony was admissible on the question of whether or not the man was "homosexually inclined or otherwise sexually perverted". Mr. Justice Hall gave these reasons:

---

[15] *Swietlinski,* 22 O.R. (2d) 604, 5 C.R. (3d) 324, 44 C.C.C. (2d) 267, 94 D.L.R. (3d) 218, 1978 CarswellOnt 52 (C.A.), affirmed, 18 C.R. (3d) 231, 55 C.C.C. (2d) 481, 34 N.R. 569, 117 D.L.R. (3d) 285, [1980] 2 S.C.R. 956, 1980 CarswellOnt 648, at (C.C.C.) p. 301.

[16] *Bleta* (1964), [1964] S.C.R. 561, 44 C.R. 193, [1965] 1 C.C.C. 1, 48 D.L.R. (2d) 139, 1964 CarswellOnt 17.

[17] (1969), [1970] S.C.R. 263, 9 C.R.N.S. 165, [1970] 2 C.C.C. 193, 9 D.L.R. (3d) 1, 71 W.W.R. 110, 1969 CarswellBC 185.

That type of evidence is very close, if not identical, to the conclusion the jury must come to in such a case if it is to find that the accused was not guilty because he did not have intent necessary to support conviction. The weight to be given the opinion of the expert is entirely for the jury, and it is the function of the trial judge to instruct the jury that the responsibility for weighing the evidence is theirs and theirs alone.[18]

The real difficulty for a jury will arise where there are two experts expressing diametrically opposed views. This means that their decision will turn not so much on which facts are proved in evidence, but on which expert the jury or judge accepts. In other words, their decision will often depend on which expert they find more credible, rather than on whose opinion is the correct one. In criminal cases, however, the difficulty for the trier may be more apparent than real. The rule is that before the judge and jury are entitled to accept the opinion of the prosecution expert over the defence expert, they must be satisfied that it is the correct one.[19]

3. OPINION AS TO THE CREDIBILITY OF A WITNESS

(a) Generally

Where the central issue at trial is whether a certain event occurred (such as a sexual assault) and the only two persons present at the event are the complainant and the accused, the trier is faced with the difficult question of determining who is telling the truth. This raises the question of whether a witness should be allowed to give evidence that one of the witnesses to the event is or is not a credible witness. Historically, opinion evidence as to the credibility of a witness was not allowed, although evidence in the form of character evidence of the witness's reputation in the community for lack of credibility was always allowed. The reason why opinion evidence was not allowed is because of the reluctance of allowing evidence on the very issue that the trier was required to decide. Another concern was that it might prolong the trial unduly by creating confusion and a multiplicity of issues.

However, 50 years ago in *Gunewardene*,[20] the English Court of Criminal Appeal accepted that an impeaching witness should no longer be confined to expressing an opinion as to the lack of veracity of a

---

[18] *Ibid.,* at pp. 279-80.
[19] *Molnar,* 76 C.R. (3d) 125, 55 C.C.C. (3d) 446, 38 O.A.C. 62, 1990 CarswellOnt 91, [1990] O.J. No. 339 (C.A.).
[20] [1951] 2 K.B. 600, [1951] 2 All E.R. 290, 35 Cr. App. R. 80 (Ct. of Crim. App.).

prosecution witness based upon that witness's general reputation. The impeaching witness was now entitled to state that from his or her knowledge of the witness, that witness was unworthy of credit. But in *Gunewardene*, the Court would not let the impeaching witness detail his reasons for that opinion, even though he was a medical witness. It took another thirteen years before that restriction was overruled. In *Toohey v. Metropolitan Police Commissioner*,[21] the House of Lords decided that a medical witness could give his reasons why the witness should not be believed. For example, the witness was allowed to say that the witness suffered from a mental defect or abnormality that made his or her evidence unreliable. In Canada, that view was finally accepted by the Ontario Court of Appeal in *Gonzague*.[22]

Three years later, the Ontario Court of Appeal went further and removed the restrictions upon a lay person giving reasons why a witness should not be believed. In *T. (S.)*,[23] it was held that the opinions of the defence witnesses that the complainants at a sexual trial ought not to be believed, and the basis of their belief, were receivable. The Court also said that reply evidence was admissible to reduce the impact of that impeaching evidence. But it was stressed that the jury should also be told that the reply evidence must not be used to bolster the credibility of the complainants.

The way in which a character witness is entitled to question the testimony of a witness who has given evidence is by the following questions:

1.   Do you know the reputation of (the witness) as to truth and veracity in the community in which he (or she) resides?

If the answer is "yes", then the witness may be asked:

2.   Is that reputation good or bad?

If the answer is "bad", the following question is permitted:

3.   From that reputation, would you believe that witness on oath?

---

[21] [1965] A.C. 595, [1965] 1 All E.R. 506, 49 Cr. App. R. 148 (H.L.).
[22] 34 C.R. (3d) 169, 4 C.C.C. (3d) 505, 1983 CarswellOnt 81 (C.A.).
[23] 18 O.A.C. 219, 57 O.R. (2d) 737, 31 C.C.C. (3d) 1, 55 C.R. (3d) 321, 1986 CarswellOnt 144 (C.A.).

The rule in *Gonzague* and *T. (S.)* was reconsiderd by the Ontario Court of Appeal in *Clarke*.[24] Rosenberg J.A., delivering the judgment of the Court, questioned the usefulness of permitting a character witness, who has not heard the evidence in the case, to predict whether another witness has told the truth under oath. He noted that a witness is sworn to tell the truth, is subject to prosecution for lying under oath, the testimony takes place before a judge and sometimes a jury, and the witness knows that he or she is subject to cross-examination. Thus, the circumstances under which a person may be willing to lie under oath are probably considerably different from the circumstances in which he or she would likely lie to an acquaintance or even acquire a reputation for lack of veracity. As far as he was concerned, counsel did not have the absolute right to ask the third question and a judge would be justified in refusing to permit it.

Although opinion evidence *discrediting* a witness's testimony is now receivable, the authorities are clear that evidence *bolstering* a witness's testimony is generally not receivable, even if it is expert testimony. For example, in *Kyselka*,[25] the Crown had called a psychiatrist who had testified that the complainant, a retarded girl who had alleged that she had been raped, was likely, because of her condition, to be a truthful witness. The Ontario Court of Appeal, however, held that evidence bolstering the testimony of a witness was not admissible because it amounted to "oath helping".[26]

(b) Child Abuse Cases

Notwithstanding these clear statements of the law, in recent years the courts have come under increasing pressure to admit medical or psychiatric evidence of the credibility of a complainant in sexual assault cases. That pressure has been strong, particularly where the complainant is a child or is mentally infirm, because of the ease with which their evidence can be attacked by the defence and the fear that such victims are not receiving the kind of protection from the courts that they need and deserve. Although the courts have continued to apply the rule prohibiting direct comment by an expert on the credibility of the complainant, such evidence has been not been rejected if it only inferentially

---

[24] 18 C.R. (5th) 219, 112 O.A.C. 233, 129 C.C.C. (3d) 1, 1998 CarswellOnt 3447, [1998] O.J. No. 3521 (C.A.).

[25] [1962] O.W.N. 160, 133 C.C.C. 103, 37 C.R. 391, 1962 CarswellOnt 13 (C.A.).

[26] See also *Burkart*, 45 C.R. 383, 50 W.W.R. 515, [1965] 3 C.C.C. 210, 1964 CarswellSask 75 (C.A.).

bolsters the complainant's credibility. For example, in *Beliveau*,[27] MacFarlane J.A. admitted the testimony of a paediatrician that the complainant, because of her age, was unlikely to have a motive to lie only because,

> These questions were necessary in assessing the validity of his opinion on an issue in the case, and not to establish that the child was a truthful witness.

In *B. (G.)*,[28] the Supreme Court was prepared to go even further. There three young offenders were charged with the sexual assault of a seven-year-old child. A psychologist specializing in the treatment of victims of sexual abuse had testified that the changes noted in the victim's behaviour, such as bed-wetting and nightmares, were characteristic of behaviour noted in victims of this type of sexual abuse. It was held that evidence of an expert as to the psychological and physical conditions that frequently arise as a result of sexual abuse of a child was admissible because it provided assistance to the trier of fact in concluding whether an assault had occurred. Since the defence was that there had been no assault, the admissibility of that evidence inferentially bolstered the complainant's credibility on that issue. Nevertheless, Madam Justice Wilson delivering the judgment of the Court, warned that:

> ...the expert evidence should not be used to bolster the credibility of witnesses or indicate that they should be believed since credibility is a matter exclusively reserved for the trier of fact.[29]

Unfortunately what amounts to a direct comment on a complainant's credibility and an inferential bolstering of that testimony is not always easy to determine. For example, in *R. (S.)*,[30] evidence was admitted on behalf of the Crown to explain why there was a delay of several months between the time that the complainant (a child) first complained of sexual abuse and the date when the charges were laid. The explanation was that a social worker believed her, but the investigating officer did not. To resolve the issue, a psychologist was called in to conduct an assessment of the child's credibility and the charges were laid. Both the social worker and the psychologist were allowed to give evidence before the child testified that they believed her. In allowing an

27   30 C.C.C. (3d) 193, 1986 CarswellBC 665 (C.A.).
28   56 C.C.C. (3d) 200, [1990] 2 S.C.R. 30, 111 N.R. 31, 86 Sask. R. 111, 77 C.R. (3d) 347, 1990 CarswellSask 20, 1990 CarswellSask 410, [1990] S.C.J. No. 58.
29   *Ibid.*, at (C.C.C.) p. 207.
30   8 O.R. (3d) 679, 15 C.R. (4th) 102, 73 C.C.C. (3d) 225, 56 O.A.C. 1, 1992 CarswellOnt 101 (C.A.).

appeal from a conviction, the Ontario Court of Appeal said that the effective purpose of the evidence was to bolster the credibility of the complainant and it was therefore not admissible. The better way to deal with the question of delay between the report and the charges was to simply tell the jury that they should not speculate about the delay, because it was not a matter that concerned them.

In *Marquard*,[31] the Supreme Court reaffirmed the general rule that the ultimate conclusion as to the credibility or truthfulness of a particular witness is for the trier of fact, and is not the proper subject of expert opinion. However, the Court went on to say that expert evidence of human conduct in the psychological and physical factors that may lead to certain behaviour relevant to credibility is admissible, provided the testimony goes beyond the ordinary experience of the trier of fact. Marquard was charged with the aggravated assault of her three-and-a-half-year-old granddaughter. It was alleged that she had put the child's face against a hot stove door in order to discipline her. The child's unsworn testimony was that her "nana" had put her in (or on) the stove. Both the accused and her husband had testified that they discovered the child early in the morning, screaming, after she had burned herself trying to light a cigarette with a butane lighter. Among the expert testimony called by both the Crown and the defence was a witness who commented on the child's credibility. The Court said that the testimony of an expert as to why children may lie to hospital staff about the cause of their injuries was clearly admissible because the witness was an expert in child behaviour. A lay jury needed expert evidence to understand the full implication of the witness's change in story. The Court said, however, that when the expert testified that she personally did not believe the child's first story, preferring the second version which the child told at trial, she crossed the line between expert testimony and human behaviour and assessment of credibility of the witness herself.

Similarly, in *B. (R.H.)*,[32] the Supreme Court re-affirmed that the use of experts to explain human behaviour is now clearly admissible to furnish the court with scientific information likely to be outside the experience and knowledge of the judge and jury. The Court said that the behaviour of a person who has been systematically abused is an example of a matter on which experts may assist. Moreover, the fact that such evidence is inadmissible for one purpose (*i.e.*, to show the truthfulness

---

[31]   25 C.R. (4th) 1, 85 C.C.C. (3d) 193, [1993] 4 S.C.R. 223, 108 D.L.R. (4th) 47, 159 N.R. 81, 66 O.A.C. 161, 1993 CarswellOnt 127, 1993 CarswellOnt 995, [1993] S.C.J. No. 119.
[32]   29 C.R. (4th) 113, 42 B.C.A.C. 161, 67 W.A.C. 161, 89 C.C.C. (3d) 193, [1994] 1 S.C.R. 656, 165 N.R. 374, 1994 CarswellBC 576, 1994 CarswellBC 1237.

of a witness) does not automatically prevent it being received for another legitimate purpose (*i.e.*, to show whether the complainant was sexually abused).

B. was charged with indecently assaulting the complainant when she was nine and sexually assaulting her when she was 16. The charges came to light when the complainant was, herself, convicted of sexually abusing young boys that she was babysitting and ordered to take counselling. At that time, the complainant revealed that she had been sexually abused as a child. At trial, the complainant said that she did not reveal the assaults when they occurred because B. was a good friend of her father. She feared that she would be disbelieved and lose her father. Her psychiatrist testified as to her condition as a consequence of what she had undergone, giving a picture of why she reacted as she did. On appeal, the accused's counsel argued that the psychiatrist's evidence went to the very root of the issue before the judge — that she had been sexually abused by the accused — which the court had to decide and usurped the function of the trial judge. The Supreme Court disagreed. The Court said that the fact that such testimony was admissible to explain human behaviour did not render it inadmissible just because it also violated the rule against oath helping and the very issue which the jury was required to decide, that is, whether the complainant was sexually abused.

In *C. (G.)*,[33] the Newfoundland Court of Appeal was prepared to sanction the admission of expert evidence to explain delayed disclosure and continued association by survivors of childhood sexual abuse, provided the proper groundwork was laid. The Court said that expert evidence about the general behaviour and psychological characteristics of survivors of childhood sexual abuse should be regarded as susceptible to admission, even when the complainant is being tried during the victim's adulthood. The Court reasoned that it assists in making an assessment of a complainant's credibility, not as a determinant of ultimate truthfulness, but to explain factors bearing on a witness's believability, provided the subject matter of the testimony likely transcends ordinary experience.

Nevertheless, the courts have said that before evidence of behavioural characteristics of child sexual abusers will be admitted, the characteristics must be of such distinctiveness that a comparison of one with the other will be of material assistance in determining guilt or innocence. For example, in *A. (G.R.)*,[34] a charge of sexual assault, the Ontario Court

---

[33]   110 C.C.C. (3d) 233, 144 Nfld. & P.E.I.R. 204, 451 A.P.R. 204, 1996 CarswellNfld 222 (C.A.).

[34]   35 C.R. (4th) 340, 1994 CarswellOnt 120, [1994] O.J. No. 2930 (C.A.).

of Appeal rejected the evidence of a psychologist that certain characteristics were usually found in child sexual abusers, namely, that abusers will be members of the family or close friends and will use bribes or threats to have the victim remain silent. The Court said that the opinion did not have that distinctiveness which would permit its use as evidence.

Similarly, in *Olscamp*,[35] the trial judge concluded that the present state of knowledge in the field of sexual abuse is such that the soundness and reliability of any expert opinion purporting to characterize behavioural symptoms as consistent with sexual abuse cannot be demonstrated. If there is any consensus to be found among the experts, it is that there is no valid profile in existence that can enable one to identify a child who has been sexually abused. While the symptoms that have often been identified as consistent with abuse may indeed be related to the fact that a child has been sexually abused, research has shown that no single symptom or constellation of symptoms have been found to have any real discriminate validity. In other words, they do not serve to single out children who have been subjected to sexual abuse from children who have suffered some other kind of abuse or trauma, or even from the population of children.

On the other hand, in *W. (A.)*,[36] the Ontario Court of Appeal held that the testimony of an abuse expert that young children do not have the motivation or sophistication, nor the mental capacity, to be elaborately deceptive and to manufacture a complex fabrication to achieve an ulterior purpose was properly received by the trial judge. Although this opinion supported the credibility of the complainant, it was not excluded by the rule prohibiting a witness, expert or otherwise, from simply asserting his or her belief in the truthfulness of a particular child in support of that child's credibility. However, the Court did say that the opinion expressed by another expert psychologist, who had examined the complainant, to the effect that she did not believe that the complainant could have fabricated the allegations, was not proper evidence for the witness to give because it went directly to an opinion as to the credibility of the witness.

---

[35]   35 C.R. (4th) 37, 95 C.C.C. (3d) 466, 1994 CarswellOnt 114 (Gen. Div.).

[36]   75 O.A.C. 130, 94 C.C.C. (3d) 441, 44 C.R. (4th) 319, 1994 CarswellOnt 1211 (C.A.), reversed, 102 C.C.C. (3d) 96, 44 C.R. (4th) 317, [1995] 4 S.C.R. 51, 96 O.A.C. 244, 206 N.R. 161, 1995 CarswellOnt 957, 1995 CarswellOnt 1181.

4. OPINION AS TO THE CREDIBILITY OF THE ACCUSED

The general rule is that the Crown is not entitled to call either experts or lay persons to give opinion evidence that the accused is not a credible witness, unless the accused puts his or her character in issue, in which case only character evidence may be called in reply. Nor is the Crown allowed to lead in-chief expert opinion about the accused's disposition to commit a crime unless it is relevant to an issue and is not being used merely as evidence of disposition.[37] The same rule applies to prevent an accused from calling experts and laymen to give their opinion that he or she is a credible witness. However, in the last twenty-five years, some authorities have allowed experts to testify as to the disposition or propensity of the accused to commit or not commit certain acts where they are relevant to a fact in issue. Unfortunately, the principles governing the admission of such evidence have not always been clearly stated.

For example, in *Lupien*,[38] the Supreme Court of Canada said that an expert could testify that an accused lacked homosexual propensities to support the accused's evidence that he did not know that his companion, who was dressed as a women was, in fact, a man. Similarly, in *McMillan*,[39] an accused charged with the murder of his child was allowed to call an expert to testify that his wife had the disposition to commit the murder. A closer examination of both these cases reveals that the evidence was admitted more to demonstrate lack of propensity of the accused, rather than to support his credibility. Again, in *Dietrich*,[40] the Ontario Court of Appeal, relying on the authority of *Lupien*, permitted an expert to testify that the accused had a psychopathic personality with a propensity for confessing to things that he did not do and should be believed when he testified that his confession was false. Although *Dietrich* is authority that an expert may give evidence bolstering the credibility of an accused, the evidence really went to establish that Dietrich had the propensity and time to confess to things that he did not do.

---

[37] *Mohan*, 29 C.R. (4th) 243, 71 O.A.C. 241, 166 N.R. 245, 89 C.C.C. (3d) 402, 114 D.L.R. (4th) 419, [1994] 2 S.C.R. 9, 18 O.R. (3d) 160 (note), 1994 CarswellOnt 66, 1994 CarswellOnt 1155.

[38] (1969), [1970] S.C.R. 263, 9 C.R.N.S. 165, [1970] 2 C.C.C. 193, 9 D.L.R. (3d) 1, 71 W.W.R. 110, 1969 CarswellBC 185.

[39] 7 O.R. (2d) 750, 23 C.C.C. (2d) 160, 29 C.R.N.S. 191, 1975 CarswellOnt 7 (C.A.), affirmed, [1977] 2 S.C.R. 824, 33 C.C.C. (2d) 360, 15 N.R. 20, 73 D.L.R. (3d) 759, 1977 CarswellOnt 474.

[40] [1970] 3 O.R. 725, 1 C.C.C. (2d) 49, 11 C.R.N.S. 22, 1970 CarswellOnt 12 (C.A.), leave to appeal refused, [1970] 3 O.R. 744n, 1 C.C.C. (2d) 68n, [1970] S.C.R. xi.

However, in *Mohan*,[41] the Supreme Court of Canada stressed that evidence of an expert witness that the accused, by reason of his or her mental make-up or condition of the mind, would be incapable of committing or disposed to commit the crime is limited in scope. The Court noted that although the exception has been applied to abnormal behaviour connoting sexual deviance, its underlying rationale was based on distinctiveness.

Sopinka J., delivering the judgment of the Court, said that before an expert's opinion as to disposition may be admitted as evidence, the trial judge must be satisfied, as a matter of law, that either the perpetrator of the crime or the accused has distinctive behavioural characteristics such that a comparison of one with the other will be of material assistance in determining innocence or guilt. Although the judge's decision should be on the basis of common sense and experience, it must not be made in a vacuum. The judge must determine whether the expert is merely expressing a personal opinion or whether the behavioural profile which the expert is putting forward is in common use as a reliable indicator of membership in a distinctive group. A finding that the scientific community has developed a standard profile for the offender who commits this type of crime will satisfy the criteria of relevance and necessity. The evidence will qualify as an exception to the exclusionary rule relating to character evidence, provided the trial judge is satisfied that the proposed evidence is within the field of expertise of the expert witness.

In *Mohan*, the defence of the accused, a doctor charged with sexually assaulting four female patients aged 13 to 16, was that what the patients said was not true. The trial judge had refused to allow the defence to call a psychiatrist who would say that the offences had unusual features that would indicate that a physician who committed them was a member of one or the other of an unusual and limited class and, that in his opinion, the accused was not a member of either class. It was held that the trial judge was correct in not allowing the admission of such evidence. There was no body of evidence that doctors who commit sexual assaults fall into a distinctive class with identifiable characteristics.

---

[41] *Supra*, note 37.

7

Admissions and Confessions

1. THE RULE

A confession is defined as a statement either in writing or given orally by a person accused of a crime that shows or tends to show that he is guilty of the crime with which he is charged. An admission is said to be distinguishable from a confession because it is only an acknowledgment of a material fact that may form a link in the chain of proof against the accused. Unlike a confession, an admission need not necessarily be in writing or made orally; it can also include conduct that could reasonably be taken to be intended as an assertion.[1] The simplest example of an admission by conduct is when a police officer asks the accused if the murder weapon belongs to him and the accused nods his head affirmatively. No words have been spoken, but his conduct is sufficient to constitute an admission that the weapon belongs to him.

Some legal scholars regard admissions and confessions as exceptions to the hearsay rule; others say they are not because they are not offered to prove a fact in issue, but only to impeach the credibility of the accused. The first view is probably correct. Admissions and confessions are exceptions to the hearsay rule because it is only logical to assume that what a person says against his or her own interest is probably true.

The distinction between a confession and an admission is not important when it comes to the rule relating to their admissibility. Both

---

[1]   *St. Lawrence*, 7 C.R. 464, [1949] O.R. 215, 93 C.C.C. 376, 1949 CarswellOnt 4 (H.C.).

are governed by the same rule, which was stated by Lord Sumner in *Ibrahim*,[2] and judicially endorsed in Canada by the Supreme Court in *Boudreau*:[3]

> It has long been established as a positive rule of English criminal law, that no statement by an accused is admissible in evidence against him unless it is shown by the prosecution to have been a voluntary statement, in the sense that it has not been obtained from him either by fear of prejudice or hope of advantage exercised or held out by a person in authority. The principle is as old as Lord Hale.

There are three reasons for this rule. The first is the concern that a confession obtained as a result of an inducement may be false; only a confession freely made should be considered reliable. The second reason is a more emotional one. Until the middle of the seventeenth century, it was a common practice for the Ecclesiastic Courts to compel anyone suspected of committing a crime against the security of the state to attend before a government official and to require him to take an oath, called the *ex officio* oath, to tell the truth to all questions that might be put to him. He was not told of the specific crime nor the names of the witnesses for the Crown. If he told the truth, he might find himself charged with a crime that would put his life in peril. If he lied, he was charged with perjury and imprisoned. If he said nothing, he was arrested, tortured and incarcerated. It was not until the famous *Lilburne* case in 1641 that the *ex officio* oath was abolished and it was recognized that no man should be required to incriminate himself — *nemo tenetur prodere se ipsum* or *nemo tenetur prodere accusare*.

There is a third reason why the courts will reject a confession that has been obtained under circumstances indicating that it is not voluntary. It is important that the public have confidence in the way that the police carry out their duty to investigate crime. Unless the court is satisfied that the confession of an accused is free and voluntary, there is the concern that the public will believe that oppressive tactics are regularly used by the police. This will result in a loss of support and respect by the community for the criminal justice system.

Thus no statement made by an accused is admissible against him unless it is found to be voluntary "in the sense that it has not been obtained from him either by fear of prejudice or hope of advantage exercised or held out by a person in authority". The onus is upon the Crown to prove that the statement is voluntary before the trial judge is

---

[2] [1914] A.C. 599, 24 Cox C.C. 174, [1914-15] All E.R. Rep. 874 (Hong Kong P.C.).
[3] 7 C.R. 427, [1949] S.C.R. 262, 94 C.C.C. 1, [1949] 3 D.L.R. 81, 1949 CarswellQue 3.

authorized to allow the jury to hear it. To pass this threshold test, the Crown must satisfy the trial judge beyond a reasonable doubt that the statement was a voluntary one.

2. FORMAL ADMISSIONS

At common law, an accused was not permitted to make a formal admission where he was charged with a felony; nor is it certain that he could even do so where the charge was a misdemeanour. Section 655 of the *Criminal Code*[4] has altered that rule. It permits an accused charged with an indictable offence to "admit *any fact* alleged against him for the purpose of dispensing with proof thereof".

Does section 655 permit the defence to admit the voluntariness of a confession? The voluntariness of a confession is a question of law and is, strictly speaking, not something that can be admitted because section 655 only permits admissions of fact. However, trial judges usually get around this dilemma by having the accused admit that all of the facts leading up to the taking of the statement are consistent with it being voluntary.

Although the admission is characterized as a factual one, it does have legal consequences. In *Park*,[5] the Supreme Court went so far as to suggest that the defence has the right to waive the usual *voir dire* held to consider the voluntariness of the statement, and the trial judge has the wide discretion to accept that waiver if he or she is satisfied that the statement is voluntary.

3. ADMISSIONS BY CONDUCT

If we can assume that what a person says against his or her own interest is probably true and should be admitted, it follows that how he or she responds when an incriminating statement is made in his or her presence should be admissible against that person if his or her actions or conduct are indicative of guilt.

Let us assume, for example, that Constable Jones, who is investigating a charge of assault, confronts the accused Brown and tells him that he has reasonable grounds to believe that he has just assaulted Smith. If Brown responds by punching the officer and running away, it would be natural to assume that his conduct is indicative of guilt and should be

---

[4] R.S.C. 1985, c. C-46.
[5] [1981] 2 S.C.R. 64, 37 N.R. 501, 21 C.R. (3d) 182 (Eng.), 26 C.R. (3d) 164 (Fr.), 59 C.C.C. (2d) 385, 122 D.L.R. (3d) 1, 1981 CarswellOnt 614.

admissible against him. However, if Brown responds by denying the charge, as one would expect an innocent person to do, then his denial is not admissible at the instance of the defence because it is self-serving. This contradiction is often difficult to understand.

Silence of the accused in the face of an accusation by the police creates another problem. Although generally silence might cause one to ask why an innocent person has not denied his guilt, the law does not permit the Crown to lead evidence of the accused's silence in the face of an accusation. The reason is that an accused's right to silence is a constitutional guarantee under the *Charter of Rights and Freedoms*. It is unfair for the police to caution an accused that he has the right to remain silent and then use that silence in the face of a question that suggested his guilt.[6]

On the other hand, silence in the face of an accusation by someone other than the police will permit an inference that the accused assented to the accusation.[7] This will depend upon whether the accused's lack of response to the accusation, in the circumstances in which it is made, is reasonable.

A denial of an accusation might in some circumstances also amount to an acknowledgment of its truth.[8] In *Baron*, Mr. Justice Martin explained that:

> A denial by an accused of an incriminating statement in his or her presence does not necessarily preclude a jury from concluding that the accused has assented to the truth of the facts contained in the statement. The denial may be so equivocal or evasive as to permit an inference that the accused by his words or conduct has assented to it. However, mere disbelief of an unequivocal denial by an accused cannot have the effect of converting such a denial into an adoption of the facts contained in such statement, in the absence of additional circumstances warranting such an inference.[9]

Understandably, the courts have always been concerned that the jury may draw an unwarranted inference from such evidence. This has imposed on the trial judge the duty of determining in advance whether there is sufficient evidence from which a jury might reasonably conclude

---

[6] *Chambers*, [1990] 6 W.W.R. 554, 119 N.R. 321, [1990] 2 S.C.R. 1293, 59 C.C.C. (3d) 321, 80 C.R. (3d) 235, 49 B.C.L.R. (2d) 299, 1990 CarswellBC 217, 1990 CarswellBC 761.
[7] *Baron* (1976), 14 O.R. (2d) 173, 31 C.C.C. (2d) 525, 73 D.L.R. (3d) 213 (C.A.).
[8] *Christie*, [1914] A.C. 545, 24 Cox C.C. 249 (H.L.).
[9] *Supra*, note 7, at (C.C.C.) p. 538.

that the accused's conducted amounted to an acknowledgment of responsibility.[10] As Chief Justice MacKeigan observed in *Thompson*:[11]

> Where an accused has denied a statement such as this, it is for the trial Judge on the *voir dire* to consider whether there is any evidence in the accused's words, conduct or demeanour from which a jury could conclude that the accused, despite words of denial, really acknowledged or admitted the truth of statement. If there is no such evidence, the statement so denied should not go to the jury.

The real difficulty arises where the accused's response is ambiguous and open to interpretation. Should the trial judge refuse to admit the accused's response, or should he admit it and leave it to the jury to draw their own conclusions? One of the earliest decision of the Ontario Court of Appeal in *Fargnoli*[12] offered little guidance. There the accused was arrested for indecently assaulting his daughter and, when asked whether he wished to say anything, replied, "You got it all there ... there is nothing more for me to say about it". Two members of the Ontario Court of Appeal held that the response amounted to an acceptance of the facts while the third dissented, holding that the response was ambiguous and ought not to have been admitted.

Nevertheless, it seems to be now accepted that it is the responsibility of the trial judge to determine whether, as a matter of law, the response of an accused to an accusation of guilt could reasonably be interpreted as an admission of guilt. If it could, then the judge must leave the issue to be decided by the jury. On the other hand, if there is some concern that its probative force is greatly outweighed by its prejudicial character, then such evidence should not be admitted.[13]

4. THE MEANING OF VOLUNTARY

A strict application of the *Ibrahim* rule means that no statement can be admitted if it was obtained as a result of a either fear of prejudice induced (threat) or hope of advantage held out (promise of favour) by a person in authority. The test that the trial judge must apply is an objective

---

[10] *Hebert*, 47 B.C.L.R. (2d) 1, [1990] 2 S.C.R. 151, 77 C.R. (3d) 145, [1990] 5 W.W.R. 1, 57 C.C.C. (3d) 1, 110 N.R. 1, 49 C.R.R. 114, 1990 CarswellBC 139 and *Warner*, 21 O.R. (3d) 136, 75 O.A.C. 288, 94 C.C.C. (3d) 540, 1994 CarswellOnt 159 (C.A.).

[11] 26 C.R.N.S. 144, 16 C.C.C. (2d) 374, 1974 CarswellNS 5 (C.A.), at (C.C.C.) p. 380.

[12] (1957), 25 C.R. 310, 117 C.C.C. 359, 1957 CarswellOnt 3 (S.C.C.).

[13] *Moore*, 15 C.C.C. (3d) 541, 5 O.A.C. 51, 1984 CarswellOnt 1178 (C.A.), leave to appeal refused, 15 C.C.C. (3d) 541n, 7 O.A.C. 320, [1985] 1 S.C.R. x .

one. What must be decided is the effect that the threat or promise of favour by the police, viewed objectively, could be expected to have on the ordinary citizen if he or she were accused of an offence.

The authorities do not require that the threat be openly made. Words or conduct which would lead an accused to believe that, unless a confession is made, violence will be used will amount to threat. Even a veiled promise of punishment will amount to a threat. Indeed, threats or promises need not be aimed directly at the suspect for them to have a coercive effect.[14] However, they must be of such a nature that when considered in the light of the relationship between the person and the accused, and all of the surrounding circumstances of the confession, it would tend to induce an accused to make an untrue statement. Thus, in considering the effect of the words or conduct of the person in authority on the accused, the trial judge must examine all of the surrounding circumstances that led to the making of the statement.

Words such as "it would be better for you if you told us what happened", or "you will be arrested if you do not tell us where the stolen goods are", or "you had better tell us the truth", or "it is necessary to give an explanation" in the past have been held to be a threat; whereas words such as "be sure to tell the truth" and "be a good girl and tell the truth" have been held not to constitute a threat. The reason is that the first group of words are considered an expression of compulsion or obligation to speak, whereas the second are not. The dividing line, however, is often difficult to draw.[15]

Recently, the Supreme Court has said that subtle veiled threats, although implying that dire consequences may flow from a refusal to talk, should not automatically require exclusion.[16] The trial judge is required to carefully examine the entire context in which the specific words are used and ask whether there is a reasonable doubt that the resulting confession was voluntary.

The background of the accused may also be a relevant factor. Someone who has never been involved with the police before may be so terrified by the predicament in which he finds himself that he may be more influenced by suggestions made by a police officer than an experienced criminal would be.

---

[14] *Oickle*, 2000 SCC 38, 36 C.R. (5th) 129, 147 C.C.C. (3d) 321, 190 D.L.R. (4th) 257, 259 N.R. 227, [2000] 2 S.C.R. 3, 187 N.S.R. (2d) 201, 585 A.P.R. 201, 2000 CarswellNS 257, 2000 CarswellNS 258, [2000] S.C.J. No. 38.
[15] See *S. (S.L.)*, 22 C.R. (5th) 71, 228 A.R. 361, 188 W.A.C. 361, 132 C.C.C. (3d) 146, 1999 CarswellAlta 88, [1999] A.J. No. 69 (C.A.).
[16] *Oickle, supra,* note 14.

A promise of favour or an inducement is anything that gives the accused some hope or expectation with respect to the charge or contemplated charge, or some other matter. That "some other matter" could be another charge against the accused or a charge against someone whom the accused might wish to help, such as his wife or child, or a close friend.[17] A promise of favour or inducement could result, not only from the police officer's words, but also from a combination of his words and those of the accused. For example, a police officer's affirmative reply to a question by an accused whether he would be released "if I give a statement" could constitute an inducement. Indeed, any explicit offer of assistance by a police officer to procure lenient treatment in return for a confession will warrant exclusion in all but exceptional cases.[18] Similarly, an offer of psychiatric assistance or other counselling for the suspect in exchange for a confession is clearly an inducement, although not as strong as an offer of leniency, and may be excluded. However, the officer must be in a position to deliver on the offer. Thus, moral or spiritual inducements that produce a confession will generally not be excluded since the inducement offered is not in the control of the officer. Similarly, a statement by the officer that convinces the suspect that he will feel better if he confesses will not be excluded since the officer has not offered anything.[19]

For forty years after *Ibrahim*, the courts applied the rule so strictly that exclusion occurred only where there was an actual threat or inducement. However, in 1956, the Supreme Court of Canada in *Fitton*,[20] finally recognized the role which compulsion or oppression could play in causing someone to make a statement. Mr. Justice Rand expressed it this way:

> The rule on the admission of confession ... at times presents difficulty of application because its terms tend to conceal underlying considerations material to a determination. The cases of torture, actual or threatened, or of unabashed promises are clear; perplexity arises when more subtle elements must be evaluated. The strength of mind and will of the accused, the influence of custody or its surroundings, the effect of questions or of conversation, all call for delicacy in appreciation of the part they have played behind the admission, and to enable a court to decide whether what was said was freely and voluntarily said, that is, was free from the influence of hope or fear aroused by them.[21]

---

[17] *Ibid.*
[18] *Ibid.*
[19] *Ibid.*
[20] [1956] S.C.R. 958, 116 C.C.C. 1, 24 C.R. 371, 6 D.L.R. (2d) 529, 1956 CarswellOnt 26.
[21] *Ibid.,* at (C.C.C.) p. 5.

This passage recognizes that oppressive conditions may cause some persons to feel compelled to make a confession. Oppressive conditions can sap a person's free will, which is a necessary element of a voluntary confession, and cause the suspect to confess in order to escape those conditions. Oppressive conditions can also overbear a suspect's will to the point that he or she comes to doubt their own memory, believe the relentless accusations made by the police and give an induced confession.[22] Since each individual has a unique psychological make-up, the court must closely examine all of the circumstances surrounding the taking of the statement, such as the length of the period of questioning, the length of time intervening between periods of questioning, whether the accused was given proper refreshment, and the individual characteristics of the accused.[23]

As has been noted:

> What may be oppressive as regards a child, an invalid or an old man or somebody inexperienced in the ways of this world may turn out not to be oppressive when one finds that the accused person is a tough character and an experienced man of the world.[24]

It is important to observe at this stage that the focus of the traditional *Ibrahim* Rule was not upon any conscious choice of an accused whether to speak or not to speak to the police; his or her rights could be viewed only negatively in the sense that there was a right not to be tortured or coerced into making a statement by threats or promises held out by a person who was, and whom the accused believed was, a person in authority. In 1979, however, the Supreme Court of Canada recognized for the first time that the focus should also be on the accused's state of mind. In *Ward*,[25] Mr. Justice Spence wrote:

> In my view, there is a further investigation of whether the statements were freely and voluntarily made even if no hope of advantage or fear of prejudice could be found in consideration of the mental condition of the accused at the time he made the statements *to determine whether or not the statements represented the operating mind of the accused.*[26]

---

22 *Oickle, supra,* note 14.
23 *Hoilett,* 121 O.A.C. 391, 136 C.C.C. (3d) 449, 26 C.R. (5th) 332, 1999 CarswellOnt 1886 (C.A.).
24 Note to *Martin v. Priestley* (1967), 51 Cr. App. R. 1.
25 [1979] 2 S.C.R. 30, 25 N.R. 514, 14 A.R. 412, [1979] 2 W.W.R. 193, 44 C.C.C. (2d) 498, 94 D.L.R. (3d) 18, 7 C.R. (3d) 153 (Eng.), 10 C.R. (3d) 289 (Fr.), 1979 CarswellAlta 192.
26 *Ibid.*, at (C.C.C.) p. 506.

Ward, who had been involved in a single car collision, was found lying unconscious outside his vehicle. His lady friend was found dead beside him. After being revived by mouth-to-mouth resuscitation at the scene of the accident, Ward was questioned by police officers but denied driving the vehicle. Thirty minutes later and again some five or six hours later at the hospital, he was questioned again and this time admitted driving the vehicle. He was charged with criminal negligence.

On the *voir dire*, Ward said that he could not remember anything from the time that he was in a hotel some hours before the accident until the afternoon or evening following the accident. His doctor testified that he could answer simple questions but was unable to tell them what happened. The Court held that the trial judge was correct in excluding Ward's answers to the police officers because they did not represent his "operating mind".

A similar result was reached in *Horvath*.[27] Horvath, a youth of 17, was charged with the murder of his mother. On the evening of his arrest, he was interrogated and cross-examined by two police officers for two and one-half hours, but the statement he gave contained nothing inculpatory. The next day, he was interviewed by another officer, a skilled interrogator, for four hours except for three brief intervals. Horvath, who was left alone during those three intervals, was observed by the officer reflecting aloud in what were called "monologues" or "soliloquies". During the second monologue, he admitted killing his mother and repeated the confession to the officer. In the third monologue, he asked his mother's forgiveness for having disclosed the incident. He then signed a confession.

The trial judge rejected the confession after accepting the opinion of a psychiatrist that Horvath had been in a hypnotic state for a large part of the interview before he signed the confession. In a split decision, the Supreme Court held that the confession, which had followed directly from the earlier statement, and which was made while under hypnosis, was not voluntary because it had been induced by conditions created earlier.

In 1986, the importance of the accused's subjective state of mind was expanded into a further consideration: whether the accused was aware of what was at stake in making any statement. In *Clarkson*,[28] the

---

[27] [1979] 2 S.C.R. 376, 7 C.R. (3d) 97, 25 N.R. 537, 44 C.C.C. (2d) 385, [1979] 3 W.W.R. 1, 93 D.L.R. (3d) 1, 11 C.R. (3d) 206 (Fr.), 1979 CarswellBC 667.

[28] [1986] 1 S.C.R. 383, 26 D.L.R. (4th) 493, 66 N.R. 114, 69 N.B.R. (2d) 40, 25 C.C.C. (3d) 207, 50 C.R. (3d) 289, 19 C.R.R. 209, 177 A.P.R. 40, 1986 CarswellNB 14, 1986 CarswellNB 104.

accused, while intoxicated, had confessed to the police to murdering her husband. The trial judge had excluded the statement because he was not satisfied that the accused was "aware of the consequences" of making the statement. The Supreme Court agreed that the judge was correct in excluding the confession, but only two of the seven members of the Court agreed with his reasons. Although the rest found that the accused had been deprived of her right to counsel, none specifically rejected the "awareness of the consequences" test. They held that it was up to the trial judge, in his or her unique position of hearing all of the witnesses, to decide that issue by balancing the probative value of the evidence in the light of the possible prejudice to the accused.

The "awareness of the consequences" test means that a statement made by an accused is not admissible if the accused is not aware that he or she is making a statement that may be used against him or her. *Clarkson* was a straightforward case involving an intoxicated accused, who, because of her condition, was found by the trial judge not to be aware of the consequences of making a statement. Should the rule be limited to persons in similar situations, such as the intoxicated or the mentally challenged or should it be extended to persons of normal cognitive ability who may not appreciate the consequences of speaking to the police?

In a series of cases since *Clarkson*, the Supreme Court has said that the "awareness of the consequences" test should only be extended to persons of limited cognitive ability. The first, *Hebert*,[29] involved an accused who had refused to give a statement to the police after he had consulted counsel, but who later unknowingly confessed to an under-cover police officer who had been placed in his cell. Madam Justice McLachlin, who delivered the majority judgment of the Court, held that the confession to the undercover officer should be excluded because the accused's right to counsel had been infringed. In other words, by placing an undercover officer in his cell, the accused's right to remain silent, which is protected as a fundamental principle of justice under section 7 of the *Canadian Charter of Rights and Freedoms*, had been breached. This was because "the guarantee of the right to counsel confirms that the essence of the right is the accused's freedom to choose whether to make a statement or not".

McLachlin J., however, went on to stress that:

---

[29]   47 B.C.L.R. (2d) 1, [1990] 2 S.C.R. 151, 77 C.R. (3d) 145, [1990] 5 W.W.R. 1, 57 C.C.C. (3d) 1, 110 N.R. 1, 49 C.R.R. 114, 1990 CarswellBC 139.

I should not be taken as suggesting that the right to make an informed choice whether to speak to the authorities or to remain silent necessitates *a particular state of knowledge on the suspect's part over and above the basic requirement that he possess an operating mind.* The Charter does not place on the authorities and the courts *the impossible task of subjectively gauging whether the suspect appreciates the situation and the alternatives.* Rather, it seeks to ensure that the suspect is in a position to make an informed choice by giving him the right to counsel. The guarantee of the right to counsel in the Charter suggests that the suspect must have the right to choose whether to speak to the police or not, but it equally suggests that the test for whether that choice has been violated is essentially objective. [Emphasis added.][30]

In other words, the mental element required by an accused before a confession will be accepted is that of an "operating mind", the *Horvath* and *Ward* test. The test is essentially an objective one with a limited subjective element. The *Clarkson* case was only referred to in her judgment in the context of the waiver of the right to silence.

The second case, *Evans*,[31] reaffirmed that distinction. The *Evans* case involved a youth of subnormal intelligence who was charged with the brutal murder of two women. The police had suspected that the accused's older brother was involved in the killings and had arrested the accused on a charge of trafficking in marijuana, in the hope that he would be able to provide evidence against his brother. When advised of his right to counsel and asked if he understood his rights, the accused said "no". During the course of his interrogation by the police, the accused became the prime suspect in the murders, but was not told that he was being detained for murder nor advised again of his right to counsel. The Court found that the statements taken from the accused had been improperly admitted by the trial judge because the accused's right to counsel had been infringed. McLachlin J., who again delivered the majority view, this time held:

In view of the appellant's subnormal mental capacity and the circumstances surrounding his arrest — the fact that no attempt was made to explain his rights to him after he indicated that he did not understand them, as well as the fact that he was subjected to a day of aggressive and at times deceptive interrogation which apparently left him feeling as if he had "no choice" but to confess — *I am not satisfied that he appreciated the consequences of making the written statement and thereby waiving his right to counsel* or, to put it another way, that he waived his right "with full knowledge of the rights

---

[30] *Ibid.,* at (C.R.) p. 183.
[31] 4 C.R. (4th) 144, [1991] 1 S.C.R. 869, 63 C.C.C. (3d) 289, 124 N.R. 278, 3 C.R.R. (2d) 315, 1991 CarswellBC 918.

> the procedure was enacted to protect and of the effect the waiver will have on those rights in the process. [Emphasis added.][32]

In other words, because of his subnormal mental capacity, the test was "an appreciation of the consequences of making the statement". This time, the *Clarkson* case was cited as authority.

In *Hebert* and *Evans*, the Supreme Court drew a distinction between a person with normal mental faculties and a person who is mentally incapacitated because of an inherited condition or one induced by alcohol (and possibly drugs). In the former, the threshold test for voluntariness is an operating mind, that is, one who understands what he or she is saying. In the latter, the threshold test appears to be higher. It includes not only one who understands what he or she is saying, but one who also appreciates that what he or she is saying may be used against them.

In *Whittle*,[33] the Supreme Court re-affirmed its earlier decision in *Hebert*. It adopted a dual test in determining whether a confession should be admitted. The first test requires a focus on the cognitive ability of the accused. The requirement should be no more than "an operating mind". The "operating mind" test includes:

> ... a limited mental component which requires that the accused have sufficient cognitive capacity to understand what he is saying and what is said. This includes the ability to understand that the evidence can be used against the accused.
>
> The same standard applies with respect to the right to silence in determining whether the accused has the mental capacity to make an active choice.
>
> In exercising the right to counsel or waiving the right, the accused must possess the limited cognitive capacity required for fitness to stand trial. The accused must be capable of communicating with counsel to instruct counsel, and understand the function of counsel and that he or she can dispense with counsel even if this is not in the accused's best interests. It is not necessary that the accused possess analytical ability. The level of cognitive ability is the same as that required with respect to the confession rule and the right to silence. The accused must have the mental capacity of an operating mind as outlined above.

The judge is not required to determine whether the accused was capable of making a good or a wise choice, or one that is in his best interests when he chooses to speak. In other words, there is no require-

---

[32]   *Ibid.,* at (C.R.) p. 164.
[33]   32 C.R. (4th) 1, 170 N.R. 16, 73 O.A.C. 201, 92 C.C.C. (3d) 11, [1994] 2 S.C.R. 914, 23 C.R.R. (2d) 6, 116 D.L.R. (4th) 416, 1994 CarswellOnt 91, 1994 CarswellOnt 1163.

ment that the accused be capable of understanding the consequences of making a statement.[34]

Once the subjective mental capacity of the accused is established, the trial judge must turn his or her attention to the second part of the test: the effect of police conduct on the accused's decision to speak. Here the issue for the judge is whether the actions of the police deprived the accused of making an effective choice by reason of coercion, trickery or misinformation or lack of information. If the judge has any doubt on the point, then the statement should not be admitted.

The question of depriving an accused of an effective choice raises the question of whether the police may, during the interrogation process, create an "atmosphere of oppression" that would deprive an accused of the effective choice whether to speak or not to speak. In *Paternak*,[35] Mr. Justice Kerans noted that there can be an atmosphere of oppression and yet no loss of cognitive ability. He observed:

> For an otherwise healthy and mature human to be deprived of an effective choice, I am inclined to the view that the influence must be so overbearing that it can be said that the detainee has lost any meaningfully independent ability to choose to remain silent, and has become a mere tool in the hands of the police. That can happen, of course. And sometimes a judge will have a doubt whether it happened, and shall refuse to admit the statement.
>
> The contextual question about effective choice will be whether a healthy and mature detainee who is reluctant to speak is deprived of effective choice when a police officer persuades him to change his mind. On the one hand, we must in this age take notice of the reality of modern torture, where a person can be "brainwashed" or totally broken by an interrogation. On the other hand, we should take notice also that all human communication can and usually does involve a degree of influence. The opinion of the hearer can be influenced in many ways, sometimes very subtly, by what the speaker says or does. Moreover, some persons are more susceptible to influence than others. In my view the Supreme Court did not intend to forbid an agent of the state even to attempt to influence the detainee to speak. On the contrary, if that were the rule, one may as well forbid the admission of *any* statements by detainees because the mere fact of detention and interrogation can influence one to speak. In other words, if there is to be absolutely no influence, there must be no communication.[36]

On further appeal to the Supreme Court,[37] the decision of the trial judge excluding the statement was restored. The Court focused on the

---

[34] *Oickle, supra,* note 14.
[35] 33 Alta. L.R. (3d) 71, 42 C.R. (4th) 292, 174 A.R. 129, 102 W.A.C. 129, 101 C.C.C. (3d) 452, 1995 CarswellAlta 281, [1995] A.J. No. 795 (C.A.).
[36] *Ibid.,* at (C.R.) p. 301.
[37] 2 C.R. (5th) 119, 110 C.C.C. (3d) 382, [1996] 3 S.C.R. 607, 187 A.R. 395, 127 W.A.C.

failure of the police to re-warn the accused concerning his right to counsel when there was a substantial change in his jeopardy and said that this was a violation of his right to counsel. It failed to deal with the question whether there can be aggressive questioning of the accused once the officer is satisfied that the accused has an operating mind and the accused has agreed to be questioned after being given his right to counsel.

Generally, the authorities do not suggest that the police should be prohibited from questioning an accused beyond the traditional "tell us what happened". Questions that are designed to influence the accused to speak freely about his or her possible involvement in the crime are not prohibited once the accused has chosen to speak. The central issue in *Hebert* and *Whittle*, and indeed, in *Paternak*, was whether the police deprived the accused of making an effective choice to speak or not to speak by reason of coercion, trickery or misinformation or lack of information. The focus of those cases was the denial of an accused's constitutional right to counsel. So long as the accused has been advised of his right to counsel and, in the absence of an indication that he is unable to make an effective choice whether or not to speak, there does not seem to be a prohibition against aggressive questioning by the police. The degree and extent of that aggressive questioning has, unfortunately, yet to be clearly defined by the Supreme Court.

5. PERSONS IN AUTHORITY

The *Ibrahim* rule said that a confession of an accused is not admissible unless it is voluntary in the sense that it was not obtained by a threat or promise held out by "a person in authority". If the person is not someone in authority, then the rule does not apply and the confession will be admissible.

The general rule is that a person in authority includes anyone who has authority or control over the accused or over the proceedings or prosecution against him.[38] In the past, people such as police officers, jailers or guards, magistrates or judges, prosecutors, informants, employers and complainants have been regarded as persons in authority.

395, 203 N.R. 250, 44 Alta. L.R. (3d) 201, 1996 CarswellAlta 948, 1996 CarswellAlta 949.

[38]   *Todd* (1901), 4 C.C.C. 514, 13 Man. R. 364 (K.B.).

In *B. (A.)*,[39] Mr. Justice Cory reviewed a number of authorities and set out the following principles:

1.   As a general rule, a person in authority is someone engaged in the *arrest, detention, examination or prosecution* of the accused; the word "examination" refers to interrogation by police officers, detention or security guards and members of the Crown Attorney's office.
2.   In some circumstances, the complainant in a criminal prosecution may be considered to be a person in authority.
3.   The parent of an infant who is the injured party or a complainant in a criminal prosecution may be a person in authority, depending upon the factual background.[40] where the fathers of the two victims confronted the accused with their children's complaints and held a knife to his throat.
4.   An inducement given by one who is not a person in authority, but made in the presence of persons in authority, may be deemed to have been given by a person in authority; in other words, a person not in authority is clothed with that authority by the presence of those in authority.

On the other hand, persons such as physicians, surgeons and psychiatrists, the father or wife of the accused, or a friend, have been held not to be persons in authority. Nevertheless, in some instances, someone such as a doctor or a psychiatrist who is called in by the Crown to examine the accused may be considered a person in authority if he or she pursues an active role in questioning the accused for the purpose of obtaining an admission or confession. Similarly, section 672.21(2) of the *Criminal Code* dealing with an accused in respect of whom a verdict of not criminally responsible on account of mental disorder has been rendered, gives an accused protection from admission into evidence of any statement made by the accused "during the course and for the purpose of an assessment or treatment directed by a disposition, to the person specified in the assessment order or disposition, or to anyone acting under that person's direction".[41]

---

[39]   13 O.A.C. 68, 50 C.R. (3d) 247, 26 C.C.C. (3d) 17, 1986 CarswellOnt 100 (C.A.), leave to appeal refused, 26 C.C.C. (3d) 17n, [1986] 1 S.C.R. v, 50 C.R. (3d) xxv.
[40]   See *Wells*, 230 N.R. 183, 127 C.C.C. (3d) 500, 163 D.L.R. (4th) 628, 18 C.R. (5th) 181, 112 B.C.A.C. 101, 182 W.A.C. 101, [1998] 2 S.C.R. 517, 57 B.C.L.R. (3d) 104, [1999] 5 W.W.R. 331, 1998 CarswellBC 1931, 1998 CarswellBC 1932.
[41]   *G. (B.)*, 240 N.R. 260, 24 C.R. (5th) 266, 135 C.C.C. (3d) 303, 174 D.L.R. (4th) 301, 63

For a long time, a perplexing question was whether a subjective or an objective test should be used in determining if the person was someone "in authority". In other words, was it enough that the person was someone in authority or was it necessary for the accused to believe as well that he or she was a person in authority? One would have thought that the answer was self-evident, at least in the case of an inducement. How can a person be affected by an inducement unless he or she believes that the person has the ability to make good on a promise? However, the case of a threat or a beating would be another matter. Here a confession would be rejected by a trial judge in exercise of his or her discretionary power to prevent the administration of justice from being brought into disrepute, rather than from the rules relating to persons in authority.

Nevertheless, that question was never settled until the decision of the Supreme Court of Canada in *Rothman*.[42] There the court held that the test was a subjective one. The real issue was whether the accused thought that the person to whom he confessed could either make good his promise or carry out his threats. Thus, if the accused confessed to someone such as an undercover officer, then that officer was not a person in authority even though he might be, from a purely objective point of view, considered to be in a position of undoubted authority.

The rule is that if a statement is made to someone who is not ordinarily engaged in the arrest, detention, examination or prosecution of an accused person, there is a duty upon the defence to raise before the trial judge the issue of the legal admissibility of a confession to that person and request a *voir dire*. In other words, in the absence of a conventional authority figure at the time when the inculpatory statement was made, the trial judge is not required to hold a *voir dire*. The defence must put the judge on notice and request a *voir dire*.[43]

On the *voir dire*, the accused will have the evidential burden of demonstrating that there is a valid issue for consideration. If the accused meets the burden, the Crown will then have the persuasive burden of demonstrating beyond a reasonable doubt that the receiver of the statement was not a person in authority. If the trial judge finds that the receiver

---

C.R.R. (2d) 272, [1999] 2 S.C.R. 475, 1999 CarswellQue 1204, 1999 CarswellQue 1205, [1999] S.C.J. No. 29.

[42]   [1981] 1 S.C.R. 640, 59 C.C.C. (2d) 30, 20 C.R. (3d) 97, 121 D.L.R. (3d) 578, 35 N.R. 485, 1981 CarswellOnt 43, 1981 CarswellOnt 611.

[43]   *Hodgson*, 230 N.R. 1, 127 C.C.C. (3d) 449, 163 D.L.R. (4th) 577, 18 C.R. (5th) 135, 113 O.A.C. 97, [1998] 2 S.C.R. 449, 1998 CarswellOnt 3417, 1998 CarswellOnt 3418, [1998] S.C.J. No. 66; *Wells*, *supra*, note 40.

of the statement was a person in authority, then the Crown will be required to establish beyond a reasonable doubt that the statement was made voluntarily.[44]

Generally, it is only the accused who can know that the statement was made to someone regarded by the accused as a person in authority. However, if the evidence viewed objectively indicates that the issue should be explored on a *voir dire*, then the trial judge has the duty to raise the matter and direct a *voir dire*.[45] Evidence that indicates a close connection between the receiver of the statement and the authorities should alert the trial judge to the need to hold a *voir dire*. In such instances, the trial judge is required to inquire of the defence whether it is prepared to discharge its evidential burden on the person in authority issue or whether it waives a *voir dire*.

6. THE RIGHT TO COUNSEL

Section 10 of the *Charter of Rights and Freedoms* guarantees everyone the right ... on arrest or detention:

(a) to be informed promptly of the reasons therefore;
(b) to retain and instruct counsel without delay and be informed of that right...

Whenever a person is detained or arrested, he or she must be informed of his or her right to retain and instruct counsel. Except in the case of a youthful offender, the mentally or physically infirm, and possibly someone who has had no experience with the police, that duty is simply to advise the detainee of his or her right to counsel and to provide the opportunity to contact a lawyer if he or she requests. The police are not required to satisfy the trial judge that the detained or arrested person understood his or her rights, unless there are circumstances that would lead him or her to believe otherwise. It is generally presumed that a person understands the meaning of the right to counsel unless that person can establish otherwise.[46]

Nevertheless, the police must advise the detainee in language that the detainee can understand, exactly what the right to counsel means. In other words, there is an obligation on the arresting officer to advise the detainee of the right to counsel in language that makes that right mean-

---

[44] *Hodgson, ibid.*

[45] *Hodgson, ibid.*; *Wells supra*, note 40.

[46] *Anderson*, 45 O.R. (2d) 225, 10 C.C.C. (3d) 417, 39 C.R. (3d) 193, 7 D.L.R. (4th) 306, 2 O.A.C. 258, 9 C.R.R. 161, 1984 CarswellOnt 45 (C.A.).

ingful and comprehensible to him.[47] Moreover, the detainee should be advised of the right to counsel when he or she is capable of understanding and appreciating that right. For example, if the detainee is ill or intoxicated, then the officer has an obligation to wait until he or she is feeling better or has sobered up.[48]

Once a person, who has been advised of his right to counsel, indicates that he wishes to exercise that right, all questioning must stop until that request is fulfilled.[49] There is also an obligation on the police to assist the detainee to contact his counsel so that he can exercise that right. This includes the duty to inform the detainee of the existence and availability of duty counsel and legal aid in the jurisdiction, particularly if he expresses a concern that his inability to afford a lawyer is an impediment to the exercise of the right to counsel.[50] Since duty counsel and legal aid are an intrinsic part of the practice of criminal law in Canada, this duty requires the police to provide information about access to counsel free of charge where an accused meets the prescribed financial criteria set by provincial Legal Aid. This duty also requires the police to provide information about access to duty counsel providing immediate, although temporary, legal advice, irrespective of financial status, as to services actually available within the jurisdiction.[51]

Although a detainee must be given a reasonable opportunity to exercise the right to counsel, that right is not an absolute one. It must be exercised with reasonable diligence.[52] An accused who requests the right to contact counsel cannot indefinitely delay consulting with him. He

---

[47] *Vanstaceghem*, 48 M.V.R. 311, 58 C.R. (3d) 121, 21 O.A.C. 210, 36 C.C.C. (3d) 142, 1987 CarswellOnt 100 (C.A.).

[48] *Clarkson*, [1986] 1 S.C.R. 383, 26 D.L.R. (4th) 493, 66 N.R. 114, 69 N.B.R. (2d) 40, 25 C.C.C. (3d) 207, 50 C.R. (3d) 289, 19 C.R.R. 209, 177 A.P.R. 40, 1986 CarswellNB 14, 1986 CarswellNB 104.

[49] *Manninen*, 76 N.R. 198, 38 C.R.R. 37, 58 C.R. (3d) 97, 21 O.A.C. 192, 34 C.C.C. (3d) 385, [1987] 1 S.C.R. 1233, 41 D.L.R. (4th) 301, 61 O.R. (2d) 736 (note), 1987 CarswellOnt 967.

[50] *Brydges*, [1990] 2 W.W.R. 220, 46 C.R.R. 236, [1990] 1 S.C.R. 190, 103 N.R. 282, 71 Alta. L.R. (2d) 145, 104 A.R. 124, 53 C.C.C. (3d) 330, 74 C.R. (3d) 129, 1990 CarswellAlta 3, 1990 CarswellAlta 648.

[51] *Prosper*, 33 C.R. (4th) 85, 118 D.L.R. (4th) 154, 92 C.C.C. (3d) 353, 133 N.S.R. (2d) 321, 380 A.P.R. 321, 172 N.R. 161, 6 M.V.R. (3d) 181, [1994] 3 S.C.R. 236, 23 C.R.R. (2d) 239, 1994 CarswellNS 25, 1994 CarswellNS 438; *Harper*, 33 C.R. (4th) 61, 6 M.V.R. (3d) 138, 118 D.L.R. (4th) 312, 172 N.R. 91, 92 C.C.C. (3d) 423, 97 Man. R. (2d) 1, 79 W.A.C. 1, [1994] 3 S.C.R. 343, 23 C.R.R. (2d) 291, 1994 CarswellMan 8, 1994 CarswellMan 381; *Pozniak*, 33 C.R. (4th) 49, 23 C.R.R. (2d) 303, [1994] 3 S.C.R. 310, 74 O.A.C. 232, 118 D.L.R. (4th) 205, 92 C.C.C. (3d) 472, 172 N.R. 72, 6 M.V.R. (3d) 113, 19 O.R. (3d) 802 (note), 1994 CarswellOnt 101, 1994 CarswellOnt 1165.

[52] *Leclair*, 91 N.R. 81, [1989] 1 S.C.R. 3, 31 O.A.C. 321, 46 C.C.C. (3d) 129, 67 C.R. (3d) 209, 37 C.R.R. 369, 1989 CarswellOnt 67, 1989 CarswellOnt 953.

must take reasonable steps to try to contact his lawyer to obtain advice.[53] If he fails to do so, then the police may proceed to question him.[54]

A person may waive his right to counsel and that waiver need not be in writing. However, the onus of establishing that the accused waived his right to counsel with full knowledge of the consequences of doing so, lies upon the prosecution. That may in some instances be onerous if it appears that the accused does not have full mental faculties, such as an accused who may be mentally ill, or is under the influence of drugs or alcohol.[55] In *Clarkson*, the Supreme Court of Canada held:

> While this constitutional guarantee cannot be forced upon an unwilling ac-cused, any voluntary waiver in order to be valid and effective must be prem-ised on a true appreciation of the consequences of giving up the right.[56]

The Supreme Court, however, seems to have drawn a distinction between mental illness or drunkenness that deprives a person of the ability to appreciate the consequences of giving up the right to counsel and a person who simply has limited cognitive ability. In *Whittle*,[57] the Court said that there is no obligation upon the Crown to prove that a person, who has the limited cognitive capacity to understand the legal process that he or she is facing and the right to communicate with counsel, is capable of making a rational decision that is personally beneficial:

> ...provided the accused possesses this limited capacity, it is not necessary that he or she be capable of exercising analytical reasoning in making a choice to accept the advice of counsellor in coming to a decision that best serves her interests.[58]

The Court concluded:

> In exercising the right to counsel or waiving the right, the accused must possess the limited cognitive capacity required for fitness to stand trial. The

---

[53] *Bartle*, 33 C.R. (4th) 1, 23 C.R.R. (2d) 193, [1994] 3 S.C.R. 173, 172 N.R. 1, 92 C.C.C. (3d) 289, 74 O.A.C. 161, 118 D.L.R. (4th) 83, 6 M.V.R. (3d) 1, 19 O.R. (3d) 802 (note), 1994 CarswellOnt 100, 1994 CarswellOnt 1164, [1994] S.C.J. No. 74.

[54] *Tremblay*, [1987] 2 S.C.R. 435, 45 D.L.R. (4th) 445, 79 N.R. 153, 25 O.A.C. 93, 37 C.C.C. (3d) 565, 60 C.R. (3d) 59, 32 C.R.R. 381, 2 M.V.R. (2d) 289, 1987 CarswellOnt 111, 1987 CarswellOnt 972.

[55] *Clarkson, supra*, note 48.

[56] *Ibid.,* at (C.R.) p. 303.

[57] 32 C.R. (4th) 1, 170 N.R. 16, 73 O.A.C. 201, 92 C.C.C. (3d) 11, [1994] 2 S.C.R. 914, 23 C.R.R. (2d) 6, 116 D.L.R. (4th) 416, 1994 CarswellOnt 91, 1994 CarswellOnt 1163.

[58] *Ibid.,* at (C.R.) p. 16.

accused must be capable of communicating with counsel to instruct counsel, and understand the function of counsel and that he or she can dispense with counsel even if this is not in the accused's best interests. It is not necessary that the accused possess analytical ability. The level of cognitive ability is the same as that required with respect to the confession rule and the right to silence. The accused must have the mental capacity of an operating mind as outlined above.[59]

The police are not required to stop all questioning of an accused after he has consulted with his lawyer. They may question him provided he is willing to be questioned.[60] Nor are they are not required to advise his lawyer that they are about to question him because, presumably, if he has consulted with his lawyer, that lawyer has advised him of his right to remain silent. If an accused consents to being questioned after consulting a lawyer, then there is nothing objectionable about the police doing so. However, the prosecution will be required to establish, as in any case where the right to counsel has been waived, that the accused agreed to the interrogation without the presence of his lawyer.

When questioning an accused, the police must not belittle his lawyer with the express goal or effect of undermining the accused's confidence in a relationship with defence counsel.[61] Nor can the police enter into a plea bargain without the participation of counsel unless the accused expressly waives that right.[62] Any plea bargain must be offered either to the accused's counsel, or to the accused while in the presence of his or her counsel, unless the accused has expressly waived the right to counsel. In *Burlingham*, Iacobucci J. for the majority of the Supreme Court noted that section 10(b) of the *Charter* mandates:

...to the extent that the plea bargain is an integral element of the Canadian criminal process, the Crown and its officers engaged in the plea bargaining process must act honourably and forthrightly.[63]

Finally, the police are required to re-advise an accused of his or her right to counsel whenever there is a fundamental and discrete change in the purpose of the investigation. This will arise where the police seek to question the accused about a different and unrelated offence or a

[59] *Ibid.*, at (C.R.) p. 21.
[60] *Hebert*, 47 B.C.L.R. (2d) 1, [1990] 2 S.C.R. 151, 77 C.R. (3d) 145, [1990] 5 W.W.R. 1, 57 C.C.C. (3d) 1, 110 N.R. 1, 49 C.R.R. 114, 1990 CarswellBC 139.
[61] *Burlingham*, 38 C.R. (4th) 265, 97 C.C.C. (3d) 385, 181 N.R. 1, 124 D.L.R. (4th) 7, 58 B.C.A.C. 161, 96 W.A.C. 161, 28 C.R.R. (2d) 244, [1995] 2 S.C.R. 206, 1995 CarswellBC 71, 1995 CarswellBC 639, at (C.R.) p. 280.
[62] *Burlingham, ibid.*, at (C.R.) p. 282.
[63] *Ibid.*

significantly more serious offence than the one contemplated at the time of the warning.[64] The rationale underlying this rule is that an accused cannot exercise the right to counsel in a meaningful way unless he or she knows the extent of the risk of self-incrimination.[65] That obligation will arise even where it is the accused, rather than the police, who initiates the shift in focus of the investigation. However, the obligation to re-advise of the right to counsel will only arise if the officer questioning the accused has knowledge of the other offence and is investigating it. If the officer has no knowledge of the other offence, he or she is entitled to ask exploratory questions to elicit some further information before deciding whether an investigation of the other offence should be under-taken. Once the officer has a realistic indication that the accused might incriminate himself in a different and unrelated offence and that an investigation is warranted, the accused must be re-advised of his right to counsel before pursuing further questioning of that offence.

7. ONUS OF PROOF

If the prosecution seeks to introduce a confession or admission, the trial judge must conduct a *voir dire*, that is a trial within a trial, in the absence of the jury. The *voir dire* may be waived where the defence admits that the statement is voluntary or does not apply to have it excluded on the basis that the accused was denied his or her right to counsel.

The onus of proof will be different depending on whether the issue is voluntariness or the right to counsel. Where the issue is the voluntar-iness of the statement, the onus is upon the Crown to prove that it was given voluntarily by the accused and proof is beyond a reasonable doubt. Where, however, the issue is whether the accused has been denied his or her constitutional right to counsel under the *Charter*, the onus is upon the defence to show firstly, that there was a *right to counsel Charter* breach, and secondly, that the admission of the statement would bring the administration of justice into disrepute. That onus, however, is not as onerous as the one upon the Crown; the defence need only establish both requirements upon a balance of probabilities.

Where the issue is the voluntariness of the statement, the prose-cution will be entitled, on the *voir dire*, to lead evidence of that issue.

[64] *Evans*, 4 C.R. (4th) 144, [1991] 1 S.C.R. 869, 63 C.C.C. (3d) 289, 124 N.R. 278, 3 C.R.R. (2d) 315, 1991 CarswellBC 918.
[65] *Sawatsky*, 9 C.R. (5th) 23, 103 O.A.C. 68, 118 C.C.C. (3d) 17, 150 D.L.R. (4th) 750, 35 O.R. (3d) 767, 47 C.R.R. (2d) 360, 1997 CarswellOnt 2994, [1997] O.J. No. 3561 (C.A.).

The defence is entitled to cross-examine the prosecution witnesses and to call witnesses on behalf of the defence, including the accused who may, in turn, be cross-examined by the prosecution. After hearing arguments from both sides, the judge will decide whether the Crown has satisfied the onus of proving that the statement was made voluntarily.

If the accused elects to testify on the *voir dire*, he or she may be cross-examined on the particular issue in dispute, that is, whether the statement is voluntary. In *DeClercq*,[66] the Supreme Court held that the right to cross-examine the accused includes the right to ask him or her whether the confession is true because the answer to that question goes to the issue of credibility. This decision, however, has been strongly criticized because it does "under the guise of 'credibility'... transmute what is initially an inquiry as to 'admissibility' of the confession into an inquisition of an accused".[67]

Moreover, the argument that the prosecution should be allowed to test an accused's credibility, by asking him on a *voir dire* whether the confession is true, is a double-edged sword. If he denies the truth of the statement, is he to be disbelieved simply because he contradicts the testimony of the police? On the other hand, if he admits that the confession is true, is he to be disbelieved when he says that it was obtained by threats or inducement? Logically, an accused who admits that the confession is true is more likely to be telling the truth when he says that the police used violence or inducements to obtain it from him. Moreover, if he does admit that the confession was true, the trial judge is put in the unenviable position of having to decide whether to exclude an important piece of evidence obtained under circumstances which the administration of justice does not condone, even though he knows that the confession is an important piece of evidence with respect to the guilt of the accused.

As indicated above, the onus of proof where the issue is the voluntariness of the statement lies upon the Crown, which must satisfy the court beyond a reasonable doubt that the statement is voluntary in the sense described earlier. This onus is not established by simply calling the interrogating officers to say that the confession was preceded by the usual caution or warning and then have the officers who took the state-

---

[66] [1968] S.C.R. 902, 4 C.R.N.S. 205, [1969] 1 C.C.C. 197, 70 D.L.R. (2d) 530, 1968 CarswellOnt 15.

[67] *Hnedish* (1958), 29 C.R. 347, 1958 CarswellSask 2 (Q.B.) at (C.R.) pp. 349-50. See also *Tessier* (2001), 41 C.R. (5th) 242, 153 C.C.C. (3d) 361, 2001 CarswellNB 120 (N.B. C.A.).

ment say that it was made freely and voluntary.[68] The officer's opinion as to whether the statement was made freely and voluntarily is irrelevant; it is the trial judge who must decide that issue. This means that all of the surrounding circumstances must be examined by the Court to ensure that the statement was made freely and voluntarily. This imposes an obligation upon the Crown to call as witnesses everyone who had anything to do with the accused while he was detained and during his interrogation, or at least make them available for cross-examination.[69]

It is not enough, in order to prove that a statement is voluntary, for a police officer to relate to the court the recorded questions and answers which the officer considered important and relevant to the prosecution. Some authorities have rejected a confession where the police officer who questioned the accused failed to keep a proper record of all of the questions which were put to the accused and the answers given by him.[70] The rationale underlying the exclusion of such statements is that, although the record need not necessarily be verbatim, it should be detailed enough to enable the court to assess all of the circumstances in which the statement was taken. In other words, where the police have editorialized the statement, the court cannot be satisfied that it is the full and correct statement of the accused and that it was given voluntarily. However, this is not a firm and fast rule, and whether the confession will be excluded will depend on all of the surrounding circumstances.[71]

There is no requirement that a confession be admitted only after a *voir dire* where the Crown has established the voluntariness of the statement beyond a reasonable doubt. In *Park*,[72] the Supreme Court of Canada recognized that an accused or his counsel could waive or dispense with the holding of a *voir dire* where the voluntariness of a confession was not in dispute. The decision whether or not to hold a *voir dire* lies with the trial judge. He may, if he is satisfied that no objection is taken to the admission of the statement without a *voir dire* and that voluntariness is not in issue, admit the statement without a *voir dire*.

As indicated earlier, where the issue is the denial of counsel, the onus is upon the defence to establish on a balance of probabilities that

[68] *Sankey*, [1927] S.C.R. 436, 48 C.C.C. 97, [1927] 4 D.L.R. 245, 1927 CarswellBC 104; *Koszulap*, 27 C.R.N.S. 226, 20 C.C.C. (2d) 193, 1974 CarswellOnt 30 (C.A.).
[69] *Thiffault*, [1933] S.C.R. 509, 60 C.C.C. 97, [1933] 3 D.L.R. 591, 1933 CarswellQue 40.
[70] *Belanger* (1978), 40 C.C.C. (2d) 335 (H.C.); *Smith* (1981), 60 C.C.C. (2d) 327, 125 D.L.R. (3d) 181 (S.C.); *Stefiuk*, 11 Man. R. (2d) 411, 1981 CarswellMan 297 (Co. Ct.).
[71] *Arkell*, 54 C.C.C. (2d) 266, 1980 CarswellBC 659 (C.A.).
[72] [1981] 2 S.C.R. 64, 37 N.R. 501, 21 C.R. (3d) 182, 59 C.C.C. (2d) 385, 122 D.L.R. (3d) 1, 1981 CarswellOnt 614.

the statement was obtained in breach of the *Charter*. Once the *Charter* breach is shown, then the defence must go on to establish under section 24(2) of the *Charter* that, "having regard to all the circumstances, the admission of it (the statement) in the proceedings would bring the administration of justice into disrepute". The test is one established in *Collins*,[73] discussed in Chapter 1. There the Supreme Court said that a person's confession, obtained in violation of a *Charter* right, "strikes at one of the fundamental tenets of a fair trial, the right against self-incrimination". This is because the confession did not exist prior to the *Charter* violation; it was conscripted evidence from an accused because of the illegal actions of the police. In such instance, the more serious the offence, the more damaging to the system's repute would be an unfair trial, in which case the evidence should be excluded.

Lamer J. (as he then was) wrote:

> The trial is a key part of the administration of justice, and the fairness of Canadian trials is a major source of the repute of the system ... If the admission of the evidence in some way affects the fairness of the trial, then the admission of the evidence would tend to bring the administration of justice into disrepute and, subject to a consideration of other factors, the evidence generally should be excluded.[74]

8. THE USE OF TRICKS

The question of police trickery is a distinct inquiry, although related to voluntariness.[75] Its more specific objective is maintaining the integrity of the criminal justice system. Here, the inquiry is not concerned with reliability, but with the authorities' conduct as regards reliability. The test is whether the conduct of the police "shocks the community". If proven, then the confessions will be excluded even though the confession is voluntary in the traditional sense and the accused's right to silence has not been infringed.

An issue that has raised a great deal of judicial discussion has been the practice of placing a police officer, disguised in plainclothes and pretending to be a suspect under arrest, in a cell with an accused for the

---

[73] [1987] 3 W.W.R. 699, [1987] 1 S.C.R. 265, 38 D.L.R. (4th) 508, 74 N.R. 276, 13 B.C.L.R. (2d) 1, 33 C.C.C. (3d) 1, 56 C.R. (3d) 193, 28 C.R.R. 122, 1987 CarswellBC 94, 1987 CarswellBC 699.

[74] *Ibid.*, at (C.R.) p. 219.

[75] *Oickle*, 2000 SCC 38, 36 C.R. (5th) 129, 147 C.C.C. (3d) 321, 190 D.L.R. (4th) 257, 259 N.R. 227, [2000] 2 S.C.R. 3, 187 N.S.R. (2d) 201, 585 A.P.R. 201, 2000 CarswellNS 257, 2000 CarswellNS 258, [2000] S.C.J. No. 38.

purpose of actively eliciting incriminating information, or even passively listening to what an accused may say. On the eve of the *Charter*, such conduct was not only accepted, but was regarded as reasonably necessary for the pursuit of shrewd and sophisticated criminals.[76]

Almost a decade of the *Charter* witnessed a reversal of that view. In *Hebert*,[77] it was held that the right to silence had to be defined broadly enough to preserve for a detained person the right to choose whether to speak to the authorities or to remain silent. To permit the authorities to trick a suspect into making a confession to them after he or she has exercised the right of conferring with counsel and has declined to make a statement, would permit the authorities to do indirectly what the *Charter* forbids them from doing directly. To do so would effectively deprive a suspect of that choice.

In *Hebert*, statements made by the accused to a plainclothes officer posing as a suspect under arrest were excluded because the accused had said, after he had consulted counsel, that he did not wish to make a statement. The Court said that the police violated his right to remain silent by using a trick to negate his decision not to speak. However, the Court also stressed that the scope of the right to silence does not go so far as to prohibit the police from obtaining confessions in all cases. The right to silence was subject to the following limits:

1. There is no duty on the police to advise an accused of the right to silence.
2. The police are not prohibited from questioning an accused in the absence of counsel after he has retained counsel. Police persuasion, short of denying the accused the right to choose or of depriving him of an operating mind, does not breach the right to silence.
3. The right to silence applies only after the accused is detained.
4. The right does not affect voluntary statements made to cellmates. The violation of the suspect's rights occurs only when the Crown acts to subvert the suspect's constitutional right to choose not to make a statement to the authorities.
5. A distinction must be made between the use of undercover agents to observe the suspect, and the use of undercover agents to actively elicit information in violation of the suspect's choice to remain silent. The right to silence is not violated where the undercover agents observe rather than actively elicit.

---

[76] *Rothman*, 25 C.R. (3d) 97, 1981 CarswellOnt 93 (S.C.C.).
[77] 47 B.C.L.R. (2d) 1, [1990] 2 S.C.R. 151, 77 C.R. (3d) 145, [1990] 5 W.W.R. 1, 57 C.C.C. (3d) 1, 110 N.R. 1, 49 C.R.R. 114, 1990 CarswellBC 139.

6.   Evidence may, where appropriate, be admitted even where a violation of the accused's right is established. It is only where the court is satisfied that its reception would bring the administration of justice into disrepute that the evidence can be rejected under section 24(2) of the *Charter*. Where the police have acted with due care for the suspect's rights, it is unlikely that the statements they obtain will be held inadmissible.

Cases that have followed *Hebert* have made it clear that not every admission made by an accused to a cellmate will be excluded as violating his right to silence. The right to silence prohibits the police from actively eliciting statements from a detainee so as to infringe his right to silence. It does not apply where a police informer has been placed in the accused's cell to obtain incriminating statements from the accused, so long as he acts independently of the police.[78] Nor will the right to silence prevent the admissibility of a confession made to an undercover officer who is placed in the accused's cell, so long as the undercover officer does not actively elicit information from the accused.[79]

The issue for the trial judge to consider is whether the accused has been deprived of the right to "make a choice" whether to speak or not. In *Whittle*,[80] Mr. Justice Sopinka proposed the test be applied this way:

> Did the action of the police authorities deprive the suspect of making an effective choice by reason of *coercion, trickery* or *misinformation* or the *lack of information*?[81]

9. EXCLUSION OF EVIDENCE OBTAINED BY AN INVOLUNTARY CONFESSION

At common law, a judge had no discretion to exclude evidence because of the manner in which it was obtained.[82] In *St. Lawrence*[83] it

[78]   *Johnston*, 5 C.R. (4th) 185, 64 C.C.C. (3d) 233, 47 O.A.C. 66, 2 O.R. (3d) 771, 1991 CarswellOnt 92 (C.A.), leave to appeal refused (1991), 67 C.C.C. (3d) vi (S.C.C.); *Gray*, 4 O.R. (3d) 33, 51 O.A.C. 81, 66 C.C.C. (3d) 6, 1991 CarswellOnt 691 (C.A.), leave to appeal refused, (1992), 69 C.C.C. (3d) vi (S.C.C.).
[79]   *Graham*, 1 O.R. (3d) 499, 3 C.R. (4th) 44, 62 C.C.C. (3d) 128, 44 O.A.C. 374, 1991 CarswellOnt 77 (C.A.), leave to appeal refused, (1992), 69 C.C.C. (3d) vi, 138 N.R. 411 (note), 56 O.A.C. 79 (note) (S.C.C.).
[80]   32 C.R. (4th) 1, 170 N.R. 16, 73 O.A.C. 201, 92 C.C.C. (3d) 11, [1994] 2 S.C.R. 914, 23 C.R.R. (2d) 6, 116 D.L.R. (4th) 416, 1994 CarswellOnt 91, 1994 CarswellOnt 1163.
[81]   *Ibid.,* at (C.R.) p. 14.
[82]   *Wray* (1970), [1971] S.C.R. 272, 11 C.R.N.S. 235, [1970] 4 C.C.C. 1, 11 D.L.R. (3d) 673, 1970 CarswellOnt 22.
[83]   7 C.R. 464, [1949] O.R. 215, 93 C.C.C. 376, 1949 CarswellOnt 4 (H.C.).

was held that where the discovery of some fact confirms the truth of an involuntary confession, the part of the confession that is confirmed by the discovery of the fact is admissible. Recently, in *S. (K.)*,[84] the Ontario Court of Appeal held that the rule was no longer valid. It was a product of a time when a trial judge had no residual discretion to exclude evidence because of the manner in which it was obtained. All of this has been overtaken by constitutional and judicial development. The Court noted that comments from the Supreme Court of Canada reflect a strong indication that using an involuntary confession is inconsistent with fundamental notions of fairness and the administration of justice. The Court said that, in the light of such developments from the Supreme Court, the rule should be modified to acknowledge that the trial judge has the discretion to exclude the evidence. Moreover, it is only in exceptional circumstances that the confession should not be excluded. Since admitting an involuntary confession runs counter to fundamental aspects of trial fairness, it is difficult to conceive of a basis for exercising the discretion in favour of admission.[85]

---

[84]   36 C.R. (5th) 198, 148 C.C.C. (3d) 247, 50 O.R. (3d) 321, 77 C.R.R. (2d) 327, 136 O.A.C. 238, 2000 CarswellOnt 3290, [2000] O.J. No. 3534 (C.A.).

[85]   But see *Oickle, supra*, note 75, where the Supreme Court held that the underlying consideration when dealing with the admissibility of a confession is the reliability of the evidence.

PART C

Proof at Trial

8

Proof at Trial

1. GENERALLY

The common law system is known as the adversary or accusatorial system, as opposed to the continental system, which is generally described as the inquisitorial system. Although both systems have many characteristics in common, such as an oral hearing with both the prosecution and the accused separately represented by counsel, and with no compulsion upon the accused to answer questions, there are distinct differences. Under the inquisitorial system, the judge takes an active role in questioning witnesses for the prosecution and in examining the accused and witnesses for the defence. Moreover, prior to trial, a brief or dossier compiled by a juge d'instruction or examining magistrate containing the examination of various witnesses is provided to the judge and jury.

The common law system may be described more as a duel between the Crown prosecutor and the defence counsel, with the judge sitting in the middle as an impartial arbiter. There are, however, some limitations on the contestants. It is the duty of counsel for the Crown to bring out all of the facts both for and against the accused. Moreover, it has been said that:

> ... the business of counsel for the Crown is fairly and impartially to exhibit all the facts to the jury. The Crown has no interest in procuring a conviction. Its only interest is that the right person should be convicted, that the truth should be known, and that justice be done.[1]

On the other hand, it is the duty of counsel for the defence to use all of the legitimate means at hand to obtain an acquittal for his or her client.

The usual steps in the process are these: opening statement by the prosecution; presentation of the prosecution's case; opening statement by the defence; presentation of the evidence for the defence; rebuttal evidence by the prosecution; summation of counsel for the prosecution and for the defence; charge to the jury by the trial judge; verdict of the jury or the judge, where the trial is by judge alone.

---

[1] *Sugarman* (1935), 25 Cr. App. R. 109, at (Cr. App. R.) pp. 114-15.

2. DISCLOSURE BY THE CROWN

(a) Generally

In a purely adversarial setting, each side would have the right until trial to withhold from the other information pertinent to the success or failure of its case. However, under the common law, the duty of the Crown is to bring out all facts both for and against the accused "so that the right person should be convicted, that truth be known and that justice be done".[2]

Unfortunately, this was not the case in the early days of common law. In fact, in the early days, there was very little, if any, disclosure. Until the seventeenth century, anyone charged with a felony was kept in close confinement until his trial. The accused was given only a copy of the indictment against him when he was asked to plead and then only discovered the evidence against him when it was produced at trial. [3]

It was not until 1848, with the passage of the *Indictable Offences Act*,[4] that a preliminary inquiry was finally held in the presence of the accused and the accused given an opportunity to cross-examine the witnesses against him and to obtain a copy of their depositions. But disclosure, even at the preliminary inquiry stage, was still the exception rather than the norm. The very nature of the adversary system relied upon the element of surprise. Courts were reluctant to allow an accused to use the preliminary inquiry to find out the case about him. As late as 1970, the Supreme Court of Canada said that the defence could not demand, as of right, the production of statements made by Crown witnesses.[5]

Today, the only statutory disclosure provisions are contained in the *Criminal Code*.[6] Section 603 allows an accused, after he or she has been ordered to stand trial, to inspect without charge the indictment, his or her own statement, the evidence and the exhibits, if any, and gives the accused the right to obtain copies of those documents (with the exception of the exhibits) upon payment of a reasonable fee. Section 604 imposes a duty upon the Crown to provide to an accused charged with treason, at least ten days before his or her arraignment, a copy of

---

[2]   *Sugarman, ibid.*
[3]   Stephen, *A History of the Criminal Law of England*, Vol. 1 (New York, Franklin reprint, 1964) at pp. 284, 350.
[4]   *Sir John Jervis's Act*, c. 42.
[5]   *Patterson*, [1970] S.C.R. 409, 10 C.R.N.S. 55, 72 W.W.R. 35, 2 C.C.C. (2d) 227, 9 D.L.R. (3d) 398, 1970 CarswellAlta 61.
[6]   R.S.C. 1985, c. C-46, ss. 603, 604

the indictment, a list of the witnesses against him or her and a copy of jury panel.

(b) Evidence in the Possession of the Crown

It was only a decade ago that the Supreme Court of Canada decided to introduce judicial reform and guidance with respect to the question of Crown disclosure. In *Stinchcombe*,[7] the Supreme Court finally rejected the argument frequently advanced by the Crown that full and frank disclosure of its case would only enable the defence to tailor its evidence to conform with the Crown's evidence. Section 7 of the *Charter*, the right to fundamental justice, the Court said, has given the common law right to Crown disclosure new vigour. The fruits of an investigation, which are in the possession of the Crown, are not the property of the Crown for its use in securing a conviction. Rather, they are the property of the public to be used to ensure that justice is done.

The issue in *Stinchcombe* was whether an accused should be allowed to see contradictory statements of Crown witnesses. Under the adversary system, a contradictory statement of a witness may be an important tool for the defence to show that a witness's testimony may not be credible. Fairness to an accused, the Court said, demands such disclosure. The Court concluded that the Crown has the duty to disclose to the defence all material evidence in its possession whether favourable to the accused or not, in order to ensure a fair trial and guarantee that an accused can make full answer and defence.

The obligation to disclose, the Court said, is triggered by a request by or on behalf of the accused and disclosure should be made even before the accused is called upon to elect his or her mode of trial. In those rare cases where an accused is unrepresented by counsel, there is a further duty upon the Crown to advise the accused of his or her right to disclosure; moreover the trial judge should not take the accused's plea until disclosure has been made. Finally, the obligation to disclose is a continuing one and must be made whenever additional information is received.

However, the Supreme Court did recognize that the obligation to disclose is not absolute. Rather, it is subject to the Crown's discretion both to the withholding of information and to the timing of disclosure, for example, with respect to the rules of privilege. That discretion is

---

[7]   (1991), [1992] 1 W.W.R. 97, [1991] 3 S.C.R. 326, 130 N.R. 277, 83 Alta. L.R. (2d) 193, 120 A.R. 161, 8 C.R. (4th) 277, 18 C.R.R. (2d) 210, 68 C.C.C. (3d) 1, 8 W.A.C. 161, 1991 CarswellAlta 192, 1991 CarswellAlta 559.

reviewable by the trial judge. Defence counsel can initiate a review and the Crown must justify its refusal to disclose. Since disclosure of all relevant information is the general rule, the Crown is required to bring itself within an exception to that rule.

(c) Evidence in the Possession of Third Parties

The *Stinchcombe* case only dealt with the question of potential evidence for the defence that was in the possession or under the control of the Crown. But what about the right of the defence to production of potential evidence, not in the possession or under the control of the Crown, but in the possession of third parties? The Supreme Court was faced with this issue four years later in *O'Connor*.[8] In *O'Connor*, the issue was whether the Court could order the production of therapeutic records of a complainant. The defence wanted to examine the records to see if there was any information in them that might be inconsistent with the evidence that the complainant was expected to give at trial.

This time, the Court drew a distinction between records in the hands of the Crown and records in the hands of a third party. The Court said that where third party records have fallen into the possession of the Crown, any concern relating to their privacy and privilege has disappeared. If the complainant is willing to release this information in order to further the criminal prosecution, then fairness requires that the accused be entitled to use it in preparation of his or her defence.

Nevertheless, the Court did accept that the rule should be somewhat different where the records were in the hands of a third party. It said that the onus was on the accused to satisfy the court that the information is *likely to be relevant*. To obtain the records, the accused had to bring a formal written application supported by an affidavit setting out the specific grounds for production, although the court could waive formal notice in the interests of justice. Notice also had to be given to the third party in possession of the documents, as well as to those who had a privacy interest in the records. The accused also had to subpoena the custodian and the records to ensure their attendance in court.

The Court pointed out that the initial application for disclosure had to be made to the judge seized of the trial, and generally before the jury were empanelled. Before ordering production, the trial judge had to be satisfied that there was a *reasonable probability* that the information

---

[8] (1995), [1996] 2 W.W.R. 153, [1995] 4 S.C.R. 411, 44 C.R. (4th) 1, 103 C.C.C. (3d) 1, 130 D.L.R. (4th) 235, 191 N.R. 1, 68 B.C.A.C. 1, 112 W.A.C. 1, 33 C.R.R. (2d) 1, 1995 CarswellBC 1098, 1995 CarswellBC 1151, [1995] S.C.J. No. 98.

was logically probative of an issue at trial or the competence of the accused to testify. The test of *likely relevance* upon an accused was not to be interpreted as an onerous burden, but rather a requirement to prevent speculative, fanciful, disruptive, unmeritorious, obstructive and time-consuming requests for production. If the records were ordered produced, it was the responsibility of the judge to examine them and weigh *the salutary and deleterious* effects of production in order to determine whether a non-production order would constitute a reasonable limit on the ability of the accused to make full answer and defence. In balancing the competing interest, the judge was required to consider: (1) the extent to which the record was necessary for the accused to make full answer and defence; (2) the probative value of the record; (3) the nature and extent of the reasonable expectation of privacy vested in the record; (4) whether production of the record would be premised upon any discriminatory belief or bias; and (5) the potential prejudice to the complainant's dignity, privacy or security that would be occasioned by production of the record.

The Supreme Court was not unanimous in its view. In a strong dissent, Madam Justice L'Heureux Dubé felt that the defence should have the onus of establishing the "likely relevance", of any record before production could be ordered for inspection by the judge. Without establishing "likely relevance" she said, applications before the court could turn into a fishing expedition that would result in the invasion of the privacy of women who have been sexually assaulted and would deter women from reporting the assault for fear of having their past dredged up in court.

The dissenting view of Madam Justice L'Heureux Dubé quickly found favour with the government of Canada and legislation was introduced to limit the right of an accused to access to third party records. On May 12, 1997, Parliament proclaimed Bill C-46 to provide statutory rules governing the production of the personal records of all witnesses where an accused is charged with certain *specific sexual offences.*[9]

Under this legislation, the defence is now required to go through a two-stage procedure to obtain production of third party records from the trial judge. In the first stage, the trial judge must conduct an *in camera* hearing and give the complainant or witness the opportunity to make submissions. The judge must then decide, without looking at the records, whether they should be produced to him or her for review. The test which the judge must adopt is whether the record is still "likely

---

[9]   Sections 278.1 to 278.91 of the *Criminal Code.*

relevant", but it has been supplemented with the further requirement that production "be necessary in the interests of justice." In deciding whether to order production, the judge is required to consider "the salutary and deleterious effects" of that decision on the accused's right to make full answer and defence and on the right to privacy and equality of the complainant or witness.[10] In effect, what the judge is expected to do in the first stage is to balance the competing interests of the right to make full answer and defence and the right to privacy *without even looking at the records*. Although attacks on the new legislation as infringing sections 7 and 11(d) of the *Charter* were successful in the trial courts of some provinces,[11] the Supreme Court of Canada upheld the new legislation. In *Mills*,[12] the Supreme Court said that the fact that section 278.2 prevents the automatic disclosure of all relevant and non-privileged information in the possession of the Crown does not deprive the accused of his right to make full answer and defence. The criterion that production be necessary *in the interests of justice* invests the trial judge with the discretion to consider the full range of rights and interests at issue before ordering production in a manner scrupulously respectful of the requirements of the *Charter*. In other words, section 278 now permits the trial judge to exercise a wide discretion in considering a variety of factors in order to preserve the complainant's privacy and equality rights to the maximum extent possible, and also ensure that the accused has access to documents required to make full answer and defence.

(d) Remedies for Failure to Disclose

Generally, the courts have been reluctant to sanction any remedy against the Crown for the failure to provide timely and complete disclosure to the defence, except an order for disclosure, an adjournment or a mistrial and the imposition of costs. A stay of proceedings has been regarded as a remedy only of "last resort", granted where the adverse effect on the ability of the accused to make full answer and defence cannot be remedied, and even then, only in the clearest of cases.[13]

---

[10] Section 278.5.

[11] *Mills*, 205 A.R. 321, 47 C.R.R. (2d) 104, 12 C.R. (5th) 138, [1998] 4 W.W.R. 83, 56 Alta. L.R. (3d) 277, 1997 CarswellAlta 762, [1997] A.J. No. 891 (Q.B.) and *Lee* (September 24, 1997), Chapnik J. (Ont. Gen. Div.).

[12] [1999] 3 S.C.R. 668, 139 C.C.C. (3d) 321, 248 N.R. 101, 28 C.R. (5th) 207, 180 D.L.R. (4th) 1, [2000] 2 W.W.R. 180, 244 A.R. 201, 209 W.A.C. 201, 75 Alta. L.R. (3d) 1, 69 C.R.R. (2d) 1, 1999 CarswellAlta 1055, 1999 CarswellAlta 1056, [1999] S.C.J. No. 68

[13] *O'Connor*, 29 C.R. (4th) 40, 89 C.C.C. (3d) 109, 20 C.R.R. (2d) 212, 42 B.C.A.C. 105, 67 W.A.C. 105, [1994] B.C.J. No. 1116, 1994 CarswellBC 575 (C.A.), affirmed (1995),

However, the loss or destruction of potential evidence that may be of assistance to the defence has been another matter. Here the Supreme Court has said that the Crown has a duty to explain what has happened to the evidence or risk a stay of proceedings. For example, in *Carosella*,[14] a social worker at a sexual abuse crisis centre, who had interviewed the complainant in a sexual assault case, shredded her notes pursuant to a policy laid down by the centre mandating the shredding of most of the contents of their files in which there was "police involvement". Neither the Crown nor the complainant was aware that this had been done. In fact, both had consented to a disclosure of the contents of the entire file to the trial judge to determine which part of the files should be disclosed to the defence. The trial judge had stayed proceedings on the basis that the destroyed notes were relevant and material, and that they would, more likely than not, assist the accused. However, the Ontario Court of Appeal had set aside the stay because the Court felt that the notes were not a verified account of what the complainant had said, did not constitute a written statement of the complainant and no realistic appraisal of the probable effect of the lost note could support the conclusion that the accused's right to make full answer and defence had been compromised.

The Supreme Court of Canada, in a majority decision, re-instated the stay of proceedings. Sopinka J., delivering the majority judgment, held that an accused who alleges a breach of his right to make full answer and defence as a result of non-disclosure or non-production is not required to show that the conduct of the defence was prejudiced. If the material that was destroyed meets the threshold test for disclosure or production, the accused's *Charter* right is breached without the requirement of showing additional prejudice. The extent to which the *Charter* violation causes actual prejudice to the accused relates only to the remedy to be fashioned pursuant to section 24(1) of the *Charter*. Sopinka J. felt that in the circumstances of the case (a 1-3/4 hour interview immediately followed by a complaint to the police), a stay of proceedings was the only appropriate remedy. The deliberate destruction of the material

---

[1996] 2 W.W.R. 153, [1995] 4 S.C.R. 411, 44 C.R. (4th) 1, 103 C.C.C. (3d) 1, 130 D.L.R. (4th) 235, 191 N.R. 1, 68 B.C.A.C. 1, 112 W.A.C. 1, 33 C.R.R. (2d) 1, 1995 CarswellBC 1098, 1995 CarswellBC 1151, [1995] S.C.J. No. 98; *Stinchcombe*, 88 C.C.C. (3d) 557, 149 A.R. 167, 63 W.A.C. 167, 30 C.R. (4th) 119, 1994 CarswellAlta 324 (C.A.), affirmed, 178 N.R. 157, 38 C.R. (4th) 42, 96 C.C.C. (3d) 318, 162 A.R. 269, 83 W.A.C. 269, [1995] 1 S.C.R. 754, 1995 CarswellAlta 27, 1995 CarswellAlta 409.

14 112 C.C.C. (3d) 289, 98 O.A.C. 81, 4 C.R. (5th) 139, [1997] 1 S.C.R. 80, 31 O.R. (3d) 575 (headnote only), 142 D.L.R. (4th) 595, 207 N.R. 321, 41 C.R.R. (2d) 189, [1997] S.C.J. No. 12, 1997 CarswellOnt 85, 1997 CarswellOnt 86. See also *MacDonnell*, 114 C.C.C. (3d) 145, 6 C.R. (5th) 80, [1997] 1 S.C.R. 305, 158 N.S.R. (2d) 1, 466 A.P.R. 1, 210 N.R. 318, [1997] S.C.J. No. 16, 1997 CarswellNS 26, 1997 CarswellNS 27.

in order to deprive the court and the accused of relevant evidence would damage the image of the administration of justice. Confidence in the system would be undermined if the court condoned conduct designed to defeat the processes of the court by an agency that receives money and whose actions are scrutinized by provincial governments.

Although *Carosella* established that there is no onus upon the defence to establish prejudicial loss where there has been a deliberate destruction of potentially relevant evidence that might be of assistance to the defence, it did not deal with the question of the failure of the authorities to record evidence that might be potentially relevant. The distinction between destroyed evidence and unrecorded interviews remained unclear until a few months later when the Supreme Court released its reasons in *La*.[15] There the accused was charged with the sexual assault of a thirteen-year-old runaway that the police were looking for. One of the runaway's conversations with a police officer was taped at police headquarters in preparation for a secure treatment application and only notes of her date of birth, address and phone numbers were made. The taped conversation was not for any criminal investigation, as the investigation into the accused's activities had not yet started. The tape was later misplaced. The trial judge had stayed proceedings.

Delivering the main judgment of the Court, Sopinka J. lifted the stay and set out the following principles dealing with disclosure by the Crown:

1. The Crown has the obligation to disclose all relevant information in its possession, inculpatory or exculpatory, whether it intends to rely upon it or not. The right of disclosure is a component of the right to make full answer and defence that is, in turn, a principle of fundamental justice embraced by section 7 of the *Charter*.
2. The Crown's obligation to disclose all relevant information in its possession gives rise to an obligation to preserve relevant evidence.
3. When the prosecution has lost evidence that should have been disclosed, the Crown has a duty to explain what has happened to it. In determining whether the Crown's explanation is satisfactory, the Court should analyze the circumstances surrounding the loss of evidence. The main consideration is whether the police or the Crown took reasonable steps to preserve the evidence for disclosure. The relevance that the evidence was perceived to have at the

---

[15] 213 N.R. 1, 116 C.C.C. (3d) 97, 148 D.L.R. (4th) 608, 200 A.R. 81, 146 W.A.C. 81, 8 C.R. (5th) 155, 44 C.R.R. (2d) 262, [1997] 2 S.C.R. 680, [1997] 8 W.W.R. 1, 51 Alta. L.R. (3d) 181, 1997 CarswellAlta 490, 1997 CarswellAlta 491, [1997] S.C.J. No. 30.

time must be considered. The police cannot be expected to preserve everything on the chance that it will be relevant in the future. Furthermore, even the loss of relevant evidence will not result in a breach of the duty to disclose if the conduct of the police is reasonable.

4.   The degree of care that is expected of the police for the preservation of the evidence will increase with the relevancy of the evidence.

5.   If the explanation satisfies the trial judge that the evidence has not been destroyed or lost owing to unacceptable negligence, then the duty to disclose has not been breached. Nevertheless, the loss of a document may be so prejudicial that it impairs the right of an accused to make full answer and defence and to receive a fair trial. To make out a breach of s. 7 of the *Charter* on the ground of lost evidence, the accused must establish actual prejudice to his or her right to make full answer and defence.

6.   If the explanation does not satisfy the trial judge, then section 7 of the *Charter* has been breached. Such a failure may also suggest that an abuse of process has occurred. Conduct amounting to abuse of process will include the deliberate destruction of material by the police or other officers of the Crown for the purpose of defeating the Crown's obligation to disclose and, even absent proof of improper motive, an unacceptable degree of negligent conduct.

7.   An accused need not establish abuse of process for the Crown to have failed to meet its section 7 *Charter* obligation to disclose.

8.   The appropriateness of a stay of proceedings depends upon the effect of the conduct amounting to an abuse of process or other prejudice on the fairness of the trial and will be best assessed in the context of the trial as it unfolds. The trial judge has a discretion whether to rule on the application for a stay immediately or after hearing some or all of the evidence. It will usually be preferable for the judge to reserve on the application unless it is clear that no other course of action will cure the prejudice that is occasioned by the conduct giving rise to the abuse. This will enable the judge to assess the degree of prejudice and whether measures to minimize that prejudice have borne fruit.

9.   Even if the trial judge rules on the motion at an early stage of the trial and the motion is unsuccessful, it may be renewed if there is a material change of circumstances.

3. THE CASE FOR THE CROWN

(a) The Opening Statement

In a jury trial, but not necessarily in a trial by judge alone, the prosecution will begin with an opening speech to the jury. The purpose of the speech is to lay before the jury a brief summary of the facts upon which the prosecution relies to establish its case and of the evidence that it expects each prosecution witness will give. The Crown must always be fair in the opening address, as well as in the prosecution in general. There is a duty to be impartial and to guard against injecting comments likely to excite or inflame the jury against the accused.

(b) The Evidence Generally

When the address of the Crown prosecutor is completed, the trial judge will call upon the prosecutor to present the case for the Crown. The prosecution will then begin by calling witnesses who will be examined in-chief. In an examination-in-chief, the prosecution must be careful not to lead the witness on matters crucial to its case. A leading question is one that suggests the answer to the witness. For example, it is not permissible to ask the witness, "Did you see the accused shoot the victim"? A leading question is one that takes for granted evidence that a witness has not yet given. The question, "When did you stop beating your wife?" is leading because it assumes that the witness has already said that he beat his wife in the past and has stopped doing so.

Although the Crown is bound by strict duty to ensure the preservation of the integrity of the criminal justice system, it must operate within the context of an adversarial procedure. So long as the Crown has given full disclosure of its case within the guidelines set down by the Supreme Court of Canada in *Stinchcombe*,[16] the responsibility for choosing what witnesses are necessary to establish its case rests upon the Crown. Neither the defence nor the trial judge have any right to dictate to the Crown what evidence it should call.[17] This fundamental principle was reaffirmed by the Supreme Court in *Cook*.[18] There, the accused was convicted of assault causing bodily harm on a male victim

[16] (1991), [1992] 1 W.W.R. 97, [1991] 3 S.C.R. 326, 130 N.R. 277, 83 Alta. L.R. (2d) 193, 120 A.R. 161, 8 C.R. (4th) 277, 18 C.R.R. (2d) 210, 68 C.C.C. (3d) 1, 8 W.A.C. 161, 1991 CarswellAlta 192, 1991 CarswellAlta 559.

[17] *V. (J.)* (1994), 91 C.C.C. (3d) 284 (Que. C.A.).

[18] 210 N.R. 197, 114 C.C.C. (3d) 481, 7 C.R. (5th) 51, 146 D.L.R. (4th) 437, [1997] 1 S.C.R. 1113, 188 N.B.R. (2d) 161, 480 A.P.R. 161, 1997 CarswellNB 125, [1997] S.C.J. No. 22.

arising out of an incident in a woman's apartment. The woman had testified, but not the male victim. On appeal, the New Brunswick Court of Appeal set aside the conviction. The Court said that an accused had a right to be faced by his accuser. Although recognizing that the Crown has the discretion to call, or not call, whatever witnesses it considers necessary for the presentation of its case, the Court said that Crown was not entitled to hold back evidence that could assist the accused. There was a duty upon the trial judge to inquire why a complainant was not being called, and to determine whether or not the witness should be called to avoid a miscarriage of justice.

The Supreme Court, however, disagreed with that view. The Court noted that, historically, fairness has been the main ground for opposing the Crown's discretionary authority to choose which witnesses to call. Since the Crown is now required to disclose all relevant information it possesses, the defence is made aware of potentially exculpatory evidence discovered by the Crown and of material inconsistencies, and has the ability to call those witnesses. The Court did not agree that an accused who is not given a free opportunity to cross-examine every potential witness, whether or not the Crown wishes to call them, is necessarily prejudiced in his or her defence. Nor could the Court accept that a failure on the Crown's part to call a witness that would result in prejudice to the accused, because of loss of the choice to address the jury last, should affect the Crown's discretion to produce the witnesses it chooses. Rather, the failure to call a witness was only a factor for the trial judge to consider in deciding whether or not he or she should call that witness. That was a matter to be left to each judge's discretion and should be exercised only in rare cases so as to avoid overly interfering with the adversarial nature of the proceedings. Unless improper motives can be imputed to the prosecution, such as the desire, for example, to hide exculpatory evidence, Crown counsel will be considered to have properly executed his or her function in the criminal trial.

(c) A Confession or Admission by the Accused

If Crown counsel intends to introduce a statement or admission made by the accused, he or she will indicate to the judge that a *voir dire* is required to determine the voluntariness of the statement or admission.[19] The defence may, however, be prepared to admit that the state-

---

[19] *Piche* (1970), [1971] S.C.R. 23, 74 W.W.R. 674, 12 C.R.N.S. 222, 11 D.L.R. (3d) 700, [1970] 4 C.C.C. 27, 1970 CarswellMan 81.

ment is voluntary, in which case a *voir dire* will not be necessary.[20] If the trial judge rules that the statement was made voluntarily by the accused, or if the defence admits that it was made voluntarily, then it will usually be introduced through the officer or person who took the statement and will be made an exhibit, if it is in writing. A statement that has been ruled by the trial judge to be involuntary may not be introduced by the Crown and is inadmissible for all purposes. For example, it cannot be used by the Crown or by a co-accused to cross-examine an accused who enters the witness stand and gives evidence inconsistent with what he or she said in their statement.

The Crown may not wish to introduce an accused's statement because it is exculpatory, but still be able to use it to cross-examine the accused if he gives evidence contrary to the contents of the statement. The courts, however, will not allow the Crown to lie in wait and permit the accused to trap himself.[21] Some courts have suggested that if the statement is relevant to a fact in issue, even if it does not directly incriminate the accused, then the statement should be advanced as part of the Crown's case in chief, unless it is marginally, minimally or doubtfully relevant.[22] The more persuasive view, however, is that although the Crown need not introduce the statement in chief, it must at least attempt to prove its voluntariness during the presentation of the prosecution case in chief.[23] If the statement is proved to be voluntary, this will at least alert the accused to the fact that it may be used by the Crown to cross-examine him if he gives evidence which conflicts with the contents of the statement.

Although a statement which has been ruled inadmissible because it was not proved by the Crown to be voluntary may not be used to cross-examine an accused who enters the witness stand, that rule will not necessarily apply where the statement has been declared inadmissible because of a breach of the accused's *Charter* rights. For example, in *Calder*,[24] the trial judge had excluded the statement of an accused which the Crown sought to introduce in chief because his right to counsel had

---

[20] *Park*, [1981] 2 S.C.R. 64, 37 N.R. 501, 21 C.R. (3d) 182, 59 C.C.C. (2d) 385, 122 D.L.R. (3d) 1, 1981 CarswellOnt 614.

[21] *Drake* (1970), 12 C.R.N.S. 220, [1971] 1 W.W.R. 454, 1 C.C.C. (2d) 396, 1970 CarswellSask 37 (Q.B.).

[22] *Bruno* (1975), 27 C.C.C. (2d) 318 (Ont. C.A.).

[23] *Lizotte*, 18 C.R. (3d) 364, 61 C.C.C. (2d) 423, 1980 CarswellQue 25 (C.A.).

[24] 32 C.R. (4th) 197, 19 O.R. (3d) 643, 74 O.A.C. 1, 23 C.R.R. (2d) 94, 92 C.C.C. (3d) 97, 1994 CarswellOnt 94 (C.A.), affirmed, 46 C.R. (4th) 133, 27 O.R. (3d) 258 (headnote only), 105 C.C.C. (3d) 1, 132 D.L.R. (4th) 577, 194 N.R. 52, 34 C.R.R. (2d) 189, [1996] 1 S.C.R. 660, 90 O.A.C. 18, 1996 CarswellOnt 1405, 1996 CarswellOnt 1405F.

been violated. When the accused gave evidence in his defence, the Crown applied to the trial judge to be allowed to use the statement to impeach his credibility. It was argued by the Crown that when an accused gives evidence, he brings his credibility into issue and cannot argue that the use of such statements for credibility violates his right against self-incrimination. Although the trial judge rejected that argument, it found favour with two of the three judges of the Ontario Court of Appeal who, however, dismissed the appeal for other reasons. On a further appeal by the Crown, the Supreme Court, in a majority decision, held that the trial judge was correct in refusing to permit cross-examination on the excluded statement.

Sopinka J., speaking for the majority, felt that since the exclusion order made by the trial judge under section 24(1) of the *Charter* was made under the authority of a constitutional provision, the condition under which the trial judge may reconsider his decision must be at least as stringent as that in respect of an order made under the authority of a statute. He rejected the notion that a distinction should be made between the prohibited use for all purposes of a statement ruled involuntary and one excluded for a *Charter* violation. He was of the view that although the rule against the admission of an involuntary statement is based primarily on reliability concerns, the law has now developed to the extent that the voluntariness rule is supported in part on fairness in the criminal process.[25]

> The effect of destroying the credibility of an accused who takes the stand in his or her defence using evidence obtained from the mouth of the accused in breach of his or her Charter rights will usually have the same effect as the use of the same evidence when adduced by the Crown in its case in chief for the purpose of incrimination. The fact that a jury carefully instructed can apply the distinction does not mean that the use for the purpose of impeachment will, in the eyes of the jury, have a less detrimental effect on the case for the accused.[26]

Nevertheless, he did not rule out the use of such evidence entirely and accepted that it could be used in "very limited circumstances". But before it could be used, the Crown was required to seek a ruling from the trial judge during its case or before cross-examining the accused. In such instance, a *voir dire* would be necessary in which the trial judge

---

[25] *Whittle*, 32 C.R. (4th) 1, 170 N.R. 16, 73 O.A.C. 201, 92 C.C.C. (3d) 11, [1994] 2 S.C.R. 914, 23 C.R.R. (2d) 6, 116 D.L.R. (4th) 416, 1994 CarswellOnt 91, 1994 CarswellOnt 1163.
[26] *Ibid.*, at p.15.

would have to consider the admissibility of the statement for the limited purpose for which the Crown intended to use the statement.

McLachlin J., in a strong dissent, disagreed that the use of a statement excluded for the breach of a *Charter* right should occur only "in very limited circumstances". As far as she was concerned, this was not a proper test because the trial judge, before excluding evidence obtained in breach of the *Charter*, is required under section 24(2) to consider "all the circumstances", not "limited circumstances". The addition of a requirement of "very limited circumstances" would contradict the plain words of the statute. She summed up her dissenting opinion this way:

> It may be seen as unfair to tender against an accused as substantive evidence a statement which the state obtained from him in violation of his Charter rights. However, where the accused chooses to take the stand and place his credibility in issue, vouching to the jury that what he is telling them is the whole truth and nothing but the truth, it is more difficult to say that it is unfair to permit the Crown to cross-examine him on his prior inconsistent statement and to put to him the vital question of which is version is true. These are important considerations which must be weighed against any unfairness arising from the way the statement was taken, if the judge is to properly determine whether admission of the statement would bring the administration of justice into disrepute.[27]

McLachlin J. felt that it is important to permit the jury to judge fairly the truthfulness of the witness. It is equally important not to permit witnesses to take the stand and fabricate lies, free from fear that they may be cross-examined on earlier contradictory statements. Thus, she argued, the trial judge must consider "all the circumstances" as required by section 24(2), not simply the "limited circumstances" suggested by the majority members of the Court.

(d) Introduction of Prior Testimony

Section 715 of the Code permits evidence given by a witness at the accused's previous trial on the same charge, or evidence of the witness taken in the investigation of the accused or on the preliminary hearing into the charge, to be read as evidence at trial if the witness refuses to be sworn or give evidence, or is dead, insane, too ill to travel or testify, or is absent from Canada. However, section 715 also gives the trial judge discretion to refuse to allow the evidence to be read if the

---

[27] *Ibid.*, at p. 27.

accused satisfies the judge that he or she did not have full opportunity to cross-examine the witness when the evidence was given or taken.

For some time, the courts felt that once the Crown complied with section 715, the trial judge was required to admit the transcript of the previous testimony. The judge had no discretion to exclude it. However, in *Potvin*,[28] the Supreme Court of Canada decided that a trial judge has the discretion to refuse to admit such evidence where it is obtained in a manner that is unfair to the accused. For example, the fact that a witness is absent from Canada will not necessarily result in the admission of the witness's testimony if the Crown could obtain his or her attendance by some minimal degree of effort. A judge might also refuse to permit the Crown to introduce transcript evidence if the Crown was aware at the time that the witness previously testified that he or she would not be available to testify at trial and failed to tell the defence so that they could use their best efforts in cross-examination.[29] Similarly, the failure of the Crown to disclose information which could have been used by the defence in cross-examination to attack the credibility of the complainant at the preliminary inquiry has been held to be a reason to deny the Crown the right to introduce transcript evidence, as a denial of the accused's right to full answer and defence.[30]

An unusual example of where the Crown was refused the right to lead transcript evidence under section 715 was *Hawkins*.[31] At issue was whether the evidence of a woman who had testified against the accused at his preliminary hearing and then subsequently married him, could be read in under section 715. The Supreme Court said that it could not. Spousal incompetency does not represent a refusal to give evidence as required by the section. The common law rule of spousal incompetency disqualifies a spouse from giving evidence regardless of the spouse's choice.

---

[28]   93 N.R. 42, [1989] 1 S.C.R. 525, 21 Q.A.C. 258, 47 C.C.C. (3d) 289, 68 C.R. (3d) 193, 42 C.R.R. 44, 1989 CarswellQue 104.

[29]   *Kaddoura*, 82 A.R. 347, 41 C.C.C. (3d) 371, 60 C.R. (3d) 393, 56 Alta. L.R. (2d) 126, [1988] 1 W.W.R. 693, 1987 CarswellAlta 251 (C.A.), leave to appeal refused (1988), 87 A.R. 160n, 60 Alta. L.R. (2d) lv, 64 C.R. (3d) xxx (S.C.C.).

[30]   *Barembruch*, 119 C.C.C. (3d) 185, 96 B.C.A.C. 215, 155 W.A.C. 215, 1997 CarswellBC 1837, [1997] B.C.J. No. 2029 (C.A.).

[31]   111 C.C.C. (3d) 129, 30 O.R. (3d) 641 (headnote only), 2 C.R. (5th) 245, 204 N.R. 241, 96 O.A.C. 81, [1996] 3 S.C.R. 1043, 141 D.L.R. (4th) 193, 1996 CarswellOnt 4063, [1996] S.C.J. No. 117.

(e) Videotape Testimony of a Child Complainant

The common law has recognized, at least since the 18th century, that an accused has the right to face his or her accuser and subject the testimony of that accuser to the test of cross-examination. That right has been constitutionally recognized by section 11(d) of the *Charter*. Section 11 guarantees an accused the right "to be presumed innocent until proven guilty according to law in a fair and public hearing by an independent and impartial tribunal". Section 7 of the *Charter* also recognizes, "the right to life, liberty and security of the person and the right not to be deprived thereof except in accordance with the principles of fundamental justice".

The Supreme Court of Canada, however, has accepted that section 715.1 of the *Criminal Code* is a legitimate exception to that right.[32] Section 715.1 allows for the reception of videotaped evidence of a complainant under the age of 18 years if he or she has been the victim of certain listed offence involving sexual abuse. There are three conditions that must be satisfied before the videotape will be admitted. The first condition is that the videotaped interview must have been made *within a reasonable time after the alleged offence.* Here, what constitutes *a reasonable time* will depend on all of the circumstances of the case. For example, in *Scott,*[33] the videotaped interview took place about four and a half months after the assault. In admitting the videotaped interview, the trial judge took into account the fact that the child in the particular circumstances of the case was reluctant to disclose the assault. The second condition is that the videotaped interview must describe "the acts complained of". *Scott* also recognized that the description of the acts may include more than the bare visible acts constituting the assault. The Court said that if the section is to serve its purpose, the complainant must be allowed to give her version of the events underlying the charge. This can include everything that happened from the time she first met her assailant until he left her, including a description of his physical features, or his name, if known to her, and any statements made by him during the assault. [34]

---

[32] *L. (D.O.),* 25 C.R. (4th) 285, 161 N.R. 1, 85 C.C.C. (3d) 289, 88 Man. R. (2d) 241, 51 W.A.C. 241, [1993] 4 S.C.R. 419, 18 C.R.R. (2d) 257, 1993 CarswellMan 348, reversing, 6 C.R. (4th) 277, 65 C.C.C. (3d) 465, 73 Man. R. (2d) 238, 3 W.A.C. 238, 1991 CarswellMan 10 (C.A.).

[33] 27 C.R. (4th) 55, 67 O.A.C. 213, 87 C.C.C. (3d) 327, 1993 CarswellOnt 142 (C.A.).

[34] *Meddoui,* 77 Alta. L.R. (2d) 97, 111 A.R. 295, 2 C.R. (4th) 316, 61 C.C.C. (3d) 345, [1991] 2 W.W.R. 289, 5 C.R.R. (2d) 294, 1990 CarswellAlta 187 (C.A.), set aside, [1991]

The final condition that must be satisfied is that the videotaped interview must be *adopted* by the complainant in his or her testimony, although what constitutes adoption for the purposes of section 715.1 has been the subject of some judicial dispute.[35]

The Supreme Court in *F. (C.)*,[36] concluded that section 715.1 is a statutory exception to the hearsay rule and "permits an out-of-court statement to be admitted for the truth of its contents provided that certain conditions are met".[37] Cory J., for the Court, recognized that a witness who could not remember the events could not be cross-examined effectively. As far as he was concerned, however, the fact that the statement had to be made within a reasonable time, that the trier can watch the entire interview and observe and assess the personality and intelligence of the child and the requirement that the child attest that he or she was attempting to be truthful when the videotaped interview was made, provided the requisite reliability of the statement. Cory J. also rejected the argument in *Meddoui* that the videotaped evidence adds nothing to the testimony when the complainant has an independent present memory of the events. Both the adopted videotaped statement together with the *viva voce* evidence given at trial are to comprise the whole of the evidence-in-chief of the complainant. As he noted:

> The admission of the videotaped statements made shortly after the events in issue may be of great assistance in augmenting a child's testimony at trial by the account of events given in the statement when the incidents were fresh in the child's mind.[38]

Cory J. felt that the primary goal of section 715.1 is to create a record of what is probably the best recollection of the event. A subsidiary aim of the section is to prevent, or reduce materially, the likelihood of inflicting further injury upon a child as a result of participating in court proceedings by reducing the number of interviews that the child must undergo and by conducting them in less overwhelming surroundings. He also stressed that videotaping may increase the accuracy of the

---

3 S.C.R. ix, [1992] 1 W.W.R. lxv (note), 6 C.R.R. (2d) 192 (note), 82 Alta. L.R. (2d) lxv (note), 69 C.C.C. (3d) vi (note), 137 N.R. 389 (note).
[35] *Meddoui, ibid.*, and *T. (W.P.)*, 14 O.R. (3d) 225, 16 C.R.R. (2d) 49, 83 C.C.C. (3d) 5, 63 O.A.C. 321, 1993 CarswellOnt 1056 (C.A.). See Chapter 3, (d) Statutory Exceptions (ii) Videotaped Evidence of a Complainant.
[36] 220 N.R. 362, 154 D.L.R. (4th) 13, 120 C.C.C. (3d) 225, 11 C.R. (5th) 209, [1997] 3 S.C.R. 1183, 104 O.A.C. 321, 1997 CarswellOnt 4448, 1997 CarswellOnt 4449, [1997] S.C.J. No. 89.
[37] *Ibid.*, at (C.R.) p. 216.
[38] *Ibid.*, at pp. 222-23.

testimony since the child may feel more comfortable and be more forth-coming.

One of the concerns often expressed by the defence, that was not adequately addressed in *F. (C.)*, is that a child may be subjected to a pre-video interview involving suggestive questioning and persistent pressure, not only by the police, but also by social workers whose primary concern will be the treatment of the child, not the prosecution of the abuser. Cory J. did say that it was preferable, where reasonably possible, that the police not conduct a pre-video interview. However, if the police felt that one was necessary, they should ask simple open-ended questions, although it may be necessary in some instances to ask the child leading questions. Nevertheless, any pre-video interviewing by the police would not affect the admissibility of the videotaped statement, only its weight. He was not prepared to grant to the trial judge the right to exclude a videotaped statement altogether where the judge was convinced that the pre-video interview questioning was so tainted by the method of questioning the child that it would be dangerous to admit it.

(f) No Case-Splitting by the Crown

The Crown is required to call all of its evidence to prove its case before the defence is called upon. This is known as the rule against case-splitting. It is based upon the principle that an accused should not be taken by surprise and need not incriminate himself until he has heard and thoroughly explored the entire case that the Crown intends to present against him. It has been said to provide "a safeguard against the importance of a piece of evidence, by reason of its late introduction, being unduly emphasized or magnified in relation to the other evidence".[39]

Although the rule requires the Crown to prove each and every element of the charge, it does not require the Crown to anticipate every defence that may be raised. For example, the Crown is not required to lead evidence-in-chief that could rebut an alibi of the accused, even if it has received notice from the defence prior to trial that the defence intends to introduce alibi evidence and has been given particulars of that alibi.[40] Nor is the Crown required to lead evidence that an accused is not suffering from a mental disorder that would exempt him from criminal

---

[39] *Per* Martin J.A. in *Campbell*, 38 C.C.C. (2d) 6, 17 O.R. (2d) 673, 1 C.R. (3d) 309, 1 C.R. (3d) S-49, 1977 CarswellOnt 5 (C.A.) at (C.R.) p. 334.

[40] *Rafferty*, [1983] 4 W.W.R. 511, 25 Alta. L.R. (2d) 334, 43 A.R. 323, 6 C.C.C. (3d) 72, 1983 CarswellAlta 69 (C.A.); *Andrews* (1979), 8 C.R. (3d) 1, 1979 CarswellBC 546 (C.A.), leave to appeal refused (1979), 28 N.R. 537n (S.C.C.).

responsibility since section 16(2) of the *Criminal Code* presumes that a person is not suffering from a mental disorder so as to be exempt from criminal responsibility "until the contrary is proved on the balance of probabilities".[41]

(g) Admissions by the Defence

The defence is entitled to admit a fact in issue thereby avoiding the necessity of the Crown proving the fact. Section 655 of the *Code* provides that:

> Where an accused is on trial for an indictable offence, he or his counsel may admit any fact alleged against him for the purpose of dispensing with proof thereof.

For example, counsel for the defence may admit that a child witness is of sufficient intelligence to give sworn testimony.[42] Similarly, the defence may admit that the statement given by the accused was voluntary, dispensing with the necessity of holding a *voir dire*.[43]

However, the Crown is not required to accept an admission by the defence where to do so might preclude the Crown from leading evidence on a vital issue. For example, in *Castellani*,[44] the accused was charged with the capital murder of his wife. She had died of arsenic poisoning after ingesting quantities of arsenic over several months prior to her death. At trial, counsel for the defence at trial wanted to admit that the accused had been having an extramarital affair with another woman to prevent the Crown from leading the evidence-in-chief that the accused and the other woman were planning to marry immediately after his wife was dead and that these plans were made while she was critically ill. In other words, the admission was to prevent the Crown from showing a motive by the accused to commit the murder. It was held by the Supreme Court of Canada that the trial judge was correct in refusing to permit the admission. It was not open for an accused to frame the Crown's allegations so as to conform to his own purpose and then insist on admitting them.

---

[41]   *Chaulk* (1990), 2 C.R. (4th) 1, 62 C.C.C. (3d) 193, 69 Man. R. (2d) 161, [1991] 2 W.W.R. 385, 1 C.R.R. (2d) 1, 119 N.R. 161, [1990] 3 S.C.R. 1303, 1990 CarswellMan 385, [1990] S.C.J. No. 139.

[42]   *Fong*, 92 C.C.C. (3d) 171, 157 A.R. 73, 77 W.A.C. 73, 1994 CarswellAlta 697 (C.A.).

[43]   *Park*, [1981] 2 S.C.R. 64, 37 N.R. 501, 21 C.R. (3d) 182, 59 C.C.C. (2d) 385, 122 D.L.R. (3d) 1, 1981 CarswellOnt 614.

[44]   (1969), [1970] S.C.R. 310, 9 C.R.N.S. 111, 71 W.W.R. 147, [1970] 4 C.C.C. 287, 11 D.L.R. (3d) 92, 1969 CarswellBC 187, 1969 CarswellBC 259.

4. CROSS-EXAMINATION BY THE DEFENCE

(a) The Nature of the Cross-examination

When the prosecution has completed its examination-in-chief of a witness, the defence may cross-examine that witness. The purpose of cross-examination is to show that the witness is mistaken or lying, or it may be directed towards bringing out facts favourable to the defence that were not brought out in chief by the prosecution. Here, questions that suggest the answer are not only permitted, they will often be put to the witness by the cross-examiner.

The general rule is that questions on cross-examination must relate either to a fact in issue or to the impeachment of the witness's credibility. Impeachment of the witness's credibility allows the cross-examiner to ask the witness questions about misconduct on unrelated matters which may not have resulted in a conviction.[45] The purpose is to suggest that the witness should not be believed because of such bad character. The witness may also be cross-examined regarding an outstanding charge against him for the purpose of showing a possible motivation to seek favour with the Crown.[46] Impeachment of the witness's credibility also allows the cross-examiner to ask the witness questions not related to a fact in issue to show that the witness may have a motive to lie, may be biased against the accused or may be a person not worthy of belief. If the question is not relevant to a fact in issue or to the witness's credibility, the trial judge has the duty to disallow it even if the opposing counsel does not object.[47]

Although the defence is entitled to cross-examine a witness about testimony that was introduced by other witnesses, what is not permitted is to ask the witness to comment upon the credibility of another witness. That calls for speculation on the part of the witness as to the motives of those witnesses and an opinion as to whether they are lying, which is irrelevant to the inquiry. It is the responsibility of the trier of fact, not the witness, to assess the credibility of the witnesses.[48]

---

[45]   *Davison* (1974), 6 O.R. (2d) 103, 20 C.C.C. (2d) 424 (C.A.), leave to appeal refused, 6 O.R. (2d) 103n, 20 C.C.C. (2d) 424n, [1974] S.C.R. viii.

[46]   *Titus*, [1983] 1 S.C.R. 259, 33 C.R. (3d) 17, 2 C.C.C. (3d) 321, 144 D.L.R. (3d) 577, 46 N.R. 477, 1983 CarswellOnt 64, 1983 CarswellOnt 806; *Gonzague*, 34 C.R. (3d) 169, 4 C.C.C. (3d) 505, 1983 CarswellOnt 81 (C.A.).

[47]   *Rowbotham (No. 5)*, 2 C.R. (3d) 293, 1977 CarswellOnt 8 (G.S.P.); *Bourassa*, 38 Q.A.C. 10, 67 C.C.C. (3d) 143, 1991 CarswellQue 130 (C.A.).

[48]   *Markadonis*, [1935] S.C.R. 657, 64 C.C.C. 41, [1935] 3 D.L.R. 424, 1935 CarswellNS 50; *Brown*, 41 A.R. 69, 1 C.C.C. (3d) 107, 1982 CarswellAlta 470 (C.A.), affirmed, [1985]

The trial judge also has the duty to prevent the cross-examiner from putting a question to the witness which is vexatious or has the effect of misleading or leaving a false impression with the court.[49] In *Rowbotham*, Judge Borins (as he then was) described that duty this way:

> The trial judge may disallow any question put in cross-examination which may appear to him vexatious and not relevant to any matter proper to be inquired into, e.g., questions as to alleged improprieties of remote date or of such a nature as not seriously to affect present credibility. Thus, the trial judge may ask himself or herself in any particular situation whether the danger of unfair prejudice against the witness and the party calling him from character impeachment outweighs the probable value of the light shed on credibility. The court has a responsibility to ensure that witnesses are dealt with fairly and to prevent victimization. It is not the witness who is on trial. Counsel who proceeds on that premise frequently fails to assess the situation carefully.[50]

If the defence intends to introduce evidence contradicting the testimony of a witness on a *significant* fact in issue, it is generally recognized that counsel for the defence has the obligation during cross-examination to put the substance of that evidence to the witness so that the witness can have the opportunity of explaining the contradiction.[51] If the witness is not cross-examined by the defence on matters that are of *significance* to the facts in issue, and the defence then leads evidence which contradicts that witness on those issues, the trier of fact may take the failure to cross-examine into consideration in assessing the credibility of that witness and the contradictory evidence offered by the other side.[52]

This rule is based on fairness to prevent a witness from being ambushed; but it does not mean that the defence is required to slog through a prosecution witness's evidence in chief putting the witness on notice of every detail that the defence does not accept.[53] The failure to challenge a witness's version of events on significant matters that are

2 S.C.R. 273, 21 C.C.C. (3d) 477, 21 D.L.R. (4th) 761, 40 Alta. L.R. (2d) 193, [1986] 1 W.W.R. 97, 62 N.R. 241, 1985 CarswellAlta 184, 1985 CarswellAlta 614; *Yakelaya*, 20 C.C.C. (3d) 193, 46 C.R. (3d) 282, 9 O.A.C. 284, 14 C.R.R. 381, 1985 CarswellOnt 105 (C.A.).

[49] *Anderson*, [1938] 2 W.W.R. 49, 46 Man. R. 97, 70 C.C.C. 275, [1938] 3 D.L.R. 317, 1938 CarswellMan 23 (C.A.); *Bourassa*, 38 Q.A.C. 10, 67 C.C.C. (3d) 143, 1991 CarswellQue 130 (C.A.); *Hehr*, 24 Alta. L.R. (2d) 59, 18 M.V.R. 244, 1982 CarswellAlta 254 (Q.B.).

[50] *Supra*, note 47, at (C.R.) p. 299.

[51] *Browne v. Dunn* (1893), 6 R. 67 (H.L.).

[52] *Paris*, 150 C.C.C. (3d) 162, 138 O.A.C. 287, 2000 CarswellOnt 4771 (C.A.), leave to appeal refused, 2001 CarswellOnt 2137, 2001 CarswellOnt 2138 (S.C.C.).

[53] *Verney*, 67 O.A.C. 279, 87 C.C.C. (3d) 363, 1993 CarswellOnt 1157 (C.A.).

later contradicted in evidence by the defence is not controlled by a hard and fast rule; it will depend on the circumstances of the case. In some circumstances, the position of the defence on a significant matter will be clear even without cross-examination; or when considered in the overall context of the case, the fact in issue may turn out to be not significant at all. On the other hand, where the central feature of a complainant's evidence is left untouched, or even implicitly accepted in cross-examination, then the absence of cross-examination may have a negative impact on the accused's credibility.

There is no requirement that a cross-examiner only put suggestions to a witness that he can prove. That issue was clearly settled in *Bencardino*.[54] There a Crown witness had given evidence incriminating the accused and then testified for the defence changing his evidence. The Crown then called a barrister who had acted for the witness on his own trial seeking to prove what the barrister had told the Crown. The trial judge had refused to allow the Crown to elicit such evidence. Jessup J.A., delivering the judgment of the Ontario Court of Appeal, said that he deprecated the tactics of the Crown counsel in implying "without evidence to support such an implication", a lack of integrity on the part of defence counsel. However, he was unable to say any illegality was involved. He went on to adopt the words of Lord Radcliffe in *Fox v. General Medical Council*,[55] where he said:

> An advocate is entitled to use his discretion as to whether to put questions in the course of cross-examination which are based on material which he is not in a position to prove directly. The penalty is that, if he gets a denial or some answer that does not suit him, the answer stands against him for what it is worth.[56]

(b) Questions as to Credibility — Rule Against Collateral Evidence

As already noted previously, impeachment of the witness's credibility allows the cross-examiner to ask the witness questions not related to a fact in issue to show that the witness may have a motive to lie, may be biased against the accused or may be a person not worthy of belief. Questions in cross-examination that are directed solely to the credibility of a witness and not to a fact in issue are said to be collateral. The rule is that except for questions in cross-examination pertaining to the wit-

---

[54] 2 O.R. (2d) 351, 15 C.C.C. (2d) 342, 24 C.R.N.S. 173, 1973 CarswellOnt 51 (C.A.).

[55] [1960] 1 W.L.R. 1017, [1960] 3 All E.R. 225 (P.C.).

[56] *Ibid.,* at (W.L.R.) p. 1023.

ness's previous criminal record and other recognized exceptions, neither the defence nor the Crown is allowed to call evidence to refute the answer given by the witness. The reason why evidence to refute a witness on a collateral issue is not permitted, even though it may show that the witness is not a believable person, is because it is too remote and may distract the jury from the main issue in the case. There is a concern that it would only encourage a series of mini-trials on the credibility of each witness and unduly prolong the length of the trial.

One statutory exception to the rule — section 12 of the *Canada Evidence Act* — relates to previous convictions and will be dealt with in the next section. Evidence that demonstrates bias or partiality by a witness is another exception to the collateral facts rule.[57] For example, in *M. (P.)*,[58] where the accused was charged with sexual assault and gross indecency involving a 12-year-old, reply evidence was permitted to show bias on the part of the complainant's mother who had lived with the accused for about six years. Medical evidence to demonstrate that a witness suffers from a mental disease or abnormality of the mind which may affect the reliability of his evidence is another exception to the collateral facts rule.[59] Here, evidence may be led, not only as to the foundation of and the reason for the diagnosis, but also the extent to which the credibility of the witness is affected. Finally, it has been recognized that evidence may be called to show that the witness cannot be believed on oath. Here the evidence is restricted. The witness may only be asked whether he or she knows the witness's reputation for veracity and whether, from such knowledge, he or she would believe the witness on oath.[60]

Occasionally a strict application of the rule will cause a miscarriage of justice and the courts will relax its strict enforcement. For example, in instances of alleged sexual abuse where there are no witnesses other than the victim and the accused, and the defence is that the assault never happened, evidence that the victim has made other false allegations would undoubtedly be relevant not only to her general credibility but

[57] *McDonald* (1959), [1960] S.C.R. 186, 32 C.R. 101, 126 C.C.C. 1, 1959 CarswellOnt 38; *Babinski*, 135 C.C.C. (3d) 1, 122 O.A.C. 1, 44 O.R. (3d) 695, 1999 CarswellOnt 1360, [1999] O.J. No. 1407 (C.A.).
[58] 42 O.A.C. 153, 1 O.R. (3d) 341, 1990 CarswellOnt 696 (C.A.).
[59] *Hawke*, 7 O.R. (2d) 145, 22 C.C.C. (2d) 19, 29 C.R.N.S. 1, 1975 CarswellOnt 4 (C.A.); *French* (1977), 37 C.C.C. (2d) 201 (Ont. C.A.), affirmed (1979), [1980] 1 S.C.R. 158, 28 N.R. 100, 47 C.C.C. (2d) 411, 98 D.L.R. (3d) 385, 1979 CarswellOnt 709F.
[60] *Toohey v. Metropolitan Police Commissioner*, [1965] A.C. 595, [1965] 1 All E.R. 506, 49 Cr. App. R. 148 (H.L.); *Gonzague, supra*, note 46. But see a criticism of the exception in *Clarke*, 18 C.R. (5th) 219, 112 O.A.C. 233, 129 C.C.C. (3d) 1, 1998 CarswellOnt 3447, [1998] O.J. No. 3521 (C.A.).

also to the issue of whether or not a sexual assault occurred. However, the courts have refused to permit the defence to call in reply evidence of other false accusations because "it would introduce a collateral issue of credibility which would be as difficult to resolve as those contained in the complaints of which the trial judge was seized".[61]

For example, in *Riley*,[62] the accused, who was charged with sexual assault, alleged that the accusation was false and that the complainant had made a false accusation against one R, who had been acquitted of a similar accusation against him. However, the trial judge had curtailed the defence's cross-examination of the complainant on the alleged false accusation and refused to allow R to be called to testify as to the falsity of the accusations against him. The Ontario Court of Appeal held that the trial judge's ruling was correct. It noted that even if they had a proper record of R's trial, a not guilty verdict, standing by itself, could not establish that the prosecution was based on fabricated evidence by the complainant.

Even a trial judge's finding that a police officer was a compulsive liar has been considered by the Ontario Court of Appeal to be nothing more than an opinion on unrelated testimony given by the witness in the context of another case.[63] In *Ghorvei*,[64] the accused, who had been convicted of trafficking and breach of recognizance, sought, on appeal, to introduce fresh evidence of the finding by the trial judge against the police officer in the form of a transcript of a previous trial of another accused. It was held that had there been a conviction of the police officer for perjury or for giving contradictory evidence under oath with respect to the facts of the other trial, that conviction could have been used on cross-examination. However, since it was nothing more than a rejection of the officer's evidence, it was a collateral issue and not admissible.

Recently, English courts have shown signs of a more liberal approach to allowing such rebuttal evidence by the defence. For example, in an English case, *Chandu Nagrecha*,[56] the accused, an owner of a restaurant, was charged with indecently assaulting the complainant, one

[61] *Riley*, 11 O.R. (3d) 151, 1992 CarswellOnt 707 (C.A.), leave to appeal refused, 154 N.R. 400 (note), 13 O.R. (3d) xvi, 64 O.A.C. 400 (note), [1993] 2 S.C.R. x, at (O.R.) p. 154; *Harper*, 149 Nfld. & P.E.I.R. 295, 467 A.P.R. 295, 1997 CarswellPEI 37, [1997] P.E.I.J. No. 41 (C.A.).
[62] *Ibid.*
[63] *Ghorvei*, 138 C.C.C. (3d) 340, 124 O.A.C. 301, 29 C.R. (5th) 102, 46 O.R. (3d) 63, 1999 CarswellOnt 2763 (C.A.).
[64] *Ibid.*
[65] [1997] 2 Cr. App. R. 401; see also *Busby* (1981), 75 Cr. App. R. 79 (C.A.); *Funderburk* (1990), Cr. App. R. 466; *Marsh* (1985), 83 Cr. App. R. 165.

of his employees. The only witnesses were the complainant and the accused. The defence was not that the complainant consented but that the alleged assault had never happened. At trial, counsel for the accused cross-examined the complainant about allegations of sexual impropriety that she had made against other men but she denied them. The trial judge then refused to allow the defence to call evidence as to the making of those complaints. The Court of Appeal held that the judge had erred. The Court said that the evidence went not merely to credit, but to the heart of the case. It could also be said that the evidence was also admissible on the basis of similar fact evidence, although the Court did not give this as a reason. In other words, the fact that the complainant had made a false complaint about other men went to the issue of whether she had made a false complaint against the accused and was relevant to her credibility.

The practice of putting questions that are directed only to credibility and are collateral to the issues in the case can often be abused. A good example was the common practice in a sexual assault prosecution before the enactment of section 276 of the *Criminal Code* of defence counsel asking the complainant whether she ever had sexual intercourse with a person other than the accused. The fact that the complainant had sexual intercourse with another male person who was not her husband was not then, nor is it now, relevant to the issue of whether she consented to intercourse with the accused. Nevertheless, the courts permitted the question under the guise that it tested her credibility, although it was more likely allowed because of the stereotypical belief that a woman who had sexual relations with someone other than her husband was more likely to have consented to having sexual relations with the accused and was, therefore, not worthy of belief. If the complainant denied it, the defence was not allowed to call evidence to refute it. It was collateral to the issue of whether she consented to sexual intercourse with the accused and the defence was bound by her answer. However, damage to the complainant's credibility was often caused by the mere asking of the question. If she answered truthfully and admitted that she had, there was the concern that she would be judged on her morality rather than her credibility. Section 276 of the *Criminal Code* has now put an end to such practice unless the defence can establish that the question is relevant to a fact in issue.

(c) Previous Criminal Record of the Witness

The one statutory exception to the rule against admitting collateral evidence is section 12 of the *Canada Evidence Act*. Section 12 allows the cross-examiner to ask a witness whether he or she has been convicted of "any offence". If the witness denies the fact or refuses to answer, the opposite party is allowed to prove the conviction, even though such evidence is strictly collateral to the facts in issue. The rationale underlying this section is that the question goes to the credibility of the witness. In other words, the fact that a witness has a criminal record goes to the issue of whether the witness is worthy of belief.[66] Presumably, it is based on the assumption that a person who has a criminal record is less likely to tell the truth than a person who does not. At the same time, the judge is required to instruct the jury that they are only entitled to consider the record of the witness for the purpose of assessing his or her credibility with respect to the issue before the court. It is assumed that the jury will honour the judge's instructions.

Section 12(1) authorizes the cross-examiner to ask the witness whether he or she "has been convicted of any offence". The plain language of the section would seem to restrict the cross-examiner to questioning the witness about the particulars of the offence and not the underlying facts resulting in the conviction. The Ontario Court of Appeal, however, has said that since section 12 is permissive in its terms, cross-examination must be limited within the bounds of relevance and propriety.[67] The Court reasoned that since cross-examination on the underlying facts of the conviction may be relevant "to discreditable conduct and associations, unrelated to the subject-matter of the testimony, as a ground for disbelieving" the witness's testimony, the trial judge could allow such cross-examination.

The expression "conviction" used in section 12 has been interpreted to include the sentence imposed by the court so that the cross-examiner may question the witness about the penalty imposed.[68] The words "any offence" in section 12 have been interpreted to mean any offence under a federal statute even though it does not truly relate to the criminal law power of the federal government.[69] Those words have also

[66] *Pleich*, 16 C.R. (3d) 194, 55 C.C.C. (2d) 13, 1980 CarswellOnt 44 (C.A.).
[67] *Miller*, 21 C.R. (5th) 178, 131 C.C.C. (3d) 141, 116 .A.C.331, 1998 CarswellOnt 4983, [1998] O.J. No. 5356 (C.A.); *Gassyt*, 127 C.C.C. (3d) 546, 114 O.A.C. 147, 1998 CarswellOnt 3241 (C.A.), leave to appeal refused (1999), 244 N.R. 400 (note), 126 O.A.C. 200 (note) (S.C.C.).
[68] *Boyce*, 7 O.R. (2d) 561, 23 C.C.C. (2d) 16, 28 C.R.N.S. 336, 1974 CarswellOnt 46 (C.A.).
[69] *Watkins*, 70 C.C.C. (3d) 341, 54 O.A.C. 200, 1992 CarswellOnt 1062 (C.A.).

been interpreted to include convictions for offences committed outside of Canada so long as the process of adjudication of guilt is of a character that would constitute a conviction under Canadian law.[70]

On the other hand, it is considered improper to cross-examine a witness with respect to a conviction for which he or she has been granted a pardon. Section 749(3) of the *Criminal Code* provides that a person granted a free pardon is deemed never to have committed the offence in respect of which the pardon is granted. Moreover, section 5 of the *Criminal Records Act* provides that a pardon is evidence of the fact that the conviction in respect of which the pardon is granted should no longer reflect adversely on the convicted person's character.[71] Similarly, section 12 does not permit cross-examination of a witness on an offence of which he or she was found guilty and granted a discharge, or a conditional discharge and the conditions were subsequently fulfilled.[72]

(d) Protection from Self-Incrimination

Section 7 of the *Charter* guarantees everyone the right to life, liberty and security of the person and the right not to deprived thereof except in accordance with the principles of fundamental justice. This right has been interpreted by the Supreme Court of Canada to encompass the right to remain silent and is broader than the common law confession rule and the rule against self-incrimination.[73] Nevertheless, a witness who is facing the same or similar charges as the accused does not have an absolute right to silence protected by section 7 if that witness is subpoenaed to testify at the accused's separate trial. In *S. (R.J.)*,[74] the Supreme Court said that although a statutory compulsion to testify engages a witness's liberty interest under section 7, that interest can only be affected in accordance with the principles of fundamental justice. The Court reasoned that since sections 11(c) and 13 of the *Charter* prevent the witness's testimony and a limited class of evidence derived from that witness's testimony being used against him or her in other

---

[70] *Stratton*, 42 C.C.C. (2d) 449, 21 O.R. (2d) 258, 3 C.R. (3d) 289, 90 D.L.R. (3d) 420, 1978 CarswellOnt 29 (C.A.).

[71] *Paterson*, 122 C.C.C. (3d) 254, 102 B.C.A.C. 200, 166 W.A.C. 200, 1998 CarswellBC 122 (C.A.), leave to appeal refused (1999), 242 N.R. 199 (note), 132 B.C.A.C. 139 (note), 215 W.A.C. 139 (note) (S.C.C.).

[72] *Danson* (1982), 35 O.R. (2d) 777, 66 C.C.C. (2d) 369 (C.A.).

[73] *Hebert*, 47 B.C.L.R. (2d) 1, [1990] 2 S.C.R. 151, 77 C.R. (3d) 145, [1990] 5 W.W.R. 1, 57 C.C.C. (3d) 1, 110 N.R. 1, 49 C.R.R. 114, 1990 CarswellBC 139.

[74] 36 C.R. (4th) 1, 26 C.R.R. (2d) 1, 177 N.R. 81, 21 O.R. (3d) 797 (note), 96 C.C.C. (3d) 1, [1995] 1 S.C.R. 451, 78 O.A.C. 161, 121 D.L.R. (4th) 589, 1995 CarswellOnt 2.

proceedings, save for proceedings in respect of perjury or for the giving of contradictory evidence, fundamental justice is satisfied.

The Court, however, did stress that the *Charter* protections contained in sections 11(c) and 13 do not authorize the Crown or the defence to engage in all types of inquisition. It noted that although the principle against self-incrimination generally finds recognition not only in section 13 but also under section 24(2) of the *Charter*, derivative evidence which could not have been obtained, or the significance of which could not have been appreciated, but for the testimony of the witness, should generally be excluded under section 7 in the interests of trial fairness. The Court reasoned that, although such evidence is not created by the accused and thus not self-incriminatory by definition, it is self-incriminatory nonetheless because the evidence could not have otherwise become part of the Crown's case. In such instance, the witness must be protected against assisting the Crown in creating a case to meet.

The Court did not feel that there should be an automatic rule of exclusion for derivative evidence. It said that exclusion should be governed by the trial judge's discretion. The exercise of that discretion should depend upon the probative effect of the evidence balanced against the prejudice caused to the accused by its admission. Moreover, the burden is on the accused to demonstrate that the proposed evidence is derivative evidence deserving of protection from being used against the accused.

5. THE REQUIREMENT FOR CORROBORATION

Although it is often said that the common law system is distinguishable from the civil law system because the court is entitled to reach a decision on the unsupported evidence of one witness, that is not the way it always was. In its infancy, the jury system required that a certain number of persons swear upon oath that an accused was guilty or not guilty, although it might be said that the witnesses were really giving evidence as to the accused's character rather than probative evidence on the question of his or her guilt or innocence. Later, as the jury system became more like what it is today, certain rules developed. One was the requirement that no prosecution for treason could succeed upon the evidence of one witness; another was that a prosecution for perjury required clear corroborating testimony. A rule of practice also developed requiring the corroboration of the testimony of accomplices, complainants in sexual cases and children.

The historical rationale requiring corroboration of an *accomplice* was stated as early as 1775 by Lord Mansfield in *Rudd*:[75]

> And though, under this practice, they are clearly competent witnesses, their single testimony alone is seldom of sufficient weight with a jury to convict the offenders; it being so strong a temptation to a man to commit perjury, if by accusing another he can escape himself.

Support for the corroboration of *women complainants* in sexual cases was based on the belief that:

> ...these cases are particularly subject to the danger of deliberately false charges, resulting from sexual neurosis, fantasy, jealousy, spite or simply a girl's refusal to admit that she consented to an act of which she is now ashamed.[76]

For the corroboration of *children*, it was argued that:

> Children are suggestible and sometimes given to living in a world of make-believe. They are egocentric, and only slowly learn the duty of speaking the truth ... a child's power of observation and memory tends to be even less reliable than that of an adult.[77]

The requirement for corroboration of the testimony of women, children and accomplices was eventually swept away by legislation and case law. The rigid rule that had been in place for over two centuries was replaced with judicial discretion. In *Vetrovec*,[78] the Supreme Court questioned the rationale for retention of the rule requiring corroboration of the testimony of an accomplice. Dickson J. (as he then was) delivering the judgment of the Court had grave doubts about the utility of its continuance. He wrote:

> None of these arguments can justify a fixed and invariable rule regarding all accomplices. All that can be established is that the testimony of some accomplices may be untrustworthy. But this can be said of many other categories of witnesses. There is nothing inherent in the evidence of an accomplice which automatically renders him untrustworthy. To construct a universal rule singling out accomplices, then, is to fasten upon this branch of the law a blind and empty formalism. Rather than attempting to pigeon-hole a witness into a category and then recite a ritualistic incantation, the trial judge might better

---

[75]   (1775), 1 Cowp. 331, 98 E.R. 1114 (K.B.), at (Cowp.) p. 336.
[76]   Glanville Williams, *Proof of Guilt*, 3rd ed. at p. 159.
[77]   *Ibid.*, at pp. 178-79.
[78]   [1982] 1 S.C.R. 811, 67 C.C.C. (2d) 1, [1983] 1 W.W.R. 193, 27 C.R. (3d) 304, 136 D.L.R. (3d) 89, 41 N.R. 606, 1982 CarswellBC 663, 1982 CarswellBC 682.

direct himself to the facts of the case and thoroughly examine all the factors which might impair the worth of a particular witness. If, in his judgment, the credit of the witness is such that the jury should be cautioned, then he may instruct accordingly. If on the other hand, he believes the witness to be trustworthy, then, regardless of whether the witness is technically an 'accomplice' no warning is necessary.[79]

Instead of a technical set instruction, what was appropriate from the trial judge was:

> . . . in some circumstances [is] a clear and sharp warning to attract the attention of the juror to the risks of adopting, without more, the evidence of the witness.[80]

Dickson J., however, recognized that there were cases where a jury might require some instruction.

> It does not, however, always follow that the presiding judge may always simply turn the jury loose upon the evidence without any assisting analysis as to whether or not a prudent finder of fact can find confirmation, somewhere in the mass of evidence, of the evidence of a witness . . . However, there is in some circumstances, particularly in lengthy trials, the need for helpful direction on the question of sifting the evidence where guilt or innocence might, and probably will, turn on the acceptance or rejection, belief or disbelief, of the evidence of one or more witnesses.[81]

Although the *Vetrovec* case seemed to suggest that the need for a warning was entirely a matter for the discretion of the trial judge who was in the best position to assess the credibility of the witness, subsequent decisions of the Supreme Court and provincial appellate courts have said that the trial judge's discretion is not untrammeled.[82] Two considerations are paramount in determining whether a warning must be given: the credibility of the witness; and the importance of the witness's evidence to the Crown's case. If a witness's evidence is highly important, a jury warning may be mandatory.

An example of where one would expect a mandatory warning is in the case of a jailhouse informant. As a matter of common sense, a

---

[79] *Ibid.*, at (C.C.C.) p. 11.
[80] *Ibid.*, at p. 17.
[81] *Ibid.*, at pp. 17-18.
[82] *Brooks*, 141 C.C.C. (3d) 321, 182 D.L.R. (4th) 513, 30 C.R. (5th) 201, 2000 SCC 11, 46 O.R. (3d) 640 (headnote only), 129 O.A.C. 205, 250 N.R. 103, [2000] 1 S.C.R. 237, 2000 CarswellOnt 292, 2000 CarswellOnt 293, [2000] S.C.J. No. 12; *Bromley*, 2001 NFCA 5, 151 C.C.C. (3d) 480, 197 Nfld. & P.E.I.R. 316, 591 A.P.R. 316, 2001 CarswellNfld 19 (C.A.).

jailhouse informant who is prepared to bargain his credibility for a lighter sentence should always be subject to an inference of untrustworthiness. However, in its most recent pronouncement on the subject, the Supreme Court has said that if the trial judge believes the witness can be trusted, then regardless of whether the witness is an accomplice or a jailhouse informant, a warning is not necessary.[83]

Legislation has swept away the requirement for corroboration of the evidence of children and of complainants in sexual cases. In 1980, section 274[84] was added to the *Criminal Code* providing that:

> Where an accused is charged with an offence under section 151, 152, 153, 155, 159, 160, 170, 171, 172, 173, 212, 271, 272 or 273, no corroboration is required for a conviction and the judge *shall not* instruct the jury that it is unsafe to find the accused guilty in the absence of corroboration.

In 1993, section 659[85] of the *Code* was amended to provide that:

> Any requirement whereby it is mandatory for a court to give the jury a warning about convicting an accused on the evidence of a child is abrogated.

Although there is no longer an obligation upon the trial judge to warn the jury about the need for corroboration, the Supreme Court has recognized that a cautionary warning may be necessary in some circumstances. In *W. (R.)*,[86] Madam Justice McLachlin, in dealing with the evidence of children, noted:

> The repeal of provisions creating a legal requirement that children's evidence be corroborated does not prevent the judge or jury from treating a child's evidence with caution where such caution is merited in the circumstances of the case. But it does revoke the assumption formerly applied to all children, often unjustly, that children's evidence is always less reliable than the evidence of adults. So if a court proceeds to discount a child's evidence automatically, without regard to the circumstances of the particular case, it will have fallen into an error.[87]

Later she said:

---

[83] *Ibid.*
[84] Chapter 125, s. 19.
[85] Section 669.
[86] 13 C.R. (4th) 257, 137 N.R. 214, [1992] 2 S.C.R. 122, 54 O.A.C. 164, 74 C.C.C. (3d) 134, 1992 CarswellOnt 90, 1992 CarswellOnt 991, [1992] S.C.J. No. 56, reconsideration refused (November 18, 1992), Doc. 21820 (S.C.C.).
[87] *Ibid.,* at (C.R.) p. 266.

It is neither desirable nor possible to state hard and fast rules as to when a witness's evidence should be assessed by reference to "adult" or "child" standards - to do so would create anew stereotypes potentially as rigid and unjust as those which the recent developments in the law's approach to children's evidence have been designed to dispel. Every person giving testimony in court, of whatever age, is an individual, whose credibility and evidence must be assessed by reference to criteria appropriate to her mental development, understanding and ability to communicate. But I would add this. In general, where an adult is testifying as to events which occurred when she was a child, her credibility should be assessed according to criteria applicable to her as an adult witness. Yet with regard to her evidence pertaining to events which occurred in childhood, the presence of inconsistencies, particularly as to peripheral matters such as time and location, should be considered in the context of the age of the witness at the time of the events to which she is testifying.[88]

The only surviving requirement for corroboration lies in prosecutions for treason,[89] perjury[90] and procuring a feigned marriage.[91] There can be no conviction for any of those offences on the evidence of one witness unless that evidence is "corroborated in a material particular by evidence that implicates the accused." Corroborative evidence is thus independent confirmatory evidence of a witness that shows or tends to show not only that a crime was committed, but also that the accused committed it. The law is that the trial judge is required to specify for the jury what items of evidence are capable of being corroborative, leaving to them the ultimate question of deciding whether such items are, in fact, corroborative. If the items viewed cumulatively, (but not alone), are capable of constituting corroboration, the trial judge must specify those items which may be considered part of the cumulative package.[92]

At common law, corroborative evidence had to be independent testimony which affected the accused by connecting or tending to connect him with the crime. The evidence could be either direct or circumstantial in nature.[93] The common law also required that the evidence emanate independently from the witness.[94]

---

[88] *Ibid.*, at pp. 267-68.
[89] *Criminal Code*, s. 47(3).
[90] *Ibid.*, s. 133.
[91] *Ibid.*, s. 292(2).
[92] *McNamara (No.1)* (1981), 56 C.C.C. (2d) 193 (Ont.C.A.), affirmed, 45 C.R. (3d) 289, 9 O.A.C. 321, 19 C.C.C. (3d) 1, 19 D.L.R. (4th) 314, 59 N.R. 241, [1985] 1 S.C.R. 662, 1985 CarswellOnt 939.
[93] *Baskerville*, [1916] 2 K.B. 658, 80 J.P. 446, 25 Cox C.C. 524, [1916-17] All E.R. Rep. 38, 12 Cr. App. R. 81 (C.A.).
[94] *Thomas*, [1952] 2 S.C.R. 344, 15 C.R. 1, 103 C.C.C. 193, [1952] 4 D.L.R. 306, 1952 CarswellOnt 16.

The common law rule has been modified in the last quarter century. Corroborative evidence need no longer emanate independently of the suspect witness.[95] The evidence need only satisfy the trier of fact that the witness is telling the truth about a salient matter in the time frame in question; it need not point specifically to the guilt of the accused.[96] Evidence given by an accomplice that is contradicted or explained by an accused may still constitute corroborative evidence; it is for the jury to decide whether the evidence, in fact, is corroborative.[97] Finally, although a piece of evidence viewed in isolation may not constitute corroboration, a number of pieces viewed collectively may constitute corroboration.

6. RE-EXAMINATION OF A CROWN WITNESS

When the defence has completed the cross-examination of the Crown witness, then Crown counsel will be permitted to re-examine the witness. The purpose of re-examination is to deal only with new evidence or clarify matters raised by the defence during cross-examination and only to reply to those new facts. The Crown is not entitled to rehash or ask the witness to repeat evidence already given by him in chief.

7. REOPENING THE CASE FOR THE CROWN

Occasionally, a prosecutor may discover that he or she has closed the case too soon and has omitted evidence crucial to the case for the Crown. The prosecutor will then apply to the trial judge to be permitted to re-open the Crown's case. Whether or not the prosecutor will be permitted to do so is a discretionary matter for the trial judge.

Historically, three stages were recognized in the trial during which the discretion of the trial judge to allow the Crown to reopen its case could be exercised. The first stage was before the Crown closed its case. Here, the trial judge had wide latitude in allowing the Crown to recall a witness to prove an omitted element of the case or correct earlier testimony. The second stage was after the Crown had closed its case. Here the trial judge had the discretion to allow the Crown to reopen its case to correct some oversight or prove a matter that it had failed to do so inadvertently, provided that there was no prejudice to the accused. How-

[95] *Murphy* (1976), [1977] 2 S.C.R. 603, 70 D.L.R. (3d) 42, [1976] 5 W.W.R. 65, 35 C.R.N.S. 44, 9 N.R. 329, 29 C.C.C. (2d) 417, 1976 CarswellBC 205.
[96] *McCaw,* 1998 CarswellOnt 724, [1998] O.J. No. 730 (C.A.), leave to appeal refused, 234 N.R. 197 (note), 118 O.A.C. 198 (note), [1998] S.C.C.A. No. 173.
[97] *McNamara (No.1), supra,* note 92.

ever, once the defence had begun to present its case, the trial judge's discretion was narrowly restricted. The Crown was only allowed to reopen its case to prove a matter, *ex improviso*, which no human ingenuity could have foreseen.[98]

Allowing the prosecution to re-open its case after the defence was called upon to meet it, was regarded as an indirect breach of the fundamental rule that an accused was not required to respond to the allegation until the Crown established that there was a "case to meet". Once there was a case to meet, then the accused could no longer remain passive and was required to answer the case against him or risk conviction.

However, in 1978, the Supreme Court of Canada seemed to sweep away these principles in *Robillard*.[99] There the Court indicated that there was absolutely no restriction on the trial judges' discretion. It said that the *ex improviso* rule did not apply to Canada and the trial judge had a wide discretion to allow the Crown to reopen its case even where the defence had been put to its election whether it intended to call evidence and had elected not to do so.

In *P. (M.B.)*,[100] the Supreme Court reconsidered its decision in *Robillard*. The Court said that although Canadian jurisprudence has not applied the strict *ex improviso* rule as it has been applied at common law, the circumstances in which the Crown may be allowed to reopen its case after the defence has begun its case should be narrow and the *Robillard* case should be construed as applying only to situations where the Crown is seeking to reopen in order to correct a matter of form. The Court gave three examples where a judge could exercise his discretion:

1.   Where the conduct of the defence, either directly or indirectly, has contributed to the Crown's failure to adduce certain evidence before closing its case.[101]

2.   Where the Crown's omission or mistake was over a non-controversial issue to do with purely formal procedural or technical matters, having nothing to do with the substance or merits of a case.[102]

---

[98]   *Cachia*, 26 C.R.N.S. 302, 17 C.C.C. (2d) 173, 1974 CarswellOnt 15 (H.C.).

[99]   [1978] 2 S.C.R. 728, 5 C.R. (3d) 186, 41 C.C.C. (2d) 1, 85 D.L.R. (3d) 449, 21 N.R. 557, 1978 CarswellQue 132.

[100]   165 N.R. 321, 29 C.R. (4th) 209, 89 C.C.C. (3d) 289, [1994] 1 S.C.R. 555, 70 O.A.C. 161, 113 D.L.R. (4th) 461, 21 C.R.R. (2d) 1, 17 O.R. (3d) 782 (note), 1994 CarswellOnt 65, 1994 CarswellOnt 1153.

[101]   *Champagne* (1969), [1970] 2 C.C.C. 273, 1969 CarswellBC 268 (C.A.); *Crawford*, 33 M.V.R. 45, 43 C.R. (3d) 80, 1984 CarswellOnt 84 (Co. Ct.).

[102]   *Kissick (No. 1)*, [1952] 1 S.C.R. 343, 14 C.R. 1, 102 C.C.C. 129, 1952 CarswellMan 1;

3.   Where the interests of the accused warrant reopening the Crown's case.[103]

It is often forgotten that there is a clear difference between an application by the Crown to reopen its case in order to call additional evidence and reply evidence called by the Crown after the defence has completed its case. When the Crown applies to reopen its case and lead additional evidence, it accepts that the additional evidence is relevant to a factual issue which was material during its case and that should have and would have been led during its case. It also offers an explanation for failing to do so, which it contends justifies departing from the normal trial format. If the evidence is an attempt to fill a gap in the Crown's case revealed by the defence, or if it effectively changes the case which the defence undertook to answer when it elected to call evidence, then the application will usually be refused, except in the rarest of cases.[104]

The right to adduce reply evidence, on the other hand, arises where the defence has led evidence which the Crown could not reasonably have anticipated. In other words, the reply evidence will take on its significance from evidence that the defence tendered during its case, not something that the Crown should have led in chief.

8. MOTION FOR DIRECTED VERDICT OR NO-CASE TO ANSWER

If the Crown has presented a *prima facie* case, the trial judge will then call upon the defence to present its case. However, the defence may ask the trial judge to direct the jury to return a verdict of acquittal on the basis that there is no *prima facie* case to answer. Where a judge presides without a jury, the defence will ask the judge to enter a verdict of not guilty him or herself.

The test that the trial judge must apply in determining if the Crown has established a *prima facie* case is whether there is any evidence upon which a reasonable jury properly instructed could convict the accused. The judge must remember that at this stage of the proceedings, the question of proof beyond a reasonable doubt does not arise. Nor is the judge entitled to take the case away from the jury and direct them to render a verdict of acquittal because he or she concludes that the evidence

---

Huluszkiw (1962), [1963] 1 O.R. 157, 37 C.R. 386, 133 C.C.C. 244, 37 D.L.R. (2d) 309 (C.A.); *Assu*, 64 C.C.C. (2d) 94, 1981 CarswellBC 724 (C.A.).
[103]   *Nelson*, [1993] O.J. No 1899, 1993 CarswellOnt 2534 (Gen. Div.).
[104]   *M. (F.S.)*, 111 C.C.C. (3d) 90, 93 O.A.C. 201, 1996 CarswellOnt 3364 (C.A.).

is manifestly unreliable. In other words, the judge is not entitled to weigh the quality of the evidence even when sitting without a jury.

Although the test appears relatively straightforward, its application to the facts of any case often creates difficulty for the trial judge. Exactly what does "any evidence" mean? In *Charemeski*,[105] where the accused was charged with the murder of his estranged wife, the trial judge had directed a verdict of acquittal on the basis that the Crown had failed to adduce evidence of *causation*. The forensic evidence had failed to establish definitely whether the deceased had died from natural causes, or as a result of an accident, suicide or homicide. In a majority judgment, the Supreme Court, however, was satisfied that the condition and position of the body as found could have led to the inference that the deceased was the victim of foul play. In dissent, McLachlin J. felt that to pass the hurdle of a directed verdict of acquittal, the Crown must adduce *sufficient* evidence on the issues of identity, causation and the requisite mental state to sustain a verdict beyond a reasonable doubt.

This means that the trial judge must, of necessity, enter into a weighing process. The judge's determination of whether there is any evidence to go to the jury requires him or her to weigh the evidence presented by the Crown to determine whether "a reasonable jury properly instructed could convict the accused". Since no reasonable jury could convict unless there was *some evidence* of substance, the judge must determine whether it is sufficient to meet this threshold test. However, in assessing the *sufficiency* of the evidence, the trial judge must never assess its *quality or reliability*. In other words, what the judge must never do is to enter the province of the jury and decide whether the testimony of the witnesses is manifestly unreliable or, where the evidence is entirely circumstantial, whether that evidence is consistent with any conclusion other than the guilt of the accused. In a jury trial, the question of the weight of the evidence on the issue of proof beyond a reasonable doubt belongs to the jury not the judge, and the judge must be careful not to usurp their function. Although, one might wonder why the same rule applies in trials by judge alone where the judge is also the trier of the facts, and is still strictly enforced.

In *Monteleone*,[106] Mr. Justice McIntyre described the rule this way:

[105] 123 C.C.C. (3d) 225, 157 D.L.R. (4th) 603, 224 N.R. 120, 15 C.R. (5th) 1, 108 O.A.C. 126, [1998] 1 S.C.R. 679, 1998 CarswellOnt 1199, 1998 CarswellOnt 1200, [1998] S.C.J. No. 23.
[106] [1987] 2 S.C.R. 154, 41 D.L.R. (4th) 746, 78 N.R. 377, 23 O.A.C. 241, 35 C.C.C. (3d) 193, 59 C.R. (3d) 97, 61 O.R. (2d) 654 (note), 1987 CarswellOnt 970 at (C.R.) p. 103.

> Where there is before the court any admissible evidence, whether direct or circumstantial, which, if believed by a properly-charged jury acting reasonably, would justify a conviction, the trial judge is not justified in directing a verdict of acquittal. It is not the function of the trial judge to weigh the evidence, to test its quality or reliability once a determination of its admissibility has been made. It is not for the trial judge to draw inferences of fact from the evidence before him. These functions are for the trier of fact, the jury.

Although some legal scholars have argued that a trial judge should go so far as to determine whether the evidence is sufficient to prove guilt beyond a reasonable doubt before it goes to the jury, that view fails to recognize and understand the different roles played by the judge and the jury in a criminal trial. They argue that such a threshold test ensures that section 7 of the *Charter*, which guarantees an accused *fundamental justice* and section 11(d), which *presumes an accused innocent until proven guilty*, can be satisfied and given their full meaning.[107]

It must be remembered, however, that the accused has chosen a jury, not a judge, to determine whether the Crown has established his or her guilt beyond a reasonable doubt and it must be assumed that the jury will obey the judge's instructions on this issue. To ask a judge to decide whether the Crown has established the guilt of the accused beyond a reasonable doubt before allowing the case to go to the jury carries the danger that if the case is allowed to go to the jury, they might feel compelled to agree with the judge's decision on that issue and find the accused guilty even if they have a reasonable doubt. Moreover, a finding of not guilty by a jury, in the face of a legal ruling by the judge that the evidence has established the accused's guilt beyond a reasonable doubt, might cause the public generally to feel that the administration of justice has been brought into disrepute.

If the judge agrees that there is no case to answer, he or she will direct the jury that, as a matter of law, they must acquit the accused. Even though the decision is a legal one, the rule until recently meant that once an accused had elected trial by jury and been placed in the jury's charge at the beginning of the trial, only the jury, not the judge, had jurisdiction to formally pronounce the verdict of not guilty and deliver him or her from that charge. This often placed the judge in an embarrassing position if the jury were reluctant to follow his or her instruction. In *Rowbotham*,[108] the Supreme Court decided to modify the

---

[107] See David Tanovich, "Annotation", 27 C.R. (4th) 174.
[108] 30 C.R. (4th) 141, 168 N.R. 220, [1994] 2 S.C.R. 463, 90 C.C.C. (3d) 449, 72 O.A.C. 98, 22 C.R.R. (2d) 193 at 195, 1994 CarswellOnt 76, 1994 CarswellOnt 2265.

rule and allow the judge to tell the jury that he or she was withdrawing the case from them and entering a verdict of acquittal. In trials by judge alone, the judge will simply render a verdict of not guilty and dismiss the charge.

9. THE CASE FOR THE DEFENCE

(a) Generally

If there is some evidence upon which a jury properly instructed could convict the accused, the judge will call upon the defence to present its case. The defence may or may not call evidence. If the defence elects to call evidence, section 651(2) of the *Criminal Code* authorizes counsel for the accused, or the accused where he or she is not represented by counsel, to make an opening address to the jury. The purpose of the opening address is to outline to the jury essentially what the defence is all about and what the defence witnesses, including the accused if it is intended to call him, are expected to say. If the defence does not intend to call witnesses, then the Crown will be directed by the trial judge to sum up its case to the jury and the defence is entitled to address the jury last.[109]

If the defence calls any witnesses, the proceedings are reversed. The witnesses will be examined in chief by counsel for the defence, or the accused if he or she is unrepresented by counsel, cross-examined by counsel for the Crown and re-examined by counsel for the accused.

(b) Alibi Evidence

Under Canadian law, everyone accused of a crime has the right to remain silent. A jury is not entitled to draw any inference against an accused because he or she chooses to exercise that right. That right, however, is not an absolute one. One exception arises where the defence is alibi. In such instance, the failure to disclose a defence of alibi in a *timely* manner may be considered by the trier in assessing the credibility of that defence.[110] The purpose of this exception is to guard against

[109] *Criminal Code*, s. 651.
[110] *Chambers*, [1990] 6 W.W.R. 554, 119 N.R. 321, [1990] 2 S.C.R. 1293, 59 C.C.C. (3d) 321, 80 C.R. (3d) 235, 49 B.C.L.R. (2d) 299, 1990 CarswellBC 217, 1990 CarswellBC 761, *per* Cory J at (C.C.C.) p. 343. See also *Russell*, 67 C.C.C. 28, [1936] 4 D.L.R. 744 (S.C.C.).

surprise alibis fabricated in the witness box that the prosecution is almost powerless to challenge.[111]

At one time, the rule required the defence to disclose an alibi immediately upon arrest.[112] However, this put the accused in an untenable position because it conflicted with the accused's right to remain silent. In *Cleghorn*,[113] the Supreme Court decided to modify the rule to define *timely disclosure* to mean "when it allows the prosecution and police to investigate the alibi evidence before trial". The Court said that the criteria of *timeliness* and *adequacy* should be evaluated on the basis of whether a meaningful investigation could have been undertaken as a result of disclosure. The new rule is that the failure to disclose an alibi at a sufficiently early time to permit it to be investigated by the police is a factor that may be considered by the trier in determining the weight to be given to it. The Court also said that timely disclosure of the alibi no longer has to be made by the accused. The right to silence at the investigative stage permits disclosure of the alibi to be made by a third party, who is a witness to the alibi.

The Court in *Cleghorn* also indicated that disclosure should be given with sufficient particularity to enable the authorities to conduct a meaningful investigation. Three pieces of information are necessary: a statement that the accused was not present at the location of the crime; the whereabouts of the accused at that time; and, the names of any witness to the alibi.The Ontario Court of Appeal has stressed that to constitute an alibi, the explanation advanced by the defence must be determinative of the final issue of guilt or innocence of the accused. In *Hill*,[114] the accused was convicted of perjury, insurance fraud and arson in connection with the burning of his boat to collect insurance money. The case for the Crown depended on the evidence of a disgruntled former employee who said that he had a meeting with the accused on a certain date at which time the accused solicited him to set fire to the boat and did so at his request. The accused testified that he could not have met with his employee on the date alleged because he was elsewhere. The trial judge charged the jury that the accused had raised an alibi defence and they could, in considering the weight to be given to the alibi, take into account the fact that it was not disclosed to the police. It was held

---

[111] *Cleghorn*, 41 C.R. (4th) 282, 100 C.C.C. (3d) 393, 186 N.R. 49, 85 O.A.C. 129, [1995] 3 S.C.R. 175, 32 C.R.R. (2d) 41, 1995 CarswellOnt 126, 1995 CarswellOnt 802.
[112] *Russell, supra*, note 110.
[113] *Supra*, note 111.
[114] 41 C.R. (4th) 299, 25 O.R. (3d) 97, 83 O.A.C. 99, 102 C.C.C. (3d) 469, 1995 CarswellOnt 127 (C.A.).

that the trial judge mischaracterized his defence as an alibi defence. At best, the accused's explanation of his whereabouts might demonstrate that the conversations could not have taken place when they were alleged to have taken place, not that they never took place. Thus the date when the accused claimed to have been elsewhere was not essential to the Crown's case against him.

Although the rationale underlying *Hill* is sound, its application to the facts in that case is difficult to understand. The facts set out in the reported judgment indicate that the case for the Crown was that the meeting between the accused and the former employee took place at a certain time and place during which the accused solicited the employee to burn his boat. The accused's defence was that he could not have met with his employee on the date alleged because he was elsewhere. Thus, the suggestion by the Court that the date when the accused claimed to have been elsewhere was not essential to the Crown's case against him and therefore not strictly alibi evidence, flies in the face of the theory of the Crown.

Where the defence has given notice to the Crown prior to trial that it intends to adduce alibi and has given details of that alibi, the Crown is not required to lead evidence-in-chief which could rebut that alibi. The Crown is entitled to wait until the accused has testified and then lead that evidence in rebuttal. The rule is that the Crown is only required to lead evidence where it is relevant to the case it is presenting; there is no obligation upon the Crown to foresee that certain evidence might later become relevant.[115]

The trial judge is required to instruct the jury that the mere fact that they disbelieve the alibi does not necessarily mean that it is concocted. It is only where they conclude that the alibi was deliberately fabricated by the accused that they are entitled to draw the inference that he did so by consciousness of guilt.[116] Although the logic of the distinction is difficult to understand, the rationale underlying the rule is that it is a necessary safeguard to prevent the jury from short-circuiting the Crown's obligation to prove guilt beyond a reasonable doubt by moving directly from disbelief to a finding of guilt.

[115] *Rafferty*, [1983] 4 W.W.R. 511, 25 Alta. L.R. (2d) 334, 43 A.R. 323, 6 C.C.C. (3d) 72, 1983 CarswellAlta 69 (C.A.); *Andrews* (1979), 8 C.R. (3d) 1, 1979 CarswellBC 546 (C.A.), leave to appeal refused (1979), 28 N.R. 537n (S.C.C.).
[116] *Carey*, 113 C.C.C. (3d) 74, 1996 CarswellQue 1070 (C.A.); *Tessier*, 113 C.C.C. (3d) 538, 87 B.C.A.C. 269, 143 W.A.C. 269, [1997] B.C.J. No. 515, 1997 CarswellBC 451 (C.A.).

10. CROSS-EXAMINATION OF DEFENCE WITNESSES

(a) Generally

Although witnesses for the defence are open to the same kind of attack as witnesses for the prosecution, an accused who testifies occupies a special position when he is being cross-examined by Crown counsel. In *Davison*,[117] Mr Justice Martin succinctly summed up that position:

> An accused who gives evidence has a dual character. As an accused he is protected by an underlying policy rule against the introduction of evidence by the prosecution tending to show that he is a person of bad character, subject of course, to the recognized exceptions to that rule. As a witness, however, his credibility is subject to attack. If the position of an accused who gives evidence is assimilated in every respect to that of an ordinary witness he is not protected against cross-examination with respect to discreditable conduct and associations. If the accused could in every case be cross-examined with a view to showing that he is a professional criminal under the guise of an attack upon his credibility as a witness it would be virtually impossible for him to receive a fair trial on the specific charge upon which he is being tried. It is not realistic to assume that, ordinarily, the jury will be able to limit the effect of such a cross-examination to the issue of credibility in arriving at a verdict. In my view the policy rule which protects an accused against attack upon his character lest it divert the jury from the issue which they are called upon to decide, namely, the guilt or innocence of the accused on the specific charge before the Court, is not wholly subordinated to the rule which permits an accused who elects to give evidence to be cross-examined on the issue of his credibility. In this area of the law, as in so many areas, a balance has been struck between competing interest, which endeavours so far as possible to recognize the purpose of both rules and does not give effect to one to the total exclusion of the other. Consequently, limitations are imposed with respect to the cross-examination of an accused which do not apply in the case of an ordinary witness...I conclude that, save for the cross-examination as to previous convictions permitted by s.12 of the Canada Evidence Act, an accused may not be cross-examined with respect to misconduct or discreditable associations unrelated to the charge on which he is being tried for the purpose of leading to the conclusion that by reason of his bad character he is a person whose evidence ought not be believed. Cross-examination, however, which is directly relevant to prove the falsity of the accused's evidence does not fall within the ban notwithstanding that it may incidently reflect upon the accused's character by disclosing discreditable conduct on his part.

---

[117] (1974), 6 O.R. (2d) 103, 20 C.C.C. (2d) 424 (C.A.), leave to appeal refused, 6 O.R. (2d) 103n, 20 C.C.C. (2d) 424n, [1974] S.C.R. viii, approved in *Stewart*, 62 C.C.C. (3d) 289, 43 O.A.C. 109, 1991 CarswellOnt 1317 (C.A.).

It is improper for the Crown to ask the accused to express an opinion whether another witness for the prosecution is lying since the opinion of one witness about the veracity of another witness is a matter solely for the court to consider, not the accused or any other defence witness.[118] Similarly, it is considered improper for the Crown to ask the accused why a complainant would make up the allegations since such questions place some obligation on the accused to provide some motive for the complainant to lie.[119]

As noted above, other witnesses for the defence do not have the same protection. They are subject to the same attack as any other witness and may be cross-examined with respect to misconduct on unrelated matters which have not resulted in a conviction[120] with a view to showing that the witness ought not to be believed because of such bad character.[121] Impeachment of the witness's credibility also allows the cross-examiner to ask the witness questions not related to a fact in issue to show that the witness may have a motive to lie, may be biased in favour of the accused or may be a person not worthy of belief.

(b) Questions as to Credibility — Rule Against Collateral Evidence

As has already been pointed out, the general rule is that questions in cross-examination must relate either to a fact in issue or to the impeachment of the witness's credibility. Generally, the Crown is entitled to call evidence in reply to refute an answer given by the accused or a defence witness to a fact in issue. However, the rule is different where the question is asked to test the credibility of the witness and does not relate to a fact in issue. Here, the prosecution is not allowed to call evidence to refute the answer given by the witness or the accused; the prosecution is bound by the answer. An exception to that rule is where the questions pertain to the previous criminal record of the accused or

---

[118] *Markadonis*, [1935] S.C.R. 657, 64 C.C.C. 41, [1935] 3 D.L.R. 424, 1935 CarswellNS 50; *Vandenberghe*, 96 C.C.C. (3d) 371, 1995 CarswellOnt 1806, [1995] O.J. No. 243 (C.A.); *Rose*, 153 C.C.C. (3d) 225, 42 C.R. (5th) 183, 143 O.A.C. 163, 53 O.R. (3d) 417, 2001 CarswellOnt 955 (C.A.).

[119] *F. (A.)*, 30 O.R. (3d) 470, 93 O.A.C. 102, 1 C.R. (5th) 382, 1996 CarswellOnt 3157 (C.A.). But see *P. (H.P.)*, 112 C.C.C. (3d) 140, 113 Man. R. (2d) 271, 131 W.A.C. 271, 1996 CarswellMan 586 (C.A.).

[120] *Davison, supra*, note 117.

[121] *Titus*, [1983] 1 S.C.R. 259, 33 C.R. (3d) 17, 2 C.C.C. (3d) 321, 144 D.L.R. (3d) 577, 46 N.R. 477, 1983 CarswellOnt 64, 1983 CarswellOnt 806; *Gonzague*, 34 C.R. (3d) 169, 4 C.C.C. (3d) 505, 1983 CarswellOnt 81 (C.A.).

242 THE PRACTICAL GUIDE TO EVIDENCE IN CRIMINAL CASES

the witness for the defence. In such instance, s. 12 of the *Canada Evidence Act* permits the cross-examiner to prove the record.

One might question the wisdom of a rule that allows one side to ask a question to test credibility but does not allow evidence in reply to prove that the witness is being untruthful on that issue. The reason for the rule is to ensure that the trier concentrates on the issue in dispute and avoids a multiplicity of proceedings. If the cross-examiner were allowed to call impeachment evidence on every question that was put to a witness, it would mean that trials would be sidetracked and unduly prolonged by a series of mini-trials to refute a witness's testimony.

(c) Criminal Record of the Accused

Section 12 of the *Canada Evidence Act* provides that a witness (which includes the accused) "may be questioned as to whether he has been convicted of any offence" and, if he or she denies the fact or refuses to answer, the opposite party may prove the conviction. When it comes to the accused, as opposed to an ordinary witness, the word "conviction" has been strictly construed. Section 12 does not permit the Crown to go beyond prior convictions and to cross-examine an accused as to discreditable conduct or association with disreputable individuals in order to attack his credibility.[122] Nor does it permit cross-examination where the accused was found guilty and granted a discharge, or a conditional discharge and the conditions were subsequently fulfilled.[123] Similarly, it is considered improper to cross-examine a witness with respect to a conviction for which he or she has been granted a pardon. Section 749(3) of the *Criminal Code* provides that a person granted a free pardon is deemed never to have committed the offence in respect of which the pardon is granted. Moreover, section 5 of the *Criminal Records Act* provides that a pardon is evidence of the fact that the conviction in respect of which the pardon is granted should no longer reflect adversely on the convicted person's character.[124]

The risk of such questions in the case of the accused, unlike a witness, is that the jury may conclude that because the accused has been convicted of an offence on a previous occasion, he or she probably committed the offence that they are trying. This imposes upon the trial

---

[122] *Davison, supra*, note 117.
[123] R.S.C. 1985, c. C-47.
[124] *Paterson*, 122 C.C.C. (3d) 254, 102 B.C.A.C. 200, 166 W.A.C. 200, 1998 CarswellBC 122 (C.A.), leave to appeal refused (1999), 242 N.R. 199 (note), 132 B.C.A.C. 139 (note), 215 W.A.C. 139 (note) (S.C.C.).

judge the responsibility of instructing the jury that they must not draw this inference against the accused. The jury must be specifically told that they may not use the accused's prior criminal record to show that the accused was likely to commit the offence charged.[125] The judge must also instruct the jury that they are only entitled to consider the criminal record of the accused for the purpose of assessing his credibility with respect to the issues before the court. The jury system assumes that the jury will honour those instructions.[126]

For some time, the law was uncertain as to whether the trial judge had any discretion to disallow questions about prior convictions where it was prejudicial to an accused, such as where the conviction was an old one, or where it bore no relationship to the issue of credibility (*i.e.*, convictions for dishonesty such as forgery, cheating and the like).[127] Some trial judges felt that the word "may" in section 12 gave the judge the discretion to disallow the question in a proper case.[128] In *Stratton*,[129] the Ontario Court of Appeal appeared to put the issue to rest when it concluded that there was no judicial discretion to exclude evidence rendered admissible by the section.

Eight years later, the Supreme Court of Canada examined the entire issue in *Corbett*.[130] There, the constitutionality of s. 12 was challenged on the basis that it infringed an accused's presumption of innocence guaranteed by section 11(d) of the *Charter*. In a majority decision, that argument was rejected. The Court said that the fact that the accused has a criminal record does not mean that he or she should not be believed. It is only a factor that may be taken into account by the trier in assessing an accused's credibility. However, it was prepared to recognize that a trial judge does have a discretion to exclude evidence of previous convictions of an accused in those cases where a mechanical application of section 12 of the *Canada Evidence Act* would undermine the right of an accused to a fair trial as guaranteed by the *Charter*.

---

[125] *Todish*, 7 O.A.C. 336, 18 C.C.C. (3d) 159, 1985 CarswellOnt 1394 (C.A.); *P. (M.)*, 151 C.C.C. (3d) 193, 139 O.A.C. 129, 52 O.R. (3d) 631, 2001 CarswellOnt 66 (C.A.).

[126] *Corbett*, [1988] 1 S.C.R. 670, [1988] 4 W.W.R. 481, 85 N.R. 81, 28 B.C.L.R. (2d) 145, 41 C.C.C. (3d) 385, 64 C.R. (3d) 1, 34 C.R.R. 54, 1988 CarswellBC 252, 1988 CarswellBC 756.

[127] *Morris* (1978), [1979] 1 S.C.R. 405, 6 C.R. (3d) 36, 43 C.C.C. (2d) 129, 91 D.L.R. (3d) 161, 23 N.R. 109, 1978 CarswellQue 38, at (C.C.C.) p. 153.

[128] *Powell* (1977), 37 C.C.C. (2d) 117 (Ont. Gen. Div.); *Skehan* (1978), 39 C.C.C. (2d) 196 (Ont. H.C.).

[129] 42 C.C.C. (2d) 449, 21 O.R. (2d) 258, 3 C.R. (3d) 289, 90 D.L.R. (3d) 420, 1978 CarswellOnt 29 (C.A.).

[130] [1988] 1 S.C.R. 670, [1988] 4 W.W.R. 481, 85 N.R. 81, 28 B.C.L.R. (2d) 145, 41 C.C.C. (3d) 385, 64 C.R. (3d) 1, 34 C.R.R. 54, 1988 CarswellBC 252, 1988 CarswellBC 756.

Chief Justice Dickson, who delivered the main majority judgment, recognized that there was always a risk that a jury, if told that the accused had a criminal record, might make more of that fact than it should. On the other hand, he also recognized that there was the risk that concealing the prior record of an accused who testified would deprive the jury of information relevant to his credibility, and create a serious risk that they would be presented with a misleading picture. Although accepting that the trial judge has a discretion to exclude prejudicial evidence in an appropriate case, he felt that often the best way to balance and alleviate these risks was to give the jury all of the information and at the same time require the trial judge to give them clear directions as to the limited use that they were to make of such information.

What factors should a trial judge consider in exercising his or her discretion to exclude all or part of an accused's criminal record? Chief Justice Dickson indicated that he regarded those factors listed by Mr. Justice La Forest in his dissenting judgment as useful. Mr. Justice La Forest recognized that it was impossible to provide an exhaustive catalogue of factors in assessing the probative value or potential prejudice of such evidence. He did begin, however, by stating that he regarded the nature of the prior conviction as among the most important considerations. A conviction which involved acts of deceit, fraud, cheating or stealing was more probative of a person's honesty and integrity than an act of violence that had little or no direct bearing on a person's veracity. Another factor creating potential prejudice was the similarity of the prior conviction to the charge before the court.[131] He felt that a trial judge should be wary of admitting such evidence unless it met the stringent test for admitting similar fact evidence. The remoteness or nearness of the previous conviction was also a factor to be considered. A conviction, even one involving an act of dishonesty, which occurred long before, should be generally excluded on the ground of remoteness.

One issue that gave Mr. Justice La Forest concern is the fairness to the Crown of prohibiting the cross-examination of an accused on prior convictions where the defence has made a deliberate attack upon the credibility of a Crown witness, particularly where the case boils down to a credibility contest between the accused and that witness. He was prepared to recognize that, in such instance, the jury was entitled to have before it the record of the person attacking the character of the Crown witness in order to determine whether he was any more worthy of belief

---

[131]   *P. (G.F.)*, 29 C.R. (4th) 315, 18 O.R. (3d) 1, 89 C.C.C. (3d) 176, 70 O.A.C. 350, 1994 CarswellOnt 67 (C.A.); *Trudel*, 60 Q.A.C. 138, [1994] R.J.Q. 678, 90 C.C.C. (3d) 318, 1994 CarswellQue 167, [1994] A.Q. No. 114 (C.A.).

than the person attacked. He felt, however, that this was not a factor that should override the concern for a fair trial.

Cases decided since *Corbett* have generally held that the test in determining whether the criminal record of an accused should be excluded is a balancing of interest, that is, a balancing of probative value against prejudicial effect. The right to a fair trial is the context in which the balancing exercise must be considered. The outcome of the balancing of probative value and prejudicial effect is the preservation of a fair trial.[132] For example, in *Saroya*,[133] the accused was charged with aggravated assault and assault causing bodily harm. It was held that the trial judge was correct in not excluding a previous conviction for attempted murder. To deprive the jury of the accused's criminal record would leave the jury with incomplete and therefore incorrect information about the accused's credibility as a witness and hinder their ability to correctly appreciate the facts. On the other hand, in *Brooks*,[134] the accused was charged with and convicted of murder in the death of a child. The trial judge had permitted the Crown to examine the accused on his entire criminal record including offences of theft under, fraud, breach of probation, failure to comply with a recognizance and assault. The only persons who could have had access to the child on the night of the murder were the accused and the child's mother. Although an appeal was dismissed, it was held that acts of violence such as assault have less bearing on a person's credibility than do acts of dishonesty, such as fraud and theft, and trial judges should be wary of admitting acts of violence to avoid the possibility that the jury might convict the accused on the basis of his disposition to commit such acts.

Whether the Crown will raise the accused's criminal record during cross-examination is usually a crucial factor in the decision of the defence whether or not to call the accused. In Ontario, it was the common practice for such applications to be raised by the defence before the accused testified and for the trial judge to hear and give a conditional ruling. Thus, for example, if an accused (with convictions for violence) entered the witness box and gave evidence suggesting that he was a peace-loving person and would not commit the offence before the court,

---

[132] *Saroya*, 36 C.R. (4th) 253, 76 O.A.C. 25, 1994 CarswellOnt 122, [1994] O.J. No. 2920 (C.A.).

[133] *Ibid.*

[134] 113 O.A.C. 201, 20 C.R. (5th) 116, 129 C.C.C. (3d) 227, 41 O.R. (3d) 661, 1998 CarswellOnt 3866, [1998] O.J. No. 3913 (C.A.), reversed, 141 C.C.C. (3d) 321, 182 D.L.R. (4th) 513, 30 C.R. (5th) 201, 2000 SCC 11, 46 O.R. (3d) 640 (headnote only), 129 O.A.C. 205, 250 N.R. 103, [2000] 1 S.C.R. 237, 2000 CarswellOnt 292, 2000 CarswellOnt 293, [2000] S.C.J. No. 12.

the trial judge would permit the Crown to bring out the convictions for violence. The trial judge would frequently inquire as to the nature of the defence and indicate that the ruling might be withdrawn if the defence changed.

Not all courts, however, agreed with this practice. In *Hoffman*,[135] the Alberta Court of Appeal said that the trial judge should not accede to a request by the defence, before an accused is sworn, for a ruling whether or not the Crown would ask him questions about his criminal record. The Court reasoned that since the trial judge's discretion to exclude such evidence was only permitted where the accused's criminal record was of minimal probative value and of such prejudicial effect that a suitable warning to the jury would not suffice against possible misuse, the exercise of his discretion would depend very much on the nature of the evidence of the accused.

The issue was eventually resolved by the Supreme Court in *Underwood*.[136] The Court said that the proper time for the defence to bring a *Corbett* application is after the close of the case for the Crown. At that time, the trial judge should decide, before calling upon the defence, whether the accused's criminal record should be revealed. The trial judge could also, if he believed it to be necessary, hold a *voir dire* and inquire what evidence the defence intended to call so that he could make a fully informed ruling on the application. The Court said that the *voir dire* is not a "defence disclosure" and does not create independent rights in the Crown. It should not be treated as an excuse for the Crown to deeply probe the case for the defence. The Court pointed out that although the defence always retains the right to lead evidence that was not disclosed at the *voir dire*, the trial judge is entitled to change his ruling if he believes that the undisclosed evidence would have had a material impact on the *Corbett* application.

The ruling in *Underwood* is based on the principle that, before the accused calls evidence in his own defence, he must have knowledge of the case to be met. The extent to which the accused's criminal record will be admissible against him will encompass part of the Crown's case. It is justified as part of the broader principle against self-incrimination, which has its roots in the presumption of innocence and the power imbalance between the state and the individual.

---

[135] 32 C.R. (4th) 396, 155 A.R. 275, 73 W.A.C. 275, 1994 CarswellAlta 325 (C.A.).
[136] 221 N.R. 161, 121 C.C.C. (3d) 117, 155 D.L.R. (4th) 13, 12 C.R. (5th) 241, 48 C.R.R. (2d) 205, [1998] 1 S.C.R. 77, 209 A.R. 276, 160 W.A.C. 276, [1999] 4 W.W.R. 326, 67 Alta. L.R. (3d) 81, 1997 CarswellAlta 1080, 1997 CarswellAlta 1081.

(d) Cross-examination of a Co-Accused

The right of an accused to full answer and defence gives him the right to cross-examine a co-accused who has testified and given damaging evidence against him.[137] In such instance, the protection given by *Davison*[138] does not apply to the co-accused. This means that it is open for an accused to cross-examine a co-accused about his character to show that the co-accused is a disreputable person not worthy of belief.[139] The policy of the law is that the right of a co-accused to full answer and defence does not allow him to hide under that umbrella of protection thereby impairing the right of an accused to full answer and defence by asking questions pertinent to his defence. It is generally assumed that a co-accused, who claims that he will be prevented from having a fair trial if the accused is allowed to cross-examine him, will apply to the court to have his trial severed from that of the accused.

Moreover, a co-accused, who exercised his right to remain silent when he was questioned by the police and who testifies at trial against an accused, cannot use the fact that he exercised that right to deprive the accused of the right to challenge his testimony by a full attack on his credibility. In other words, he cannot immunize himself from an attack by the accused to the effect that he said nothing when questioned by the police.[140] However, although an accused can cross-examine his co-accused on the fact that he remained silent when questioned by the police for the purpose of dispelling any evidence given by the co-accused implicating him, he cannot go further. An accused is not permitted to ask the trier of fact to consider the evidence of the co-accused's silence as positive evidence of his guilt on which the Crown may rely to convict him.

Ironically, the right to attack a co-accused who has exercised the right to remain silent places that co-accused in an anomalous situation. As was noted by McLachlin J. in *Creighton*,[141] it obliges the co-accused to make a prior consistent statement in order to avoid cross-examination on his silence. However it renders him unable to tender that evidence in

---

[137] *Creighton*, 37 C.R. (4th) 197, 179 N.R. 161, 81 O.A.C. 359, 96 C.C.C. (3d) 481, 27 C.R.R. (2d) 1, [1995] 1 S.C.R. 858, 22 O.R. (3d) 288 (note), 1995 CarswellOnt 12, 1995 CarswellOnt 523.

[138] (1974), 6 O.R. (2d) 103, 20 C.C.C. (2d) 424 (C.A.), leave to appeal refused, 6 O.R. (2d) 103n, 20 C.C.C. (2d) 424n, [1974] S.C.R. viii.

[139] *Jackson*, 9 C.R. (4th) 57, 51 O.A.C. 92, 68 C.C.C. (3d) 385, 1991 CarswellOnt 119 (C.A.), affirmed, 26 C.R. (4th) 178, [1993] 4 S.C.R. 573, 162 N.R. 113, 86 C.C.C. (3d) 385, 68 O.A.C. 161, 109 D.L.R. (4th) 318, 1993 CarswellOnt 136, 1993 CarswellOnt 997.

[140] *Creighton, supra*, note 137.

[141] *Ibid.*

support of his own credibility because the law of evidence precludes the admission of a prior consistent statement to bolster his credibility. She would have precluded the accused from attacking the co-accused's exercise of the right to silence. As far as she was concerned, pre-trial silence was either a right or it was not a right. If it was a right, the trier of fact should not be permitted to draw an adverse inference from its exercise. She stressed that if adverse inferences are permitted, the right to silence is effectively lost, for no accused who wishes to preserve the possibility of putting forth his story at trial can afford to exercise it. The right to silence, she said, if it means anything, means that a suspect has a right to refuse to talk to the police and not be penalized for it. Moreover, once an accused has been informed by the police of his right not to speak, the exercise of this right cannot logically found an inference as to his credibility if he later testifies.

11. REBUTTAL EVIDENCE FOR THE PROSECUTION

The general rule as to the order of proof is that the prosecution must introduce all evidence in its possession that it relies upon to establish its case before it closes. The rule ensures that the defence knows exactly what case it has to meet in response to the case for the Crown.[142] The rule is intended to prevent an accused from being taken by surprise, and to enable him to investigate by cross-examination the reliability of such evidence before he is called upon to introduce his defence. It is also intended to prevent the undue emphasis or magnification of evidence in relation to other evidence by reason of its late introduction.[143]

The Crown is not expected, however, to anticipate what the defence may be and to lead evidence to refute that defence in advance. For example, the Crown is not required to lead evidence in chief to rebut the defence of alibi, even where the defence has given notice that it intends to raise that issue when called upon. The Crown is entitled to wait until the defence has called its alibi evidence and lead its evidence by way of rebuttal.[144] Similarly, where the onus is upon the accused to raise the defence, such as a defence under section 16 of the *Criminal Code* that

[142] *Krause*, 7 B.C.L.R. (2d) 273, [1987] 1 W.W.R. 97, [1986] 2 S.C.R. 466, 71 N.R. 61, 54 C.R. (3d) 294, 29 C.C.C. (3d) 385, 14 C.P.C. (2d) 156, 33 D.L.R. (4th) 267, 1986 CarswellBC 330, 1986 CarswellBC 761.
[143] *Campbell*, 38 C.C.C. (2d) 6, 17 O.R. (2d) 673, 1977 CarswellOnt 5 (C.A.), varied, 17 O.R. (2d) 673 at 699, 38 C.C.C. (2d) 6 at 32, 1977 CarswellOnt 6 (C.A.).
[144] *Andrews* (1979), 8 C.R. (3d) 1, 1979 CarswellBC 546 (C.A.), leave to appeal refused (1979), 28 N.R. 537n (S.C.C.); *Rafferty*, [1983] 4 W.W.R. 511, 25 Alta. L.R. (2d) 334, 43 A.R. 323, 6 C.C.C. (3d) 72, 1983 CarswellAlta 69 (C.A.).

the accused is not responsible because he was suffering from a mental disorder, the Crown is not required to lead evidence that he was not suffering from a mental disorder as part of its case in chief.[145]

Generally speaking, rebuttal evidence is restricted to evidence to meet new facts presented by the defence. But the accused's mere denial of the prosecution's case during the course of his testimony does not constitute new facts permitting the prosecution to repeat its case or to introduce additional evidence to support it. However, the trial judge does have the discretion to admit, in reply, evidence relevant to the Crown's case as a result of defence evidence that the prosecution could not reasonably be expected to anticipate.

For example, evidence that is of marginal importance during the Crown's case may take on added significance as a result of the defence evidence. If that evidence was not a live issue at the end of the Crown's case, then the Crown may be permitted to call evidence in reply to that issue, if the admission of the evidence would not work an unfairness to the accused.[146] Rebuttal evidence will also be admitted where it is related to an essential issue which may be determinative of the case and which the Crown could not have foreseen would be necessary to prove its case.[147]

An example is *Aalders*.[148] There, the accused, who was charged with first degree murder in the course of a break-in at the victim's residence and theft of the victim's belongings, had testified that the money found in his possession when he was arrested came in part from his welfare allowance. By way of reply, the trial judge had allowed the Crown to call two welfare workers to testify that the accused had never received social assistance. It was held that the trial judge had not erred in doing so, even though the accused had admitted the robbery. Evidence as to the details of the robbery formed an integral part of the Crown's case, and it was important that any confusion with regards to the accused's statement and testimony on this essential issue be clarified. The Court said that evidence from the welfare officials that the accused had never received welfare payments was relevant and important because it

---

[145] *Chaulk* (1990), 2 C.R. (4th) 1, 62 C.C.C. (3d) 193, 69 Man. R. (2d) 161, [1991] 2 W.W.R. 385, 1 C.R.R. (2d) 1, 119 N.R. 161, [1990] 3 S.C.R. 1303, 1990 CarswellMan 385, [1990] S.C.J. No. 139.

[146] *P. (G.)*, 95 O.A.C. 200, 112 C.C.C. (3d) 263, 4 C.R. (5th) 36, 31 O.R. (3d) 504, 1996 CarswellOnt 4538 (C.A.).

[147] *Aalders*, 21 C.R. (4th) 141, 103 D.L.R. (4th) 700, 55 Q.A.C. 161, [1993] 2 S.C.R. 482, 82 C.C.C. (3d) 215, 154 N.R. 161, 1993 CarswellQue 13, 1993 CarswellQue 158.

[148] *Ibid.*

would establish that the robbery was, in all probability, the source of all the money in his possession at the time of his arrest.

Atikian[149] is a straightforward example of the Crown improperly splitting its case and calling, by way of rebuttal, evidence that should have been lead in chief. In *Atikian*, the parents of a 17-month-old infant, who had died from malnutrition and bronchial pneumonia, were charged with failing, without lawful excuse, to provide the infant with the necessaries of life thereby causing her death. Their defence was that they were simply following the advice of an herbalist and honestly believed that this advice would restore their child to good health. After the defence completed its case, the Crown was allowed by the trial judge to call, by way of rebuttal, the accused's 16-year-old daughter who had given to the police a prior statement in which she told them that her father did not believe in herbalists and that he was constantly urging her mother to take the baby to a doctor or to a hospital. It was held by the Ontario Court of Appeal that the trial judge erred in allowing the Crown to split its case this way. The reply evidence went to the very heart of the case. It was unfair to allow the Crown to lead that evidence in reply when neither parent had been confronted with their daughter's statement during cross-examination, nor given the opportunity to refute it.

A good example of where rebuttal evidence was held to be properly introduced is *Sparrow*,[150] a murder case. There, the accused's car was found containing shell cartridges from the same type of gun used to kill the deceased. Blood stains from the same grouping as the deceased were also found on the trunk of the car. The accused, during the course of his cross-examination, "guessed" that the bloodstains were as a result of a fistfight between the deceased and a friend several days before the killing. The Crown was allowed to call in reply a professor of *criminalistics* to testify as to the age of the bloodstains because that issue was not a live one until the accused testified.

However, the rule is not always easy to apply. Appellate courts often disagree as to what constitutes evidence properly the subject of rebuttal, and evidence of facts relevant to prove guilt that should have been called by the Crown during its case in chief. For example, in *Biddle*,[151] the accused was charged with two counts of assault causing bodily harm and two counts of choking, arising out of two separate

---

[149]   1 O.R. (3d) 263, 3 C.R. (4th) 77, 42 O.A.C. 214, 62 C.C.C. (3d) 357, 1990 CarswellOnt 70 (C.A.).
[150]   12 C.R. (3d) 158, 51 C.C.C. (2d) 443, 1979 CarswellOnt 55 (C.A.).
[151]   36 C.R. (4th) 321, 22 O.R. (3d) 128 (note), 178 N.R. 208, 96 C.C.C. (3d) 321, 79 O.A.C. 128, [1995] 1 S.C.R. 761, 123 D.L.R. (4th) 22, 1995 CarswellOnt 7, 1995 CarswellOnt 521.

attacks on women. The victim of the second incident testified that she was attacked in her apartment building between 10:00 p.m. and 10:30 p.m. The accused testified that he was at a show from around 7:30 p.m. to 9:15 p.m. He claimed that after he left the show, he walked his dog and went to visit a friend who was not at home. He then drove to two bars and left his car at a parking garage around 11:25 p.m. and was arrested upon returning to it. The Crown was allowed by the trial judge to call, by way of rebuttal, the evidence of a woman who claimed to have been followed by the accused in his car around 8:30 p.m. while she was driving to the garage of her apartment building. Although that evidence did not directly relate to the time of the attack on the victim, its admission cast doubt on the credibility of the accused with respect to where he was at the time of the attack.

The Ontario Court of Appeal was of the view that the trial judge had not erred in permitting the Crown to call reply evidence. The Supreme Court of Canada, however, disagreed and ordered a new trial. The Court said that since the accused had given an explanation to the police as to his whereabouts that evening, the Crown therefore knew that the defence intended to challenge the identification evidence of the victim and should have called the evidence of the woman who saw him at 8:30 p.m. in chief. Presumably, if the accused had not given an explanation of his whereabouts to the police and offered that explanation for the first time at trial, the evidence of the woman would have been admissible in reply because it could not have been anticipated by the Crown.

Another example of appellate disagreement as to the appropriateness of reply evidence is *Melnichuk*.[152] There the accused borrowed money from the complainant representing that the loan would be secured by a valid mortgage on his cottage property. The accused gave the complainant a document that he said was a mortgage on the cottage property and represented that he would see that it was registered. However, the document was a forgery and was never registered. The accused then obtained a mortgage from a third party and registered it on his property as a first mortgage. The accused defaulted on the complainant's mortgage. As part of its case in chief, the Crown called a lawyer who testified that the purported mortgage was a forgery and had not been prepared by his office. In his testimony, the accused said that he believed

---

[152]   104 C.C.C. (3d) 160, 87 O.A.C. 336, 1995 CarswellOnt 911 (C.A.), leave to appeal refused (1996), 105 C.C.C. (3d) vi, 94 O.A.C. 80 (note), 204 N.R. 74 (note) (S.C.C.), reversed, [1997] 1 S.C.R. 602, 209 N.R. 321, 114 C.C.C. (3d) 503, 99 O.A.C. 218, 146 D.L.R. (4th) 686, 1997 CarswellOnt 798, 1997 CarswellOnt 799.

the complainant's mortgage had been registered and that he was led to believe that the third party mortgage was a second mortgage on his property. This belief, he said, was based on a letter that he received from the lawyer and he then produced the letter. However, the letter had not been shown to the lawyer during his cross-examination by defence counsel. The trial judge had allowed the Crown in reply to call the lawyer to say that he would not have placed a second mortgage on the property and was certain that the accused had advised him that the third party's mortgage was to be a first mortgage. The majority of the Court held that the introduction of the letter for the first time by the accused could not have been reasonably anticipated by the Crown. In dissent, Doherty J.A. held that the issue of whether the third party mortgage was a first mortgage or a second mortgage was part of its case and that such evidence should have been led in chief. A further appeal by the accused was allowed by the Supreme Court of Canada[153] who held, relying on the reasons given by Doherty J.A., that the trial judge had erroneously permitted the Crown to call reply evidence.

As was pointed out previously, rebuttal evidence is only allowed where the evidence relates to a fact in issue. The Crown is not allowed to call rebuttal evidence to contradict a collateral matter. Again, the purpose of the rule is to ensure that the trier of fact concentrates on the issue in dispute and is not sidetracked by a collateral matter. Thus, if an accused goes into the witness box and gives evidence about a matter that is not relevant to a fact in issue, he cannot be contradicted by evidence in reply. The Crown is bound by his answer.

Unfortunately, the rule allows an accused to go into the witness stand and make all kinds of unfounded allegations against the witnesses for the Crown that cannot be refuted by evidence in reply. It does not mean that the trier has to accept the evidence given by the accused. It only means that the Crown cannot call evidence to directly contradict the accused on that issue.

A example of where this occurred is *Krause*.[154] In *Krause*, a murder case, it was alleged that the killing arose out of a drug deal between the accused and the deceased. At trial, the accused testified that it was a regular thing during the investigation for the police to take him down to the police station and for them to threaten to harass other drug dealers

---

[153]   [1997] 1 S.C.R. 602, 209 N.R. 321, 114 C.C.C. (3d) 503, 99 O.A.C. 218, 146 D.L.R. (4th) 686, 1997 CarswellOnt 798, 1997 CarswellOnt 799.

[154]   7 B.C.L.R. (2d) 273, [1987] 1 W.W.R. 97, [1986] 2 S.C.R. 466, 71 N.R. 61, 54 C.R. (3d) 294, 29 C.C.C. (3d) 385, 14 C.P.C. (2d) 156, 33 D.L.R. (4th) 267, 1986 CarswellBC 330, 1986 CarswellBC 761.

and say that they had been given the dealer's names by the accused. He also testified that the police had shown him a gory photograph of the deceased on the first interview. The trial judge had permitted the Crown to call evidence to rebut the allegations. The Supreme Court of Canada held that he had erred in doing so. Evidence as to police integrity and their conduct in relation to the accused during the investigation was collateral to the main and only issue in the case, that is, whether the accused had killed the deceased, and should not have been admitted by the trial judge.

12. SURREBUTTAL BY THE DEFENCE

As a general rule, the Crown is allowed the last opportunity to call evidence by way of rebuttal to new facts raised by the defence that the Crown could not have reasonably anticipated. However, some authorities have extended this right of rebuttal, or what might be more properly called surrebuttal, to the defence. A closer look at those authorities reveals that they have not created new law. They have merely given the defence the right to rebut facts raised by the Crown for the first time in response to a defence that must be raised by an accused, such as a mental disorder that renders him incapable of appreciating the nature and quality of his act or omission or of knowing that it was wrong.

As Chief Justice Lamer noted in *Chaulk*[155] where the defence was insanity (now not guilty by reason of mental disorder):

> First, the Crown cannot be expected to adduce evidence as part of its case-in-chief to meet a defence that the accused might possibly raise; this principle is not altered by the fact that the accused may warn the Crown that it intends to raise a particular defence. Secondly, a requirement that the Crown adduce evidence in chief to establish the sanity of the accused would defeat the presumption contained in s. 16(4).[156]

For example, in *Ewart*,[157] the accused, who was charged with first degree murder, raised the defence of insanity and called a psychologist who testified that the accused was suffering from a particular disease of the mind. In reply, the Crown called three psychiatrists who said that the accused did not have that particular disease of the mind, but had a psychopathic personality. Following that testimony, the accused at-

[155] (1990), 2 C.R. (4th) 1, 62 C.C.C. (3d) 193, 69 Man. R. (2d) 161, [1991] 2 W.W.R. 385, 1 C.R.R. (2d) 1, 119 N.R. 161, [1990] 3 S.C.R. 1303, 1990 CarswellMan 385, [1990] S.C.J. No. 139.
[156] *Ibid.*, at (C.R.) p. 52.
[157] 52 C.C.C. (3d) 280, 1989 CarswellBC 598 (C.A.).

tempted to re-call its expert to reply to that evidence, but was refused by the trial judge. It was held by the British Columbia Court of Appeal that since the Crown's evidence was not a denial of the thesis advanced by the defence, but an alternative explanation of the accused's conduct, the rules regarding the permissible scope of surrebuttal must be applied liberally in order to allow the accused to make full answer and defence.

Similarly, in *Rhodes*,[158] the accused was charged with first degree murder based on an allegation of a killing during the commission of a rape. The defence called expert evidence to show that the accused did not suffer from a predisposition to engage in sexual assaults. By way of rebuttal, the Crown was then allowed to call a witness who said that she had been raped by the accused two months before the killing. However, the defence was denied the right to call evidence to rebut the witness's allegations. It was held that since such reply evidence went to show the pre-disposition that the defence psychiatrist had rejected, the trial judge erred in refusing the accused the right to call witnesses in surrebuttal as to the rape allegations.

One final matter should be noted in respect of surrebuttal evidence. Surrebuttal will not, as a general proposition, cure the improper admission by a trial judge of rebuttal evidence by the Crown that should have been introduced in chief.[159] In other words, where the Crown has been allowed to lead evidence in rebuttal that should have been led in chief, the Crown cannot argue that the defence has not been prejudiced by the admission of such evidence because it has been allowed to call surrebuttal evidence in reply to that evidence.

13. ADDRESSES OF COUNSEL AND THE CHARGE TO THE JURY

When all of the evidence is completed, counsel, or the accused where unrepresented by counsel, are entitled to address the jury or, in the case of trial by judge alone, the judge. Section 651(1) of the *Criminal Code* requires the accused, or his or her counsel where he or she is represented by counsel, to address the jury first if the defence has called any evidence, including the accused. The same rule usually applies where the accused has elected trial by judge alone, although the trial judge may order otherwise. If the defence has called no evidence, then section 651(3) of the *Code* gives the defence the right to address the jury last. The same practice is generally followed where the trial is by judge alone, subject to the discretion of the trial judge.

Crown counsel is only entitled to put before the jury matters which are supported by the evidence presented at trial, not from his or her personal experiences or observations.[160] Moreover, it is improper for the Crown to express a personal opinion about the veracity of any witnesses, particularly the accused, or to express an opinion about the guilt of the accused.[161]

There are two reasons for this rule. The first is that it is irrelevant; the veracity of the witnesses or the guilt of the accused is a matter for the jury or judge. For that reason, similar submissions by the defence are not permitted. The second is that such comments made by a representative of the Crown may unfairly influence the jury.

In the charge to the jury, the judge is required to review the evidence presented at trial and instruct the jury on the law which they are to apply to that evidence. Although the judge is entitled to express an opinion about the importance of any evidence presented or the credibility of any witness, it must be made clear to the jury that they are not bound to accept that opinion. The judge must remember the enormous influence that he or she has with the jury and must try to maintain a balance of fairness. On the other hand, the judge does have the duty to stress to the jury that while they are the sole judges of the facts and the weight to be given to the evidence presented, they must accept the law that he or she has given them.

The trial judge must explain to the jury that the burden of proof throughout is on the Crown and that they must, as a matter of law, acquit the accused if they have a reasonable doubt as to his or her guilt. In assessing whether the Crown has met that burden of proof, the jury must be told that they must consider the evidence as a whole.[162] It is improper for the judge to tell the jury that they must be satisfied beyond a reasonable doubt with respect to each piece of evidence upon which the Crown relies to prove the accused's guilt. That rule also applies with respect to any statement or admission made by the accused.[163] The trial judge must also outline to the jury what verdicts they are entitled to return on each count with respect to possible included offences. It is improper, however,

[160] *Pisani* (1970), [1971] S.C.R. 738, 1 C.C.C. (2d) 477, 15 D.L.R. (3d) 1, 1970 CarswellOnt 210, 1970 CarswellOnt 210F.
[161] *Boucher* (1954), [1955] S.C.R. 16, 110 C.C.C. 263, 20 C.R. 1, 1954 CarswellQue 14.
[162] *Morin*, 66 C.R. (3d) 1, [1988] 2 S.C.R. 345, 88 N.R. 161, 30 O.A.C. 81, 44 C.C.C. (3d) 193, 1988 CarswellOnt 82, 1988 CarswellOnt 967.
[163] *MacKenzie*, 18 C.R. (4th) 133, [1993] 1 S.C.R. 212, 146 N.R. 321, 118 N.S.R. (2d) 290, 327 A.P.R. 290, 78 C.C.C. (3d) 193, 1993 CarswellNS 12, 1993 CarswellNS 270.

for the judge to ask the jury to particularize their verdict, as is common in England. In England, the jury are frequently asked to explain the basis of their verdict in manslaughter prosecutions so that the judge will know upon what factual basis to sentence the accused.[164] The Canadian rule is that since the jury are entitled to arrive at a unanimous verdict for different reasons and on separate evidential bases, they have right to return a general verdict and need not explain it.[165]

Upon completion of the charge to the jury, they will then be asked to retire to consider their verdict. In the case of a judge alone, the judge may deliver his or her verdict at the conclusion of argument by counsel or the judge may reserve and deliver judgment at a future time.

14.   REOPENING THE CASE FOR THE DEFENCE

The defence is entitled to apply to the judge to re-open the case in order to permit the defence to introduce further evidence on behalf of an accused at any time before the jury (or the judge, in a case of trial by judge alone) has rendered its verdict. Although such an application may also be made after a conviction has been entered in a case of trial by judge alone, no such application may be made after the jury has rendered its verdict. The reason in the latter case is that once a jury has rendered its verdict, the trial judge becomes functus.

If the application is made before conviction, the judge must first be satisfied that the proposed evidence is relevant to a material issue in the case.[166] Once it is determined that the witness has relevant evidence, the judge must consider the potential prejudice to the other party should the defence be permitted to re-open the evidence. Finally, the judge must consider the effect of re-opening the evidence on the orderly and expeditious conduct of the trial. If the application to re-open the evidence is based on nothing more than a desire to reverse an earlier tactical decision, then the judge is entitled to refuse the application as being detrimental to the orderly conduct of the trial proceedings.

Once the trial judge has convicted the accused, a more rigorous test is required to protect the integrity of the process, including the enhanced interest in finality. Here the judge is usually required to apply the criteria for admissibility of fresh evidence on appeal.[167] Under that

---

[164]   *Solomon*, [1984] Crim. L.R. 433, 6 Cr. App. R. 120 (C.A.).
[165]   *Tuckey*, 46 C.R. (3d) 97, 9 O.A.C. 218, 20 C.C.C. (3d) 502, 1985 CarswellOnt 100 (C.A.).
[166]   *Hayward*, 86 C.C.C. (3d) 193, 67 O.A.C. 379, 1993 CarswellOnt 1162 (C.A.).
[167]   *Kowall*, 50 C.R. (4th) 271, 108 C.C.C. (3d) 481, 92 O.A.C. 82, 1996 CarswellOnt 3091 (C.A.), leave to appeal refused, 98 O.A.C. 400 (note), 208 N.R. 319 (note), [1997] 1 S.C.R. viii.

test, evidence will generally not be admitted if, by due diligence, it could have been adduced at trial subject to the recognition that this general principle will not be applied as strictly in a criminal case as in a civil case. The evidence should also be relevant in the sense that it bears upon a decisive or potentially decisive issue in the trial. It should also be credible in the sense that it is reasonably capable of belief. Finally, the evidence should be such that, if believed, it could reasonably, when taken with other evidence adduced at trial, be expected to have affected the result.

9

Presumptions and Burdens of Proof

1. PRESUMPTIONS GENERALLY

Everyone involved in the field of criminal law knows that there is a fundamental rule that a person accused of a crime is presumed innocent, and that there is a burden of proof upon the Crown to establish the guilt of an accused beyond a reasonable doubt. These well-known examples of presumptions and burdens of proof, however, do not easily explain the distinction between the two.

An instructive definition was offered by Chief Justice Dickson of the Supreme Court of Canada in *Oakes*:[1]

> In determining the meaning of these words, it is helpful to consider in a general sense the nature of presumptions. Presumptions can be classified into two general categories: presumptions without basic facts and presumptions with basic facts. A presumption without a basic fact is simply a conclusion which is to be drawn until the contrary is proved. A presumption with a basic fact entails a conclusion to be drawn upon proof of the basic fact...
>
> Basic fact presumptions can be further categorized into permissive and mandatory presumptions. A permissive presumption leaves it optional as to whether the inference of the presumed fact is drawn following proof of the basic fact. A mandatory presumption requires that the inference be made.
>
> Presumptions may also be either rebuttable or irrebuttable. If a presumption is rebuttable, there are three potential ways the presumed fact can be rebutted. First, the accused may be required merely to raise a reasonable doubt as to its existence. Secondly, the accused may have an evidentiary burden to adduce sufficient evidence to bring into question the truth of the

---

[1] [1986] 1 S.C.R. 103, 26 D.L.R. (4th) 200, 65 N.R. 87, 14 O.A.C. 335, 24 C.C.C. (3d) 321, 50 C.R. (3d) 1, 19 C.R.R. 308, 53 O.R. (2d) 719, 1986 CarswellOnt 95, 1986 CarswellOnt 1001.

presumed fact. Thirdly, the accused may have a legal or persuasive to prove on a balance of probabilities the non-existence of the presumed fact.

Finally, presumptions are often referred to as either presumptions of law or presumptions of fact. The latter entail 'frequently recurring examples of circumstantial evidence' ... while the former involve actual legal rules."[2]

Presumptions are thus really aids to assist a court in determining the issue before it. They are not, in themselves, either evidence or argument, although they may be based on general experience or probability, or even on policy and convenience. A few examples using the categories outlined by Chief Justice Dickson offer assistance.

Section 354(1) of the *Criminal Code*[3] makes it an offence for anyone to have in his or her possession any property knowing that it was obtained by the commission in Canada of an indictable offence. To succeed on this charge, the Crown must establish the following: firstly, that the accused had the property in his or her possession; secondly, that the property was obtained by the commission in Canada of an offence punishable by indictment (usually stolen); and thirdly, that the accused knew that it was obtained by the commission in Canada of an indictable offence, in other words, that he or she knew that it was stolen.

The doctrine of recent possession, a common law rule, states that where an accused is found in possession of goods proved to have been *recently* stolen, the judge or jury, as the case may be, may infer not only that the accused had possession of the goods knowing them to have been stolen, but also that he or she participated in whatever offence was committed to obtain them. On the prosecution of the accused, all that the Crown has to establish is that the goods were found in the possession of the accused and that they were recently stolen. Common experience tells us that people in possession of goods that were recently stolen or obtained illegally should have some knowledge of how they were obtained.

The law then casts upon the accused a presumption of guilty knowledge unless, during the course of the trial, an explanation is offered. The rule is that the judge must tell the jury (or him or herself if trying the case alone) that they *may*, not that they *must*, in the absence of an explanation that might reasonably be true, find the accused guilty.[4]

This is a permissive presumption. It leaves optional the question whether the inference of the presumed fact (that is, guilty knowledge)

---

[2]   *Ibid.*, at (C.C.C.) pp. 330-31.
[3]   R.S.C. 1985, c. C-46.
[4]   *Ungaro*, [1950] S.C.R. 430, 96 C.C.C. 245, 9 C.R. 328, [1950] 2 D.L.R. 593, 1950 CarswellBC 5.

should be drawn following proof of the basic fact (possession by the accused of goods recently stolen). It does not require the inference to be drawn.

Another example may assist in understanding what is meant by a mandatory presumption. Section 354(2) of the *Code* specifically provides that where an accused is found in possession of a motor vehicle that has the identification number wholly or partially obliterated, two presumptions will arise: the first is that the vehicle was obtained by the commission of an indictable offence; the second is that the accused knew that the vehicle was obtained by the commission of an indictable offence. However, this statutory presumption, unlike the common law doctrine of recent possession, is a mandatory presumption of law because section 354(2) provides that where the basic facts are established (possession of a motor vehicle by the accused with the identification number wholly or partially obliterated), this will amount to *proof* that the accused had the vehicle in his possession *knowing* that it was obtained by the commission of an indictable offence. Unlike a permissive presumption, a mandatory presumption requires the judge or jury to conclude that the presumed fact has been established unless there is evidence to the contrary. It is true that the evidence to the contrary need only raise a reasonable doubt. However, if the accused fails to raise a reasonable doubt, the judge is required to instruct the jury that they *must*, not simply *may*, convict the accused.[5]

Before leaving this area, two important presumptions should be discussed briefly.

2. SPECIFIC PRESUMPTIONS

(a) The Presumption of Innocence

The presumption of innocence has been long recognized under the common law. In *Woolmington v. Director of Public Prosecutions*,[6] Viscount Sankey L.C. wrote:

> Throughout the web of the English Criminal Law one golden thread is always to be seen, that is the duty of the prosecution to prove the prisoner's guilt subject to what I have already said as to the defence of insanity and subject also to any statutory exception. If, at the end of and on whole of the case,

---

5   *Boyle*, 41 O.R. (2d) 713, 35 C.R. (3d) 34, 5 C.C.C. (3d) 193, 148 D.L.R. (3d) 449, 5 C.R.R. 218, 1983 CarswellOnt 88 (C.A.).
6   [1935] A.C. 462, 25 Cr. App. R. 72 (H.L.)

there is a reasonable doubt, created by the evidence given by either the prosecution or the prisoner ... the prosecution has not made out the case and the prisoner is entitled to an acquittal. No matter what the charge or where the trial, the principle that the prosecution must prove the guilt of the prisoner is part of the common law of England and no attempt to whittle it down can be entertained.[7]

This principle has received international recognition in the Universal Declaration of Human Rights adopted December 10, 1948 by the General Assembly of the United Nations and by the International Covenant on Civil and Political Rights, 1966, article 14(2). It has also been given constitutional guarantee in Canada by section 11(d) of the *Charter Rights and Freedoms*. Section 11(d) provides:

Any person charged with an offence has the right

...

(d) to be presumed innocent until proven guilty according to law in a fair and public hearing by an independent and impartial tribunal.

The presumption of innocence simply means that there is no obligation upon an accused to respond either by giving evidence personally or by calling other witnesses. It is a presumption that remains with the accused from the very beginning of the trial until the very end. There is no burden of proof upon the accused. That burden is on the Crown to prove the accused's guilt beyond a reasonable doubt.

(b) The Presumption of No Mental Disorder

Section 16(1) of the *Criminal Code* provides that "no person is criminally responsible for an act committed or an omission made while suffering from a mental disorder that rendered the person incapable of appreciating the nature and quality of the act or omission or of knowing that it was wrong". However, section 16(2) goes on to provide that "every person is presumed not to suffer from a mental disorder so as to be exempt from criminal responsibility by virtue of subsection (1), unless the contrary is proved on the balance of probabilities".

Both the Crown and the defence have a right to raise the question of whether the accused is suffering from a mental disorder. However, section 16(3) says that whoever raises it must bear that burden of proof. It has been held that this shift of onus to the accused to prove that he or she is suffering from a mental disorder is an unconstitutional infringe-

---

[7]   *Ibid.*, at (A.C.) pp. 481-82.

ment of an accused's presumption of innocence as guaranteed by section 11(d) of the *Charter* but is saved by section 1 of the *Charter* as a reasonable limitation on that presumption.[8]

3. BURDENS OF PROOF

The close relationship between presumptions and burdens of proof often make it difficult to distinguish between the two. It is probably easier to state what the burden of proof is rather than to define it. In a dispute between parties, the burden of proof is the evidentiary burden that the court imposes on one side or the other. The general rule is that the burden of proof lies on the party who asserts the affirmative of the issue or question in dispute. The extent of that burden will vary depending on the nature of the trial.

For example, in a civil trial, where A is suing B for breach of contract, the burden of proof is upon A to establish that breach. In civil cases, the onus of proof is simply on a balance of probabilities. The most vivid example of that onus is the tipping of scales slightly in favour of the person who has the burden. If A tips the scales in his favour, ever so slightly, he wins. If the scales are tipped in favour of B, then A loses because he has failed to discharge the burden. A also loses if, at the end of the trial, the scales remain evenly balanced.

In a criminal case, the burden is always upon the prosecution and never shifts to the accused. The burden is also more onerous. That burden is to establish the guilt of the accused beyond a reasonable doubt. The trial judge is required to make it clear to the jury that the Crown is required to do more than prove the accused guilty on a balance of probabilities.[9]

A traditional formula that judges often used in defining reasonable doubt for the jury was:

> A reasonable doubt is an honest doubt, a fair doubt, one based upon reason and common sense. It is a real doubt, not some imaginary or frivolous doubt conjured up in the mind of a juror to avoid an unpleasant or painful duty.[10]

---

[8] *Chaulk* (1990), 2 C.R. (4th) 1, 62 C.C.C. (3d) 193, 69 Man. R. (2d) 161, [1991] 2 W.W.R. 385, 1 C.R.R. (2d) 1, 119 N.R. 161, [1990] 3 S.C.R. 1303, 1990 CarswellMan 385, [1990] S.C.J. No. 139.
[9] *Starr*, 2000 SCC 40, 36 C.R. (5th) 1, 147 C.C.C. (3d) 449, 190 D.L.R. (4th) 591, [2000] 11 W.W.R. 1, 148 Man. R. (2d) 161, 224 W.A.C. 161, 258 N.R. 250, [2000] 2 S.C.R. 144, 2000 CarswellMan 449, 2000 CarswellMan 450, [2000] S.C.J. No. 40.
[10] *Roloson* (1978), 42 C.C.C. (2d) 262 (Ont. C.A.); *Tuckey* (1985), 20 C.C.C. (3d) 502 (Ont. C.A.).

In the past, the courts felt that the term "reasonable doubt" was self-defining and the trial judge need not go any further. In *Campbell*,[11] Martin J.A. wrote:

> The term 'reasonable doubt' is, to a great extent, self defining and its meaning is, I think, generally well understood by the average person. Attempts to further amplify its meaning have often proved unsuccessful and, as a general rule, it is both undesirable and unnecessary to elaborate upon its meaning by departing from the traditional and accepted formulations.[12]

However, in *Starr*,[13] the Supreme Court held that an effective way to define the reasonable doubt standard for the jury is to explain that it falls much closer to absolute certainty than to proof on a balance of probabilities. The Courts have also frowned on the use of such adjectives such as "lingering" or "nagging" applied to doubt in a charge on reasonable doubt.[14]

Trial judges have run into difficulties when they have attempted to give the jury examples from everyday experience. For example, in *Bisson*,[15] the trial judge gave the jury as an example the steps in detail that should be taken to determine the level of oil in an automobile. He suggested that when proper checks had been done, a person could feel certain "beyond a reasonable doubt" that there was enough oil in the car to enable it to run. The Supreme Court said that the trial judge should not have done so and ordered a new trial. To suggest that jurors may apply examples from everyday life in determining proof beyond a reasonable doubt could be misleading and lower the requisite standard. Often, those everyday decisions made by ordinary persons are made by using a standard of probability. Moreover, examples tend to be applied subjectively and will vary with the life experiences and background of every individual juror.

In *W. (D.)*,[16] Cory J. said that, ideally, a trial judge should instruct a jury along these lines:

11 38 C.C.C. (2d) 6, 17 O.R. (2d) 673, 1 C.R. (3d) 309, 1 C.R. (3d) S-49, 1977 CarswellOnt 5 (C.A.), varied, 17 O.R. (2d) 673 at 699, 1 C.R. (3d) S-49, 38 C.C.C. (2d) 6 at 32, 1977 CarswellOnt 6 (C.A.).
12 *Ibid.*, at (C.C.C) p. 25.
13 2000 SCC 40, 36 C.R. (5th) 1, 147 C.C.C. (3d) 449, 190 D.L.R. (4th) 591, [2000] 11 W.W.R. 1, 148 Man. R. (2d) 161, 224 W.A.C. 161, 258 N.R. 250, [2000] 2 S.C.R. 144, 2000 CarswellMan 449, 2000 CarswellMan 450, [2000] S.C.J. No. 40.
14 *Scott*, 140 O.A.C. 95, 153 C.C.C. (3d) 87, 2001 CarswellOnt 287 (C.A.).
15 222 N.R. 365, 155 D.L.R. (4th) 531, 121 C.C.C. (3d) 449, [1998] 1 S.C.R. 306, 14 C.R. (5th) 1, 1998 CarswellQue 66, 1998 CarswellQue 67, [1998] S.C.J. No. 21.
16 3 C.R. (4th) 302, 63 C.C.C. (3d) 397, 122 N.R. 277, 46 O.A.C. 352, [1991] 1 S.C.R. 742, 1991 CarswellOnt 80, 1991 CarswellOnt 1015, [1991] S.C.J. No. 26.

First, if you believe the evidence of the accused, obviously you must acquit.

Secondly, if you do not believe the testimony of the accused but you are left in a reasonable doubt by it, you must acquit.

Third, even if you are not left in doubt by the evidence of the accused, you must ask yourself whether, on the basis of the evidence which you do accept, you are convinced beyond a reasonable doubt by that evidence of the guilt of the accused.[17]

In *Lifchus*,[18] Cory J. went further and indicated what should and what should not be said to a jury about reasonable doubt. He felt that the following references to the required standard of proof should be avoided:

1. Describing the term "reasonable doubt" as an ordinary expression which has no special meaning in the criminal law context;
2. Inviting jurors to apply to the task before them the same standard of proof that they apply to important, or even the most important, decisions in their own lives;
3. Equating proof "beyond a reasonable doubt" to proof "to a moral certainty";
4. Qualifying the word "doubt" with adjectives other than "reasonable", such as "serious", "substantial" or "haunting", which may mislead the jury; and
5. Instructing jurors that they may convict if they are "sure" that the accused is guilty before providing them with a proper definition as to the meaning of the words "beyond a reasonable doubt".

Cory J. said that the trial judge should explain that:

1. The standard of proof beyond a reasonable doubt is inextricably intertwined with that principle fundamental to all criminal trials, the presumption of innocence;
2. The burden of proof rests on the prosecution throughout the trial and never shifts to the accused;
3. A reasonable doubt is not a doubt based upon sympathy or prejudice; rather, it is based upon reason and common sense;
4. It is logically connected to the evidence or absence of evidence;

[17] *Ibid.*, at (C.R.) p. 310.
[18] 9 C.R. (5th) 1, 118 C.C.C. (3d) 1, 216 N.R. 215, 150 D.L.R. (4th) 733, 118 Man. R. (2d) 218, 149 W.A.C. 218, [1997] 3 S.C.R. 320, [1997] 10 W.W.R. 570, 1997 CarswellMan 392, 1997 CarswellMan 393, [1997] S.C.J. No. 77, amended (1998), 120 C.C.C. (3d) vi (S.C.C.).

5.   It does not involve proof to an absolute certainty. It is not proof beyond any doubt nor is it an imaginary or frivolous doubt;

6.   More is required than proof that the accused is probably guilty — a jury which concludes only that the accused is probably guilty must acquit.

Cory J. went on to suggest that instructions to the jury might be given along the following lines:

> The accused enters these proceedings presumed to be innocent. That presumption of innocence remains throughout the case until such time as the Crown has on the evidence put before you satisfied you beyond a reasonable doubt that the accused is guilty.
>
> What does the expression "beyond a reasonable doubt" mean?
>
> The term "beyond a reasonable doubt" has been used for a very long time and is part of our history and our traditions of justice. It is so ingrained in our criminal law that some think it needs no explanation, yet something must be said regarding its meaning.
>
> A reasonable doubt is not an imaginary or frivolous doubt. It must not be based upon sympathy or prejudice. Rather, it is based on reason and common sense. It is logically derived on the evidence or absence of evidence.
>
> Even if you believe the accused probably guilty or likely guilty, that is not sufficient. In those circumstances you must give the benefit of the doubt to the accused and acquit because the Crown has failed to satisfy you of the guilt of the accused beyond a reasonable doubt.
>
> On the other hand you must remember that it is virtually impossible to prove anything to an absolute certainty and the Crown is not required to do so. Such a standard of proof is impossibly high.
>
> In short, if, based upon the evidence or *lack of evidence*, you are sure that the accused committed the offence you should convict since the evidence demonstrates that you are satisfied of his guilt beyond a reasonable doubt.

Unfortunately, he fell into error in the last paragraph of the model charge that has been italicized. Clearly, a jury should not be satisfied of guilt of the accused because of a "lack of evidence". That error was later corrected.[19]

4. CONSTITUTIONAL GUARANTEES

As was pointed out earlier, section 11(d) of the *Charter* guarantees every person charged with an offence the right "to be presumed innocent until proven guilty according to law in a fair and public hearing by an

---

[19]   (1998), 120 C.C.C. (3d) vi.

independent and impartial tribunal". Since the enactment of that section, there have been a number of cases in Canada attacking presumptions, both permissive and legal, as breaching section 11(d). These presumptions, described as reverse onus provisions, have been attacked on the basis that they have whittled down the presumption of innocence. The position of the Crown has generally been that these presumptions have been created by statute because there is a close connection between the basic fact and the presumed fact. Unless the presumption is allowed to stand, there will be instances where the Crown may be unable to prove its case. It has been argued that section 1 of the *Charter* protects presumptions as a reasonable limit in a free and democratic society.

In *Downey*,[20] Cory J., delivering the majority judgment of the Supreme Court, summarized the principles governing the constitutionality of statutory presumptions:

1. The presumption of innocence is infringed whenever the accused is liable to be convicted despite the existence of a reasonable doubt.
2. If by the provisions of a statutory presumption, an accused is required to prove or disprove on a balance of probabilities either an element of an offence or an excuse, then it contravenes section 11(d) of the *Charter*. Such a provision would permit a conviction in spite of a reasonable doubt.
3. Even if a rational connection exists between the established fact and the presumed fact, this would be insufficient to make valid a presumption requiring the accused to disprove an element of the offence.
4. Legislation which substitutes proof of one element for proof of an essential element will not infringe the presumption of innocence if, as a result of the proof of the substituted element, it would be unreasonable for the trier of fact not to be satisfied beyond a reasonable doubt of the existence of the other element. In other words, a statutory presumption will be valid if proof of the substituted fact leads inexorably to the proof of the other. The statutory presumption will infringe section 11(d) if it requires the trier of fact to convict in spite of a reasonable doubt.
5. A permissive assumption from which a trier of fact *may* but not *must* draw an inference of guilt will not infringe section 11(d) of the *Charter*.

---

[20] 2 Alta. L.R. (3d) 193, 136 N.R. 266, 125 A.R. 342, 14 W.A.C. 342, 90 D.L.R. (4th) 449, [1992] 2 S.C.R. 10, 13 C.R. (4th) 129, 9 C.R.R. (2d) 1, 72 C.C.C. (3d) 1, 1992 CarswellAlta 56, 1992 CarswellAlta 467.

6.   A provision that might have been intended to play a minor role in
      providing relief from conviction will none the less contravene the
      Charter if the provision (such as the truth of a statement) must be
      established by the accused.

In *Oakes*,[21] the Supreme Court set out the test that should be applied
in determining whether or not a section of a statute that breaches the
Charter is saved by section 1. One consideration was whether the measures adopted were carefully designed to achieve the objective in question. In other words, a presumed fact in a statute could not be saved by
section 1 unless it was rationally connected to the basic fact. At issue in
the *Oakes* case was whether the former section 8 of the *Narcotic Control
Act*[22] (now the *Controlled Drugs and Substances Act*)[23] which required
an accused found in possession of a narcotic to disprove on a balance of
probabilities that he had the narcotic in his possession for the purpose
of trafficking, violated section 11(d) of the *Charter* and was not saved
by section 1. The Court found that section 8 did violate section 11(d). It
was held that there was no rational connection between the basic fact of
possession and the presumed fact of possession *for the purpose of trafficking* since the reverse onus clause could give rise to unjustified and
erroneous convictions for drug trafficking of persons guilty only of
possession of a small quantity of narcotics. Section 8 was held to be
unconstitutional as infringing the presumption of innocence in section
11(d).

In *Boyle*,[24] which involved the constitutionality of the presumption
in section 354(2) of the *Criminal Code*, the Court of Appeal of Ontario
considered the rationality of the connection between the basic fact (possession of a motor vehicle with a wholly or partially obliterated identification number) with the two presumed facts (that the vehicle was
obtained by the commission of an indictable offence and that the accused
had guilty knowledge) and found the first presumed fact constitutionally
valid but not the second. It was held that the only conceivable reason
for removing or obliterating a vehicle identification number was to
conceal the fact that it had been stolen or had been obtained by the
commission of an indictable offence. On the other hand, since the pre-

---

21   [1986] 1 S.C.R. 103, 26 D.L.R. (4th) 200, 65 N.R. 87, 14 O.A.C. 335, 24 C.C.C. (3d) 321,
     50 C.R. (3d) 1, 19 C.R.R. 308, 53 O.R. (2d) 719, 1986 CarswellOnt 95, 1986 CarswellOnt
     1001.
22   R.S.C. 1985, c. N-1.
23   S.C. 1996, c. 19.
24   41 O.R. (2d) 713, 35 C.R. (3d) 34, 5 C.C.C. (3d) 193, 148 D.L.R. (3d) 449, 5 C.R.R. 218,
     1983 CarswellOnt 88 (C.A.).

sumption of guilty knowledge was not restricted to persons such as car dealers, who might reasonably be presumed to be knowledgeable with respect to the location of vehicle identification numbers and to be alive to the desirability of making an examination to ascertain whether there had been obliteration of such numbers, there was no rational connection between the basic fact and the presumed fact.

10

Particular Problems of Proof

1. JUDICIAL NOTICE

Not every fact in issue need be proved by the introduction of evidence. The law has long recognized that some matters are so notorious they do not require formal proof. As one judge said,

> Courts will take judicial notice of what is considered by reasonable men of that time and place to be indisputable either by resort to common knowledge or to sources of indisputable accuracy easily accessible to men in the situation of members of that court.[1]

This does not mean that the matter can never be disputed. Judicial notice is nothing more than a *prima facie* recognition of the matter as true without requiring the side who asserts it to prove it. However, the other side is not required to accept the matter as being proved. They are entitled to dispute it if they believe it to be disputable.[2]

Judicial notice may be taken of the law or of a certain fact. For example, the common law requires courts to take judicial notice of the common law and all public statutes without those statutes being specifically pleaded. Legislative expression of this rule is contained in sections 17 and 18 of the *Canada Evidence Act*.[3] Sections 20 to 27 of the Act also provide a method of proving Imperial proclamations, orders in council, treaties, orders, warrants, licences, certificates, rules, regula-

---

[1] *Bennett*, 15 C.R.N.S. 28, 4 C.C.C. (2d) 55, 1971 CarswellNS 5 (N.S. Co. Ct.) *per* O'Hearn J. at (C.C.C) p. 66.
[2] *Zundel*, 18 O.A.C. 161, 58 O.R. (2d) 129, 35 D.L.R. (4th) 338, 31 C.C.C. (3d) 97, 56 C.R. (3d) 1, 29 C.R.R. 349, 1987 CarswellOnt 83 (C.A.), leave to appeal refused, 23 O.A.C. 317n, 61 O.R. (2d) 588n, 56 C.R. (3d) xxviii, [1987] 1 S.C.R. xii.
[3] R.S.C. 1985, c. C-5.

tions or other Imperial records, Acts or documents, as well as those issued by the Governor General, the Governor in Council and the lieutenant governor or lieutenant governor in council of a province, judicial proceedings and official or public documents. In all other cases, the common law requires formal proof. However, the *Canada Evidence Act* does not restrict a party to proving such documents under that Act. Documents may be still be proved at common law or by resorting to an applicable provision of another statute.[4]

What constitutes common knowledge of a fact will be judged by reference to that which is common knowledge in the community where and when the issue is being tried, even though it may be unknown elsewhere.[5] For example, a judge sitting in the City of Kitchener may take judicial notice of the fact that Kitchener lies within the Regional Municipality of Waterloo, but not necessarily that a small village lies within the boundaries of the Region.[6] Other examples where judicial notice has been taken are that whisky, beer and wine are intoxicating,[7] that a large screwdriver is an instrument capable of being used for housebreaking,[8] and that bridges are publicly owned property.[9] On the other hand, courts are not yet allowed to take judicial notice of a distinctive cultural characteristic in the absence of evidence of that characteristic.[10]

Although a judge is entitled to take judicial notice of a fact, he is not necessarily required to do so, even if it is generally known and accepted. A judge is entitled to refuse to take judicial notice of a fact that is essential to the Crown's case where to do so would gravely prejudice the case for the defence.[11]

2. IDENTITY

It has been long recognized and accepted by the courts that identification based on personal impressions, that is, human observation and

---

[4] *P. (A.)*, 109 C.C.C. (3d) 385, 92 O.A.C. 376, 1 C.R. (5th) 327, 1996 CarswellOnt 3150, [1996] O.J. No. 2986 (C.A.).

[5] *Potts*, 36 O.R. (2d) 195, 66 C.C.C. (2d) 219, 14 M.V.R. 72, 26 C.R. (3d) 252, 134 D.L.R. (3d) 227, 1982 CarswellOnt 56 (C.A.), leave to appeal refused, 66 C.C.C. (2d) 219n, 134 D.L.R. (3d) 227n, [1982] 1 S.C.R. xi.

[6] *Eagles* (1976), 31 C.C.C. (2d) 417 (Ont. H.C.).

[7] *Moxley*, 38 Man. R. 27, 50 C.C.C. 408, [1929] 1 D.L.R. 202, [1928] 3 W.W.R. 537, [1928] 3 W.W.R. 576, 1928 CarswellSask 130 (Man. C.A.).

[8] *Robert*, [1969] 3 C.C.C. 165, 1968 CarswellBC 241 (C.A.).

[9] *Rese*, [1967] 2 O.R. 451, 2 C.R.N.S. 99, [1968] 1 C.C.C. 363, 1967 CarswellOnt 13 (C.A.).

[10] *W. (S.)*, 6 C.R. (4th) 373, 1991 CarswellOnt 105 (C.A.).

[11] *Zundel*, *supra*, note 2.

recollections, is notoriously unreliable. When a witness says "that is the man" without pointing out any distinctive features which single him out from others, that kind of identification will be given little weight or value. Why? The reason is because of the possibility of honest error.[12] Experience has shown that even honest persons can be mistaken as to identification and recognition.

The trial judge is thus required to warn the jury (and him or herself) of the special need for caution when assessing the quality of identification evidence and the reason for the need of such a warning. For example, the judge might tell the jury that a mistaken witness can be a convincing one and that even a number of such witnesses can all be mistaken. Secondly, the judge must direct the jury to examine closely the circumstances of the identification. For example, matters such as how long the witness had the accused under observation, at what distance, in what light and whether the witness's observation was impeded in any way, should be considered. Another factor that should be considered by the trier is whether the witness ever saw the accused before, and if so, how often and whether there was any reason to remember the accused. Finally, the trial judge must remind the jury of any specific weaknesses that had appeared in the identification evidence.[13] Although recognition of a person known to the witness may be more reliable than the identification of a stranger, the judge must remind the jury that mistakes can even occur in the recognition of a person that the witness knows, such as relatives and friends.

The most common example of identification evidence considered to be valueless is where a witness identifies an accused for the first time while the accused is sitting in the prisoner's dock. Another is where a witness is asked to look at the accused to see if he or she can recognize the accused as the person who committed the offence. Such identification has been called "unfair and unjust".[14] In *Browne*,[15] the British Columbia Court of Appeal described that kind of identification as:

---

[12] *Sutton* (1969), [1970] 2 O.R. 358, 9 C.R.N.S. 45, [1970] 3 C.C.C. 152, 1969 CarswellOnt 30 (C.A.); *Spatola*, [1970] 3 O.R. 74, 10 C.R.N.S. 143, [1970] 4 C.C.C. 241, 1970 CarswellOnt 4 (C.A.).

[13] *Keane* (1977), 65 Cr. App. R. 247; *Turnbull*, [1976] 3 All E.R. 549, 63 Cr. App. R. 132, [1976] 3 W.L.R. 445, Crim. L.R. 565, [1977] 1 Q.B. 224 (C.A.); *Edwardson*, 77 B.C.L.R. (2d) 362, 22 B.C.A.C. 230, 38 W.A.C. 230, 79 C.C.C. (3d) 508, 1993 CarswellBC 77 (C.A.).

[14] *Smierciak* (1946), 2 C.R. 434, 87 C.C.C. 175, [1946] O.W.N. 871, [1947] 2 D.L.R. 156, 1946 CarswellOnt 26 (C.A.) at (C.C.C.) p. 177.

[15] 11 C.R. 297, 1 W.W.R. (N.S.) 449, 99 C.C.C. 141, 1951 CarswellBC 25 (C.A.).

... valueless in the sense that it is dangerous for a Court to act upon it in any respect. Its inherent tendencies towards honest mistake and self-deception are so pervasive that they destroy any value that could otherwise attach to it in a lesser role of 'some evidence'.[16]

The trier will thus be asked to look at *other evidence* that supports that identification before a finding of guilt may be made. For example, were there any distinguishing features, either physical, or in speech, or dress, which singled out that person from others? Unless there is some unusual or distinguishing feature that supports or confirms the initial identification, the trial judge must warn the jury (and him or herself where sitting alone) that a conviction based on such evidence is generally unsafe.

Where identity is in issue, the usual practice is for the police to show the witness a series of photographs, called a photo-lineup, and ask the witness whether "anyone looks familiar to him or her". Alternatively, if a suspect is believed to have committed the offence, the police may conduct a lineup of individuals (an identification parade) including the suspect and ask the witness whether he or she can identify anyone. Appellate courts have stressed the need for constant watchfulness on the part of trial judges and Crown counsel to see that nothing unfair to an accused person is done or put in evidence in connection with identification procedure.[17]

The courts have also said that the police have a duty to ensure the integrity of the identification process by following procedures that tend to minimize the inherent dangers of eye-witness identification.

In *Goldhar*,[18] the Ontario Court of Appeal stressed that when conducting an identification parade, two matters should be clearly kept in mind:

> First, it should appear that there has been nothing whatever done to indicate to the witness the person in the line-up who is suspected by the police, either by showing the photograph or by description, or an indication of the position in the line-up. In the second place, it should appear that the selection of the other persons to form the line-up has been made fairly, so that the suspect will not be conspicuously different from all the others in age or build, colour or complexion or costume or in any other particular.[19]

---

[16] *Ibid.*, at (C.C.C.) pp. 149-50.
[17] *Miaponoose*, 30 O.R. (3d) 419, 110 C.C.C. (3d) 445, 93 O.A.C. 115, 2 C.R. (5th) 82, 1996 CarswellOnt 3386 (C.A.).
[18] 76 C.C.C. 270, [1941] 2 D.L.R. 480 (Ont. C.A.).
[19] *Ibid.*, at (C.C.C.) pp. 271-72.

In such instance, the court must be satisfied that the identification of the accused by the witness out of a series of photographs or out of a lineup was not influenced by any suggestion.

A witness who is giving testimony is routinely asked by the prosecutor whether he or she sees the accused in court and, if so, to point him or her out. If this is the first opportunity for the witness to identify the accused in the dock, or if the witness made a prior identification that was influenced by suggestion rendering the identification in court worthless, the question arises whether the trial judge has the right under the *Charter of Rights* to exclude the identification evidence altogether as a breach of section 7 (fundamental justice) or section 11(d) (presumption of innocence). In other words, will a lineup procedure which is so fatally flawed amount to a breach of the accused's *Charter* rights entitling an accused to the exclusion of the evidence altogether under section 24(2), or is it a matter that simply goes to the weight of the evidence and not its admissibility?

That issue was first addressed by the Supreme Court of Canada in *Mezzo*,[20] a rape trial. There the trial judge had directed a verdict of acquittal because the identification procedures carried out by the police had been flawed, casting serious doubt on the accuracy and reliability of the complainant's identification of the accused as her attacker. The Court ordered a new trial. McIntyre J., for the majority of the Court, regarded the issue as one of weight rather than of admissibility. He was of the view that to do otherwise:

> ... blurs or even obliterates the clear line separating the functions of judge and jury. Questions of credibility and the weight that should be given to evidence are peculiarly the province of the jury.[21]

Although the Court ordered a new trial on the basis that there was some evidence that should have been left to the jury with a proper charge by the trial judge, Madam Justice Wilson in a separate concurring decision (concurred in by Chief Justice Dickson), suggested that the proper procedure to consider improprieties was by way of a motion to exclude the evidence either under a trial judge's common law discretion to exclude prejudicial evidence having little or no probative value or under section 24 of the *Charter*. To date, similar views have been expressed

---

[20] [1986] 1 S.C.R. 802, 30 D.L.R. (4th) 161, 68 N.R. 1, [1986] 4 W.W.R. 577, 43 Man. R. (2d) 161, 27 C.C.C. (3d) 97, 52 C.R. (3d) 113, 1986 CarswellMan 327, 1986 CarswellMan 403.
[21] *Ibid.*, at (C.C.C.) pp. 107-8.

by the Courts of Appeal of British Columbia in *Thomas*,[22] and of Ontario in *D'Amico*,[23] although in none of those cases was the accused successful.

3. INTENT

As was pointed out in Chapter 1, one of the issues that the Crown must prove is that the accused intended to commit the prohibited act. The problem is that what goes on in a person's mind is often difficult, if not impossible, to ascertain. The courts, however, have found no difficulty in making that determination. As Bowen L.J. said in *Edgington v. Fitzmaurice*:[24]

> ... the state of a man's mind is as much a fact as the state of his digestion. It is true that it is very difficult to prove what the state of a man's mind at a particular time is, but if it can be ascertained it is as much a fact as anything else...

Some of the ways that a person's intent can be proved are by what he or she says or admits to others, or what he or she does. The most common method is by what is known as the presumption of intent. This presumption says that a man is presumed to have intended the natural consequences of his acts. In other words, if X shoots a gun at Y, it is open for the court to draw the inference that X did so intending to kill or injure Y. Such a presumption, however, is not considered to be a presumption of law, merely one of good common sense. As Roach J.A. pointed out in *Giannotti*:[25]

> ... a man is usually able to foresee what are the natural consequences of his acts, so it is, as a rule, reasonable to infer that he did foresee them and intend them. But, while that is an inference which may be drawn, it is not one which must be drawn. If on all the facts of the case it is not the correct inference, then it should not be drawn.

---

[22] 24 C.R. (4th) 249, 32 B.C.A.C. 209, 53 W.A.C. 209, 1993 CarswellBC 506 (C.A.) and *Fraser*, 80 C.C.C. (3d) 539, 26 B.C.A.C. 58, 44 W.A.C. 58, 15 C.R.R. (2d) 44, 1993 CarswellBC 1145 (C.A.), leave to appeal refused (October 28, 1993), Doc. 23663 (S.C.C.).

[23] 16 O.R. (3d) 125, 67 O.A.C. 396, 19 C.R.R. (2d) 309, 1993 CarswellOnt 1087 (C.A.).

[24] (1885), 29 Ch. D. 459 (C.A.) at p. 483.

[25] [1956] O.R. 349, 115 C.C.C. 203, 23 C.R. 259, 1956 CarswellOnt 11 (C.A.) at (C.C.C) p. 213.

4. MOTIVE

Motive must be distinguished from intent. Although the two words are often used interchangeably, they mean different things in the criminal law. Intent or *mens rea* refers to the mental element that the Crown must prove the accused possesses to establish its case. Intent, in criminal law, has been defined as "the exercise of a free will to use particular means to produce a particular result".[26] It may also, in some circumstances, refer to a foresight of consequences. In other words, an accused may not intend the consequences of his or her actions, but may be reckless as to the consequences and the courts will find criminal intent in this attitude.[27]

Motive, on the other hand, has been distinguished from intent as "that which precedes and induces the exercise of the will".[28] Motive may be the reason why a crime has been committed. Motive, in the words of Professor Glanville Williams:

> . . . is ulterior intention — the intention with which an intentional act is done (or, more clearly, the intention with which an intentional consequence is brought about). Intention, when distinguished from motive, relates to the means, motive to the end ...[29]

Unlike intention, the Crown need not prove that the accused had a motive to commit the crime in order to succeed in its prosecution. Nevertheless, motive may be relevant and an important element along with other evidence to establish the three elements of every crime — the act; the identity of the perpetrator; and the perpetrator's intent.[30] As Chief Justice Duff noted in *Barbour*:

> If you have acts seriously tending, when reasonably viewed, to establish motive for the commission of a crime, then there can be no doubt that such evidence is admissible, not merely to prove intent, but to prove the fact as well.[31]

In *Lewis*, Mr. Justice Dickson summed up the law as to motive this way:

---

[26] *Lewis*, [1979] 2 S.C.R. 821, 98 D.L.R. (3d) 111, 27 N.R. 451, 12 C.R. (3d) 315 (Fr.), 47 C.C.C. (2d) 24, 10 C.R. (3d) 299 (Eng.), 1979 CarswellBC 520, 1979 CarswellBC 531, at (C.R.) p. 308.

[27] *Sault Ste. Marie (City)*, [1978] 2 S.C.R. 1299, 85 D.L.R. (3d) 161, 21 N.R. 295, 7 C.E.L.R. 53, 3 C.R. (3d) 30, 40 C.C.C. (2d) 353, 1978 CarswellOnt 24.

[28] *Lewis, supra,* note 26.

[29] *Criminal Law: The General Part*, 2nd ed. (1961), p. 48.

[30] *Barbour*, [1938] S.C.R. 465, 71 C.C.C. 1, [1939] 1 D.L.R. 65, 1938 CarswellNB 25.

[31] *Ibid.*, at (C.C.C.) pp. 19-20.

1. As evidence, motive is always relevant and hence evidence of motive is admissible.

2. Motive is no part of the crime and is legally irrelevant to criminal responsibility. It is not an essential element of the prosecution's case as a matter of law.

3. Proved absence of motive is always an important fact in favour of the accused and ordinarily worthy of note in a charge to the jury.

4. Conversely, proved presence of motive may be an important factual ingredient in the Crown's case, notably on the issues of identity and intention, when the evidence is purely circumstantial.

5. Motive is therefore always a question of fact and evidence and the necessity of referring to motive in the charge to the jury falls within the general duty of the trial judge not only to outline the theories of the prosecution and defence but to give the jury matters of evidence essential in arriving at a just conclusion.

6. Each case will turn on its own unique set of circumstances. The issue of motive is always a matter of degree.[32]

5. CONSPIRACY

As was pointed out in Chapter 3, although what one accused says about his co-accused out-of-court is not evidence of the co-accused's guilt, there is an exception to that rule where an accused is charged with conspiracy. That exception allows the acts and declarations of one conspirator in furtherance of the common design to be given in evidence against all of the other conspirators, even though such evidence is hearsay.[33] However, before such evidence may be considered, the trier must first be satisfied that the accused is *probably* a member of the conspiracy by evidence directly admissible against him without relying upon the hearsay exception. Once the trier is satisfied as to this *probability*, then the trier is entitled to consider the acts and declarations of co-conspirators on the final issue of whether the Crown has proven the guilt of the accused *beyond a reasonable doubt.*[34]

One might logically assume that because of this exception to the hearsay rule, conspiracy cases create a two-stage trial: the first stage involving evidence directly proving membership of the accused in the conspiracy and a determination by the trier of the probability of that membership; and then a second stage where hearsay evidence is allowed

---

[32] *Supra.* note 26 at (C.C.C.) pp. 34-38.

[33] *Koufis*, [1941] S.C.R. 481, 76 C.C.C. 161, [1941] 3 D.L.R. 657, 1941 CarswellNS 24.

[34] *Carter*, [1982] 1 S.C.R. 938, 31 C.R. (3d) 97, 137 D.L.R. (3d) 387, 46 N.B.R. (2d) 142, 121 A.P.R. 142, 47 N.R. 288, 67 C.C.C. (2d) 568, 1982 CarswellNB 13, 1982 CarswellNB 55.

of the acts and declarations of co-conspirators to determine whether, based on all of the evidence, the accused's guilt has been proven beyond a reasonable doubt. Such a requirement would be fairer to each accused and ensure that the jury do not erroneously consider hearsay evidence during their deliberation in the first stage. However, in *Carter*,[35] the Supreme Court of Canada held that this was not necessary because "the exigencies of the trial would make a chronological separation of the evidence impossible".[36] The Court said that it was only necessary for the trial judge to instruct the jury (and himself where he sits without a jury) that they were to sift through the evidence and carry out the following three-step process:

1.   Consider whether on all the evidence, they are satisfied beyond a reasonable doubt that the conspiracy charged in the indictment existed. In other words, what must be considered at this stage is the existence of the conspiracy, not the individual membership in it;

2.   If they are so satisfied, then they must go on to decide whether "on the basis of the evidence directly admissible against the accused" the accused was probably a member of the conspiracy;

3.   Only if they conclude that the accused was probably a member of the conspiracy can they then go on to apply the hearsay exception and consider the acts and declarations performed and made by co-conspirators, in furtherance of the conspiracy, to determine along with the other evidence whether the accused was, beyond a reasonable doubt, a member of the conspiracy.

However, the distinction between what is direct evidence and what is hearsay evidence can be confusing for the jury, since it will generally depend upon the stage of their deliberations. For example, if X, one of the alleged conspirators, declares that he, along with Y and Z, are part of a conspiracy to traffic in drugs, such evidence is direct evidence of the existence of a conspiracy and may be considered by the jury during their deliberations in step one. However, such evidence is also hearsay evidence and may only be considered on the issue of the membership of Y and Z in the conspiracy if the jury reach step three.

---

[35]   [1982] 1 S.C.R. 938, 31 C.R. (3d) 97, 137 D.L.R. (3d) 387, 46 N.B.R. (2d) 142, 121 A.P.R. 142, 47 N.R. 288, 67 C.C.C. (2d) 568, 1982 CarswellNB 13, 1982 CarswellNB 55.

[36]   *Ibid.*, at (C.R.) p. 105.

The *Carter* formula has been criticized as confusing where there are only two alleged conspirators. In *Comeau*,[37] the Quebec Court of Appeal pointed out that where the conspiracy involves only two people, step one answers all the questions and steps two and three become irrelevant. In other words, the jury could not be satisfied of the existence of a conspiracy beyond a reasonable doubt without also finding the accused to be one of the conspirators beyond a reasonable doubt. Mr. Justice Tyndale summed it up this way:

> There cannot be a conspiracy of one person; two is a minimum; so if at step one the jury is satisfied beyond a reasonable doubt that the alleged conspiracy in fact existed, they must have found that the accused was a member, because he was one of the two members necessary to create the conspiracy.[38]

Although the logic of that criticism is compelling, unfortunately, the law of conspiracy is further confused by the rule that even in a two-person conspiracy, it is open for the jury to convict one accused but not the other.[39]

Thus where the indictment alleges a two-person conspiracy, it has been held that the three-step procedure set out in *Carter* must be appropriately modified to ensure that the jury are not unduly confused.[40] The jury should be told that although it may seem inconsistent to convict A and not B in a two-person conspiracy, that inconsistency arises because there may be sufficient evidence against A to establish his guilt beyond a reasonable doubt, but not sufficient evidence against B to prove his participation.

---

[37] (1991), 44 Q.A.C. 93, [1992] R.J.Q. 339, 1991 CarswellQue 283 (C.A.), affirmed, 144 N.R. 229, 51 Q.A.C. 213, [1992] 3 S.C.R. 473, 1992 CarswellQue 129, 1992 CarswellQue 129F. See also *Viandante*, 40 C.R. (4th) 353, 102 Man. R. (2d) 126, 93 W.A.C. 126, 1995 CarswellMan 10, [1995] M.J. No. 269 (C.A.), leave to appeal refused, 206 N.R. 154 (note), 115 Man. R. (2d) 160 (note), 139 W.A.C. 160 (note), [1996] S.C.C.A. No. 243.

[38] *Comeau, ibid.*, at (R.J.Q.) p. 348.

[39] *Barrow*, [1987] 2 S.C.R. 694, 87 N.S.R. (2d) 271, 222 A.P.R. 271, 45 D.L.R. (4th) 487, 81 N.R. 321, 38 C.C.C. (3d) 193, 61 C.R. (3d) 305, 1987 CarswellNS 344.

[40] *Viandante, supra*, note 37.

Index